GOVERNORS STATE UNIVERSITY LIBRARY

W9-BDS-919
3 1611 00150 0690

Psychophysics:
The Fundamentals

Third Edition

Psychophysics:
The Fundamentals

Third Edition

George A. Gescheider
Hamilton College

GOVERNORS STATE UNIVERSITY
UNIVERSITY PARK
IL 60466

LAWRENCE ERLBAUM ASSOCIATES, PUBLISHERS
1997   Mahwah, New Jersey   London

QP 431 .G473 1997

Gescheider, George A.

Psychophysics

Copyright © 1997 by Lawrence Erlbaum Associates, Inc.
All rights reserved. No part of this book may be reproduced in any form, by photostat, microform, retrieval
system, or any other means, without the prior written
permission of the publisher.

Lawrence Erlbaum Associates, Inc., Publishers
10 Industrial Avenue
Mahwah, New Jersey 07430

Library of Congress Cataloging-in-Publication-Data

Gescheider, George A.
Psychophysics : the fundamentals / George A. Gescheider.
— 3rd ed.
        p. cm.
    Includes bibliographic references and index.
    ISBN 0-8058-2281-X (alk. paper)
    1. Senses and sensation—Testing. 2. Psychophysics.
  3. Psychophysiology—Methodology. I. Title.
    QP431.G473 1997
    96-41791   152.1—dc20
                                          CIP

Books published by Lawrence Erlbaum Associates are
printed on acid-free paper, and their bindings are chosen
for strength and durability.

Printed in the United States of America
10 9 8 7 6 5 4 3 2 1

This book is dedicated to my wife, Annie,
with whom I happily share my life,
to my daughters, Mary and Meg,
of whom I am very proud,
to my mother, Mary,
who has always made me feel special,
and to my good friend, Obie

Contents

Preface

Psychophysics is the scientific study of the relation between stimulus and sensation, and therefore the problems of psychophysics constitute some of the most fundamental problems of modern psychology. For centuries thinkers have recognized the importance of understanding sensation. In fact, experimental psychology developed as an independent science largely because of the recognition that the scientific study of sensation could yield insight into the workings of the human mind.

Experimental psychology was established as an independent science when, in Leipzig, 1879, Wilhelm Wundt founded the first laboratory for experimental work exclusively directed toward understanding psychological processes. The work of Wundt and other early experimental psychologists evolved from the British empiricist and associationist schools of philosophy, which had firmly established the idea of the senses as the key to human understanding. This idea was reinforced by advances in sensory physiology, which suggested that the problem might yield to scientific investigation.

But perhaps the single most important historical antecedent of experimental psychology was psychophysics. Thus, for some psychologists the most significant date in psychology is not 1879, the founding date of Wundt's laboratory, but 1860, the date of the publication of Fechner's *Elements of Psychophysics*. Fechner's work, in providing methods and theory for the measurement of sensation, gave psychology basic tools for the study of mind.

Today psychophysics remains a central part of experimental psychology. Important recent changes in psychophysics are the development of the theory of signal detection and the refinements of methods for directly scaling sensory magnitude. These two advances have greatly broadened the applicability of psychophysics to areas far beyond the original problems of measuring sensory thresholds. Modern psychophysics can be credited with contributions to the solution of problems in such diverse realms as sensory processes, memory, learning, social behavior, and esthetics.

This book describes the methods, theories, and applications of classical and modern psychophysics. It was written for advanced undergraduate students with some background in statistics; graduate students may also find it useful for obtaining an overview of the field. I hope *Psychophysics: The Fundamentals* will be useful for courses in perception, general experimental psychology, and quantitative methods.

Twelve years have passed since the publication of the second edition of this book. In this third edition, I have included many of the methodological and theoretical contributions made in the field during this time period. I have also expanded on some of the topics found in the first and second editions. The major additions found in this book are descriptions of adaptive procedures for measuring thresholds, context effects in scaling, theory of quantal fluctuations, multidimensional scaling, nonmetric scaling of sensory differences, and the relationship between the size of the DL and the slope of the sensation magnitude function. New methods have also been included for measuring the observer's sensitivity and criterion and the discussion of category scaling has been expanded to include the range frequency model and verbally labeled categories. Methods used to control the observer's nonlinear use of numbers in magnitude estimation such as line-length scaling, magnitude matching, master scaling and category-ratio scaling are described. Finally, a glossary of terms is added.

ACKNOWLEDGMENTS

I wish to acknowledge the special efforts of Sandy Bolanowski, Gene Galanter, Neil Macmillan, Larry Marks, Joe Sturr, and John Swets in providing me with their constructive criticism and helpful suggestions after reading various versions and sections of the manuscript. I would also like to thank my students for their support and helpful suggestions, Nancy Wichmann for her typing and help in putting the final manuscript together, Chris Ingersoll for her excellent artwork, and Marcy Pruiksma, Book Production Editor, for coordinating different facets of this project.

—*George A. Gescheider*

Psychophysical Measurement of Thresholds: Differential Sensitivity

Prior to a century ago the approach to psychological problems consisted primarily of philosophical speculation. The transition of psychology from a philosophical to a scientific discipline was greatly facilitated when the German physicist G. T. Fechner introduced techniques for measuring mental events (1860). The attempt to measure sensations through the use of Fechner's procedures was termed psychophysics and constituted the major research activity of early experimental psychologists. Since this time psychophysics has consisted primarily of investigating the relationships between sensations (ψ) in the psychological domain and stimuli (ϕ) in the physical domain.

Central to psychophysics is the concept of a *sensory threshold*. The philosopher Herbart (1824) had conceived of the idea of a threshold by assuming that mental events had to be stronger than some critical amount in order to be consciously experienced. Although measurement is not a part of this description of the threshold, scientists eventually were able to see the implication of such a concept for psychological measurement. In the early nineteenth century, for example, German scientists such as E. H. Weber and G. T. Fechner were interested in the measurement of the sensitivity limits of the human sense organs. Using measurement techniques of physics and well-trained human observers, they were able to specify the weakest detectable sensations in terms of the stimulus energy necessary to produce them. The *absolute threshold* or *stimulus threshold* (RL for the German *Reiz Limen*) was defined as the smallest amount of stimulus energy necessary to produce a sensation. Since an organism's sensitivity to external stimuli tends to fluctuate somewhat from moment to moment,

1

several measurements of the threshold value of the stimulus are averaged to arrive at an accurate estimation of the absolute threshold. When a stimulus above absolute threshold is applied to the sense organ, the intensity of this stimulus must be increased or decreased by some critical amount before a person is able to report any change in sensation. The *difference threshold* (DL for the German *Differenz Limen*) was defined as the amount of change in a stimulus ($\Delta\phi$) required to produce a *just noticeable difference* (jnd) in the sensation. If the intensity of the stimulus is 10 units, and the stimulus must be increased to 12 units to produce a just noticeable increment in the sensation, then the difference threshold would be 2 units.

Sensation intensity is only one of several ways in which sensations can differ, and DL's have also been measured for other dimensions of sensation. It is generally agreed that sensations can differ on at least four basic dimensions—intensity, quality, extension, and duration. The dimension of quality refers to the fact that sensations may be different in kind. The different sensory modalities have unique kinds of sensations; for example, seeing is an entirely different kind of experience than hearing. Within sensory modalities, sensations also vary in quality. A sound becomes higher or lower in pitch as the vibration frequency of the stimulus is changed. Variations of the wavelength of light are accompanied by changes in hue. A cutaneous sensation may be felt as pain, warmth, cold, or simply a pressure. If the underlying stimulus dimensions for a sensation are known, the difference thresholds can be measured to find the changes in these dimensions necessary to produce just noticeable changes in the sensation. For example, in auditory pitch discrimination the DL for changes in frequency has been measured. In color discrimination the DL for the perception of changes in the wavelength of light has been measured. Since sensations can vary along the dimension of extension, the DL can be measured for variation in spatial aspects of physical stimuli, such as size, location, and separation. And, finally, since sensations last for varying periods of time, the DL for stimulus duration has been of interest to psychophysicists.

Much work in psychophysics has consisted of investigating how the absolute and difference thresholds change as some aspect of the stimulus (wavelength, frequency, adaptation time, intensity level, etc.) is systematically varied. The resulting relations are called *stimulus critical value functions*, since they describe how the threshold (critical stimulus value) changes as a function of other aspects of the stimulus.

DIFFERENTIAL SENSITIVITY

One of the first stimulus critical value functions to be investigated was the relation between the difference threshold for intensity and the intensity level of a stimulus. If, for example, the difference threshold is 2 units when the intensity level of the stimulus is 10 units, what would the difference threshold be for intensity when the stimulus is set at 20, 30, 40, or 50 units? Working mainly with the discrimination of lifted weights, the German physiologist E. H. Weber (1834) discovered that two relatively heavy weights must differ by a greater amount than two relatively light weights for one weight to be perceived as heavier than the other; that is, heavier weights are harder to discriminate and are associated with larger DL's. More precisely, the size of the difference threshold was a linear function of stimulus intensity. Thus, increases in the intensity of the stimulus that were just noticeably different to the observer were always a constant fraction of the stimulus intensity. For weights placed on the skin, this fraction is about ⅓₀.

The size of Weber's fraction is quite different, however, for other stimulus conditions and sense modalities. What is significant is that whether the stimulus is applied to the eye, ear, skin, nose, tongue, or other sense organs, there appears to be a lawful relationship between the size of the difference threshold and the stimulus intensity level. This relationship is known as *Weber's law*: the change in stimulus intensity that can just be discriminated ($\Delta\phi$) is a constant fraction (c) of the starting intensity of the stimulus (ϕ):

$$\Delta\phi = c\phi \quad \text{or} \quad \Delta\phi/\phi = c. \tag{1.1}$$

As seen graphically in our hypothetical situation, the size of the difference threshold is one-fifth of the starting stimulus intensity at all intensity levels (Fig. 1.1). If Weber's law is valid, we would expect, $\Delta\phi/\phi$ to be constant as intensity level is varied ($\Delta\phi/\phi = c$). This prediction is typically confirmed for a fairly wide range of stimulus intensities. However, the Weber fraction, $\Delta\phi/\phi$, tends to increase greatly at extremely low intensities. In Figure 1.2 the relationship between the Weber fraction and intensity is shown for an experiment on lifted weights (Engen, 1971). The observer was required to successively lift weights with one hand, and the value of $\Delta\phi$ was determined for six different values of ϕ. The results for each of two observers indicate that $\Delta\phi/\phi$ is nearly constant for all but the lightest weights.

Technically, the Weber fraction is an extremely useful calculation providing an index of sensory discrimination which can be compared across different conditions and different modalities. It is impossible, for example, to compare meaningfully the $\Delta\phi$ for vision in luminosity units with the $\Delta\phi$ for audition in sound pressure units, but the relative sensitivities for the two modalities can be gauged through a comparison of Weber fractions. Some of the results from two classic studies on intensity discrimination are presented in Figures 1.3 and 1.4. In the study

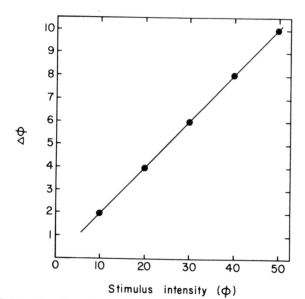

FIG. 1.1. The relationship between Δφ and φ according to Weber's law.

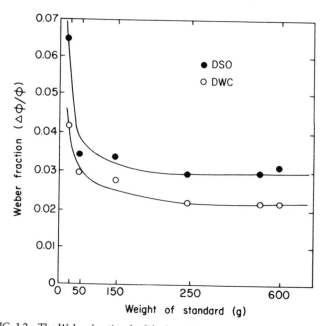

FIG. 1.2. The Weber fraction for lifted weights. The value of Δφ/φ for each of two observers was nearly constant over the stimulus range, except for the lowest stimulus values. (From Engen, 1971.)

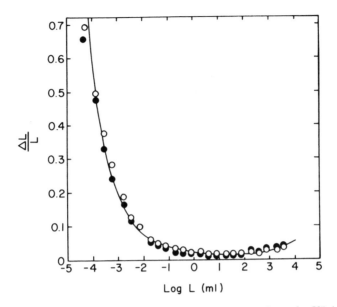

FIG. 1.3. Relation between $\Delta\phi/\phi$ and log luminance as shown by König (open circles) and Brodhun (solid circles). (From König & Brodhun, 1889; after Hecht, 1934, Fig. 27, p. 769.)

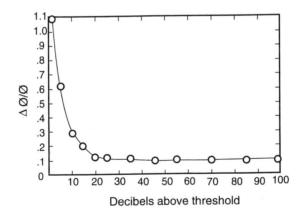

FIG. 1.4. Relation between $\Delta\phi/\phi$ and the intensity of auditory noise expressed as decibels above the absolute threshold. (From Miller, 1947.)

5

by König and Brodhun (1889), the observer viewed a split field in which the two sides could be made to differ in intensity by various amounts. The difference in intensity necessary for discrimination of a brightness difference between the two sides was determined for nearly the full range of visual intensities. Figure 1.3 contains data from separate experiments by König and Brodhun on the discrimination of intensity differences in white light. At low intensities, $\Delta\phi/\phi$ decreased as intensity increased, but then became approximately constant for the higher intensity values.

In a similar study, Miller (1947) determined the intensity difference in a burst of white noise necessary for discrimination at various intensity levels. We see again from the results presented in Figure 1.4 that $\Delta\phi/\phi$ first decreased as a function of ϕ, and then becomes approximately constant. A comparison of the lowest Weber fractions in Figure 1.3 and Figure 1.4 reveals that brightness discrimination is somewhat keener than loudness discrimination.

A modification of Weber's law more closely corresponding to empirical data states

$$\frac{\Delta\phi}{\phi + a} = c \quad \text{or} \quad \Delta\phi = c(\phi + a), \tag{1.2}$$

where a is a constant that usually has a fairly small value. The empirical values of $\Delta\phi/(\phi + a)$ obtained in a discrimination experiment are often approximately the same for all values of ϕ when the correct value of a has been chosen. Since the original version of Weber's law does not correspond to the data for intensity values near absolute threshold, it would seem that the constant a, which brings Weber's law into line with the data, must be related to the operation of sensory systems near threshold. The exact significance of a has not been determined, but it may represent the amount of sensory noise that exists when the value of ϕ is zero. The actual stimulus intensity which effectively determines $\Delta\phi$ may not be ϕ, but rather ϕ plus the continuously fluctuating background noise level of the nervous system. Since sensory noise as spontaneous activity in the nervous system exists as a background to stimulation, its level may greatly influence the value of $\Delta\phi$ for very low intensity values. When the level of sensory noise is taken into account, Weber's law may be essentially correct.

The hypothetical results shown in Figure 1.5 illustrate the effects of employing an additive constant a when describing how $\Delta\phi$ changes as ϕ increases. In the top graph $\Delta\phi/\phi$ is approximately constant over most of the range of ϕ values with the exception of the substantial deviation at low values of ϕ. When a constant a is added to all values of ϕ and $\Delta\phi/(\phi + a)$ is plotted as a function $\phi + a$, the results are described by Weber's law over the entire range of ϕ values.

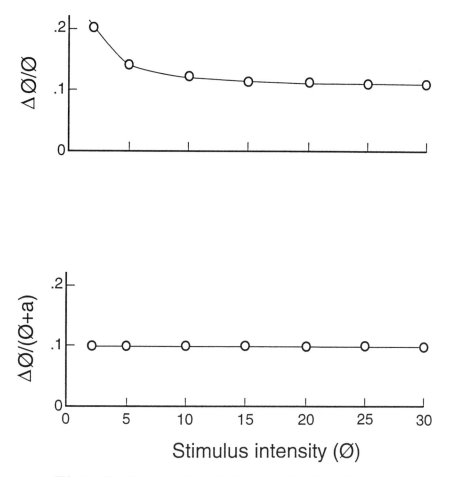

FIG. 1.5. Hypothetical results in which $\Delta\phi/\phi$ is plotted as a function of ϕ(top) and $\Delta\phi/(\phi + a)$ is plotted as a function of ϕ (bottom).

One advantage of the previous interpretation of the constant a is that the concept of sensory noise provides a unifying principle for under-standing absolute and difference thresholds. The absolute threshold can be regarded as the value of ϕ needed to increase the neural activity level above the sensory noise level by some critical amount. The difference threshold can be thought of as the change in ϕ needed to produce a critical difference in neural activity level associated with two intensities of stimu-lation. Thus, both the absolute threshold and the difference threshold involve the discrimination of differences in levels of neural activity. The importance of the concept of sensory noise will become increasingly apparent in our subsequent discussions of psychophysical theory.

Noise in a psychophysical experiment may originate from outside as well as from inside the observer. One source of external noise is uncontrolled fluctuations in the stimulus. Attempts to determine the difference threshold for the sense of smell have illustrated the large effects that such external noise can have on psychophysical experiments. For many years the highest reported values of $\Delta\phi$ were for the sense of smell. The intensity of an odorant typically had to be changed by 25% to 35% for the perceived intensity of the smell to change (e.g., Gamble, 1898). A high Weber fraction for smell is surprising, since absolute thresholds for detecting odorants are among the lowest measured for any sensory modality. Cain (1977) has argued that the high difference thresholds for the sense of smell are an artifact of uncontrolled fluctuations in the concentrations of the olfactory stimulus. In olfactory psychophysics, substances are placed in an apparatus designed to deliver odorants to the observer's nose. The change in concentration of these substances required to produce a just noticeable difference in smell is the difference threshold. This procedure would be acceptable only if the changes in concentration of an odorant *at the nose* of the observer were entirely determined by changes in concentrations of the substance *in the apparatus*. Cain, however, demonstrated that, although the concentration of the substance in the apparatus may be constant, the concentration at the nose of the observer will vary greatly from one presentation to the next. When this "noise" at the nose was taken into account, Weber fractions for smell were found to be as low as 4%, which is about one-tenth the value commonly accepted. Cain's research illustrates the importance of precise stimulus control in psychophysics. Measurement of the stimulus should always be made as close to the sensory receptors as possible. Cain's analysis of the olfactory stimulus teaches us the important lesson that failure to control the stimulus at the receptors can lead investigators to make false conclusions about the nature of a sensory system.

Although Weber's law, at all but the lowest stimulus values, provides an excellent description of most intensity discrimination data, there are notable exceptions that have been repeatedly observed for the auditory discrimination of pure tones and tactile discrimination of vibration. For example, Riesz (1928) determined the intensity increment in an auditory tone necessary for discrimination at various intensity levels and at various frequencies. Because the frequency of 4000 Hz yielded the lowest values of $\Delta\phi$, only the data for this frequency are presented in Figure 1.6. We can see that the value of $\Delta\phi/\phi$ first decreases rapidly as a function of ϕ, but, instead of becoming constant as it did with white noise, $\Delta\phi/\phi$ continues to decrease gradually with further increases in ϕ. This gradual decrease in $\Delta\phi/\phi$ that can be observed even at the highest intenstiy levels, because it is so slight, has become known as the "near miss" to Weber's

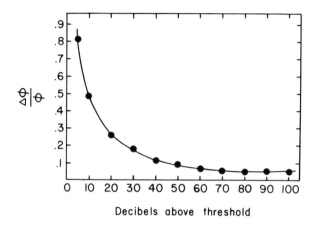

FIG. 1.6. Relation between $\Delta\phi/\phi$ and the intensity of a 4000-Hz tone. The intensity of the tone is expressed in decibels above absolute threshold. (From Riesz, 1928.)

law (McGill & Goldberg, 1968a, b). As yet, there are no widely agreed on explanations for this phenomenon. The near miss to Weber's law has also been observed for vibratory stimulation of the palm near the base of the thumb, and the results for 250 Hz sinusoidal stimulation and vibratory noise are seen in Figure 1.7. It is curious that the near miss has been found when random noise stimulation is presented to the skin as well as when sinusoidal stimuli are applied (Gescheider, Bolanowski, Verrillo, Arpajian, & Ryan, 1990). Recall that, in hearing, Weber's law describes intensity discrimination of white noise and the near miss is observed only for sinusoidal stimulation of pure tones. Perhaps the explanation for the near

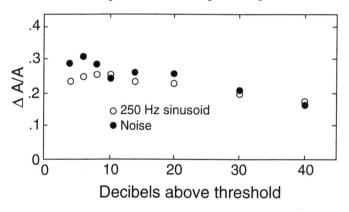

FIG. 1.7. Relation between $\Delta\phi/\phi$ and the intensity of a vibrotactile stimulus expressed as decibels above the absolute threshold. (From Gescheider, Bolanowski, Verrillo, Arpajian, & Ryan, 1990.)

miss to Weber's law will eventually come from a careful comparison of the conditions under which the phenomenon is observed in the auditory and tactile modalities.

FECHNER'S PSYCHOPHYSICS

It was from Weber's work on the DL that Fechner extracted the theoretical implication which led to his formulation of the discipline called psychophysics. Fechner's investigations, originating from an attempt to establish a precise relationship between the physical and mental, were published in 1860 as *Elements of Psychophysics*. In this work, Fechner was concerned with the problem of measuring private experience. For example, if a room appeared to become brighter, a sound louder, or an injury more painful, Fechner wanted to find a way to give the brightness, loudness, or painfulness a number that represented the experience. As a result of his background in physics and mathematics, he approaches these problems in a quite different manner than those who preceded him. In the last 35 years of his life, Fechner's work focused on the idea that mind and matter are equal and are merely two alternative ways of regarding the universe. His psychophysics was a small, but highly significant, part of this concept.

Seeking proof for his ideas about the equivalence of mind and matter, Fechner tried through measurement and quantification to derive a mathematical equation to describe the relationship between physical events and conscious experience. Fechner's first insights into the problem came when he proposed that an arithmetic series of mental intensities might correspond to a geometric series of physical energies. He later realized this principle was exactly what Weber's results seemed to imply: that as the stimulus intensity increases, it takes greater and greater changes in intensity to change the sensation magnitude by some constant amount. Fechner proposed that sensation magnitude could be quantified indirectly by relating the values of $\Delta\phi$ on the physical scale to the corresponding values of the just noticeable difference (jnd) in sensation on the psychological scale. His central assumption was that all jnd's were equal psychological increments in sensation magnitude, regardless of the size of $\Delta\phi$. Fechner's proposed relationship between the size of $\Delta\phi$ in physical units (from Weber's law) and the size of the jnd in psychological units is illustrated in Figure 1.8. It is very important to understand that two independent dimensions exist in this relationship—the stimulus dimension, ϕ, and the sensation dimension, ψ. Fechner was saying that, regardless of its size in physical units, the jnd is a standard unit of sensation magnitude because it is the smallest detectable increment in a sensation and is therefore always psychologically the same size. As is the case with any scale of

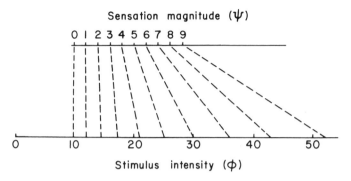

FIG. 1.8. Relation between Weber's law and Fechner's law. Stimulus values that are marked off according to Weber's law were assumed by Fechner to result in equal steps in sensation magnitude.

measurement, once a basic unit is established, one has only to count up units in order to specify the amount of a measured property. Thus, Fechner developed a scale of sensation magnitude by counting jnd's, starting at absolute threshold. The intensity in physical units of a stimulus at absolute threshold, which represents the transition between sensation and no sensation, was assumed to correspond to the zero point on the psychological scale of sensation magnitude. A sensation produced by a stimulus 20 jnd's above absolute threshold should therefore have a psychological magnitude twice as great as a sensation produced by a stimulus that is only 10 jnd's above absolute threshold.

In order to determine empirically the number of jnd's above absolute threshold corresponding to values of the physical stimulus, one would have to undertake the arduous task of starting at absolute threshold and measuring successive values of $\Delta\phi$ along the physical continuum. The first $\Delta\phi$ above the absolute threshold would be measured, and the stimulus intensity value for one jnd above absolute threshold would be recorded and used as the starting stimulus for the measurement of the next $\Delta\phi$. The measurement of the second $\Delta\phi$ would provide a stimulus value two jnd's above the absolute threshold; this value would then be recorded and used as the starting stimulus for the measurement of the third $\Delta\phi$, and so on. Once the physical intensity values had been determined for successive jnd's over the range of energies to which the sensory system responds, the relationship between stimuli in physical units (ϕ) and sensation magnitude in psychological units (number of jnd's above absolute threshold) could be specified in terms of a graph or an equation.

Rather than employing the laborious procedure of experimentally determining successive $\Delta\phi$ values along the entire physical dimension, Fechner, by assuming the validity of Weber's law, was able to calculate the number of jnd's above absolute threshold for specific values of the stimulus. For example, if $\Delta\phi/\phi$ is $\frac{1}{5}$, and the absolute threshold is 10, then the stimulus value corresponding to the first jnd would be $10 \times \frac{1}{5} + 10 = 12$. The stimulus value corresponding to the second jnd is obtained by the same procedure ($12 \times \frac{1}{5} + 12 = 14.4$). This method of successive calculation provides the basis for Table 1.1. This table contains stimulus intensity values and the corresponding number of psychological units (number of jnd's). The results of this procedure are presented graphically in Figure 1.9. If the number of jnd's above absolute threshold is a valid measure of sensation magnitude, then it is apparent from Figure 1.9 that equal increments in sensation correspond to larger and larger increases in stimulus intensity as stimulus intensity increases. In fact, if sensation magnitude is plotted against the logarithm of stimulus intensity, the relationship is linear (Fig. 1.10). A considerable amount of labor would be saved if the equation were known for this logarithmic relationship. The sensation magnitude produced by some specific stimulus intensity could then be quickly calculated. Fechner derived a general formula from Weber's law by integration over a series of ϕ values; it has become known as Fechner's law:

$$\psi = k \log \phi. \tag{1.3}$$

In the formula, ψ is the sensation magnitude, ϕ is the intensity of the stimulus in units above absolute threshold, and k is a constant multiplier, the value of which depends upon the particular sensory dimension and modality.

In evaluating Fechner's law, we must consider the two main assumptions which he had to make to derive the equation. First, Fechner's law

TABLE 1.1
Number of jnd's Above Threshold
Corresponding to Stimulus Intensity Values

Number of jnd's	Stimulus intensity	Log stimulus intensity
0	10.00	1.000
1	12.00	1.079
2	14.40	1.158
3	17.28	1.238
4	20.79	1.316
5	24.89	1.396
6	29.86	1.476
7	35.83	1.554
8	43.00	1.633
9	51.60	1.713

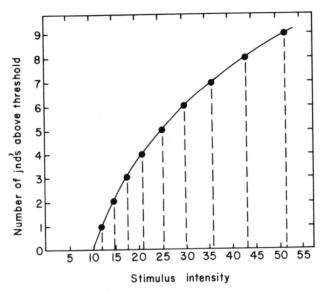

FIG. 1.9. Number of jnd's above threshold plotted against stimulus intensity. The points are from Table 1.1, which contains the calculated values based on the assumption that the Weber fraction is $\frac{1}{5}$ and the absolute threshold is 10 units.

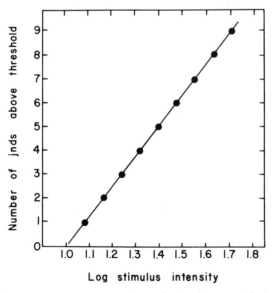

FIG. 1.10. Number of jnd's above threshold plotted against the logarithm of stimulus intensity. The calculated values are in Table 1.1.

is valid only to the extent that Weber's law is correct, and we have already seen that the Weber fraction is not a constant at the low end of the stimulus range. Thus, the generality of the law is necessarily restricted to ranges of stimulus intensity over which $\Delta\phi/\phi = c$. In the second place, Fechner's law rests upon the assumption that the jnd is an equal increment in sensation at all levels of stimulus intensity. This assumption is basic to the entire concept of scaling sensations by using the jnd as the unit measurement. However, experimental tests have shown that jnd's along the intensive dimension are psychologically unequal (S. S. Stevens, 1936). A sound 20 jnd's above absolute threshold is judged to be much more than twice as loud as a sound 10 jnd's above absolute threshold.

In another experiment, Durup and Piéron (1933) had observers adjust the intensities of blue and red lights so that they appeared equal in brightness. Contrary to Fechner's notion that all jnd's are subjectively equal, the two stimuli no longer appeared to have the same brightness when their intensities were increased by the same number of jnd's. If jnd's are subjectively equal, then two stimuli that appear equal in subjective magnitude should continue to appear so when their intensities are both increased by the same number of DL steps. For example, increasing the intensity of both stimuli by 10 DL steps should increase the sensation magnitude of both stimuli by 10 subjectively equal jnd's. According to Fechnerian thinking, the sensation magnitudes of both stimuli, in this situation, have been raised by the same amount and therefore the two stimuli should still appear subjectively equal. Because this prediction was not confirmed, it follows that jnd's are not subjectively equal and therefore cannot be used as the basic unit for measurement of sensation magnitude.

For more than 100 years, Fechner's equation was widely accepted in psychology and, to some extent, in other fields, such as physiology and engineering. Today, it is not considered an accurate statement of the relationship between stimulus intensity and sensation magnitude. However, the fact that experimental results have not led to the verification of Fechner's law does not detract from the overall significance of his work. The importance of his accomplishments lies in the direction he took while trying to deal with problems of mental events. The concept of measurement, a primary goal of science, became a part of psychological investigation through Fechner's work.

PROBLEMS

1.1. Using Weber's formula $\Delta\phi = c\phi$ calculate $\Delta\phi$ for ϕ values of 10, 15, 20, 25, and 30, when c is .1 and when it is .2. On the same graph plot $\Delta\phi$ as a function of ϕ for the two values of c. On another graph plot $\Delta\phi/\phi$ as a function of ϕ for the two values of c.

1.2. If, in an experiment, you found $\Delta\phi$ to be 2.4 when ϕ was 10.0, and you assumed the validity of Weber's law, $\Delta\phi = c\phi$, what values of $\Delta\phi$ would you expect if you repeated the experiment for ϕ values of 3.0, 5.0, 20.0, and 30.0? Plot the expected values of $\Delta\phi$ as a function of ϕ.

1.3. Experimentally determined values of $\Delta\phi$ can seldom be accurately predicted from the equation $\Delta\phi = c\phi$. For example, the values of $\Delta\phi$ presented below could represent the typical results of a discrimination experiment.

ϕ	$\Delta\phi$
3.0	1.0
5.0	1.4
10.0	2.4
20.0	4.4
30.0	6.4

On the graph used for problem 1.2, plot these experimentally determined values of $\Delta\phi$ and compare them to those predicted from the Weber equation, $\Delta\phi = c\phi$

1.4. For the experimentally determined values of $\Delta\phi$ given in problem 1.3, calculate the Weber fraction, $\Delta\phi/\phi$, and plot it as a function of ϕ. How does this function deviate from that expected from the Weber equation $\Delta\phi/\phi = c$?

1.5. Test the hypothesis that the equation $\Delta\phi/(\phi + a) = c$ is a better description of the hypothetical data of problem 1.3 than the Weber equation $\Delta\phi/\phi = c$. Assume a value of 2.0 for a and calculate c from $\Delta\phi/(\phi + a) = c$ for each value of ϕ. Plot $\Delta\phi/(\phi + a)$ as a function of ϕ.

1.6. In deriving his law, Fechner assumed Weber's equation, $\Delta\phi = c\phi$ was correct. Assuming c to be .1, determine the values of ϕ corresponding to the first 10 jnd's above an absolute threshold of 5.0. Using the logic of Fechner, make a graph of sensation magnitude, ψ, as a function of stimulus intensity, ϕ. Repeat the procedure for $c = .2$.

1.7. Convert the ϕ values of problem 1.6 to logarithms and plot sensation magnitude as a function of log ϕ. Write equations for the functions obtained for the two values of c in the Weber equation.

1.8. Upon what two basic assumptions is Fechner's law based? Evaluate the validity of these assumptions.

2

Psychophysical Measurement of Thresholds: Absolute Sensitivity

The measurement of the absolute threshold, though perhaps not as important for the development of psychology as Fechner's insights into difference thresholds, has led to many significant advances in understanding sensory systems. Before considering in detail the various psychophysical methods for measuring DL's and RL's, let us consider examples of how measuring absolute thresholds has facilitated our understanding of vision, audition, touch, and olfaction.

The Absolute Sensitivity of the Eye

The eye is an extremely light-sensitive instrument capable of responding to almost unbelievably small amounts of light energy. However, a simple answer cannot be given to the question: How sensitive is the eye to light? The absolute sensitivity of the eye cannot be gauged by a single threshold value, since the minimum amount of light necessary for vision has been found to depend on the conditions of stimulation. Therefore, the absolute sensitivity of the visual system is best understood by examining the functional relationships between the absolute threshold and the conditions that determine its value.

The value of the absolute threshold depends upon previous stimulation. Exposing the eye to intense light greatly decreases the absolute sensitivity of the eye. Sensitivity is recovered gradually if the eye is subsequently kept in darkness. Nearly complete recovery of sensitivity occurs after about one hour in the dark. The dark adaptation curve is traced out by measuring an observer's absolute threshold periodically during the recovery period and plotting its value as a function of time in the dark. The threshold at the beginning of dark adaptation may be as much as 100,000 times as high (5 log units) as the threshold after complete dark adaptation.

In an experiment by Hecht, Haig, and Chase (1937), the test stimulus was presented to a region of the retina containing both rods and cones, and the dark adaptation curve was found to be biphasic (Figure 2.1). The first phase shows a relatively rapid reduction in the absolute threshold as a function of time in the dark and shows the threshold stabilizing after 5–8 min. The second phase, starting after about 10 min in the dark, was a relatively gradual decrease in the threshold which was complete after about 40 min. The point on the curve where the second phase begins is called the rod–cone break. The biphasic curve is caused by the intersecting of the cone and rod recovery curves, which start at different intensity levels, change at different rates, and approach different asymptotes. Before the rod–cone break, the absolute threshold of the rods is so high that the adaptation curve is determined completely by the changing sensitivity of the cones. The rod–cone break represents the point where rod sensitivity finally begins to exceed cone sensitivity, and thereafter the remainder of the dark adaptation curve is determined by the continuing recovery of the rods.

Under most conditions, the electromagnetic radiation is visible when its wavelength is between 400 and 750 nanometers (nm). However, the

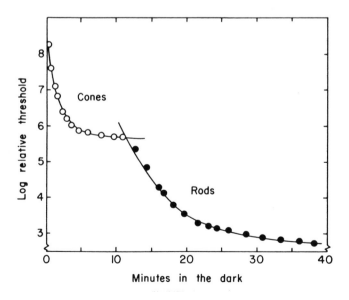

FIG. 2.1. Biphasic curve for dark adaptation. The logarithm of the threshold intensity is plotted against time in the dark. (From Hecht, Haig, & Chase, 1937.)

eye is not equally sensitive to light of all wavelengths. Spectral sensitivity curves showing the absolute threshold as a function of stimulus wavelength have been obtained for cone (photopic) and rod (scotopic) vision. In one such experiment, Wald (1945) measured the absolute thresholds of 22 observers for detecting a 1.0°, 40-msec test stimulus of variable wavelength presented either within the fovea or 8° above the fovea. Figure 2.2 illustrates that light in the extreme blue or red regions on the visual spectrum is relatively ineffective in producing visual responses. The periphery of the retina is most sensitive to light with a wavelength of approximately 500 nm, and the fovea is most sensitive when the stimulus wavelength is about 560 nm. For all wavelengths, the stimulus flash at threshold appeared to be colored for foveal stimulation, indicating the operation of cones, but all threshold stimuli appeared achromatic for peripheral stimulation, indicating the operation of rods. That rods are considerably more sensitive than cones at all but the longest wavelengths is illustrated by the fact that much less energy is required at threshold for peripheral stimulation than for foveal stimulation. The difference between rod and cone thresholds is clearly illustrated by gradually increasing the intensity of a colored light presented to an extrafoveal region of the retina containing both rods and cones. When the rod threshold is reached, the light appears colorless; however, with continued increases in intensity, a point is reached where the light is above the cone threshold, and color is finally perceived. The difference between the rod and cone thresholds measured in this way is called the photochromatic interval. It is an interval on the stimulus intensity scale in which a colored light is perceived, but as colorless. As Figure 2.2 shows us, the size of the photochromatic interval varies with wavelength, being smallest for the long wavelengths and becoming larger for shorter wavelengths.

In physics, it has been shown that light can be described as both a wave and a particle, or quantum. Prior to this development it was thought that energy varied on a continuum. We now know that—due to its quantal nature—energy, including light, changes in discrete steps. The light quantum, also known as a photon, is the smallest possible unit of light energy. It has been determined that vision occurs when the number of quanta absorbed by retinal receptors exceeds some small critical number.

The receptors are able to summate energy over space, as indicated by the fact that, within certain spatial limits, the total number of quanta is constant at threshold, whether they are distributed sparsely over a large area (up to about 10 min of arc in the fovea and 1° in the periphery of the eye) or are concentrated in a small area. This process is called *spatial summation*. Likewise, the visual receptors are able to summate energy over time up to about .1 sec, since it has been found that the total number of quanta at threshold is the same when exposing the eye to a weak

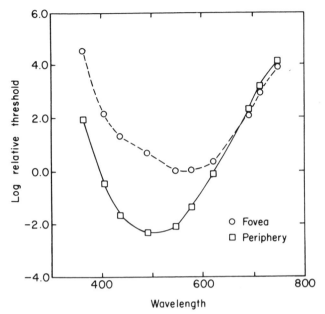

FIG. 2.2. Relative thresholds for detection of light as a function of wavelength and location of the stimulus on the retina. (From Wald, 1945. Copyright 1945 by the American Association for the Advancement of Science.)

stimulus for a long time as when exposing it to a strong stimulus for a short time. This process is called *temporal summation*. Because the eye is unable to summate energy completely over time intervals exceeding .1 sec or areas exceeding about 10 min in diameter, beyond these limits a greater number of quanta are required at absolute threshold.

In what has become a classic experiment in visual science, Hecht, Shlaer, and Pirenne (1942) determined the amount of light at the retina necessary for vision under conditions yielding optimal sensitivity. The following steps were taken to provide optimal conditions for visual sensitivity: (a) the retina was dark-adapted for at least 30 min prior to the making of threshold measurements; (b) stimuli were presented on the temporal retina 20° from the fovea, since this area contains a maximum concentration of rods; (c) a very small test field (10 min in diameter) was employed to ensure that within the visual system there would be complete spatial summation of the stimulus[1]; (d) similarly, the exposure time was

---

[1]For stimuli smaller than 1° presented to the periphery of the dark-adapted eye there exists a perfect reciprocal relation between stimulus size and stimulus intensity at the threshold of detectability (Graham, Brown, & Mote, 1939); that is, the total effective energy for the eye is determined by the product of stimulus intensity and stimulus area for areas up to 1° diameter.

very short (.001 sec) so temporal summation would operate; (e) a light of 510 nm was used because of the optimal scotopic sensitivity to light of this wavelength; and (f) so that he would be maximally set for each stimulus, the observer operated the shutter through which the stimulus was presented.

Stimulus intensity was measured by a thermopile which was substituted for the observer's pupil. A thermopile is a thin strip of metal which exhibits an increase in temperature when struck by light. The increment in temperature was then converted into units of light intensity. Thresholds were defined as the stimulus energy resulting in a sensation 60% of the time. They were measured over a period of months for seven observers and ranged between 2.1×10^{-10} and 5.7×10^{-10} ergs at the cornea. These minute amounts of energy represent between 54 and 148 quanta of light.

To specify the number of quanta absorbed at threshold by the photochemical pigment of the visual receptors (rhodopsin), the threshold values measured at the cornea were corrected for losses of light within the eye. Approximately 4% of the light reaching the cornea is reflected back instead of entering the eye. Ludvigh and McCarthy (1938) found that 50% of the light of 510 nm entering the eye is absorbed by the ocular media before reaching the retina. Finally, it has been estimated that at most only 20% of the light reaching the retina is absorbed by the rhodopsin of the receptors, the remainder being absorbed by other tissues such as blood vessels. The threshold value of 54 to 148 quanta measured at the cornea, when corrected for the above factors, is only 5 to 14 quanta absorbed by rhodopsin. In the 10-min retinal area stimulated, there are approximately 500 rods, thus making it highly unlikely that more than one quantum will strike a single rod at threshold levels of intensity. On this basis, Hecht et al. (1942) concluded that, in order to see, it is necessary for only one quantum of light to be absorbed by a single molecule of photochemical pigment in each of 5 to 14 rods. The maximum sensitivity of the eye approaches a limit imposed by the nature of light.

It is of considerable interest that in order to exceed the observer's absolute threshold, 5 to 14 rods must each be activated by the absorption of a single quantum of light. Given the exquisite sensitivity of these visual receptors, why is a single quantum absorption by a single rod not sufficient for seeing? The answer is that, as discussed earlier in this chapter with regard to the measurement of differential sensitivity, sensory thresholds are limited by the presence of internal noise in the nervous system. In the case of vision, at any moment, rods, in the absence of light, spontaneously send neural signals to the brain. Thus, because the visual system, with its ever present spontaneous neural activity, is inherently noisy, it is not possible for the observer to discriminate the neural activity generated by an external light stimulus from that generated internally as spontaneous background noise unless the light produces neural activity in at least 5 to 14 rods. When encountering the Theory of Signal Detection in Chapter 5, the reader becomes increasingly aware of the fundamental importance of the concept of internal noise to our understanding how we detect environmental stimuli. At this point, it suffices to say that, because of internal noise, absolute and differential sensitivity are very similar. In both cases, the observer must discriminate between two things. In the measurement of differential sensitivity it is the difference between two stimuli that must be discriminated, whereas in absolute sensitivity it is the difference between a stimulus and internal noise that must be discriminated.

The Absolute Sensitivity of the Ear

The remarkable sensitivity of the eye under optimal conditions of stimulation has been found to be nearly matched by that of the ear. Under normal conditions, a young person can hear sound when its frequency of vibration is between 20 and 20,000 Hz. However, the auditory system is most sensitive to vibrations between 2000 and 4000 Hz and is least sensitive to vibrations at the extremes of the audible range of frequencies. In Figure 2.3, the absolute threshold in decibels (dB) sound pressure level[2] is plotted for the frequencies that are employed in standard hearing tests. This graph, prepared by the International Organization for Standardization, is based on the combining of results from a number of studies in which an attempt was made to determine normal hearing for young people (Davis & Krantz, 1964). The extremely low thresholds for the middle frequencies can be better appreciated when the physical effects of such low sound pressure on the eardrum are determined. Wilska (1935) attached one end of a light wooden rod to the eardrum and the other end to a loudspeaker coil. The rod was vibrated, and voltage across the speaker coil was adjusted, so that a tone could hardly be heard. The vibration amplitude of the rod, and thus the amplitude of the in–out movement of the eardrum, was then measured under stroboscopic illumination with a microscope. Direct measurements of the movement of the rods could be made only for the low frequencies of vibration. At high frequencies, the movement was so slight at threshold that it had to be calculated from larger movements of the rod at low frequencies.

---

[2]Sound pressure is often expressed on a logarithmic scale as the number of decibels above a reference sound pressure. The most frequently used reference is .0002 dyne per square centimeter. The number of decibels can be computed by the formula

$$N_{dB} = 20 \log p_1/p_0,$$

where p_0 is a sound pressure of .0002 dyne/cm^2 and p_1 is the measured sound pressure.

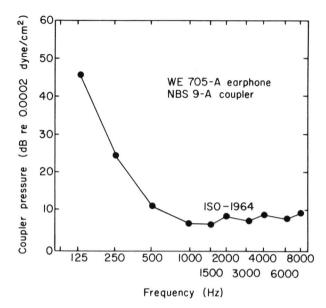

FIG. 2.3. Absolute threshold in decibels sound pressure level for the detection of pure tones as a function of stimulus frequency. (From Davis & Krantz, 1964.)

The results of the study indicate that, for frequencies of between 2000 and 4000 Hz, the eardrum has to move only 10^{-9} cm in order for a sound to be heard. This amount of movement is less than the diameter of a hydrogen molecule. By using a highly precise laser interferometer to measure vibration amplitude of the cat's eardrum at threshold, Tonndorf and Khanna (1968) were able to confirm Wilska's findings. Peak displacement amplitude at threshold was 10^{-10} cm at 1000 Hz and close to 10^{-11} cm at 5000 Hz.

It has also been estimated that the hair cells serving as sensory receptors in the inner ear, when vibrated at 2000–4000 Hz by presenting a tone to the ear, must also be moved by less than the diameter of a hydrogen molecule for hearing to occur. These remarkably low psychophysical thresholds for detection of sound suggest that, as in vision, the sensitivity of the auditory system may be approaching a limit imposed by the nature of the stimulus.

Is the sensitivity of the ear limited by its construction and physiological efficiency, or is it limited by the nature of air as a transmitting medium for sound? Sivian and White (1933) calculated the sound pressure generated by the constant random movement of individual air molecules within the frequency range of 1000–6000 Hz. These calculations indicate that a constant sound pressure exists which is only 10 dB lower than the average auditory threshold of approximately .0002 dyne/cm^2 for sounds within this frequency range. Furthermore, people with excellent hearing have thresholds which are approximately the same as the constant sound pressure from the random movement of air molecules. Therefore, for people with excellent hearing, having more sensitive ears would be useless because of the thermal noise continuously present in the air.

The Absolute Sensitivity for Touch

One way of measuring tactile sensitivity is to determine the smallest amplitude of vibration of the skin that can be detected by an observer. Vibrotactile thresholds depend on stimulus factors such as the locus of stimulation, the size of the stimulated skin area, the duration of the stimulus, and the frequency of vibration. An experiment by Verrillo (1963) will serve to illustrate the relationship which is found for the absolute threshold for vibration and the frequency of the vibratory stimulus. In Verrillo's experiment, a stimulator attached to a vibrator was placed in contact with the skin of the prominence on the palm at the base of the thumb. The stimulator protruded up into a hole in a rigid surface upon which the observer's hand rested. There was a 1-mm gap between the circularly shaped stimulator and the rigid surrounding surface. The small gap between the stimulator and the rigid surface upon which the hand rested served to control the area of stimulation by confining the vibration to the area of the stimulator. The data presented in Figure 2.4 were obtained when the size of the stimulator was varied over a range of .005 cm^2 to 5.1 cm^2.

It can be seen in Figure 2.4 that when the stimulator was larger than .02 cm^2, vibrotactile sensitivity was a U-shaped function of frequency and that sensitivity was greatest in the frequency region around 250 Hz where the amplitude of vibration needed to exceed threshold was approximately .1 micron (μm) for the largest contactor. Thus, under the best conditions in which large areas of skin on a relatively sensitive part of the body are stimulated, vibration amplitude had to be 10^{-5} cm for the mechanical disturbance to be detected. This vibration threshold, although impressive, does not compare favorably with a vibration threshold of 10^{-11} cm for movement of the eardrum necessary for hearing a 5000-Hz tone. The superiority of auditory sensitivity may be due to the greater efficiency of the auditory system in conducting mechanical disturbances to the receptors and/or the greater sensitivity of the auditory receptors.

Variation of the size of the stimulator had an interesting effect in Verrillo's study. Increasing the size of stimulators larger than .02 cm^2 resulted in a proportional decrease in the threshold. This finding indicated that the tactile system is capable of summating stimulation over a relatively large area. For stimuli that were .02 cm^2 or smaller, no spatial

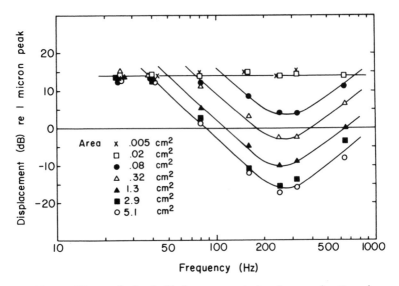

FIG. 2.4. Vibrotactile thresholds for seven contactor sizes as a function of vibration frequency. (From Verrillo, 1963.)

summation was observed. Furthermore, it can be seen that the frequency curve for these small stimulators is not U shaped, but rather that the threshold is uniformly high at all frequencies. Verrillo concluded from these findings that the skin contains at least two receptor systems which are involved in the detection of mechanical disturbances. One system summates energy over space and accounts for the U-shaped frequency function obtained when all but the smallest stimulators are used. The other system, which is not capable of spatial summation, accounts for the flat frequency function when thresholds are measured for very small contactors. By comparing psychophysical data with data on the electrophysiological response of individual tactile receptors, Verrillo (1966) was able to identify the Pacinian corpuscle as the receptor responsible for spatial summation and the U-shaped frequency response curve. There is remarkable correspondence between the U-shaped psychophysical function and the neural response of a Pacinian corpuscle (Figure 2.5). More recently, the flat portion of the psychophysical curve has been associated with other mechanoreceptors, such as Meissner corpuscles and Merkel discs.

Vibrotactile thresholds for stimuli presented within a much wider frequency range than employed in the earlier study by Verrillo are seen in Figure 2.6. These results obtained by Bolanowski, Gescheider, Verrillo, and Checkosky (1988) provided the basis for a four channel model of mechanoreception. The data points are average thresholds for five ob-

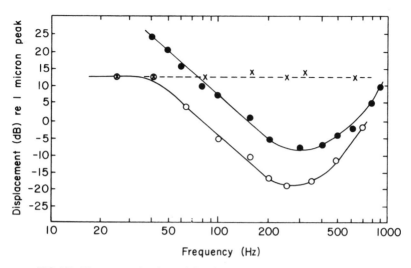

FIG. 2.5. Human psychophysical thresholds for the detection of vibrotactile stimuli (unfilled points) compared with the electrophysiological response of the Pacinian corpuscle in the cat (filled points). The flat curve is obtained when skin containing no Pacinian corpuscles is stimulated or when very small contactors are used. (From Verrillo, 1975. From *Experimental Sensory Psychology* by Bertram Scharf. Copyright © by Scott, Foresman, and Company. Reprinted by permission of the publisher.)

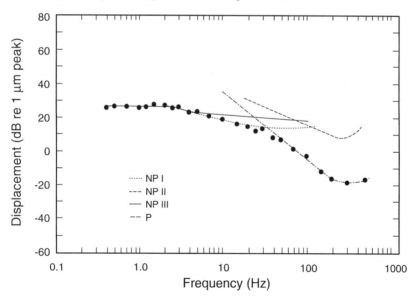

FIG 2.6. Vibrotactile thresholds as a function of frequency (filled data points). The curves are the frequency characteristics of each of four tactile information processing channels. (From Bolanowski, Gescheider, Verrillo, & Checkosky, 1988.)

servers and each of the four curves describes how the threshold of a neural channel is thought to change as vibration frequency changes. According to the model, the psychophysical threshold of the observer, measured at a particular vibration frequency, is determined by the neural channel with the lowest threshold at that frequency. Thus, thresholds, at high frequencies, are determined by the P channel with Pacinian corpuscles as receptors. Thresholds within the midrange of frequencies, between 2 and 40 Hz, are determined by the NPI channel with Meissner corpuscles as receptors, and thresholds at low frequencies (between .4 and 2 Hz) are determined by the NPIII channel with its Merkel receptors. Only when Pacinian corpuscles are absent, defective, or are inadequately stimulated with a very small contactor would the psychophysical threshold for high frequency vibration be determined by the NPII channel with Ruffini end organs as receptors.

Each of the receptor types for touch just described consists of a single sensory nerve fiber surrounded by a specialized end organ that contributes to the overall sensitivity level and frequency tuning of the neural channel. The Pacinian corpuscle, for example, consisting of many layers of tissue, each separated by fluid, is known to greatly attenuate the vibrating stimulus such that the amplitude of vibration at the outer surface of the corpuscle is always much greater than that at the nerve fiber surrounded by the corpuscle. So great is this attenuation of the stimulus that it appears that movement of the nerve fiber required to detect the stimulus may be approximately as low as that observed in hearing (Petrus & Bolanowski, 1996). Thus, mechanoreceptive nerve fibers, whether for hearing or for touch, appear to have extremely low thresholds. The function of the corpuscle surrounding a Pacinian nerve fiber may be to keep the highly sensitive fiber from being overstimulated by intense stimulation in the natural environment.

The four channel model was developed to account for the detection of mechanical stimuli applied to the glabrous, hairless, skin of the palm of the hand. When the hairy skin of the forearm, an area containing a different set of receptors than those found in glabrous skin, was studied, only three channels were discovered (Bolanowski, Gescheider, & Verrillo, 1994) and thresholds were generally higher than those observed for glabrous skin.

In conclusion, the absolute sensitivity of touch depends on a number of factors. From our discussion it is clear that the threshold is greatly influenced by the size of the contactor used to stimulate the skin, the frequency of vibration and the type of skin stimulated. Four separate types of mechanoreceptors in glabrous skin and three types in hairy skin seem to underlie the detection of mechanical stimulation of the skin. The most sensitive of these receptors, optimally responsive to high frequency vibration of approximately 250 Hz, is the Pacinian corpuscle.

The Absolute Sensitivity for Smell

An experiment reminiscent of the work of Hecht et al. (1942) on vision was performed by Stuiver (1958), a Dutch investigator. After determining the smallest number of molecules of a substance that must enter the nose to be detected, Stuiver calculated the number of molecules that had to be absorbed by the olfactory receptors within the nose. Calculations were based on experiments with a physical model of the nasal cavity, which revealed that only 2% of the molecules entering the nose make contact with the olfactory receptors, while the remaining 98% are absorbed in mucus, are carried in air streams that never make contact with the receptor area, or are carried in air streams over the receptor area without affecting it. From his psychophysical data, Stuiver estimated that each of 40 receptor cells had to absorb only a single molecule for a substance to be detected. The sensitivity of the nose, like that of the eye and the ear, approaches a limit imposed by the nature of the stimulus. In other words, under the very best conditions these systems are as sensitive as any sensing device could possibly be for detecting certain specific forms of energy.

TWO FUNCTIONS OF PSYCHOPHYSICS

From the discussions of threshold measurement, it should be apparent that psychophysics serves two basic functions. One function is descriptive and involves the specification of sensory capacities; the other is analytical and involves the testing of hypotheses about the underlying biological mechanisms that determine sensory capacity.

Descriptive Psychophysics

The descriptive function of psychophysics is illustrated by the experiment of Wald (1945), the results of which were seen in Figure 2.2. Through this experiment, we know how the visual threshold changes as the wavelength of light changes for stimuli presented to the fovea or to the periphery of the retina. It is evident from the results of this experiment that vision occurs only within a narrow band of wavelengths within the electromagnetic spectrum which ranges from approximately 350 to 750 nm. It can also be seen that, within this narrow range of visible energy, sensitivity of the visual system changes greatly as the wavelength of light changes; that we are more sensitive to lights presented peripherally than to those presented centrally; and that the most effective wavelength for vision is about 560 nm (yellow) for the fovea and 500 nm (green) for the periphery. In the discussion of visual sensitivity, we also saw that other properties of the visual system, such as adaptation, spatial summation, and temporal summation, could be studied by measuring the threshold as a function of time in the dark after light exposure, size of the stimulus, and duration of the stimulus, respectively. In addition to increasing our understanding of human sensory capacity, knowing this kind of information has had significant practical benefits. For example, an architect must have knowledge of visual sensitivity in order to design a lighting system that will properly illuminate the rooms in a building as inexpensively as possible. In fact, the design of any environment or instrument in which vision is used must take into account the psychophysical capacities of the visual system. In the production of television sets, microscopes, and even in the publication of this book, the characteristics of the human visual system have been a central consideration.

Psychophysics has also been successful in providing quantitative descriptions of the capacities of the other sensory modalities, and such information has been helpful in designing environments and equipment for people's use. For example, the function relating the auditory threshold to the frequency of sound seen in Figure 2.3 has been indispensable in designing rooms for listeners, such as concert halls and classrooms. This function is also essential in designing any system that converts sound into some other form of energy and then back to sound again, such as a radio, phonograph, or telephone. The function tells us that the ear, in acting as a filter, can process information only within a limited range of frequencies. Thus, it is the frequencies of sound within this range that must be faithfully transmitted to the ear in a good sound system. Anything short of fulfilling this requirement will mean that some information in the form of audible sound in the original message will be missing in the transmitted message received by the listener. The consequences of this loss of information will depend on how much information is lost, where in the frequency spectrum the loss occurs, and the objectives of the listener. For example, if the listener is trying to comprehend a verbal message coming over a telephone, the essential information can be transmitted through a telephone, which fails to transmit very low and very high audible frequencies in the voice. On the other hand, if the objective is to listen to recorded music that sounds much like it did in the concert hall in which it was recorded, records, discs, or tapes should be played through a hi-fidelity system capable of transmitting all audible frequencies in the original sound.

Threshold functions for the detection of vibration on the skin, such as the one seen in Figure 2.6, have been useful in designing vibrotactile communication systems for deaf and blind people. For example, much of the early research on vibrotactile communication systems focused on the problem of developing devices capable of transducing speech and music into mechanical vibrations capable of being felt by the skin. In such a system, speech sounds might be converted through a microphone to electrical signals which, after amplification, are converted back to mechanical energy through a vibrator placed in contact with the skin. The design was based on the evolutionary fact that the eardrum, which does so well at responding to the wide range of frequencies present in speech, is a descendant of the skin. Thus, it was thought that we should be able to train the skin to do what the eardrum does (Gault, 1926). The results were disappointing. Although observers could learn to recognize certain speech sounds through their skin, performance was generally poor and unreliable.

A comparison of the psychophysical thresholds for detecting movement of the skin and movement of the eardrum reveals one reason for the skin's relatively poor ability in speech perception (Figure 2.7). The amplitudes of vibration of the skin needed to feel the stimulus are much higher than the amplitudes of vibrations of the eardrum needed to hear. This difference in sensitivity, however, could be compensated for through amplification. A more serious deficiency of the skin is seen in the inability of observers to detect vibrotactile stimuli of frequencies above about 1000

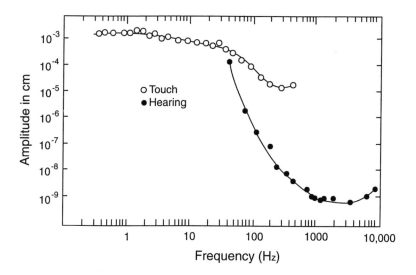

FIG. 2.7. Amplitude of vibration of the skin of the hand needed to feel the stimulus (Bolanowski, Gescheider, Verrillo, & Checkosky, 1988) and amplitude of vibration of the eardrum needed to hear (Wilska, 1935.)

Hz. Since frequencies of vibration contained in speech extend well above 1000 Hz, an accurate representation of speech cannot possibly be transmitted through the skin to the brain. On the other hand, as shown in Figure 2.7, the auditory system can detect very small movements of the eardrum for frequencies up to 10,000 Hz or higher. In addition to having a restricted frequency range, the skin is very poor in discriminating changes in frequency (Goff, 1967). The difference threshold for detecting changes in vibration frequency (ΔF) is plotted as a function of frequency for the skin and for the ear (Figure 2.8). Compared to the ear, the skin, although reasonably good at detecting changes in low frequencies, is poor in discriminating high frequencies. In the range of frequencies important for speech perception, the performance of the skin is very poor compared to that of the ear. For example, when the frequency of vibration is 200 Hz, an increase in frequency of only 2 or 3 Hz is detectable by the ear, while the required increase in frequency for the skin is over 100 Hz. Because of the relatively narrow frequency range and poor frequency discrimination of the skin, it will probably never be possible to "hear" speech through the skin by directly converting the sound to tactile vibration. Attempts are currently being made, however, to design tactile communication systems that operate within the frequency range and frequency discriminative capacities of the tactile sense. If successful, these systems will be a great help to deaf people.

Our brief treatment of descriptive psychophysics illustrates, through a few examples, the use of psychophysical measurements to define the sensitivity of a sensory system. It should be evident that this information can often be used for practical purposes.

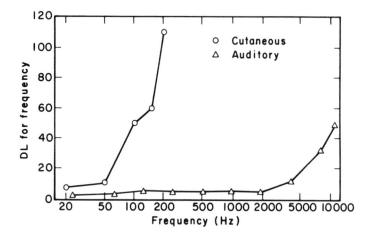

FIG. 2.8. Auditory and tactile difference thresholds for discriminating changes in frequency of vibration. (From Goff, 1967.)

Analytical Psychophysics

The second function of psychophysics has been the testing of hypotheses about the nature of biological mechanisms underlying sensory experience. The work of those investigators who use psychophysics in this way is based on the assumption that there is a basic correspondence between neural activity and perception. The *Principle of Nomination*, as Marks (1978a) has called it, declares that identical neural events give rise to identical psychological events. Thus, according to the principle, when stimulus A and stimulus B produce the same neural response, they will yield the same sensory experience. The reflexive form of the Principle of Nomination states that, when stimulus A and stimulus B produce the same sensory experience, they produce the same neural response. This principle, used in conjunction with those psychophysical procedures in which different stimuli are adjusted to yield identical sensations, constitutes a powerful tool for discovering the neural events that determine sensory experience.

The results of Wald (1945) plotted in Figure 2.2 provide an example of the use of the reflexive Principle of Nomination. In Wald's experiment, identical sensations of colorless light were experienced when the observer detected lights of different wavelengths presented to the peripheral retina. In other words, the rod (scotopic) spectral sensitivity curve gives the physical intensities of stimuli of different wavelengths needed to produce identical sensations. According to the reflexive Principle of Nomination, these combinations of wavelengths and intensity of light will produce identical responses in the nervous system. Indeed, it has been discovered that the number of photons that must be absorbed by the photochemical pigment in rods, rhodopsin, is identical at any wavelength—about 10 photons—for the observers to detect light. Specifically, as illustrated in Figure 2.9(a), the number of photons incident on the cornea of the eye at the detection threshold varies as a function of the wavelength of the stimulus. Since the lens and other ocular media of the eye absorb light, the number of photons at the retina needed for detection must be less than that measured at the cornea. The number of photons at the retina can be calculated at all wavelengths from the absorption spectrum of the ocular media (b). The values in (a) multiplied by the corresponding values in (b) gives the number of photons absorbed by the ocular media. Subtracting these values from (a) gives the number of photons at the retina needed for vision. The results of this calculation are plotted in (c). Of the photons reaching the retina, the number absorbed by the photochemical pigment rhodopsin (e) is determined for each wavelength of light by multiplying the number of photons at the retina needed to exceed threshold (c) by the absorption spectrum of rhodopsin (d). It can be seen in Figure 2.9(e) that

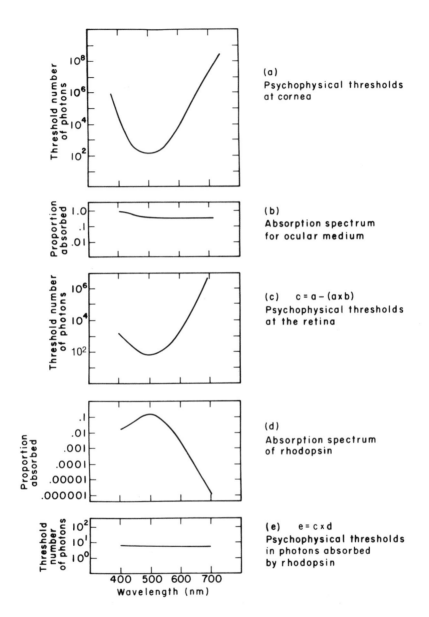

FIG. 2.9. Absolute threshold measured at the cornea of the eye as a function of the wavelength of light (a). Absorption spectrum of the ocular medium of the eye (b). Absolute threshold at the retina of the eye as a function of wavelength of light (c). Absorption spectrum of rhodopsin (d). Absolute threshold expressed as photons absorbed by the photochemical pigment rhodopsin contained in rod receptors in the retina (e).

the number of photons that must be absorbed by rhodopsin in order to exceed the threshold for vision is exactly the same at all wavelengths of light. Thus, combinations of stimulus intensity and wavelengths that produce identical sensations also produce identical photochemical reactions. A fundamental fact of visual science was discovered through integration of data from two fields as different as psychophysics and photochemistry.

More generally, it is by assuming the reflexive Principle of Nomination that it is possible to bridge the gap between psychophysical and biological facts. Because identical sensations are based on identical physiological reactions, a physiological hypothesis can be tested by a psychophysical procedure. Without this principle, the task of correlating sensory experience with physiology would probably be impossible. A biochemist studying visual pigment and a visual psychophysicist studying absolute thresholds would have no common language through which to inter-relate their findings. Because of differences in language, the two scientists would be restricted to working on problems within their own mutually exclusive subdisciplines of visual science. The research described above on the photochemical basis of the spectral sensitivity curve illustrates how the language barrier can be crossed. The hypothesis that changes in an observer's visual sensitivity with changing wavelengths of light are caused by corresponding changes in the degree to which the ocular media and photochemical pigments of the visual receptors absorb light was tested through the *method of response invariance*. In this method, termed by Rodieck (1973), the investigator seeks to discover, not how the response changes as the stimulus is varied, but rather the combinations of stimulus variables that generate identical responses. Threshold responses are considered identical because, within an experiment, the same criterion of performance (e.g., detecting the stimulus 50% of the time) is always used. The intensities of light needed to produce threshold responses were determined for a wide range of wavelengths of light. These combinations of light intensities and wavelengths were also found to result in identical physiological responses (10 photons absorbed by the photochemical pigment of the receptors).

Another name for the method of response invariance is the *criterion response technique*. When it is used to determine the spectral sensitivity of the visual system, the resulting graphed function is called an *action spectrum*. The action spectrum of rods, determined by measuring psychophysical thresholds for detecting lights of various wavelengths, can be compared to the one determined by measuring the number of photons required at each wavelength for a criterion number of photons absorption by rhodopsin. In addition, these two action spectra can be compared with one obtained through electrophysiology, in which the number of photons at each wavelength needed to cause a criterion neural response from rods is measured. A hypothetical set of results is seen in Figure 2.10, in which the action spectra have the same forms when measured psychophysically, photochemically, and electrophysiologically. An implication that has been drawn from the finding that the action spectra are essentially identical when measured in these three ways is that the spectral sensitivity of the observer, as revealed through threshold measurements made at various wavelengths of light, is determined by the spectral sensitivity of the neural responses of rods that, in turn, is determined by the spectral sensitivity of the visual pigment, rhodopsin, found in rods.

Although this approach has been known for many years, it was Brindley (1960) who first explicitly stressed its importance for psychophysics. Brindley distinguished between two general types of psychophysical observations, termed Class A and Class B observations (Figure 2.11). Class A observations are those in which the two stimuli are adjusted so that they elicit the same response from the observer. Threshold experiments and matching experiments in which two stimuli are adjusted to produce identical sensations consist of Class A observations. In both cases, the experimenter determines stimulus conditions needed to produce identical responses and, according to the reflexive Principle of Nomination, identical neural responses. Any observation that cannot be expressed as the identity or nonidentity of two sensations is a Class B observation.

The difference between Class A and Class B observations can be illustrated by examples from research in visual perception. Using Class A

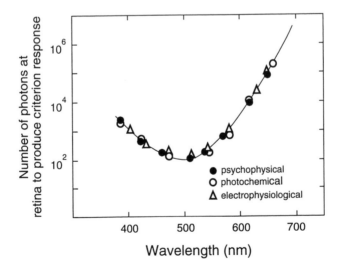

FIG. 2.10. Psychophysical, photochemical, and electrophysiological action spectra. Results are hypothetical but typical of those obtained from actual experiments.

Class A Observation

Stimulus A → Neural Response X → Sensation Y

Stimulus B → Neural Response X → Sensation Y

Class B Observation

Stimulus A → Neural Response X → Sensation Y

Stimulus P → Neural Response Q → Sensation R

FIG. 2.11. Distinction between Class A and Class B observations as described by Brindley (1960).

observations, it is possible for an observer to adjust the intensity and wavelength of a yellow light so that when it is projected on a surface, it produces, in the observer, a yellow sensation identical in brightness and hue to that of a mixture of red and green light projected adjacent to it. For example, with proper adjustment of light intensity, the yellow hue and brightness of a 565-nm light will appear identical to the mixture of a 590-nm red light and a 510-nm green light.

In contrast to Class A observations, Class B observations are when the observer's adjustments of two stimuli, although achieving a match over some dimension of perception, do not make the two sensations indiscriminable. For example, if you match two different hues, say, red and green, so that they appear equal in brightness, then you are making a Class B observation. The two sensations are still different by virtue of their differences in hue, although they are matched on the brightness dimension. Because the two sensations are not identical you cannot apply the reflexive principle of nomination. Thus, although valuable information may be obtained through Class B observations, they have limited implications for determining underlying physiological events.

In many Class B observations, the experimenter determines how the sensory response of the observer changes as the stimulus changes. Included as Class B observations are all those in which an observer reports that his sensation changes from blue to green when the wavelength of light is changed, or that a light has become twice as bright when its intensity is increased. That observers can reliably make these kinds of judgments forms the basis of many of the psychophysical scaling procedures discussed in chapters 9 through 14. Although Class B observations can be made reliably, they lack what Brindley calls a *psychophysical linking hypothesis*, which would provide a rigorous means by which psychophysical observations could be used to test hypotheses about underlying physiological mechanisms. Class A observations, on the other hand, coupled with the assumption that identical sensations are based on identical physiological events, provide a means for testing a physiological hypothesis with a psychophysical procedure. By using the method of response invariance for both the domains of sensation and physiology, it is possible to look for physiological responses that are absolutely identical when different stimuli produce sensations that are absolutely identical. Many psychophysicists have argued that it is only from such invariances that the physiological bases of sensation will be discovered. At the very least, the method of response invariance has made explicit certain methodological implications of the philosophy of materialism and has provided a powerful tool for the scientific study of sensory processes.

A second example of the use of the method of response invariance is seen in the work of Verrillo on the neurophysiological basis of the detection of vibration of the skin. In examining the absolute sensitivity for touch, we saw that the threshold for detecting vibration is independent of stimulus frequency at low frequencies and is a U-shaped function of frequency for higher frequencies (Figure 2.4). To account for this observation, Verrillo (1963) proposed a duplex theory of mechanoreception, in which he hypothesized that one type of receptor was responsible for detecting low frequencies and another for detecting high frequencies.

A sharp break in a psychophysical threshold function often represents a transition from the operation of one type of sensory receptor to another. In using psychophysical threshold functions to identify receptor systems, the assumption is made that the psychophysical threshold is always determined by the receptors that have the lowest threshold. Recall that the initial segment of the dark adaptation curve of Figure 2.1 was determined by cones because immediately after exposure to the adapting light their thresholds are lower than rod thresholds. However, after several minutes in the dark, the reverse was true and rods determined the threshold for the remainder of the experiment.

Verrillo (1966) subsequently identified the Pacinian corpuscle as the receptor responsible for detecting high frequency vibration. Verrillo's comparison of psychophysical threshold functions for human observers with neural threshold functions of Pacinian corpuscles is an example of the method of response invariance. Both functions seen in Figure 2.5 represent combinations of stimulus intensity and frequency needed to produce threshold responses. Because of the close correspondence between the U-shaped segment of the psychophysical function and the neural threshold function, Verrillo concluded that high frequency vibration is detected exclusively through stimulation of Pacinian corpuscles. Recent evidence strengthening this argument comes from Bolanowski and Verrillo (1982), who compared psychophysical thresholds for humans with neural thresholds for Pacinian corpuscles of cats. As in the Verrillo (1966) study, the relationship between threshold and stimulus frequency was examined. In addition, the skin temperature of the observer's hand and the temperature of the bathing solution of the cat's Pacinian corpuscles were experimentally varied. The results seen in Figure 2.12 show that variation in temperature has a strikingly similar effect on psychophysical and neural thresholds. In both cases, the frequency of maximum sensitivity (i.e., the frequency with the lowest threshold) shifted to higher frequencies as temperature increased. Thus, a correspondence between psychophysical and neural threshold functions was observed over a wide range of temperatures, even though the shape of the functions changed with temperature. This result is expected if a single receptor-type mediates the detection of high frequency vibration. When the frequency response of the Pacinian corpuscle is changed by manipulation of a variable such as temperature, there should follow a corresponding change in psychophysical thresholds. Bolanowski and Verrillo's findings strongly support this hypothesis.

When it is not possible to compare psychophysical and neural threshold functions, the full power of the method of response invariance cannot be exploited. Nevertheless, in the absence of neural response data it may be possible to identify underlying neural mechanisms from psychophysical data. For example, the *method of selective adaptation* has been used to study the properties of sensory receptors. When using this method, the assumption is made that, by exposing the observer to a carefully selected adapting stimulus, the thresholds of all types of receptors but one are sufficiently elevated so that the one type of receptor that remains sensitive will determine the psychophysical threshold. This method has been successfully used to study how the sensitivity of visual receptors changes as the wavelength of light changes (Stiles, 1959; Wald, 1964). Spectral sensitivity curves, as determined psychophysically under conditions of adaptation, were found to be in substantial agreement with those determined physiologically for individual receptors. Figure 2.13 illustrates a typical threshold function where small stimuli are presented exclusively to the fovea, an area of the retina containing only cone receptors. The three segments of the curve reveal the wavelengths at which each of the three types of cone, blue sensitive, green sensitive, and red sensitive, have their lowest thresholds. Because the threshold curves for each type of cone overlap substantially, it is not possible, in this experiment, to determine the entire curve for each of the individual cone types. One can, however, examine the threshold curve of one cone type if the threshold of the other two are elevated by selectively

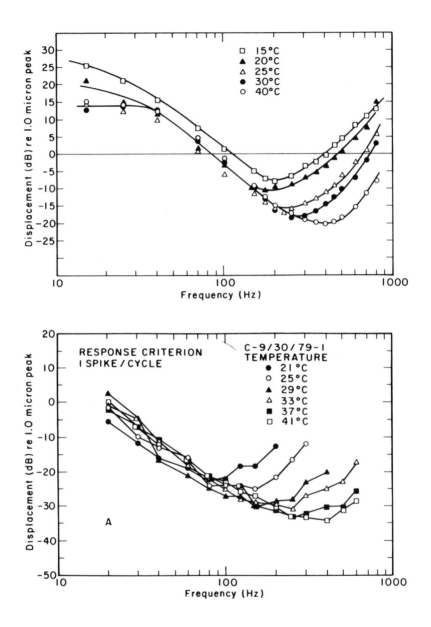

FIG. 2.12. Psychophysical threshold for detection of vibration on the hand as a function of frequency and skin temperature (top). Neural threshold of Pacinian corpuscle as a function of frequency and temperature of bathing solution (bottom). (From Bolanowski & Verrillo, 1982.)

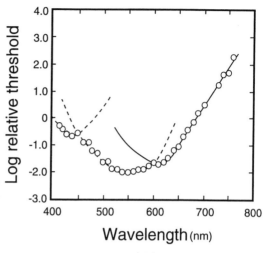

FIG. 2.13. Logarithm of relative threshold as a function of the wavelength of a stimulus presented to cones in the fovea. (Data from Hsia & Graham, 1952.)

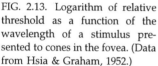

adapting them. Figure 2.14 illustrates typical results obtained with this procedure when the fovea is exposed to short wavelength light that elevates the threshold of the blue- and green-sensitive cones but has no effect on the thresholds of the red-sensitive cone. The thresholds obtained in this experiment reveal how the threshold of the red-sensitive cone varies over a wide range of wavelengths. The procedure of selective adaptation is based on the principle that the psychophysical threshold is always determined by the receptor with the lowest neural threshold. In the present example, the blue-sensitive and green-sensitive cones are adapted so that, over a wide range of wavelengths, the threshold of the red-sensitive cone is lowest, and therefore determines the psychophysical thresholds. Thus, it is possible, by measuring for a wide range of wavelengths, the psychophysical threshold for detecting light, to determine the spectral sensitivity curve for the red-sensitive receptor. We turn now to a specific experiment in which

FIG. 2.14. Logarithm of relative threshold after adaptation of the eye to short wavelength light. Thresholds mediated by red-sensitive cones along the unadapted segment of the curve were unaffected by the adapting stimulus. Thresholds mediated by blue-sensitive and green-sensitive cones were elevated through exposure to the adapting stimulus.

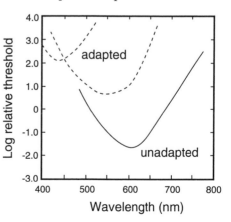

George Wald measured the spectral sensitivity curves for each of the three cone types.

In Wald's (1964) experiment, the observer was required to detect a small circle (1.0°) of variable wavelength presented against a larger (3.5°) illuminated background of fixed wavelength. By having the observer visually fixate a small point where the test stimulus was presented, no rods, and only the cones of the fovea, were stimulated. The objective of the experiment was to measure, through psychophysical procedures, the spectral sensitivity of each of the three types of cones in the fovea.

Spectral sensitivity curves, where sensitivity is plotted as a function of the wavelength of the test stimulus, had to be determined for each type of cone. The wavelength and intensity of the background were carefully chosen so that the background, through sensory adaptation, would cause substantial elevations in the thresholds of two types of cones, but have little effect on the third. Thus, measurements of psychophysical thresholds for detecting test stimuli of varied wavelength should reveal the spectral sensitivity of a single type of cone. The psychophysical thresholds for detecting light would always be determined by the cone with the lowest neural threshold.

To obtain the spectral sensitivity curve for the blue-sensitive cone, Wald's observers detected stimuli of variable wavelength presented against a bright yellow background containing all visible wavelengths longer than 550 nm. A yellow background stimulus such as this should elevate the neural thresholds of red-sensitive and green-sensitive cones, while having little effect on the thresholds of blue-sensitive cones. Psychophysical thresholds for detecting stimuli of varied wavelength presented against the yellow background should reveal the spectral sensitivity of the blue-sensitive cone. On the other hand, having the observer detect the test-lights against a blue background should elevate the thresholds of the blue-sensitive and green-sensitive cones, while having little effect on the sensitivity of the red-sensitive cone. The spectral sensitivity of the red-sensitive cone should be revealed by measuring psychophysical thresholds for detecting lights of varied wavelength presented against the blue background. Finally, to isolate the spectral sensitivity of the green-sensitive cone, Wald had observers detect lights of varied wavelength presented against a purple background containing wavelengths in both the blue and red regions of the visual spectrum. In this condition, the green-sensitive cone should be much more sensitive than the adapted blue-sensitive or red-sensitive cones, and consequently, the psychophysical thresholds should reveal the spectral sensitivity of the green-sensitive cones.

The results obtained for one of Wald's observers are presented in Figure 2.15. Sensitivity was expressed as the reciprocal of the measured threshold (1/threshold). The logarithm of sensitivity is plotted as a function of the wavelength of the test stimulus. The absolute height of each curve was not

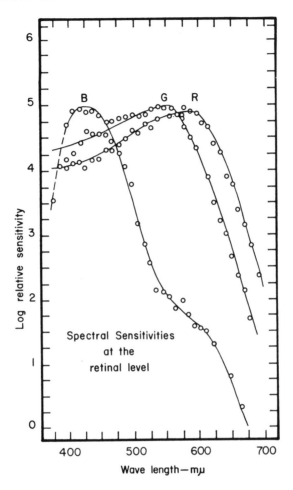

FIG. 2.15. Visual sensitivity (1/threshold) for stimuli presented to the fovea after adaptation. The blue curve (B) represents the psychophysical thresholds measured after adaptation to a yellow light. The green curve (G) represents the psychophysical thresholds measured after adaptation to a purple light. The red curve (R) represents the psychophysical thresholds measured after adaptation to blue light. (From Wald, 1964.)

determined, and thus a measure of relative sensitivity (i.e., sensitivity changes of a cone with changes in wavelength) was plotted. It can be seen that foveal spectral sensitivity curves obtained with different adapting backgrounds peaked at different wavelengths of the spectrum. After adaptation by yellow light, the curve peaked in the blue region of the spectrum. Presumably, this curve was determined entirely by the blue-sensitive cone. When the eye was adapted to purple light, the curve peaked in the green region of the spectrum, presumably reflecting the sensitivity of the green-sensitive cone. Adaptation to blue light resulted in a spectral sensitivity curve which peaked in the red region of the spectrum. Presumably, this curve was determined by the red-sensitive cone.

It must be pointed out that the measurements of light corresponding to the absolute threshold were made at the cornea of the eye and not inside the eye at the receptors. Consequently, the spectral sensitivity curves in Figure 2.15 might not be entirely accurate indicators of the spectral sensitivity of the cones. Wald thought that each of the three spectral sensitivity curves obtained in the presence of adapting background stimuli reflected the sensitivity curve of the cone plus the filtering action of non-neural structures in the eye. In other words, the psychophysical threshold measured at the cornea, in addition to being influenced by the sensitivity of the receptor, was also influenced by how much light reached the receptor after passing through the eye. Wald used absorption curves for non-neural structures in the eye (e.g., cornea, lens, ocular media, and non-visual pigments of the fovea) to correct psychophysical thresholds measured at the cornea, so that they became psychophysical thresholds at the receptors. Under conditions of selective adaptation, having specified the amount of light of various wavelengths that must reach the receptor in order for the observer to see, Wald was able to estimate the spectral sensitivity curve of the cone. Psychophysically measured spectral sensitivity curves for the three types of cones are seen in Figure 2.16.

The method of selective adaptation has also been used to study the characteristics of mechanoreceptors in the skin (Gescheider, Frisina, & Verrillo, 1979; Hollins, Goble, Whitsel, & Tommerdahl, 1990; Verrillo & Gescheider, 1977). In the study by Verrillo and Gescheider (1977), psychophysical thresholds for detecting vibration on the hand were measured before and after adaptation. Adaptation consisted of applying an intense 10-Hz stimulus to the skin for a period of 10 min. It can be seen in Figure 2.17 that adaptation by the 10-Hz stimulus had the selective effect of elevating thresholds at low, but not high, frequencies. Presumably, the low frequency adapting stimulus elevated the thresholds of all receptors except Pacinian corpuscles. Under these conditions, the frequency response of a single receptor type—the Pacinian corpuscle—could be examined over a wide range of frequencies through the measurement of psychophysical thresholds. As a consequence of elevating the thresholds of the non-Pacinian receptors, the flat portion of the psychophysical curve was eliminated, and what remains is the entire U-shaped threshold curve of the Pacinian corpuscle.

From this brief exposure to analytical psychophysics, it should be clear how the reflexive Principle of Nomination that identical sensations produced by stimuli are mediated by identical neural responses has provided the philosophical foundation for a very ambitious approach to psycho-

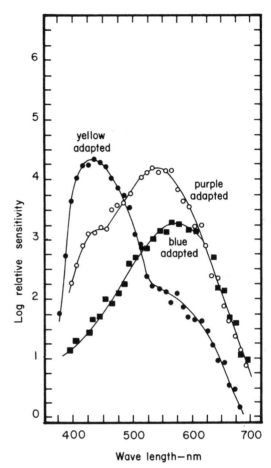

FIG. 2.16. Visual sensitivity corrected for absorption of light by elements of the eye before the retina. The three curves represent sensitivity functions for blue-, green-, and red-sensitive cones in the fovea of the human eye. (From Wald, 1964.)

physics, the goal of which is no less than to determine the neural basis of sensation. According to the analytic psychophysicist, the method of response invariance must be used to determine combinations of stimulus variables that result in identical sensations. Identical sensations are specified through invariant sensory responses, such as the absolute threshold or a psychophysical match of sensations above absolute threshold. Thus, the experimental data always consist of measurements of properties of the stimulus (e.g., intensity and wavelength) that correspond to a constant sensory response. Only after the stimulus conditions that produce identical sensation have been determined is it possible to discover the underlying neural response. After the psychophysical measurements are made, the investigator may then proceed to search for neural responses that remain constant under the same stimulus conditions that resulted in constant sensation. The discovery of such invariances in neural response

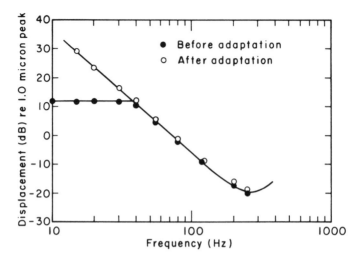

FIG. 2.17. Vibrotactile thresholds on the hand as a function of frequency measured before and after adaptation. (From Verrillo & Gescheider, 1977.)

has greatly enhanced our understanding of the neural basis of sensation and has provided strong support for the basic assumption and procedures of analytic psychophysics.

We have considered the methodological assumptions for investigating the biological bases of psychophysical responses. It is appropriate to turn now to the various techniques for measuring sensory thresholds.

PROBLEMS

2.1. Below are the neural thresholds for hypothetical neural systems A and B at various wavelengths of light. Plot these values and draw a smooth curve indicating the predicted psychophysical thresholds.

					Wavelength in nm						
	400	420	440	460	480	500	520	540	560	580	600	620
System A	80	52	40	38	37	37	36	36	38	40	43	48
System B	140	108	80	56	38	20	10	7	8	12	15	30

2.2. Draw the curve describing absolute thresholds for detecting vibration on the hand as a function of vibration frequency. Assuming that the four-channel model is correct, draw the threshold function for each of channels (see Figure 2.6). Now draw the threshold curve predicted after adaptation of the P channel with a 250 Hz adapting stimulus.

3

The Classical Psychophysical Methods

The experiments described in Chapters 1 and 2 are examples of how psychophysics has been used to determine the sensitivity of perceptual systems to environmental stimuli. In Chapter 3, the specific methods for measuring sensitivity are discussed in detail.

Presenting a stimulus to observers and asking them to report whether or not they perceive it is the basic procedure for measuring thresholds. Biological systems are not fixed, however, but rather are variable in their reaction. Therefore, when an observer is presented on several occasions with the same stimulus, he or she is likely to respond yes on some trials and no on other trials. Thus, the threshold cannot be defined as the stimulus value below which detection never occurs and above which detection always occurs. The concept of the threshold has obviously been, and still is, useful, since it affords a technique for quantifying the sensitivity of sensory systems. But since reactions to stimuli are variable, the threshold must be specified as a statistical value. Typically, the threshold has been defined as the stimulus value which is perceptible in 50% of the trials.

Fechner recognized the statistical nature of thresholds and the necessary methodological consequences. Psychologists are indebted to him for developing three methods of threshold measurement: the methods of constant stimuli, limits, and adjustment. Each of these methods consists of an experimental procedure and a mathematical treatment of data. These extremely valuable techniques for obtaining absolute and difference thresholds (RL's and DL's) are still used today.

METHOD OF CONSTANT STIMULI

Absolute Thresholds

The method of constant stimuli is the procedure of repeatedly using the same set of stimuli (usually between five and nine different values in the set) throughout the experiment. The 50% threshold is located somewhere within the range of stimulus values—the lower end of which should be a stimulus that can almost never be detected, and the upper end of which should be a stimulus that is almost always detected. As the intensity level is increased within this range, the likelihood of detecting the stimulus will systematically increase. Through the method of constant stimuli, the percentage of detections as a function of stimulus intensity, ϕ is determined.

Preliminary observations are made for locating the approximate range of values in which the stimulus of lowest intensity is seldom perceived, and the stimulus of highest intensity is almost always perceived. The procedure requires that each stimulus be presented repeatedly, usually 100 times or more, but in a random order. During the experiment, a count of the number of yes or no responses for each stimulus intensity level is kept. For each stimulus value, the proportion (p) of yes responses is then computed, and a graph called a *psychometric function* is constructed. Stimulus intensity is plotted on the abscissa, and the proportion of yes responses is plotted on the ordinate. A psychometric function for a hypothetical experiment using nine stimulus intensities is seen in Figure 3.1. In this

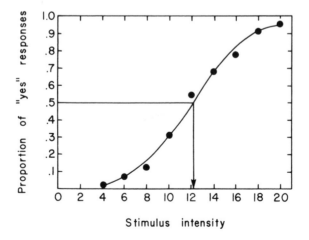

FIG. 3.1. Typical psychometric function obtained when the absolute threshold is measured by the method of constant stimuli. An ogive curve has been fitted to the points. The threshold is the stimulus intensity that would be detected 50% of the time.

example, the absolute threshold (defined as the stimulus intensity for which the proportion of trials resulting in yes responses is .5) does not correspond to any of the stimuli used in the experiment. Therefore, a curve must be fitted to the nine data points and the threshold estimated by reading, from the curve, the stimulus intensity for the .5 point. In our example, the threshold is 12.3 units. It should be noted that the best fitting curve for the data points is an S-shaped function. If enough measurements are made, psychometric functions often follow a particular S shape called an *ogive*.

The procedure of fitting ogives to the points on a psychometric function is supported by theory as well as by experimental findings. Variation of biological and psychological measurements tends to be normally distributed; when the frequencies or proportions of measurements of various magnitudes are plotted against the dimension on which variation is occurring (e.g., height, weight, IQ, or sensory sensitivity), the result is usually the bell-shaped normal distribution curve. The ogive curve is a cumulative form of this distribution and describes how the proportion of cases below a point on the normal distribution increases as the magnitude of the measurement increases. Various techniques for fitting ogive functions to threshold data range from simply drawing the curve by eye to employing various elaborate mathematical techniques.

One useful technique for fitting a particular mathematical function to pairs of numbers is to transform the numbers into units that should be linearly related if the mathematical function is appropriate. An ogive psychometric function has the convenient feature of becoming a linear function when the proportion of responses for each stimulus-value is transformed into a z score (Table 3.1). A normal distribution table is used to convert p values into z scores. The z-score values in Table 3.1 were

TABLE 3.1
Proportion of Detections and Corresponding z Scores for
Various Stimulus Intensity Values (Hypothetical Data)

Stimulus intensity (ϕ)	Proportion detected	z score
4	.04	−1.75
6	.07	−1.48
8	.13	−1.13
10	.31	−.50
12	.55	+.13
14	.66	+.41
16	.78	+.77
18	.93	+1.48
20	.98	+2.05

obtained by using the abridged version of the normal distribution table found in Table A of the appendix of this book. The p values in Table A represent the proportion of the area under the normal distribution curve below a particular z-score value on the abscissa of this curve.

Figure 3.2 illustrates the reason that the shape of the cumulative normal distribution, where p is plotted as a function of X, changes from an ogive to a straight line when p values are converted to z scores. In this example, the values of X, a hypothetical set of measurements, are normally distrib-

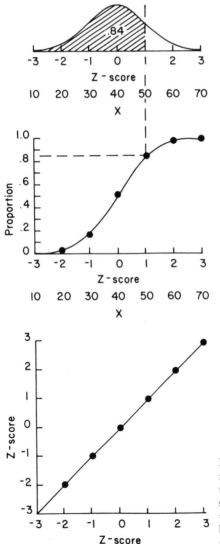

FIG. 3.2. Derivation of an ogive function from the normal distribution curve. Each point on the ogive specifies the proportion of the total area under the normal distribution that is below (to the left of) a specific point.

uted. Thus, the abscissa of the normal distribution curve is expressed in both z scores and X units. The ogive curve in Figure 3.2 results when z scores are converted to p values and plotted as a function of corresponding z-score and X values. For example, it can be seen from Table A that a p value of .84 is associated with a z score of .99. The p value of .84 and the z score of .99 define a point on the ogive function. Furthermore, the p value of .84 constitutes the proportion of the area under the normal distribution that falls below a z score of .99 and an X value of 50. As the z scores and X values become higher, the proportion of area under the normal curve below z and X increases and approaches 1.0. The ogive, therefore, is a description of how the proportion of cases below a point on the abscissa of the normal distribution increases as z and X increase. The second graph in Figure 3.2 shows the linear relationship that must occur when p values are transformed back into z scores and plotted against themselves. It is noteworthy that z plotted against X is also linear. It is only when the relationship between p and X is an ogive that transforming p values to z scores results in a linear function. Consequently, a psychometric function where p is plotted against X can be identified as an ogive if the relationship between p and X becomes linear when p values are expressed as z scores.

In our problem, the proportion of detections, whether expressed as a z score or plotted on a normal probability ordinate, is seen to be a linear function of intensity, and therefore the ogive assumption is correct (Figure 3.3). A straight line can be drawn by eye through the data points to obtain the psychometric function. Given that threshold is defined as a stimulus

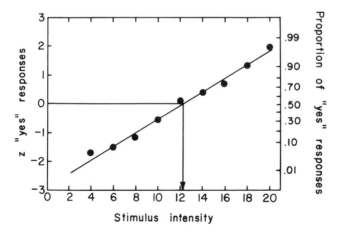

FIG. 3.3. Psychometric function in which the proportions of "yes" responses are expressed as z scores or are plotted on a normal probability ordinate. The linearity of the function indicates that the relation between the proportion of detections and stimulus intensity is an ogive.

which is detected in half of the trials, the measured threshold is the stimulus value for a z score of zero.

The psychometric function can be determined more precisely by determining the best-fitting straight line through a mathematical technique known as the *method of least squares*. In this method, the constants a and b of a straight-line equation $y = ax + b$ are determined. The resulting equation describes a line through the data points which minimizes the squared deviations of the empirical y values from the line. The following equations are used to determine a and b:

$$(\text{intercept})\ b = \frac{(\Sigma\,X^2)\,(\Sigma\,Y) - (\Sigma\,X)\,(\Sigma\,XY)}{N(\Sigma\,X^2) - (\Sigma\,X)^2}\,, \tag{3.1}$$

$$(\text{slope})\ a = \frac{N(\Sigma\,XY) - (\Sigma\,X)\,(\Sigma\,Y)}{N(\Sigma\,X^2) - (\Sigma\,X)^2}\,. \tag{3.2}$$

The value of b is equal to the Y intercept (the value of Y when X is zero) of the best-fitting straight line. The value of a is equal to the slope of the best-fitting straight line.

In our particular problem, X would be the ϕ value, Y would be the corresponding z-score value, and N would be the number of pairs of ϕ and z-score values. When a and b have been calculated, the equation for a straight line that best fits the graph of z scores plotted against stimulus intensity is

$$z = a\phi + b. \tag{3.3}$$

The ϕ values for particular z scores can be determined by using the equation

$$\phi = \frac{z - b}{a}. \tag{3.4}$$

The threshold value would then be determined by calculating ϕ when $z = 0.0$.

Difference Thresholds

The method of constant stimuli can also be used to measure difference thresholds. The observer's task is to examine pairs of stimuli and to judge which stimulus produces a sensation of greater magnitude. One of the stimuli of the pair is given a fixed value and is called the *standard stimulus* (St). The value of the other stimulus, called the *comparison stimulus* (Co), is changed from trial to trial, being sometimes greater than, sometimes less than, and sometimes equal to the value of the standard stimulus. Usually five, seven, or nine values of the comparison stimulus, separated by equal distances on the physical scale, are employed. The values of the comparison stimuli are chosen so that the stimulus of greatest magnitude is almost always judged greater than the standard, and so that the stimulus of least magnitude is almost always judged less than the standard. There are usually an equal number of comparison stimulus values above and below the value of the standard stimulus. In a random sequence, each of the comparison stimuli is paired several times with the standard stimulus, and the observer reports which stimulus has the greater sensory value.

Under ideal conditions, standard and comparison stimuli would be presented together in space and time to permit optimal discriminability. This ideal is impossible, however, because sensations occurring at the same time and initiated at the same receptive areas would blend together and become completely indiscriminable. Therefore, the two stimuli must be presented to different receptive areas at the same time, or to the same receptive area, but at different times. The particular circumstances of an experiment usually determine whether the stimuli are presented simultaneously or successively and to the same or different receptive areas. In experiments on visual brightness discrimination, for example, stimuli are often presented simultaneously to adjacent or nearby areas of the retina; conversely, loudness discrimination is frequently measured by successively presenting the standard and comparison stimuli.

The necessity of presenting stimuli for comparison to different receptors or at different times may lead to certain errors of measurement, unless special precautions are taken in designing the experiment. If stimuli are presented to different receptive areas, judgments may be affected by differences between the receptive areas as well as differences between stimuli. In other words, it may be difficult or impossible to conclude anything about an observer's ability to discriminate stimuli. To control for the effects of the *space error*, the standard stimulus may be presented on half of the trials to one receptor area and on half of the trials to the other receptor area. In an experiment on the discrimination of line length, for example, the standard line would be presented equally often to the left and right of the comparison line, so that the effects of spatial location would be neutralized when the DL was determined. A *time error* may also confound experimental results when the standard and comparison stimuli are presented successively. In one form of the time error, the proportion of times for which the comparison stimulus is judged greater than the standard stimulus is found to be higher when the comparison stimulus is presented second than when it is presented first (Hellström, 1985). Successive presentation makes it necessary for the observer to compare the second stimulus with the memory image of the first. In one interpretation of the time error, it is assumed that since the memory image may rapidly fade, the first stimulus may be judged less than the second stimulus, even when the physical intensities of the two stimuli are identical. Again, since the aim of the discrimination experiment is to study the ability of observers to detect differences in stimuli, certain precautions must be taken to eliminate the biasing effects of time errors. The most common procedure is to present the standard stimulus first on half of the trials and second on the other half of the trials. The method of counterbalancing spatial location or temporal order of standard and comparison stimuli is based on the assumption that, when the results from all of the trials are combined, the effects of the space or time errors will cancel, providing an unbiased estimate of the DL.

To understand the application of the method of constant stimuli, consider a hypothetical example where the purpose of the experiment is to measure the DL for weight discrimination when the standard stimulus is 80 gm and the comparison stimuli are 72, 74, 76, 78, 80, 82, 84, 86, and 88 gm. In this kind of experiment, care must be taken to make the weights identical in size and shape, so that the observer's discrimination will be based exclusively on heaviness. A blindfolded observer is asked to lift a weight placed in his hand. After the weight is removed, he is required to lift a second weight and to compare it with his impression of the first. Since the stimuli are presented successively, it is necessary to control for the effects of time errors. This control is established by presenting the standard stimulus (80-gm weight) first and the comparison stimulus second on half the trials and by using the reverse order on the other half of the trials. The standard stimulus must be paired with each comparison stimulus a sufficient number of times to obtain a reliable estimate of the proportion of "greater" responses for each comparison stimulus. The psychometric function with the proportion of greater responses plotted against values of the comparison stimuli is usually an ogive curve, as seen in Figure 3.4.

In a discrimination experiment, when the observer cannot perceive any difference, we expect the proportions of greater and less responses to be about equal. This .5 point on the psychometric function is called the *point of subjective equality* (PSE) and represents the value of the comparison stimulus which, over a large number of trials, is perceived subjectively as equal to the standard stimulus. In most cases, the PSE does not correspond exactly to the physical value of the standard stimulus. In our present example, the standard is 80 gm, but the PSE is 80.6 gm. The difference between the standard stimulus and the PSE is a psychophysical quantity called the *constant error* (CE):

$$CE = PSE - St. \tag{3.5}$$

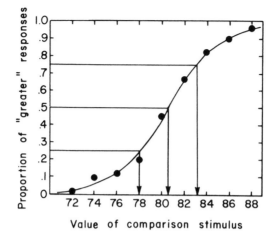

Value of comparison stimulus

FIG. 3.4. Typical psychometric function obtained when the difference threshold is measured by the method of constant stimuli. An ogive curve has been fitted to the points.

A constant error reflects some uncontrolled factor's systematic influence on the measurements being taken, so that numbers are consistently either too high or too low by a certain amount. Space and time errors are constant errors, since they systematically affect the observer's judgments. In the present example, a large negative constant error would probably occur if the standard weight were always presented first and the comparison weight second. The proportion of "greater than" responses for all comparison stimuli would tend to be too high because of a tendency to underestimate the sensory magnitude of the previously presented standard stimulus. The PSE would therefore have a value lower than that of the standard stimulus.

Because the PSE represents a complete lack of discrimination, and because 0 or 1.0 greater than responding is perfect discrimination, the intermediate proportion points of .25 and .75 have been used to find the DL. It is possible to determine two DL's, an upper and a lower. The upper difference threshold (DL_u) is the stimulus range from the PSE to the .75 point. In our example, $DL_u = 83.3 - 80.6 = 2.7$ gm. The difference between the .25 point and the PSE yields a lower difference threshold (DL_l) of 2.6 gm. This method provides a measurement of one DL above the PSE and one below; therefore, the two are often averaged to give one DL for a particular standard stimulus.

The steepness of a psychometric function depends on the observer's differential sensitivity. From the manner in which the DL is derived from plotted data, it should be evident that psychometric functions with steep slopes yield small DL's. Therefore, the slope of the psychometric function and the DL are sometimes used interchangeably as measures of sensitivity.

As was true for measuring absolute thresholds, the psychometric function for the difference threshold can be expressed in z-score units as well as in response proportions. The advantage of the z-score plot, again, is in the ease of curve fitting, since the data points almost always form a straight line. The linear z-score psychometric function of Figure 3.5 indicates that our hypothetical data have the ogival form of the cumulative normal distribution. When this form is obtained experimentally, the most common interpretation is that fluctuations in differential sensitivity are normally distributed.

The line can be fitted to the data by eye or by a more precise technique, such as the method of least squares. The PSE corresponds to a z score of zero. The values of the lower and upper DL's can be determined by drawing vertical lines from the psychometric function when z is −.67 (.25 point) and +.67 (.75 point). If a and b for the equation $z = a(\text{Co}) + b$ have been calculated by the method of least squares, then the Co values corresponding to z values of zero, −.67, and +.67, can be determined by using the equation

$$\text{Co} = \frac{z - b}{a}. \qquad\qquad (3.6)$$

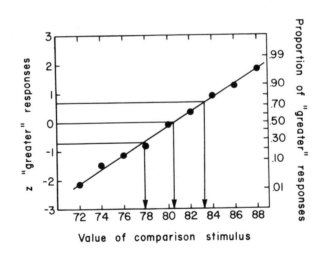

FIG. 3.5. Psychometric function for the measurement of the difference threshold in which the proportions of "greater" responses are expressed in z scores or are plotted on a normal probability ordinate. The linearity of the function indicates that the relation between the proportion of "greater" responses and the value of the comparison stimulus is an ogive.

METHOD OF LIMITS

The method of limits is perhaps the most frequently used technique for determining sensory thresholds. It is an extremely efficient means of threshold measurement and usually yields satisfactory results if proper controls are used to correct for certain constant errors characteristic of the method. The method is less precise than the method of constant stimuli, but it is far less time consuming and is therefore used much more extensively. Furthermore, when choosing the values to be used for applying the method of constant stimuli, a few minutes taken to estimate the location of the threshold by the method of limits would be well spent.

Absolute Thresholds

In the measurement of absolute thresholds by the method of limits, the experimenter starts by presenting a stimulus well above or well below threshold; on each successive presentation, the threshold is approached by changing the stimulus intensity by a small amount until the boundary of sensation is reached. The stimuli are manipulated in either an *ascending series* or a *descending series*. If the series is ascending, the experimenter begins by presenting a very weak subthreshold stimulus to the observer. On each successive trial, the intensity of the stimulus is increased by a small amount until the observer eventually reports the presence of the sensation; at this point, the series is terminated. If the series is descending, the value of the stimulus is decreased in successive steps until the observer reports the disappearance of the sensation. Each transition point obtained from a number of ascending and descending series can be considered an estimation of the threshold, and the threshold is then designated as the average of these values.

The method of limits is often used in audiometry (i.e., the measurement of hearing) to determine the absolute threshold for hearing pure tones of various frequencies. Measurement of the threshold for perception of a 1000-Hz tone might be accomplished by applying a 1000-Hz signal generated by a pure tone oscillator to earphones worn by an observer. The intensity of the signal, as measured in decibels (dB), could be varied systematically by the experimenter. Typical results of the determination of an observer's hearing threshold for a 1000-Hz tone are shown in Table 3.2. Alternate ascending (A) and descending (D) series were administered for a total of ten series. In the case of the ascending series, the transition point between sensation and no sensation is taken as the point on the physical dimension which falls midway between the stimuli for the last no response and the first yes response. In the case of a descending series, the transition point is taken as midway between the last yes response and

TABLE 3.2
Determination of the Absolute Threshold
for Hearing by the Method of Limits[a]

Stimulus intensity (dB)	A	D	A	D	A	D	A	D	A	D
10						Y				
9		Y				Y				Y
8		Y				Y				Y
7		Y		Y		Y				Y
6		Y		Y	Y	Y		Y		Y
5	Y	Y		Y	N	Y	Y	Y		Y
4	N	Y	Y	N	N	N	N	Y	Y	N
3	N	N	N				N	Y	N	
2	N		N				N	N	N	
1	N		N				N		N	
0	N		N				N		N	
−1	N		N				N			
−2	N						N			
−3	N						N			
−4	N									
−5	N									
−6	N									
−7	N									
−8	N									
−9	N									
−10	N									
Transition points =	4.5	3.5	3.5	4.5	5.5	4.5	4.5	2.5	3.5	4.5

[a]Mean threshold value = 4.1

the first no response. In Table 3.2, the mean of the transition points was 4.1 dB, and the variability was considerable—the highest value being 5.5 dB and the lowest 2.5 dB. Here again, as is the case for the method of constant stimuli, the observer's behavior is characteristically variable.

Two constant errors may influence results obtained in using the method of limits. Since the stimulus is gradually changed in the direction of threshold over several trials, there may be a tendency for an observer to develop a habit of repeating the same response. This habit may result in his continuing to make the response for a few trials after the threshold point has been reached. The constant errors resulting from this tendency are called *errors of habituation* and affect the data by falsely increasing thresholds on ascending trials and by falsely decreasing thresholds on descending trials. In opposition to this constant error, an observer may falsely anticipate the arrival of the stimulus at his threshold and prematurely report that the change has occurred before it really has, thus making an *error of expectation*. In this case, thresholds on ascending trials will be deceptively low, and thresholds on descending trials will be too high. If errors of habituation and expectation were of equal magnitude, they would cancel each other, but this condition is unlikely in most experimental situations. One technique to prevent anticipatory tendencies is to vary the starting point for successive series, so that the observer cannot predict the number of trials necessary for reaching threshold. To minimize habitual tendencies, experimenters often try to avoid the use of excessively long trial series. Preliminary training and careful instructions may also help to eliminate, or at least to minimize, the effects of these two tendencies.

Difference Thresholds

The method of limits is also useful for measuring difference thresholds. For this application, standard and comparison stimuli are presented in pairs, and on successive presentations the comparison stimulus is changed by a small amount in the direction of the standard stimulus. For example, if the standard is a 20-dB tone, the experimenter might start with a 15-dB tone and move in .5-dB increments, or might start with a 25-dB tone and move in .5-dB decrements. During each series, whether ascending (A) or descending (D), two transition points are obtained which are termed the *upper limen* (L_u) and *lower limen* (L_l). The upper limen is the point on the physical dimension where "greater" responses change to "equal" responses. Similarly, the lower limen is the point where the "less" responses change to "equal" responses. If an ascending series is given, for example, the first tone would be obviously weaker than the standard, and the observer would say "less" and would continue to say "less" until the experimenter had increased the comparison stimulus sufficiently to be indiscriminable from the standard, at which point the response would change to "equal." The physical value of the stimulus at this point would define the lower limen. As the experimenter further increased the intensity of the comparison stimulus, the observer would continue to say "equal" until the comparison stimulus became discriminably louder than the standard. The response would then change to "greater," which would establish the upper limen and end the series.

Table 3.3 contains results of an experiment in which the DL was measured for loudness when the standard stimulus was a 20-dB, 1000-Hz tone. The mean upper limen was 22.00 dB, indicating that on the average the observer perceived a 22.00-dB tone as just noticeably louder than a 20-dB tone. On the average, a tone of 17.95 dB (the lower limen) was perceived as just noticeably weaker than the 20-dB standard. The range on the stimulus dimension over which an observer cannot perceive a difference between the comparison and the standard stimuli is called the *interval of uncertainty* (IU) and is computed by subtracting the mean lower

TABLE 3.3
Determination of the Difference Threshold
for Hearing by the Method of Limits[a]

Stimulus intensity (dB)	A	D	A	D	A	D	A	D	A	D
24.5						G				
24.0		G				G	G			
23.5		G				G	G			G
23.0		G		G	G	G	G			G
22.5		G	G	G	E	G	G	G		G
22.0	G	E	E	G	E	G	E	G	G	E
21.5	E	E	E	E	E	G	E	E	E	E
21.0	E	E	E	E	E	E	E	E	E	E
20.5	E	E	E	E	E	E	E	E	E	E
20.0	E	E	E	E	E	E	E	E	E	E
19.5	E	E	E	E	E	E	E	E	E	E
19.0	E	E	E	E	E	E	E	E	E	E
18.5	E	L	E	E	E	E	E	E	E	E
18.0	E		E	L	E	L	E	L	E	E
17.5	L		L		E		L		L	L
17.0	L		L		L		L		L	
16.5	L		L		L		L		L	
16.0	L				L				L	
15.5	L				L				L	
Upper limen	21.75	22.25	22.25	21.75	22.75	21.25	22.25	21.75	21.75	22.25
Lower limen	17.75	18.75	17.75	18.25	17.25	18.25	17.75	18.25	17.75	17.75

[a]Interval of uncertainty = IU = $\overline{L}_u - \overline{L}_l$ = 22.00 − 17.95 = 4.05. Difference limen = DL = ½ IU = ½ (4.05) = 2.025. Point of subjective equality = PSE = ½$(\overline{L}_u + \overline{L}_l)$ = ½ (22.00 + 17.95) = 19.97.

limen $(\overline{L}_l)$ from the mean upper limen $(\overline{L}_u)$. The best estimate of the difference limen (DL) is taken as half the IU [DL = ½$(\overline{L}_l - \overline{L}_u)$], and the point of subjective equality is obtained by finding the midpoint of the IU [PSE = ½$(\overline{L}_u + \overline{L}_l)$]. In the present example, the IU was 4.05; the DL is therefore half of this value, or 2.025, and the PSE is 19.97.

It is important to note that in measuring the DL, as in measuring absolute thresholds by this method, care must be taken to control for the effect of errors of habituation and of expectation. In addition, since two stimuli are presented to the observer for comparison when this method is used to measure DL's, controls must be employed to prevent contamination of results by space and time errors. The same procedures suggested for use with the method of constant stimuli—counterbalancing spatial position or temporal order of stimuli—should also be sufficient when using the method of limits.

Figure 3.6 further illustrates calculation of the IU, DL, and PSE. This example presents the average results from an experiment in which the

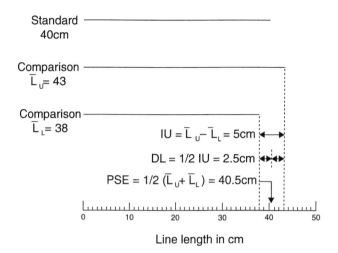

FIG. 3.6. Hypothetical results from a line length discrimination experiment.

observer judged the length of a comparison line relative to the length of a standard line, 40 cm in length. As seen in the figure, the lengths of the comparison lines corresponding to $\bar{L}_l$ and $\bar{L}_u$ were 38 and 43 cm, respectively. The DL of 2.5 cm was found by subtracting $\bar{L}_l$ from $\bar{L}_u$ to obtain the value of IU, which was then multiplied by ½. The PSE of 41.5 cm, the midpoint of the IU, was found by obtaining the sum of $\bar{L}_l$ and $\bar{L}_u$, which was then multiplied by ½.

Variations of the Method of Limits

A variation of the method of limits is the *up-and-down* or *staircase method* (Cornsweet, 1962). One begins by presenting a sequence of stimuli which progressively increase or decrease in value. When the observer's response changes, the stimulus value is recorded, and the direction of the stimulus sequence is reversed from ascending to descending, or vice versa. For example, when the observer first says yes in an ascending sequence, the experimenter will start a descending sequence which is terminated when the observer first says no, at which point the sequence is reversed again. This procedure continues until a sufficient number of response-transition points has been recorded. The threshold is taken as the average of the transition points. The size of the steps used in the staircase method must be chosen with care. If the steps are too large, the precision of the measurements will be compromised because large steps up will result in upper transition points well above the threshold and the same size step down will result in a series of transition points well below the threshold. On the other hand, if the steps are too small, many presentations of the stimulus may be required to reach a transition point, and under these conditions, the task may become tedious with no corresponding increase in accuracy (Cornsweet, 1962). The method is illustrated in Figure 3.7, where the intensity of the stimulus was started below threshold and increased in steps until the first transition point was reached. A total of 12 transition points were determined and the threshold is taken as the average stimulus intensity at the transition points. This method saves time because stimuli that are much below or above threshold are never presented. Because of its efficiency, the staircase method has been of value to clinicians.

The staircase method resembles the *threshold tracking method* Békésy (1947) used with an audiometer to test hearing. However, in the threshold tracking method the stimulus is continuously variable. The observer controls its intensity, and the results are usually recorded by a graphic recorder. Observers track their own threshold continuously. As long as the observer presses a switch, the stimulus will gradually decrease in intensity; as long as the observer keeps the switch open, the stimulus will gradually increase in intensity. If the trial starts with the switch depressed, the observer will keep it depressed until the sensation first disappears, at which time the switch is released, which causes the intensity of the stimulus to begin to gradually increase. When the stimulus is again detected, the observer presses the switch and keeps it closed until the stimulus can no longer be detected. The observer continues in this manner until performance becomes stable for some specified period of time.

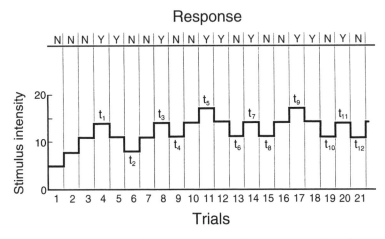

FIG. 3.7. Illustration of the staircase method. Responses are indicated as "yes" (Y) or "no" (N) and the resulting changes in stimulus intensity are plotted below as a function of trials.

Threshold is estimated by averaging the stimulus intensities corresponding to response reversals. A record of the up and down fluctuations in stimulus intensity produced by the observer's tracking is made by a graphic recorder. A sample record from a Békésy audiometer is seen in Figure 3.8. Since the output of an audiometer that is applied to an earphone can be made to change frequency continuously over a 125–10,000-Hz range in a period of a few minutes, a complete record of the observer's threshold as a function of frequency can be made in a very short time. The method has been extremely useful in clinical audiometry, and it also has been successfully adapted to measure thresholds in modalities other than hearing.

The method of threshold tracking has also been useful in animal psychophysics inasmuch as animals can be trained to make a different response when a stimulus is detected than when it is not detected. After training pigeons to peck one key when a light was visible and another key when it was not visible, Blough (1958) obtained a dark-adaptation curve as the bird tracked its threshold in a dark chamber following exposure to intense light. The training procedure involved reinforcing pecking one response key when a light was visible and reinforcing pecking another when it was off. During testing, the pecks sent signals to the light source to control its intensity. When the bird pecked on the key that had been associated, during the training period, with the presence of light, the intensity was decreased, but when it pecked the key previously associated with darkness the intensity increased. Thus, if the bird could see the stimulus, it pecked the key associated with light, causing the stimulus

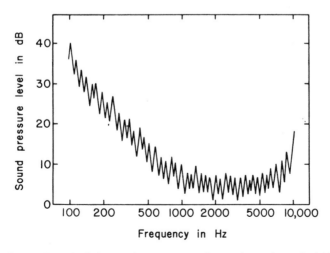

FIG. 3.8. Record of observer's responses as he continuously tracked his auditory threshold as the frequency changed.

to dim and eventually to become invisible. Then it would peck the key associated with darkness and the light would increase in intensity until it became visible again. Because this cycle repeated itself over and over again the light intensity oscillated up and down around the bird's absolute threshold (Fig. 3.9).

Another variation of the method of limits is the *forced-choice method* first used by Blackwell (1953) for experiments on vision and by Jones (1956) for experiments on taste and smell. The observer's task is to choose among several carefully specified observations, only one of which contains the stimulus. Observations may be sequential, as in *temporal-forced choice*, where they are made one after another; or observations may be simultaneous, as in *spatial-forced choice*, where they are made at several different locations. In a four-interval, temporal-forced choice experiment, the observer would be required to make four observations and then to choose the observation which contained the stimulus. In a spatial-forced choice experiment, the observer might be required to view a display on which a stimulus would be presented in one of four quadrants. In this case, the task would be to choose which quadrant contained the stimulus. In both cases, stimulus intensity is increased by discrete steps on successive trials. The stimulus intensity corresponding to a specified performance level, such as two correct responses in succession, is defined as the threshold. The method can be used to measure the difference threshold as well as the absolute threshold by presenting the comparison stimulus for one observation and the standard stimulus for all other

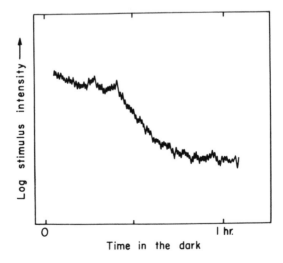

FIG. 3.9. Record of pigeon's responses during dark adaptation. (From Blough, 1958. Copyright 1958 by the Society for the Experimental Analysis of Behavior, Inc.)

observations. The observer is required to pick the comparison stimulus from among the several observations.

The development of forced-choice methods represented an advance in the attempt to solve a fundamental problem in psychophysics—the elimination of the observer's *response bias* from the outcome of the experiment. It was clear to the early psychophysicists that individuals greatly differed in how much they tended to report the presence of a stimulus when none was presented or when it was below threshold. The tendency to report the presence of subthreshold or absent stimuli was referred to as *response bias.* Because response bias can cause inaccuracies in the measurement of thresholds, it had to be controlled. To this end, the observer was given extensive training to eliminate any tendency to report the presence of a stimulus during *catch trials* containing no stimulus. To prevent the observer from knowing when these catch trials would occur, they were randomly mixed in with stimulus trials. When observers reported the presence of stimuli on catch trials, they were corrected by the experimenter. It was thought that, in this way, tendencies to report stimuli when they were not detected could be reduced to an insignificant level.

The problem with this approach, and a major criticism of classical psychophysics, is that observers, after extensive training, were trusted to report honestly whether or not they perceived a stimulus. When an observer fails to report honestly in whether a stimulus was perceived, the measurement of the threshold will be inaccurate. For example, how can one be sure that the thresholds of some observers are very low because they are extraordinarily sensitive or because of their tendencies to report the presence of stimuli that are below their thresholds of awareness? In other words, the results of the classical methods do not allow one to separate response bias from the observer's sensitivity, and unfortunately, in the testing situation, both of these factors can determine the value of the measured threshold.

Thus, in the classical psychophysical methods—such as the methods of constant stimuli, limits, and the yet to be described method of adjustment—the measured threshold may fail to provide a true measurement of sensitivity. Instead, the value of the measured threshold, although largely determined by the observer's sensitivity, may be contaminated by the effects of response bias by some unknown amount.

The development of forced-choice psychophysical methodology provided a way to estimate the value of a "true" threshold uncontaminated by the effects of response bias. Today, in psychophysical laboratories throughout the world, the observer's sensitivity is routinely measured with modern versions of the forced-choice procedure. Various adaptations of the forced-choice method are discussed in chapter 7, but here the discussion is restricted to the logic of how forced-choice psychophysics eliminates the problem of response bias.

Response bias, as the tendency of the observer to report stimuli when they are below threshold, is eliminated in the forced-choice procedure because the observer has no choice reporting a stimulus. The observer, instead, is forced to choose, on each trial, which observation contains the stimulus. When the stimulus is too weak to be detected, performance will be at chance level in the task. For example, when there are two observations from which to choose, chance performance in choosing the correct observation will be 50%. Only when the intensity of the stimulus is increased to a level where the stimulus becomes detectable on some trials, will performance rise above chance. *Threshold* is defined as the stimulus intensity resulting in a specified performance level somewhere between chance and 100% correct performance, such as 75% correct responding. Because the observer is forced to demonstrate the ability to discriminate between an observation containing a stimulus and one where the stimulus is absent, the measured threshold is not contaminated by the effects of response bias.

METHOD OF ADJUSTMENT

The method of adjustment has been used primarily for measuring difference thresholds but can also be applied to problems of absolute sensitivity. One of the main features of this method is the opportunity afforded an observer to control the changes in the stimulus necessary to measure a threshold.

Absolute Thresholds

In measuring absolute thresholds by the method of adjustment, the general procedure is to set the stimulus intensity level either far below or far above threshold and to ask the observer either to increase the intensity level until it is just perceptible, or to decrease the intensity until the sensation just disappears. Usually, the stimulus intensity is continuously variable, but it may also be varied in discrete steps. Experiments generally require an observer to make a fairly large number of ascending and descending settings, and the absolute threshold is taken as the mean of these settings. One advantage of this method is that it gives the observer an unusually large amount of active participation in the experiment, which may help to prevent boredom and, therefore, to maintain high performance.

When using this method, as with the method of limits, it is important to randomize the starting points to avoid errors of expectation and habituation. However, even when this precaution is taken, the same response bias seen in the methods of constant stimuli and limits may contaminate the results. For example, if the observer has a tendency to report the presence of stimuli when they are not detectable, the measured value of the threshold will be falsely low. In this situation, the observer, on descending trials, will continue to adjust the intensity of the stimulus down even after it has become undetectable. On ascending trials, the same observer may tend to set the stimulus intensity to a level that has not yet exceeded threshold. For this reason, the method of adjustment is generally considered to be too inaccurate for research purposes. It is, however, sufficiently accurate to be used as a clinical means of diagnosing sensory loss and for preliminary estimates of thresholds in research studies in which more accurate methods, such as the forced-choice methods, are used to make the final measurements.

Difference Thresholds

When the method of adjustment is applied to the measurement of difference thresholds, the observer is instructed to adjust a comparison stimulus until it seems equal to some standard stimulus. This is often called the *method of average error*, since the experimenter is primarily interested in the discrepancies between the observer's settings of the comparison stimulus and the physical value of the standard stimulus. In a large number of settings, an observer will sometimes underestimate and sometimes overestimate the standard by a considerable amount, but most of the matches typically tend to cluster closely around the value of the standard stimulus. As is true for the hypothetical data in Figure 3.10, a frequency distribution of the results will most likely be a symmetrical and, if enough trials have been administered, will approximate a normal distribution.[1] The mean ($\overline{X}$) of this distribution (the mean of all the settings of the comparison stimulus) is the PSE. If there are no constant errors, the PSE should correspond closely to the value of the standard. The constant error (CE) is computed by subtracting the value of the standard from the PSE (CE = PSE − St).

Whether or not there is a constant error, the frequency distribution will have a high degree of central tendency when discrimination is good; when discrimination is poor, the settings will tend to be quite variable. A measure of dispersion such as the standard deviation (σ), therefore, is used as the DL. One frequently used formula for the standard deviation is

$$\sigma = \sqrt{\frac{N \Sigma X^2 - (\Sigma X)^2}{N^2}} \ . \tag{3.7}$$

---

[1] A normal distribution of comparison stimulus settings is sometimes obtained only after some transformation is made on the stimulus units. Often a logarithmic transformation of the stimulus values results in a normal distribution of responses.

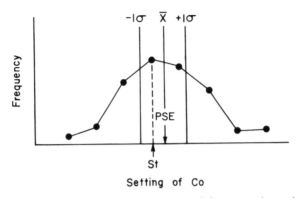

FIG. 3.10. Frequency distribution of setting of the comparison stimulus when the method of adjustment is used to measure the difference threshold. The mean of the distribution is the point of subjective equality, and the standard deviation is used as the difference threshold.

where X is the value of a particular Co setting and N is the number of settings. A large standard deviation would indicate that, over a wide range of stimulus values, the two stimuli appeared equal and that discrimination was poor. If discrimination is precise, the two stimuli will appear equal only over a narrow range of stimulus values; judgments will tend to cluster together, and the standard deviation of the distribution of judgments will be relatively small.

The method of adjustment is difficult to apply when stimuli are not continuously variable, or when pairs of stimuli cannot be presented simultaneously. When stimuli are varied in steps rather than continuously, DL measurements are somewhat inaccurate. In experiments in which the standard stimulus must be presented first and is followed by the comparison stimulus for the observer to adjust, it is impossible to counterbalance or measure stimulus order effects. A final shortcoming of the method results from giving the observer control of the stimulus: this procedure makes it difficult to maintain constant conditions during threshold measurement.

APPLICATION OF CLASSICAL PSYCHOPHYSICAL METHODS TO PROBLEMS OF STIMULUS MATCHING

A stimulus critical value function, in which absolute threshold is plotted against some property of the stimulus, can be thought of as an *equal sensation contour*. The function describes how stimulus intensity must be adjusted to maintain sensory intensity at absolute threshold as other properties of the stimulus are changed. Figure 2.3 illustrates how sound pressure must be changed in order to keep the sensory magnitude of the sound at a just audible level as the frequency of the stimulus is changed. Often, it is in our interest to determine an equal sensation contour for suprathreshold levels of stimulation. In the case of hearing, the function would specify the sound pressure necessary at various frequencies to keep the psychological loudness of the sound at some constant level.

Figure 3.11 illustrates equal loudness contours obtained by Robinson and Dadson (1956). Each contour represents a different loudness level. Loudness level, in units called *phons*, is the sound pressure level in dB of a 1000-Hz tone which sounds equal in loudness to a given tone. In determining equal loudness contours, a 1000-Hz tone is set to a particular loudness level, and the intensity of a comparison tone of another frequency is adjusted so that its loudness matches that of the standard 1000-Hz tone of fixed intensity. This procedure is repeated for a number of comparison tones of different frequencies, and the plotted results constitute one equal loudness contour. The results of Robinson and Dadson indicate that, to maintain sound at the same loudness level, both low- and high-frequency tones must be considerably more intense than those in the midrange of frequencies. The shapes of the equal loudness contours are not unlike that of the threshold curve. However, it can be seen that

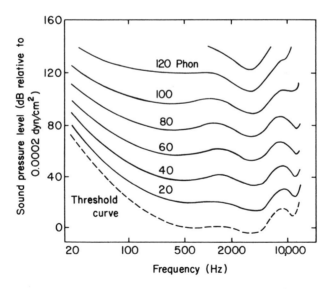

FIG. 3.11. Equal loudness contours. Each curve describes the intensity levels to which tones of various frequencies must be adjusted to keep loudness constant. Each curve was obtained at a different loudness level. (From Robinson & Dadson, 1956. Copyright 1956 by the Institute of Physics.)

the equal loudness contours become somewhat flatter at higher loudness levels. The results of this experiment indicate that the relative deficiency of the auditory system at low frequencies is much more severe at low intensity levels of stimulation. For this reason, high quality stereophonic sound equipment is usually designed to produce a relatively more intense bass response when the volume control is turned down.

The method of adjustment provides perhaps the most efficient technique for determining an equal sensation contour. As in measuring the DL, an observer is required to adjust the value of a comparison stimulus to match that of the standard stimulus. The values plotted on the equal sensation contour would consist of PSE values for several different stimuli that had been matched to the standard stimulus. The PSE values could also be obtained by other psychophysical methods, such as the method of limits or the method of constant stimuli.

In constructing equal sensation contours, psychophysical matching procedures are employed to determine the stimulus values necessary to keep sensation magnitude constant for various conditions of stimulation. All matches of a number of comparison stimuli are made to a common standard stimulus of constant value. Therefore, each match should yield a value of the comparison stimulus that produces the same sensation magnitude as that of the standard stimulus. Another equally useful matching method is to employ a single comparison stimulus which is adjusted by the observer to match changing sensation magnitude as some parameter of the standard stimulus is changed. For example, increasing the loudness of a tone as its duration is increased could be specified in terms of the intensity of a comparison stimulus of fixed duration needed to match the loudness of tones of fixed intensity and variable duration.

The measurement of loudness enhancement also provides an example of matching with a single comparison stimulus. A sound may be perceived as louder when paired with a more intense sound than when presented alone. Loudness enhancement refers to the increment in loudness of a sound caused by the presentation of another sound. For example, Zwislocki and Sokolich (1974) found that the loudness of a 10-msec tone burst was enhanced by preceding it with a more intense burst. By requiring the observer to adjust the intensity of a comparison stimulus so that its loudness was the same as that of a test stimulus, Zwislocki and Sokolich measured the loudness-enhancing effects of a conditioning stimulus. The test stimulus was presented within a 500-msec period following the presentation of the conditioning stimulus (Figure 3.12). Loudness enhancement was indicated when the observer adjusted the comparison stimulus to an intensity that was higher in the presence than in the absence of the conditioning stimulus. The amount of loudness enhancement was the difference in intensity of the matches made to the test stimulus in the

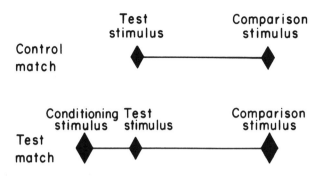

FIG. 3.12. Stimulus-matching method for investigating sensation magnitude enhancement.

presence and in the absence of the conditioning stimulus. Enhancement was found to be greatest when the conditioning and test stimuli were nearly simultaneous. The result indicates that persisting aftereffects of brief sounds may outlast the stimulus by as long as 400 to 500 msec and have the effect of enhancing the loudness of other sounds.

Analogous experiments on the perception of brief vibrotactile stimuli applied to the hand reveal an interesting similarity between auditory and tactile modalities. For both hearing and touch, enhancement was maximal when the frequencies of the two stimuli were identical and the time between them was brief (Gescheider, Verrillo, Capraro, & Hamer, 1977; Verrillo & Gescheider, 1975). As seen in Figure 3.13, when the conditioning stimulus was on the finger and the test stimulus was on the fleshy pad below the thumb (thenar eminence), the sensation magnitude of the test stimulus was suppressed for trials with very short time intervals between stimuli and enhanced for trials with longer time intervals between stimuli. Suppression was not observed when both stimuli were on the thenar eminence. These results suggest that the psychophysically measured interaction effects between sensory tactile stimuli are based on inhibitory and excitatory neural processes.

CONCLUSION

The temptation to conclude that sensations can be directly measured by the procedures outlined in this chapter must be avoided; sensations cannot be measured in units of sensory magnitude by using these methods. Instead, sensation must be expressed in terms of the amount of stimulus energy necessary to prompt specific changes in the observer's responses. Sensation is thus treated as a concept which must be defined in terms of

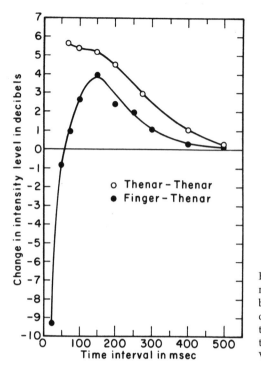

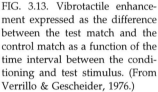

FIG. 3.13. Vibrotactile enhancement expressed as the difference between the test match and the control match as a function of the time interval between the conditioning and test stimulus. (From Verrillo & Gescheider, 1976.)

stimulus-response relationships. Inferences about the operation of sensory processes within the observer from measurements of thresholds or values of a matching stimulus are only as valid as the care in measurement and control over conditions employed in the experiment.

Techniques for measuring psychophysical responses are continually being improved upon, and recent advances in this area are described in chapters 5 through 8. Chapters 4 through 8 provide descriptions of how failure of the classical threshold concept and the emergence of the theory of signal detection resulted in improved techniques for measuring an observer's sensitivity to stimulation.

PROBLEMS

3.1. In a hypothetical experiment, the method of constant stimuli was used to measure the absolute threshold. The results are presented below.

	Stimulus Intensity								
	2	4	6	8	10	12	14	16	18
p yes	.04	.05	.20	.34	.53	.72	.94	.96	.99

Plot the psychometric function. Fit a smooth curve to the data points and estimate the absolute threshold.

3.2. Convert the p yes values in problem 3.1 to z-score units and plot the psychometric function. Determine the best-fitting straight line for the data by the method of least squares and write the equation. Draw the line through the data points. Estimate the absolute threshold.

3.3. In an experiment on discrimination, the method of constant stimuli was used to measure the DL. The results are presented below.

Comparison Stimulus

	60	70	80	90	100	110	120	130	140
p greater	.02	.08	.15	.30	.53	.68	.87	.91	.98

Convert p values to z scores. Plot the psychometric function in z-score units. Determine the best-fitting straight line by the method of least squares. Determine PSE, CE, upper DL, lower DL, and mean DL. The standard stimulus had a value of 100.

3.4. In the table below are the results of a discrimination experiment in which the method of limits was used. The value of the standard stimulus was 100.

Stimulus Intensity	A	D	A	D	A	D
140				G		
135		G		G		G
130		G		G	G	G
125	G	G		G	E	G
120	E	G		G	E	E
115	E	E	G	E	E	E
110	E	E	E	E	E	E
105	E	E	E	E	E	E
100	E	E	E	E	E	E
95	E	E	E	E	E	E
90	L	E	L	E	E	E
85	L	L	L	E	L	E
80	L		L	L	L	E
75	L		L		L	L
70	L		L		L	
65					L	
60						

Determine IU, PSE, CE, and mean DL.

3.5. In an experiment on discrimination, the method of adjustment was used to determine the DL. The standard stimulus was 100, and the settings of the comparison stimulus are in the table below.

Setting of the Comparison Stimulus				
85	105	97	95	98
105	110	98	104	82
112	95	107	109	96
65	93	102	91	108
94	108	138	79	117
98	125	102	131	94
118	99	85	100	99
135	80	73	107	104
102	115	96	120	101
88	103	67	104	94

Determine the DL, PSE, and CE.

4

Classical Psychophysical Theory

The application of the methods described in Chapter 3 yields a quantity which is expressed in physical units and called the threshold. The concept of the threshold as an index of absolute and differential sensitivity has been extremely useful in the study of sensory systems. Through the use of this quantity, investigators have been able to discover the stimuli to which our sensory systems are the most and the least sensitive. But psychophysicists have not restricted their work to this descriptive level: they have also gone beyond this level to propose theories concerning the underlying mechanisms of sensory thresholds. Each theory was proposed to account for empirical data obtained in psychophysical experiments. The theorists hoped to describe the neurophysiological or psychological processes within the observer which may have determined the observer's behavior. The validity of each theory must be evaluated by determining the degree to which precise quantitative deductions from the theory are confirmed by experimental data.

CLASSICAL THRESHOLD THEORY

Early threshold theories were based upon the assumption that the measurements obtained in psychophysical experiments were estimates of a neural threshold in the observer which could not be measured directly. It was thought that the threshold was a sharp transition point between sensation and no sensation, and that a specific, critical amount of neural activity must result from stimulation for the threshold to be exceeded. The value of the threshold was assumed to vary with properties of the stimulus (such as duration, area, and wavelength) and to vary also according to the condition of the sensory nervous system (such as state of adaptation and level of background activity). If all the factors affecting the threshold level could be maintained exactly the same from measurement to measurement, and if the application of the stimulus energy to the receptors could be exactly replicated, a particular stimulus would be expected to either always or never produce a sensation, depending upon whether the stimulus produced enough neural activity to exceed threshold.

Since the level of neural activity increases with the intensity of the stimulus, the predicted psychometric function would jump sharply from 0% to 100% detection when the stimulus intensity was set at a level that produced the threshold amount of neural activity (Figure 4.1). Empirical psychometric functions do not follow this form but are typically ogive curves, where the proportion of yes responses gradually increases with stimulus intensity. The step-like function of Figure 4.1, however, is a theoretical curve representing predicted results in a hypothetical situation where perfect control is maintained over all of the stimulus and biological variables affecting the level of neural activity in the sensory system. Since

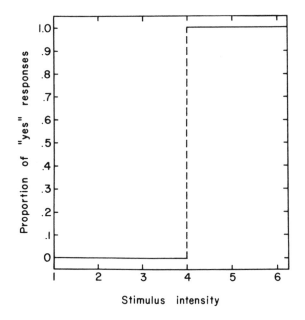

Stimulus intensity

FIG. 4.1. Psychometric function predicted from classical threshold theory for an idealized situation in which all stimulus and biological factors are under perfect experimental control. Under these conditions the threshold is represented as the stimulus intensity corresponding to an abrupt increase from zero to one in the proportion of "yes" responses.

perfect control cannot be achieved, the function remains a theoretical formulation of the outcome which would be achieved under ideal conditions if the assumptions of the classical threshold theory are correct.

Inasmuch as it has been impossible to test the theory by examining the relationship between proportion of detections and stimulus intensity when all stimulus and biological factors are perfectly controlled, proponents of the theory are obliged to account for results obtained under imperfect conditions. A primary assumption in classical threshold theory is that the threshold varies over time. Although an observer's threshold may be a sharp boundary at a particular instant in time, in an experiment it may appear to be constantly changing. Factors affecting the threshold fluctuate randomly from moment to moment, and, therefore, repeated applications of a stimulus of a particular intensity should result in a detection response only on those trials when the *momentary threshold* is exceeded.

This concept is first illustrated in Figure 4.2, in which step-like psychometric functions are seen at two separate times. At time 1, the value of the momentary threshold is 3 units and at time 2, because of randomly fluctuating factors, it has risen to 5 units. The consequence of this variation in the threshold is that the observer's performance in the detection task is no longer predicted to be all-or-none, but instead the same stimulus, when repeatedly presented on several trials, will be detected on some trials but not on others. In the present example, had a stimulus with an

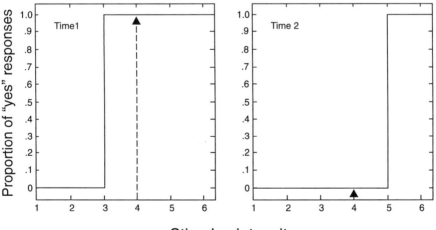

Stimulus intensity

FIG. 4.2. Hypothetical step-like psychometric functions at two separate times. Due to variability in the location of the momentary threshold, a stimulus with an intensity of 4 units will be detected at time 1 when the threshold is 3 units but not at time 2 when it is 5 units.

intensity of 4 units been presented at time 1, it would have been detected, but had it been presented at time 2 it would not have been.

The proportion of trials where the momentary threshold is exceeded should increase as an ogival function of stimulus intensity if the variation of momentary thresholds is normally distributed. Curve A of Figure 4.3 illustrates a hypothetical frequency distribution of momentary thresholds expressed in units of stimulus intensity. The ordinate of the frequency distribution indicates the relative likelihood of occurrence of each value of the threshold as it fluctuates over time. In this example, the most frequently occurring thresholds cluster around the mean value of 4 units with lower and higher values occurring less frequently. A detection re-

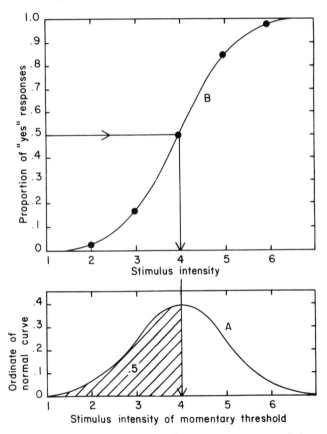

FIG. 4.3. Derivation of the ogive psychometric function from classical threshold theory. Curve A is a theoretical normal distribution of momentary thresholds. Curve B is the predicted proportion of "yes" responses for each stimulus intensity value. The predicted proportion of "yes" responses corresponds to the proportion of the area under curve A that is below a particular stimulus intensity value.

sponse would be expected only when stimulus intensity is equal to or greater than the momentary threshold value. The proportion of times that a stimulus will exceed threshold is equal to the proportion of the area under curve A that is below the value of the stimulus. For example, a weak stimulus of 2 units would exceed momentary thresholds of 2 units or less only 2% of the time. The first point on the psychometric function, curve B of Figure 4.3, would be .02 for a stimulus of 2 units. A stimulus of 3 units should be detected on .16 proportion of the trials, since momentary thresholds are 3 units or less on 16% of the trials. The second point on the psychometric function can now be plotted. When stimulus intensity is 4 units, the momentary threshold will be equal to or less than this value on exactly 50% of the trials, and this stimulus will be detected on .5 proportion of the trials. Thus, the .5 point on the psychometric function corresponds to the mean of the momentary threshold values. It should now be clear why the early psychophysicists chose 50% detection as the best estimate of the threshold. The proportion of trials on which stimulus intensity is equal to or above momentary threshold is .84 for a stimulus of 5 units and .98 for a stimulus of 6 units.

To further clarify this explanation of the psychometric function, Figure 4.4 shows the frequency distribution of momentary thresholds at each of the five points on the function. The unshaded area within a distribution corresponds to the proportion of times a repeatedly presented stimulus of a particular intensity will exceed the momentary threshold. For example, when a stimulus of 2 units of intensity is presented it should be detected .02 proportion of the time because only .02 proportion of the time, as indicated by the unshaded area of the distribution of momentary thresholds, will this stimulus be equal to or above the momentary threshold. At higher values of stimulus intensity, the unshaded area of the distribution increases as does the proportion of yes responses on the psychometric function.

According to classical threshold theory, the mean and variability of the distribution of momentary thresholds can be determined from the psychometric function. Figure 4.5 illustrates how two psychometric functions having the ogive form of the cumulative normal distribution indicate different distributions of momentary thresholds. Since the steepness of the two psychometric functions is the same, the variance of the hypothesized distributions of momentary thresholds is the same. On the other hand, because the stimulus detected .5 proportion of the time was different for the two observers, the means of the distributions of momentary thresholds of the two observers are also different. In Figure 4.6, the steepness of psychometric functions for observers C and D differ, but in both cases the stimulus detected .5 proportion of the time was 4. Thus, the distributions of momentary thresholds of observers C and D have the same mean

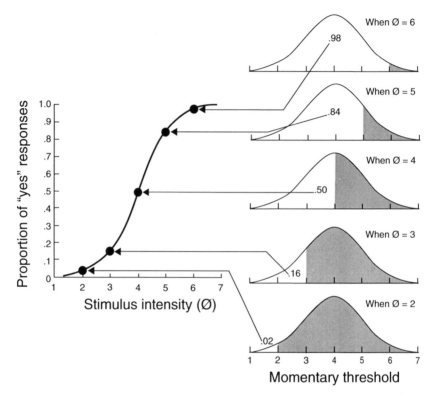

FIG. 4.4. Psychometric function explained by the distribution of momentary thresholds at each value of stimulus intensity. The unshaded area in each distribution corresponds to the proportion of times that the stimulus will be at or above the momentary threshold.

but different variances. The standard deviations of the distributions of momentary thresholds can be estimated from the psychometric functions. The intensity of a stimulus detected .16 proportion of the time is 1.0 standard deviation below the mean of the hypothesized distribution of momentary thresholds, and the intensity of a stimulus detected .84 proportion of the time is 1.0 standard deviation above this mean. In our example, the standard deviation of distributions of momentary thresholds is .5 units of stimulus intensity for observer C and 1.0 units of stimulus intensity for observer D.

Classical threshold theory is often identified as the *phi–gamma hypothesis*, with phi referring to the probability of a response and gamma referring to stimulus intensity. The phi–gamma hypothesis states that the psychometric function in which response probability is plotted against stimulus magnitude should have the ogival form of the cumulative normal distribution. The prediction of an ogive psychometric function follows directly from the

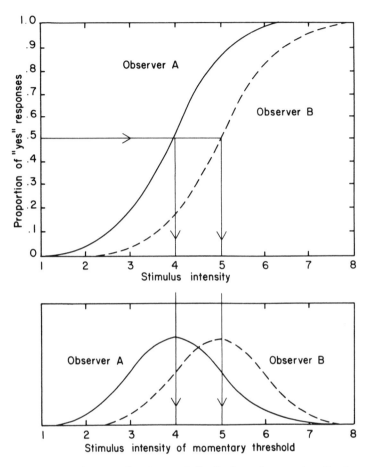

FIG. 4.5. Psychometric functions and distributions of momentary thresholds for two observers. The mean momentary thresholds of the two observers are different.

assumption that momentary thresholds are normally distributed over time. When testing the phi–gamma hypothesis, care must be taken to select an appropriate unit of measurement for the stimulus: in some cases different physical scales can be used to measure intensity—some of which may not be linearly related to each other. Sound energy is not proportional to sound pressure, for example, but is instead proportional to sound pressure squared. The cumulative normal distribution cannot possibly describe the psychometric function when sound intensity is expressed in pressure units and also when it is expressed in energy units.

Which unit of stimulus intensity is appropriate for testing the theory? Whenever possible, stimulus intensity should be expressed in units that

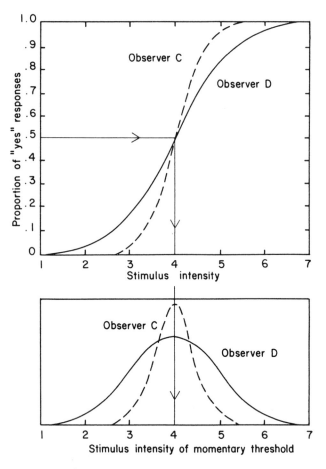

FIG. 4.6. Psychometric functions and distributions of momentary thresholds for two observers. The variability of the momentary thresholds is different for the two observers.

best reflect the operating characteristics of the sensory system. Thurstone was aware of this problem as early as 1928. He noted that for classical threshold theory to predict correctly an ogival psychometric function, the stimulus should be expressed in psychological units instead of in physical units. If fluctuations in sensitivity were normally distributed along a psychological dimension of intensity, they would not be normally distributed when expressed in units of stimulus intensity, unless stimulus values were transformed to reflect psychological intensity. Thurstone made the assumption that Fechner's law is correct and proposed the *phi–log–gamma hypothesis*. According to this hypothesis, the psychometric function should have the ogival form of the cumulative normal distribution when response probability is plotted as a function of log stimulus magnitude. Since the range of stimulus values is unfortunately so small, the predicted psychometric functions form the phi–gamma hypothesis and the phi–log–gamma hypothesis are so similar that data precise enough to differentiate between the two hypotheses have not yet been obtained.

Because similar ogival psychometric functions have been obtained in detection and discrimination experiments, classical threshold theory has been applied to the measurement of the difference threshold. Investigators assumed that the neural activity for two sensations must differ by some threshold amount to be perceived as different. The size of the stimulus difference required to exceed threshold was assumed to vary randomly from trial to trial, and, therefore, the probability of detecting a difference should increase as an ogival function of the size of the stimulus difference. A detailed description of the application of classical threshold theory to the problem of sensory discrimination can be found in Boring (1917).

In summary, classical threshold theory was the first attempt to make inferences about the nature of processes within the observer from psychophysical data. Empirically determined psychometric functions have thus been used to make inferences about the underlying nature of sensory mechanisms. The ogival psychometric functions, so frequently observed in psychophysical investigations, have led to the logical inference that fluctuations in momentary sensory thresholds are normally distributed along some sensory continuum within the observer.

QUANTAL FLUCTUATIONS

In the classical threshold theory, it is assumed that the form of the psychometric function reflects the underlying variability of the momentary threshold. Thus, in this explanation of the psychometric function, all of the variability in trial to trial performance is attributed to variability within the observer. For example, if a stimulus of fixed intensity is detected on a certain proportion of the trials, it is assumed that, on those trials, the stimulus was above the fluctuating threshold. An alternative interpretation, and one proposed by Hecht, Shlaer, and Pirenne (1942) to account for their results on the absolute threshold for vision, is that it is the threshold, not the stimulus, that is fixed and, as a result of fluctuations from trial to trial in the stimulus, the stimulus exceeds the fixed threshold and is detected on a certain proportion of the trials. On the remaining trials, the stimulus intensity is below the fixed threshold and the stimulus is not detected. In Figure 4.7, the concept of the fixed threshold is illustrated and contrasted with the momentary threshold theory. In the top of the figure, the *fixed threshold theory*, in which the threshold, ϕ_0, remains unchanged during an experimental session, is illustrated for a situation

Fixed threshold ($\emptyset_0$) and variable stimulus ($\emptyset$)

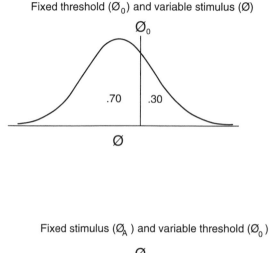

Fixed stimulus ($\emptyset_A$) and variable threshold ($\emptyset_0$)

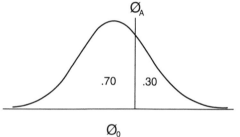

FIG. 4.7. Prediction of the proportion of trials on which the observer will detect a stimulus. In the top illustration, the threshold is fixed and the stimulus is variable. In the bottom illustration, the stimulus is fixed in intensity and the threshold is variable.

in which a stimulus, ϕ, is repeatedly presented. Although the stimulus is nominally the same from trial to trial, its value, ϕ, because of randomly fluctuating factors, varies. The result, in this example, is that the variable stimulus will exceed the fixed threshold and be detected on .30 proportion of the trials and be below threshold and fail to be detected on .70 proportion of the trials. In the bottom of the figure, the momentary threshold theory, with which the reader is already familiar, is illustrated. In the momentary threshold theory, the value of the stimulus, ϕ_A, does not fluctuate from trial to trial, but the value of the momentary threshold, ϕ_O, does. In this example, ϕ_A exceeds the randomly fluctuating value of the momentary threshold on .30 proportion of the trials and fails to exceed threshold on .70 proportion of the trials.

To evaluate the fixed threshold theory as applied to the absolute threshold for vision, it is necessary to consider the nature of light as a visual stimulus. Light consists of discrete particles called quanta or photons that result when an electron shifts from one energy state to another. The shifting of a single electron from one state to another is a random process and therefore cannot be predicted exactly. Thus, the total number of quanta emitted from a light source, set at a fixed level, randomly fluctuates from one time to another. The variability in the number of quanta contained in a flash of light can be described as a frequency distribution of a particular kind called a *Poisson distribution* as seen in Figure 4.8. Notice that when the mean of the distribution is 1 quantum, because of the impossibility of having counts of quanta less than zero, the distribution is highly asymmetrical with a skew toward a greater number of quanta than the mean. As the mean of the distribution increases, its form approaches that of a normal distribution. Recall from our discussion in Chapter 2 of the Hecht, Shlaer, and Pirenne experiment that, for vision to occur, only 5 to 14 quanta must be absorbed by the visual pigment rhodopsin contained in the rod receptors within the retina. These thresholds were derived from psychometric functions obtained through the use of the method of constant stimuli. Hecht and his associates attempted to determine whether the variability in the observer's behavior at each point on the psychometric function was entirely due to quantal fluctuations in the stimulus.

Assuming that there is no variability in the observer and that the threshold is fixed, it is possible to predict the form of the psychometric function from known variability in the stimulus. For example, assume that the observer has a fixed threshold of 5 quanta. It is now possible to predict the psychometric function of this observer from the Poisson distributions of quantal fluctuations of the stimulus (Fig. 4.9). The psychometric function at the bottom of the figure plots the predicted proportion of "yes" responses as a function of the mean number of quanta per flash. For example, suppose that the apparatus is set so that the mean

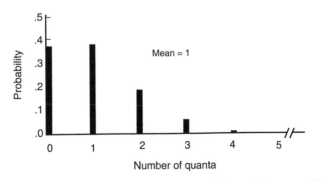

FIG. 4.8. Poisson distribution of quanta emitted from a light source. The mean of this particular distribution is 1 quantum.

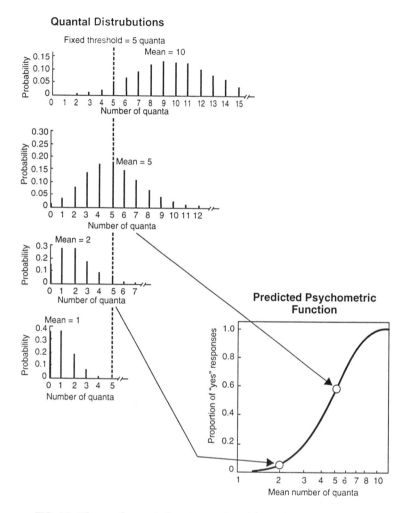

FIG. 4.9. The psychometric function predicted from the Poisson distributions of quantal fluctuations of light flashes of various intensities.

number of quanta absorbed by the visual pigment is 2. By examining the Poisson distribution with a mean of 2 quanta, we see that the probability of 5 or more quanta being generated by the stimulus is equal to the sum of the probabilities of 5, 6, 7 . . . N quanta being generated that is .04 + .02 + .01 = .07. The value of .07, in representing the proportion of times that the light flash will result in 5 or more quanta absorbed by the visual pigment, provides the predicted proportion of "yes" responses on the psychometric function for a stimulus intensity having a mean of 2 quanta. According to the theory of quantal fluctuations, the fixed threshold of 5 quanta will be exceeded by this stimulus on .07 proportion of the trials.

Likewise, the predicted proportion of "yes" responses for a flash with a mean number of quanta of 5 is equal to the sum of the probabilities of 5, 6, 7 . . . N quanta being generated that is .18 + .15 + .11 + .07 + .045 + .02 + .015 + .01 + = .60. To obtain the entire predicted psychometric function for this hypothetical observer having a fixed threshold of 5 quanta, this analysis would be repeated for each of the Poisson distributions corresponding to each flash intensity used in the experiment. The entire predicted curve is seen in the figure.

The psychometric function of Figure 4.9 was calculated for an observer with a fixed threshold of 5 absorbed quanta. This procedure can be repeated assuming other values of the fixed threshold. The results of these calculations are seen in Figure 4.10. The curve for a threshold of 5 or more quanta is the same predicted psychometric function as seen in Figure 4.9. Hecht and his associates plotted the actual curves for their observers to see how they compared with the predicted ones. The data of one of the observers, as seen in Figure 4.11, corresponds closely to the psychometric function predicted from the assumed fixed threshold of 7 quanta. The actual measured threshold of this observer was 8 quanta. Because the measured threshold and the threshold of 7 quanta derived from the theory of quantal fluctuations were nearly identical, Hecht et al. (1942) concluded that the fixed threshold-variable stimulus model accounted for the data. Thus, it appears that at least some component of the variability in the observer's performance in detecting visual stimuli at absolute threshold is due to quantal fluctuations in the stimulus that are an intrinsic characteristic of the nature of light. It is unlikely, however, that all of the variability of the observer is the result of quantal fluctuations in the stimulus. It is now known that the visual system, as a result of spontaneous neural activity, is inherently noisy. Because the magnitude of this internal noise, which limits the observer's ability to detect the stimulus, fluctuates over time, the observer's performance in the detection task

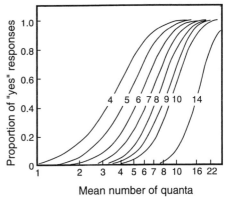

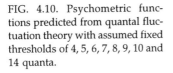

FIG. 4.10. Psychometric functions predicted from quantal fluctuation theory with assumed fixed thresholds of 4, 5, 6, 7, 8, 9, 10 and 14 quanta.

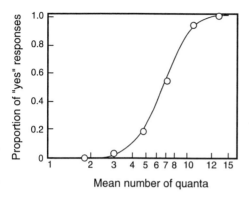

FIG. 4.11. Psychometric function predicted from quantal-fluctuation theory in which the assumed fixed threshold is 7 quanta. The data points are from one of the observers in the experiment by Hecht, Shlaer, and Pirenne (1942).

must also fluctuate over time. Thus, it appears that the variability of the observer's performance, revealed in the psychometric function, must be due to both variability in the stimulus and variability within the nervous system of the observer.

NEURAL QUANTUM THEORY

The central assumptions of classical threshold theory are that fluctuations in threshold are random and that the sensory dimension is continuous. The sensory dimension, in fact, may not be a continuum but instead may be a series of discrete steps. Under these circumstances, psychometric functions for difference thresholds could deviate from the ogival form. In fact, not all psychometric functions obtained during measurement of difference thresholds follow the ogival form. Infrequently obtained psychometric functions, where response probability increases from 0 to 1.0 as a linear function of stimulus magnitude, therefore became the basis of a new theory of sensory discrimination. The *neural quantum theory*, first made explicit by Stevens, Morgan, and Volkmann (1941), is an attempt to derive a linear psychometric function from the assumption that discrimination occurs along a sensory dimension within the observer which is made up of small discrete (quantal) steps. Neurophysiology provides no conclusive evidence regarding the nature of the sensory dimension. In the nervous system, receptor potentials and postsynaptic potentials vary as a continuous function of stimulus intensity, while action potentials constitute all-or-none responses to changes in stimulus intensity. It is also known, however, that sensory nerve fibers have thresholds below which the stimulus is too weak to elicit an action potential, and above which the stimulus is of sufficient strength to elicit this response. Furthermore, within a sensory nerve, these thresholds can vary considerably for different nerve fibers. Consequently, as the stimulus is increased, the thresholds of more fibers are exceeded, and the number of fibers responding increases. It is possible that an observer, in a carefully controlled psychophysical experiment, can detect these small quantal increases in neural activity. The final answers are not supplied by psychophysics, but it is significant that the psychometric functions reported by a handful of investigators are remarkably consistent with the neural quantum concept.

In the simplest form of neural quantum theory, it is assumed that an observer can detect an increment, $\Delta\phi$, in a stimulus, ϕ, only when it is large enough to excite one additional neural unit (Figure 4.12). The size of the necessary stimulus increment will depend on how much the first stimulus is above the threshold of the last excited neural unit. The greater the excess over the threshold of the last unit, the smaller the increment will need to be in order to excite the next unit.

The first evidence in support of a quantal theory of discrimination was reported by Békésy (1930). A standard tone lasting .3 sec was presented to an observer and was followed immediately by a .3-sec comparison tone of a different intensity. On each trial, the observer reported whether or not he detected a loudness difference between the two tones. The linear psychometric functions in this experiment were interpreted as support for the quantal nature of loudness discrimination. Similar results were obtained by Stevens, Morgan, and Volkmann (1941) for both loudness and pitch. Some of the linear psychometric functions found in these experiments are presented in Figure 4.13.

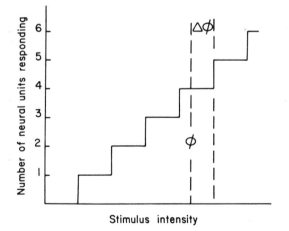

FIG. 4.12. Illustration of neural quantum theory. As stimulus intensity increases, the number of active neural units increases in an all-or-none fashion. To detect an increase in stimulus intensity, the change in stimulus intensity ($\Delta\phi$) must be large enough to exceed the threshold of the next neural unit.

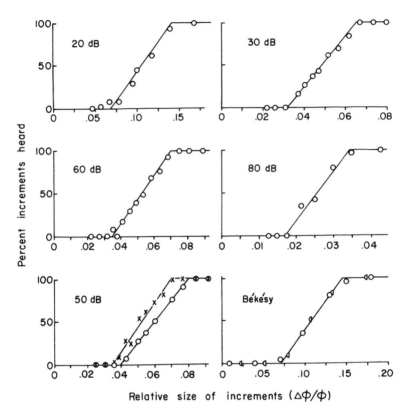

Relative size of increments ($\Delta\phi/\phi$)

FIG. 4.13. Psychometric functions for the detection of an intensity increment added to a 1000-Hz tone of five different intensity levels. Békésy's data are also presented for the detection of increments (circles) and decrements (half circles). The theoretical curves were drawn with the restriction that they be straight lines with intercepts that stand in a 2-to-1 relation. (From Stevens, Morgan, & Volkmann, 1941.)

S. S. Stevens (1972a) reviewed the data from about a dozen investigations carried out over a span of 40 years. Some 140 step-like functions for auditory loudness and pitch and for three types of visual patterns were reproduced in Stevens' paper as support for neural quantum theory. In the experiments that were reported, observers were presented with a standard stimulus followed immediately by a comparison stimulus which produced an incremental change in stimulation. Observers were required to respond when they detected the incremental change between the first and second stimuli. During a single session, sufficient data were obtained to determine the proportion of detections for several sizes of stimulus increments.

Stevens pointed out that there are three features of the data from these experiments which have special importance for neural quantum theory:

(a) stimulus increments below a critical size produce no response; (b) above that critical value, the number of increments detected is a linear function of the size of the increment; and (c) increments are always detected when the increment reaches a second critical size, which is twice the size of the largest increment that is never detected. These characteristic results are clearly seen in the data of Stevens et al. (1941) presented in Figure 4.13. The importance of these findings should become clear when the elements of the neural quantum model are understood.

According to the neural quantum model, a stimulus of a particular intensity stimulates a certain number of neural quantum units. As illustrated in Figure 4.14, some intensity levels may include a stimulus surplus (p) which is insufficient to exceed the threshold of the next unit, but is available to combine with a stimulus increment ($\Delta\phi$). When a stimulus increment occurs, it adds to p; and if their sum is large enough to excite one or more additional quantal units, the stimulus increment is detected.

In its current form, neural quantum theory relies upon the validity of two assumptions: that the observer's random sensitivity fluctuations are large compared to (Q), the size of the stimulus increment that will always succeed in exciting an additional neural unit; and that these fluctuations are slow compared to the time required for the experimenter to present the stimulus increment. The relatively large fluctuations in sensitivity cause considerable variability in the *total number* of excited neural units. As a result of this large random variability over a range of many neural

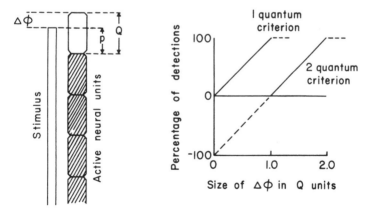

FIG. 4.14. The diagram on the left illustrates the basic concepts of the neural quantum model. The stimulus activates a certain number of neural units. The stimulus has a surplus p that is insufficient to exceed the threshold of the next unit unless the stimulus increment $\Delta\phi$ is added. (From Békésy, 1930.) The diagram on the right is the psychometric function predicted for a 2-quantum criterion. (From S. S. Stevens, 1972a. Copyright 1972 by the American Association for the Advancement of Science.)

quantal units, one value for the stimulus surplus p is as likely as any other for the presentation of a particular stimulus; consequently, the frequency distribution p for a particular standard stimulus is rectangular. Thus, if Q is the stimulus increment that will always succeed in exciting an additional neural quantum, then the value of $\Delta\phi$ that is just sufficient to excite one additional neural quantum is given by

$$\Delta\phi = Q - p. \tag{4.1}$$

A given $\Delta\phi$ will excite an additional neural unit whenever $\Delta\phi = Q - p$. Since p is uniformly distributed over the neural quantum, and since the greater the value of $\Delta\phi$ the more likely $\Delta\phi$ plus p is to exceed threshold, the proportion of times that $\Delta\phi$ will excite one additional neural quantum is given by

$$r_1 = \Delta\phi/Q. \tag{4.2}$$

Equation (4.2) indicates that, for a particular Q size, the proportion of increment detections (r_1) increases as a linear function of $\Delta\phi$. The function starts at the origin and reaches 100% when $\Delta\phi$ is equal to Q, as seen in Figure 4.14 for the one-quantum criterion. If $\Delta\phi/Q$ equals .8, then, on 80% of the trials, p will be equal to or greater than the value which must be added to $\Delta\phi$ in order to exceed threshold. When $\Delta\phi$ is further reduced so that the value of $\Delta\phi/Q$ is only .5, on only 50% of the experimental trials should the value of p be equal to or greater than the value necessary to exceed threshold when combined with $\Delta\phi$.

The use of Equation (4.2) predicts the behavior of the observer as he adopts a judgment criterion for reporting an increment in stimulation whenever one additional neural unit is excited. Psychophysical data, however, are more consistent with the hypothesis that the observer reports a stimulus increment when two additional neural quanta are excited. According to S. S. Stevens (1972a), the two-quantal criterion is necessary because the random fluctuations in sensitivity produce randomly occurring one-quantum increments and decrements in neural activity. The observer would have to adopt a two-quantum criterion in order to distinguish the presence of the stimulus from the background activity of the nervous system. The prediction from the neural quantum theory for a two-unit threshold is given by

$$r_2 = \frac{\Delta\phi - Q}{Q}. \tag{4.3}$$

In Equation (4.3), the proportion of detections first exceeds zero when $\Delta\phi$ is greater than Q, and this proportion becomes 1.0 when $\Delta\phi$ is equal to

$2Q$ (see Figure 4.14). Thus, the value of $\Delta\phi$ when the proportion of detections first becomes 1.0 should be exactly twice the value of $\Delta\phi$ when the proportion of detections first becomes greater than zero. The data reviewed by S. S. Stevens (1972a) are remarkably consistent with this prediction.

It is significant that data in support of neural quantum theory have been obtained under a variety of conditions using both auditory and visual stimuli. Stevens argued that the generality of this finding is consistent with the hypothesis that the operation of the neural quantum may be a central neural mechanism of sufficient generality to process information from all sensory modalities under a great variety of stimulus conditions. According to this hypothesis, sensory inputs would eventually converge on the same neural center in the brain. A quantal jump in neural activity level would occur when $\Delta\phi$ is large enough to exceed the threshold of some switching mechanism in the center.

The difficulty of obtaining linear psychometric functions has been attributed to a lack of precise experimental control over such randomly fluctuating factors as the observer's motivation, attention, and fatigue. Since neural quanta are very small, their operation in the detection or discrimination experiment is often masked by the much larger effects of the fluctuation of these uncontrolled factors on the observer's judgments. Fluctuation of the uncontrolled factors is likely to be normally distributed, and the ogive psychophysical function is therefore obtained. Because it is not precisely clear in this instance what constitutes an acceptable experiment, although Stevens (1972a) attempted to define the essential conditions, neural quantum theory is difficult to reject. When the data do not fit the theory, one can argue that something was wrong with the experiment. Stevens, however, identified some conditions that seem to be necessary for the production of linear psychometric functions:

1. The stimulus must be carefully controlled. When the standard and the comparison stimuli were bursts of white noise and thus varied randomly over time, a normal ogive rather than a linear function was obtained (G. A. Miller, 1947). A jittering stimulus, such as white noise which is constantly changing in amplitude and frequency spectrum, would be expected to obscure the stepwise quantal function, since large random variations between presentation of standard and comparison stimuli would greatly influence the observer's judgments.

2. If the observer is unable to maintain a constant criterion during an experimental session, the psychometric function will tend to be an ogive rather than a straight line. It is no easy task to maintain a fixed criterion during a 1- or 2-hour session in which a thousand or more stimuli are presented. According to Stevens, some observers simply cannot concen-

trate well enough to produce linear functions. Best results are often obtained when highly motivated investigators serve as observers.

3. The transition from the standard to the comparison stimulus must be rapid. If the delay between the two stimuli is long, the observer's sensitivity may not be the same for each stimulus presentation. Under these conditions, random changes in sensitivity will be reflected in an ogive psychometric function. For an adequate test of the neural quantum theory, the transition from the standard to the comparison stimulus must be nearly instantaneous.

It is only under the most stringent conditions, therefore, that we can expect neural quanta, if they exist, to manifest themselves in an observer's performance of a discrimination task. Thus, it is not surprising that most psychometric functions have the ogival rather than the linear form. Although Stevens makes a good case for the hypothesis that a well-trained, highly motivated observer under strictly controlled stimulus conditions can make discrimination judgments based on a precise two-quantum criterion, the position of the theory would be made more secure by supporting data from sensory modalities other than vision and audition and by a further delineation of the conditions under which linear psychometric functions are obtained.

A serious criticism of neural quantum theory comes from Wright (1974), who has argued that the special procedures employed by neural quantum theorists bias the observer to be very conservative in reporting weak stimuli. He has shown that the results predicted from neural quantum theory can also be predicted from the theory of signal detection if it is also assumed that observers adopt conservative judgment criteria in which they report a stimulus increment only when they are sure one occurred. (The theory of signal detection will be extensively discussed later in this chapter.) Furthermore, Wright was able to show that, as the observer's judgment strategy becomes more conservative, the results predicted from the theory of signal detection more closely approach those predicted from neural quantum theory. Thus, it is not possible to decide between the two alternative explanations of the data without further experimental investigation. It is unlikely, however, that the neural quantum theory will be adequately tested in the near future. Little research on the problem has been conducted during the last 20 years, and, with the death of S. S. Stevens, the theory is left without a major defender. In a 1973 paper, Norman pointed out that the rise of the theory of signal detection has led to an almost complete lack of attention to problems concerning the ways observers respond in noise-free situations (Norman, 1973). It is unlikely that a satisfactory answer to the question will come as a side effect in the study of detection and discrimination in noisy situations, since such experiments would surely obscure neural quanta if they do exist. What is needed, and will come with a revival of interest in the problem, are experiments specifically designed to test neural quantum theory.

While neural quantum theory was developed to account for discrimination data obtained in a relatively noise-free situation, the theory of signal detection applies to situations in which the observer must detect weak stimuli presented against a noisy background. In psychophysics today, perhaps the most powerful arguments that sensation changes on a continuum rather than in discrete steps come from the proponents of the theory of signal detection. Before describing this theory in detail, some evidence will be presented in support of the hypothesis that, in most situations, an observer's judgments of weak stimuli are not determined by the abrupt discontinuity in neural activity implied by the absolute threshold concept, but instead are determined by an adjustable judgment criterion.

EVIDENCE AGAINST THE THRESHOLD CONCEPT

The concept of the absolute threshold as a boundary or limit below which no sensation can occur is cast in doubt by the results of many recent psychophysical experiments. It is apparent that threshold measurement does not consist of an observer simply reporting the presence or absence of sensations. Experimenters have therefore directed their attention to the problem of discovering exactly what it is that observers do when they detect stimuli.

Early psychophysicists assumed a close correspondence between the verbal reports of a well-trained observer and concurrent neurological changes in the sensory system caused by stimulation. They worked to obtain results that were pure sensory functions uncontaminated by factors not directly related to the sensory system (e.g., the observer's attitudes and expectations concerning the task). Experimenters assumed that in a well-controlled psychophysical experiment the probability of a yes response [p(yes)] for a particular stimulus presentation was entirely a function of the stimulus and the biological state of the sensory system. Since these experimenters were interested mainly in the sensory system, this assumption simplified matters considerably. The results of recent experiments, however, indicate that many nonsensory variables, even when well-trained observers are used, strongly influence performance in the detection situation.

One nonsensory variable consistently found to affect the p(yes) is the probability of stimulus occurrence [p(S)]. In the early psychophysical experiments, p(S) was always 1.0, because a stimulus was presented on every trial. It seems likely that even for the most conscientious observers, the extremely high expectation of stimulus occurrence associated with the presentation of a stimulus on every trial would itself influence the probability of saying yes when a stimulus is presented. In fact, when $p(S)$ is systematically varied, p(yes) is found to increase with $p(S)$. Put simply, the more often the signal is actually presented, the greater the likelihood that the observer will say "yes, I detected it." In such an experiment, fairly weak stimuli are typically used, and during a session several hundred trials may be administered. The observer's task is to report whether or not a stimulus occurred on a particular trial. A value of $p(S)$ is chosen, and the trials on which the stimulus is presented are determined randomly. Several sessions are usually conducted in which different values of $p(S)$ are used.

Consider the possible outcomes of a single trial in the detection situation. When the stimulus is present, the observer may report yes (a *hit*), or he may report no (a *miss*). On trials when the stimulus is absent, the observer will make either a *false alarm* by saying yes, or he will make a *correct rejection* by saying no. A 2 × 2 table containing the experimentally obtained proportions for each of the four possible outcomes summarizes the results of a series of trials for a particular set of stimulus conditions. In an experiment on $p(S)$, we would have a 2 × 2 table for each of the values of $p(S)$. Table 4.1 shows the kind of results such an experiment might yield. We need only consider p(yes), since p(no) is equal to 1.0 minus p(yes) and is therefore not an independent measure of performance in a two-choice situation. It is quite clear that the probability of a yes response when the stimulus is present increases as the probability of occurrence of the stimulus is made higher. This relationship has been found to exist for weak, moderate, and strong stimuli.

TABLE 4.1
Response Proportions in a Signal Detection Situation
in Which Stimulus Probability Is a Variable

$p(S)$	Number of stimulus trials	Number of no stimulus trials		Response Yes	No
.90	180	20	Stimulus	.99	.01
			No stimulus	.95	.05
.70	140	60	Stimulus	.91	.09
			No stimulus	.64	.36
.50	100	100	Stimulus	.69	.31
			No stimulus	.31	.69
.30	60	140	Stimulus	.36	.64
			No stimulus	.09	.91
.10	20	180	Stimulus	.05	.95
			No stimulus	.01	.99

The relationship between the probability of reporting yes when the stimulus is present [p(yes | stimulus)] and the probability of reporting yes when it is absent [p(yes | no stimulus)] can be illustrated by a graph called a *receiver-operating characteristic curve* or *ROC curve* (Figure 4.15). The term *receiver operating characteristic* (ROC) was originally developed in the early 1950s in the field of engineering to describe the operating characteristics of various electronic sensing devices. A few years later, in the 1950s, this term was adopted for use in psychophysics to describe the performance of human observers. More recently, Swets (1973) renamed ROC curves in psychophysics as *relative operating characteristic*. For the purpose of our discussion, the term ROC can stand for either the original receiver operating characteristic or for the Swets modification. In both cases, the ROC curve represents a graphic description of how the hit rate of an observer changes as a function of changes in the false alarm rate. In the present example, each point on the ROC curve represents the data obtained under a specific p(S) condition.

Each ROC curve represents data obtained for a stimulus of fixed intensity. Thus, the ROC curve is a means of illustrating the often dramatic

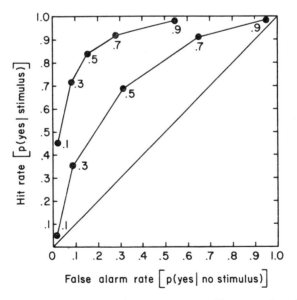

FIG. 4.15. Receiver-operating characteristic curve. The proportion of yes responses when a stimulus is presented is plotted against the proportion of yes responses when no stimulus is presented. Each data point corresponds to a different probability of stimulus occurrence. The points on a single curve result from the presentation of a stimulus of a particular intensity. The top curve is based on detecting a stimulus of higher intensity than that of the bottom curve.

effects of a nonsensory factor on performance in the detection task. As seen in Figure 4.15, increasing the stimulus intensity influences the function by making it arch higher, and a decrease in intensity results in a curve approaching the 45° line. Each individual ROC curve shows the tremendous influence of the observer's expectations about the stimulus. The shifting points along the ROC curve result from the observer being told the value of $p(S)$ at the beginning of each testing period (Tanner, Haller, & Atkinson, 1967). The higher the observer's expectation that the stimulus will be presented on a particular trial, the higher will be both the hit rate and the false alarm rate. The observer rapidly adapts to changing situations such that when $p(S)$ is high, the hit rate will be maximized at the expense of a high false alarm rate, and when $p(S)$ is low, the correct rejection rate will be maximized at the expense of a low hit rate. This strategy of the observer makes sense because it maximizes the number of correct responses. For example, when the stimulus comes frequently, the observer says "yes" frequently, yielding a high number of correct responses on trials when the stimulus is presented (hits) and a few errors on the rare occasions in which it was absent (false alarms). On the other hand, when the stimulus is presented infrequently, the observer says "no" most of the time, yielding a high number of correct responses on trials when the stimulus is absent (correct rejections) and a few errors on the rarely presented stimulus trials (misses).

Since the probability of observers' yes responses are affected by their expectancies about the occurrence or nonoccurrence of the stimulus, it is difficult to see how absolute thresholds can be measured by using conventional psychophysical methods. For example, psychometric functions are lowered and raised depending on the observer's expectations about the stimulus, and, of course, the absolute thresholds derived from the functions are different. In other words, the physical value of the stimulus to which the observer says yes 50% of the time depends on $p(S)$, a nonsensory variable. Figure 4.16 shows that the psychometric function for the detection of vibration on the fingertip was elevated by increasing $p(S)$ (Gescheider, Wright, Weber, & Barton, 1971). Changing $p(S)$ had a strong biasing effect on the conventional threshold measurement. The threshold was 1.0 μm when $p(S)$ was .7 and 1.5 μm when $p(S)$ was .3. Furthermore, when the stimulus is absent, $p(yes)$ is considerably above zero, depending on $p(S)$. According to threshold theory, a well-trained, honest observer should rarely, if ever, report a sensation when a stimulus has not been presented.

When a person is required to indicate the presence or absence of stimuli, whether in the laboratory or in the natural environment, there may be serious consequences related to his response. Consider the person who watches a radar scope for the detection of enemy aircraft. Since the stimulus

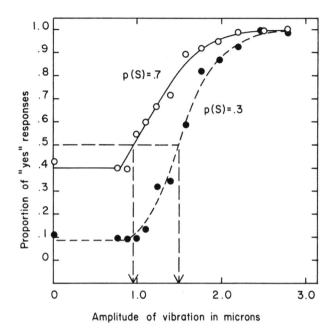

FIG. 4.16. Psychometric functions for the detection of 60-Hz vibration on the fingertip when $p(S)$ was .3 and when $p(S)$ was .7. It is apparent that $p(S)$ has a large effect on the measured threshold. (From Gescheider, Wright, Weber, & Barton, 1971.)

probability is low, the observer's stimulus expectancy is low, and therefore we expect the probability of a correct detection to be low. But since the value of a correct detection and the cost of failing to detect a stimulus are very high, the probability of a hit is kept high and the probability of a miss low. Thus, if the payoff for correct detections and the punishment for misses are made great enough, accurate detection can be maintained even in situations where stimulus occurrence is extremely infrequent. But what happens on occasions when the stimulus is not present? Since the payoff for correctly detecting stimuli is high, the radar scope observer will frequently say yes in the absence of a stimulus (false alarm). Thus, when response consequences are changed, $p(\text{yes} \mid \text{stimulus})$ and $p(\text{yes} \mid \text{no stimulus})$ tend to change together. This principle is also evident when false alarms are punished and correct identifications of stimulus-absence are rewarded. In this case, the probability of yes-responding when there is no stimulus is kept low, but at the same time, the probability of yes-responding in the presence of a stimulus is kept low.

If stimulus intensity and stimulus probability are held constant in a psychophysical experiment, an ROC curve can be generated by manipulating the *costs* and *values* in the detection situation. Typically, at the start of an experimental session the observer is told the stimulus probability and payoff conditions. The payoff conditions are specified by a *payoff matrix* such as the one shown in Table 4.2. Money is often used to reward correct responses, while loss of money is used to punish incorrect responses. It is the various combinations of costs and values which, by changing the likelihood of reporting a stimulus on a particular trial, result in different data points on an ROC curve. If the value of reporting a stimulus when it is presented is high, and the cost of incorrectly reporting it when it is absent is low, the observer will exhibit a high probability of reporting stimuli. However, if the cost is high for incorrectly reporting a stimulus, and the value is low for correctly reporting it, the probability of reporting stimuli will be low. It is significant that ROC curves that have been generated by changing payoff conditions have exactly the same form as those generated by changing stimulus probability. It seems that the two variables affect the same psychological process. Some investigators have identified this process as *response bias*.

Thus, at least two nonsensory factors—stimulus probability and response consequences—have large effects on detection. The evidence for the effects of nonsensory variables on detection performance strongly suggests that the absolute threshold concept does not apply to stimulus detection behavior. If thresholds do in fact exist, it is almost impossible to measure them using classical psychophysical techniques. Human judgments about sensory information are plainly biased by the prevailing conditions of the detection situation.

The early psychophysicists were well aware that response biasing factors such as expectancies and payoff contingencies could contaminate their experimental results. Attempts to control for the effects of biasing factors were made in several ways. Extensive training prior to the experiment, which teaches the observer to maintain a consistent approach in making judgments, was one way of eliminating or at least reducing response bias.

Another technique frequently employed to control response bias was the application of statistical procedures to the data. Early experimenters assumed that detection responses would occur on a certain proportion of trials where the stimulus did not exceed threshold. These detection re-

TABLE 4.2
Payoff Matrix in a Signal Detection Situation

	Response	
	Yes	*No*
Stimulus	5¢	−2¢
No stimulus	−2¢	5¢

sponses were considered false and were attributed to guessing due to response bias. Such false detection responses were often observed when *catch trials* containing no stimulus were presented. It was assumed that sensory events on catch trials never exceeded threshold and, therefore, that the proportion of false alarms on catch trials would give a good estimation of the guessing rate. The proportion of hits observed in an experiment was thought to be the sum of the proportion of trials where threshold was exceeded by the stimulus plus the proportion of trials where the stimulus did not exceed threshold, but where the observer guessed anyway and made the detection response. The following equation describes this relationship:

$$p(\text{hits}) = p^*(\text{hits}) + \{p(\text{false alarms})[1 - p^*(\text{hits})]\}. \qquad (4.4)$$

The empirically obtained proportion of hits, $p(\text{hits})$, is equal to the proportion of hits when threshold is exceeded, $p^*(\text{hits})$, plus the proportion of hits when threshold was not exceeded, $p(\text{false alarms})[1 - p^*(\text{hits})]$. The proportion of hits when threshold was not exceeded is the proportion of stimulus trials when threshold was not exceeded, $1 - p^*(\text{hits})$, multiplied by the guessing rate as estimated by the proportion of false alarms on catch trials, $p(\text{false alarms})$.

The relation between Equation (4.4) and the threshold concept is illustrated in Figure 4.17. According to classical threshold theory, all catch

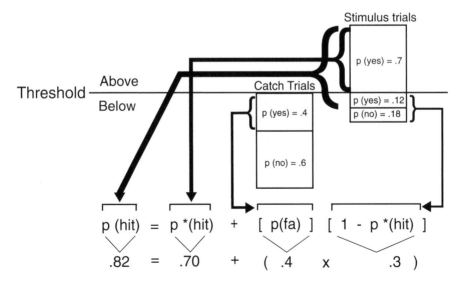

FIG. 4.17. Illustration of relation between Equation (4.4) and threshold theory.

trials result in events that are below threshold. Thus, it was assumed that internal noise is never sufficiently intense to exceed threshold and consequently to be perceived. This being the case, the reporting of the stimulus on catch trials was attributed to guessing. Thus, in the present example, the false alarm, p(fa) of .4 would be entirely attributed to guessing. This guessing tendency observed during catch trials, quantified as p(fa) in the equation, becomes the means of estimating the proportion of stimulus trials on which the stimulus is below threshold, yet is reported by the observer. To accomplish this, $[1 - p^*(\text{hit})]$, the proportion of trials on which the stimulus is below threshold is multiplied by p(fa), $[p(\text{fa}) \times [1 - p^*(\text{hit})]$ $= .4 \times .3 = .12]$. Finally, this proportion of .12, consisting of lucky guess stimulus trials, must be added to .7, the legitimate and true proportion of hits, $p^*(\text{hit})$, consisting of the proportion of stimulus trials on which the stimulus is above threshold.

Rearrangement of Equation (4.4) yields a correction for guessing that can be applied to the proportion of hits obtained in an experiment:

$$p^*(\text{hits}) = \frac{p(\text{hits}) - p(\text{false alarms})}{1 - p(\text{false alarms})}. \qquad (4.5)$$

Implicit in the use of this equation to determine the proportion of hits corrected for guessing, $p^*(\text{hits})$, is the assumption of classical psychophysics that a threshold exists. Thus, the equation was not merely a statistical tool used by early psychophysicists, but was a theoretical statement as well. Fortunately, this theoretical statement can easily be tested. Equation (4.4) states that the relation between the empirically determined proportion of hits and the proportion of false alarms should be linear. The straight lines start from various values of p(yes | stimulus) when p(yes | no stimulus) is zero. The higher the signal strength, the higher the value of p(yes | stimulus) will be. As the observer's guessing rate increases, p(yes | stimulus) and p(yes | no stimulus) should increase linearly until both become 1.0. A family of ROC curves predicted from threshold theory is seen in Figure 4.18. It is unfortunate for the proponents of threshold theory that ROC curves have been found to deviate consistently from linearity. The curved shape of empirically obtained ROC curves is thought to constitute powerful evidence for rejection of the threshold concept in favor of a new conception of the observer's behavior in the detection situation (Swets, 1961).

Another way of evaluating classical threshold theory is to examine the influence of the false alarm rate on the psychometric function. Seen in Figure 4.19 are two hypothetical psychometric functions in which the proportion of yes responses of an observer is plotted as a function of stimulus intensity. Assume the functions were obtained under identical

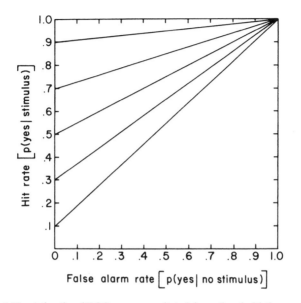

FIG. 4.18. A family of ROC curves predicted from threshold theory. Each line represents changes in p(yes | stimulus) and p(yes | no stimulus) caused by changes in the guessing rate for the detection of a stimulus of a particular intensity.

conditions with the exception that in one case the observer expected the stimulus to be presented on 70% of the trials, but in the other case the stimulus was presented on only 30% of the trials. When the probability of stimulus presentation, p(S), was .7, the proportion of yes responses on trials when no stimulus was presented yielded a false alarm rate of .43. When p(S) was .3, the false alarm rate was only .11. Furthermore, the hit rate on trials when a stimulus was presented was much higher when the observer expected the stimulus to be presented frequently. According to classical threshold theory, the high rate of reporting a stimulus when its presentation is expected is due to a high rate of guessing that the stimulus was presented when one could not be detected. To obtain a measurement of the absolute threshold in this situation, it is essential that the psychometric function be corrected for guessing. In classical threshold theory, threshold is defined as the stimulus intensity that is detected half of the time when the false alarm rate is zero. To determine the threshold, the proportion of yes responses when the stimulus was presented, p(hit), must be corrected by Equation (4.5) to obtain p^*(hit), the proportion of times the observer would have detected the stimulus if the false alarm rate had been zero. In our hypothetical example, when the values of p(hit) of both

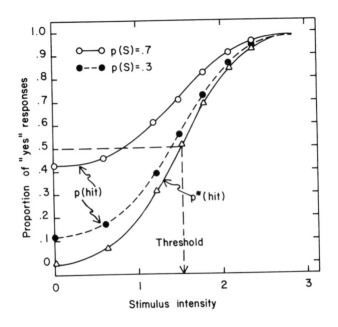

FIG. 4.19. Hypothetical psychometric functions with different false alarm rates. When the false alarm rates are used to correct the p(hit) values for guessing, the corrected values, p^*(hit), produce a single psychometric function for both false alarm rates.

psychometric functions in Figure 4.19 are corrected for guessing using Equation (4.5), a single psychometric function with a false alarm rate of zero is found. The absolute threshold is derived from the corrected function as the stimulus intensity corresponding to a p^*(hit) value of .5. The hypothetical data in this example are the results expected if classical threshold theory were true. According to the theory, threshold is invariant after the correction for guessing has been made. Once the bias caused by guessing has been removed, the psychometric functions obtained under different false alarm rates should all be identical. Results from actual experiments, however, have not confirmed this hypothesis derived from threshold theory.

The psychometric functions obtained in the experiment by Gescheider et al. (1971) and seen in Figure 4.16 indicate that when p(S) was .7 the false alarm rate and the hit rate were much higher than when p(S) was .3. Equation (4.5) was used to correct the proportions of yes responses for guessing, and the corrected results are plotted in Figure 4.20. It is clear that the corrected psychometric functions are not superimposed and give

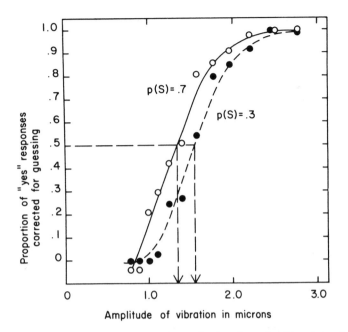

FIG. 4.20. Psychometric functions obtained when the probability of signal presentation was .3 and when it was .7. Through the false alarm rate, the p(hit) values seen in Figure 4.16 have been corrected for guessing.

different thresholds. This result is similar to that of Swets, Tanner, and Birdsall (1961), who examined psychometric functions for the detection of visual stimuli. The results of these experiments, in conjunction with those obtained by plotting ROC curves, constitute a very strong case against the validity of classical threshold theory. Thus, we must discard the theory of a threshold that is exceeded only when a stimulus of sufficient strength is presented. However, the concept of a lower threshold which is frequently exceeded by spontaneous activity in the nervous system is not in disagreement with experimental findings. Low threshold theory is discussed in chapter 6.

PROBLEMS

4.1. Draw an underlying distribution of momentary thresholds that is negatively skewed (longer tail at low than at high end of the distribution). Draw your best estimation of the predicted psychometric function.

4.2. The Poisson distribution of quantal fluctuations with a mean of 2 quanta is now presented:

Number of Emitted Quanta	Probability
0	.13
1	.26
2	.26
3	.17
4	.09
5	.03
6	.015
7	.008

If the observer's fixed threshold is 3 quanta, what is the probability that the stimulus will be detected?

4.3. Draw a psychometric function and an underlying distribution of momentary thresholds for observer A who has a relatively low average threshold with great variability of thresholds and for observer B who has a relatively high average threshold with little variability of thresholds.

4.4. Assume that high threshold theory is correct. For p^*(hits) values of .20 and .50 determine the values of p(hits) corresponding to p(false alarms) values of .00, .20, .40, .60, .80, and 1.00. Plot an ROC curve for each of the two p^*(hits) values.

5

The Theory of Signal Detection

The discovery that expectancy and payoff have such a dramatic influence upon detection behavior was incorporated into a new theoretical conception of the detection situation. Tanner and Swets (1954) proposed that statistical decision theory and certain ideas about electronic signal-detecting devices might be used to build a model closely approximating how people actually behave in detection situations. The model is called the *theory of signal detection* (TSD) and is described in detail by Green and Swets (1966). Fundamental to TSD is the concept of noise.

DISTRIBUTIONS OF NOISE AND SIGNAL PLUS NOISE

Signals (stimuli) are always detected—whether by electronic devices or by humans—against a background of activity. The level of this background activity, called *noise*, is assumed to vary randomly and may be either external to the detecting device or caused by the device itself (e.g., physiological noise caused by spontaneous activity of the nervous system). In the detection situation, the observer must therefore first make an *observation* (x) and then make a decision about the observation. On each trial, the observer must decide whether x is due to a signal added to the noise background or to the noise alone. When a weak signal is applied, the decision becomes difficult, and errors are frequent. One factor contributing to the difficulty of the problem is the random variation of background noise. On some trials, the noise level may be so high as to be mistaken for a signal, and on other trials it may be so low that the addition of a weak signal is mistaken for noise. This state of affairs can

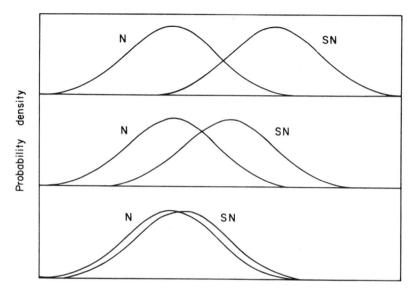

Magnitude of sensory observation (𝒙)

FIG. 5.1. Theoretical frequency distributions of noise and signal noise for three different values of signal strength.

be represented graphically by two probability distributions describing the random variation of noise (N) and the signal plus noise (SN) (Figure 5.1). Since the signal is added to the noise, the average sensory observation magnitude will always be greater for the *signal-plus-noise distribution*, SN, than for the *noise distribution*, N. However, the difference between the means becomes smaller and smaller as the signal strength is decreased, until the distributions are essentially the same. It is when the two distributions greatly overlap that decision making becomes difficult.

THE LIKELIHOOD RATIO

On any given trial the observer makes a sensory observation x which consists of a random sample from one or the other of the two distributions. Based on its sensory magnitude, the observer decides whether x was sampled from the N or the SN distribution. The ordinate of N gives the *probability density*,[1] or likelihood, of x occurring when only noise is pre-

---

[1]The term *probability density* is used because x is continuous rather than discrete. If x had a limited number of discrete values, each could be described as having a particular probability of occurrence. In either case, the ordinate gives the relative likelihood of a particular value of x.

sented. Similarly, the ordinate of SN gives the likelihood of x occurring when a signal is presented. Each value of x can now be expressed in terms of these two likelihoods or probability densities. For each value of x there exists a particular *likelihood ratio, $l(x)$*, defined as

$$l(x) = \frac{\text{ordinate of SN}}{\text{ordinate of N}}. \tag{5.1}$$

The likelihood ratio provides the observer with a basis for making a decision, since it expresses the likelihood of x in the SN situation relative to the likelihood of x in the N situation. Even though x may vary on several dimensions (e.g., hue, saturation, brightness, shape), each x can be located on a single dimension of likelihood ratio, since for each x there exists a single ordinate value of N and a single ordinate value of SN. Thus, the observer's final decision of whether x is due to N or SN can be based on a single quantity, the likelihood ratio.

Figure 5.2 illustrates how the value of the likelihood ratio, $l(x)$, changes as the value of the sensory observation, x, changes. At a point on the sensory observation dimension where the noise and signal-plus-noise distributions cross, the ordinate values for the two distributions are the same, resulting in a likelihood ratio of 1.0. This likelihood ratio of 1.0 indicates that a sensory observation, x, located at this point on the sensory observation dimension, is equally likely to result from noise as it is from signal plus noise. When the value of x is higher than this point, the likelihood ratio is greater than 1.0; and when the value of x is below this point, the likelihood ratio is less than 1.0. A likelihood ratio greater than 1.0 indicates that it is more likely that the sensory observation resulted from signal plus noise than from noise alone. A likelihood ratio less than 1.0 indicates that it is more likely that the sensory observation resulted from noise alone than from signal plus noise.

THE OBSERVER'S CRITERION

One of the assumptions of TSD is that an observer establishes a particular value of $l(x)$ as a cutoff point, or criterion (β), and that the decision will be determined by whether a particular observation, x, is above or below the criterion. Proponents of the theory assume that the observer operates by a *decision rule*: when $l(x)$ is equal to or greater than β, the observer chooses SN, and when $l(x)$ is below β, the observer chooses N. If the observer properly sets the criterion, performance will be optimal in a long series of observations. For example, in many situations it would be best for the observer to set a criterion so that the value of β was equal to 1.0. Since sensory observations having likelihood ratios greater than 1.0 are

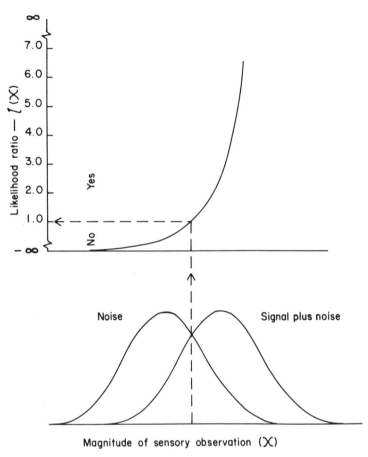

FIG. 5.2. Change of likelihood ratio as a function of the value of x.

more likely to have resulted from signal plus noise than from noise alone, the observer should always choose SN when $l(x)$ is greater than 1.0. When $l(x)$ is less than 1.0, the observer should always choose N, because sensory observations having likelihood ratios less than 1.0 are more likely to be the result of noise than signal plus noise. Figure 5.2 illustrates how an observer should report "yes, a signal was presented" when the likelihood ratio is greater than 1.0, and report "no, a signal was not presented" when the likelihood ratio is less than 1.0.

Figure 5.3 illustrates a case in which the observer has set a criterion at a point on the sensory observation dimension where β is equal to 1.0 (the ordinates of the N and SN distributions are equal). When sensory observations are above the criterion, the observer reports "yes, there is a signal." When the sensory observation is below the criterion, the observer reports

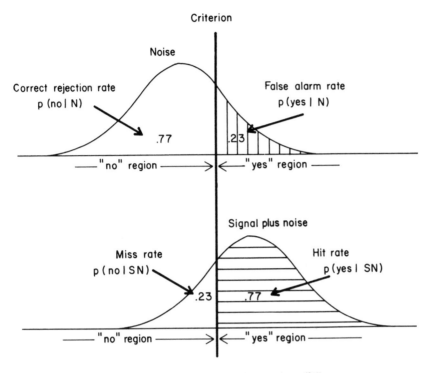

FIG. 5.3. Theoretical frequency distributions of noise and signal plus noise. The location of the observer's criterion determines whether a particular sensory observation, x, results in a no or a yes response.

"no, there is no signal." Sometimes, the observer will be correct and report yes when the signal is presented (hit) and no when only noise is present (correct rejection). Sometimes, however, the observer will be incorrect and report yes when only noise is present (false alarm) and no when the signal is presented (miss).

In a typical signal detection experiment, there are many trials in which the signal is presented, and there are many trials in which no signal is presented. The order of presentation of SN and N trials is random. The intensity of the signal is usually the same on each SN trial. On each trial, the observer must report whether or not a signal was presented. The hit rate is the proportion of SN trials in which the observer reported the signal, and the false alarm rate is the proportion of N trials in which the observer reported a signal. If such an experiment were conducted with the observer whose N and SN distributions and criterion are depicted in Figure 5.3, it would be possible to predict the hit and false alarm rates.

The predicted proportion of hits, the hit rate [p(yes | SN)], is the proportion of the SN distribution above the criterion. The hit rate in this example is .77. The predicted proportion of false alarms, the false alarm rate [p(yes | N)], is the proportion of the N distribution above the criterion. In this example, this rate is .23. For this observer, the location of the criterion on the sensory observation dimension, and the location of the N and SN distributions, were known in advance; therefore, it was possible to predict the hit and false alarm rates for an experiment. More typically, the reverse is done; that is, the location on the sensory observation dimension of the criterion, and N and SN distributions, are derived from the observer's experimentally determined hit and false alarm rates. It is here that the power of TSD lies. If the theory is correct, it becomes possible, through analysis of experimentally obtainable hit and false alarm rates, to specify quantitatively the processes going on inside the observer that are the bases of sensory decision making.

Swets et al. (1961) consider the detection situation to be analogous to a game of chance in which three dice are thrown. Two of the dice are ordinary, but the third is a special die with three spots on each of three sides and no spots on the other three sides. When the dice are thrown, the player is told only the total number of spots on all three dice. This information is analogous to the information given for each observation in a detection situation. On the basis of the total number of spots showing, the player must decide whether the unusual die showed a zero or a three. Similarly, in the detection situation the observer must decide whether an observation was a product of noise alone or of signal plus noise. To come out ahead in the long run, the player of the dice game would compute the probability of occurrence of each of the possible totals (2 to 12) when the unusual die shows zero, and likewise, the probabilities of each of the totals (5 to 15) when the unusual die shows three. The results can be plotted as two probability distributions and should be thought of as the analogs of the noise and signal-plus-noise distributions (Figure 5.4). Furthermore, as in the detection situation, a criterion can be set so that if the total number of spots were greater than some number the player would say "three," and if the total were less than the number he would say "zero." In our example, where the probabilities of a three and a zero are both .50 and the costs and values are the same for the various decision outcomes, the optimal criterion is the point where the two curves cross. In a detection situation, where the stimulus probability is .50 and the costs and values are equal for the various decision outcomes, the optimal criterion is also the point on the observation magnitude dimension where the two distributions cross.

It can be demonstrated mathematically that in the dice game the optimal cutoff point changes when the conditions of the game are changed.

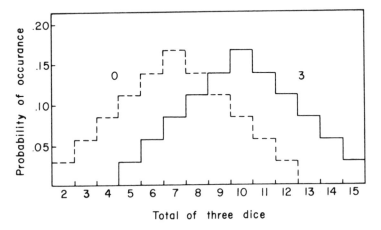

FIG. 5.4. Probability distributions for the dice game. (From Swets, Tanner, & Birdsall, 1961. Copyright 1961 by the American Psychological Association. Reprinted by permission.)

For example, if the unusual die were changed to one having three spots on five of the six sides and no spots on only one side, the probability of obtaining three spots would be .83 instead of .50, and the optimal criterion would be lowered. A good player would lower the cutoff point for saying "three." Likewise, the optimal criterion would be raised if only one side of the die had three spots and the other five sides had none. In the detection situation, changing the stimulus probability is assumed to have a similar effect on the observer's criterion. In order to perform optimally in a situation where stimulus occurrence is highly probable, an observer will report a signal after a less intense sensory observation than when the stimulus is relatively improbable.

The location of the optimal cutoff point in the dice game is also influenced by changes in the payoff conditions. For example, if the reward is great for correctly saying "three" and the punishment slight for saying "three" when "zero" is correct, the optimal criterion will, of course, be relatively low for saying "three." Rewards and punishments in the detection situation are assumed to have a similar effect on the observer's criterion. A radar scope observer, for instance, maintains a low criterion for reporting signals because of the extreme importance of detecting enemy aircraft and the possible disastrous consequences of failing to do so.

The criterion set in the dice game will also be influenced by the degree of overlap of the two distributions. If the number of spots on the unusual die is made zero or four instead of zero or three, the distributions will overlap less because the distribution, when four is correct, will be shifted further up the scale, and the game becomes easier. Since the point where the two distributions cross is also shifted up the scale, the optimal criterion will be higher. This manipulation in the dice game can be translated into an increase in stimulus intensity in the detection situation. When the signal-plus-noise distribution is shifted to a higher point on the observation magnitude dimension, detection becomes easier, and the optimal criterion is higher.

In summary, the detection of energy changes in our environment involves, according to TSD, the establishing of a decision rule in the same way as the efficient playing of a game of chance does. The decision rule is the setting of a criterion determining which hypothesis about a given piece of information will be accepted and which rejected. High criteria are used to minimize false alarms and maximize correct rejections, whereas low criteria are used to minimize misses and maximize hits. The location of optimal criterion is a function of (a) the probabilities of the N and SN presentations, and (b) the costs and values for the various decision outcomes.

In the detection situation, where the costs and values of the various decision outcomes and the probability of signal presentation are precisely known, the optimum value of the criterion, β_{opt}, can be calculated by

$$\beta_{opt} = \frac{p(N)}{p(SN)} \times \frac{\text{value(correct rejection)} - \text{cost(false alarm)}}{\text{value(hit)} - \text{cost(miss)}}. \quad (5.2)$$

β_{opt} is the value of the likelihood ratio, $l(x)$, which, when used as the criterion, will result in the largest possible winnings in the long run; $p(N)$ is the probability of a noise trial; $p(SN)$ is the probability of a signal-plus-noise trial; value is the amount given to the observer for each correct decision, and cost is the amount taken away from the observer for each incorrect observation. Costs are entered into the equation as negative numbers. For example, if a nickel were taken away for each false alarm, the cost of a false alarm would be –5.

When the value of β, as calculated from the judgments of observers, is compared with β_{opt}, it is generally found that observers do fairly well at optimizing their winnings. An exception to this rule occurs, however, when β_{opt} is very small or very large, in which case β will not be as extreme as β_{opt}, and the observer will fail to optimize his winnings. Observers tend not to set extremely low or extremely high criteria, even in situations where these strategies would lead to optimal performance.

An interesting early application of setting the optimal criterion is seen in Pascal's famous "wager." In 1670, Blaise Pascal, a French mathematician, claimed that to believe in God was rational. He noted that there are two possibilities, existence of God or nonexistence of God, and two possible responses, belief in God or disbelief in God. Pascal argued that, even if the probability of God's existence is extremely small, the gain (value) of asserting His existence and the cost of denying it make belief in God the rational choice. In TSD terms, the decision criterion should be set infinitely low because the value of a hit is infinitely high as is the cost of a miss, and at the same time there is no cost to a false alarm and no value to a correct rejection. Thus, "If you gain, you gain all; if you lose, you lose nothing. Wager, then, without hesitation that He is" (Pensée No. 233, Pascal, 1958).

THEORETICAL SIGNIFICANCE OF THE
RECEIVER-OPERATING CHARACTERISTIC CURVE

One of the main sources of evidence supporting TSD comes from the experimental manipulation of variables resulting in data plotted as ROC curves. In fact, shapes of ROC curves for various stimulus intensities can be generated from the theory and checked against empirical data. It should be recalled that the high threshold theory was rejected because of its failure to predict empirical ROC curves.

The manner in which ROC curves are predicted from TSD is illustrated in Figures 5.5, 5.6, and 5.7. The ROC curve in Figure 5.5 represents a situation where the signal strength is sufficient to result in only a slight overlap of the N and SN probability distributions. The vertical lines represent the locations of the criterion that might be associated with specific conditions of stimulus probability and payoff. Each point on an ROC curve, according to the theory, is determined by the location of the observer's criterion on the x dimension. If an observation is to the right of the criterion, the observer will say yes. The proportion of the area under the curve to the right of the criterion gives the proportion of yes decisions. Therefore, the hit rate [p(yes I SN)] and the false alarm rate [p(yes I N)] can be determined by finding the areas under the SN and N distribution curves, respectively, which are located to the right of the criterion. As the criterion is changed from high to low, the false alarm rate and the hit rate increase and, when plotted, form an ROC curve. The illustration in Figure 5.6 shows the ROC curve predicted from TSD when the signal strength is so weak as to result in considerable overlap of the N and SN distributions. Figure 5.7 is the predicted ROC curve when there is no separation between the N and SN distributions. In this case, the signal is too weak to have an effect on the nervous system. Comparing the ROC curves of Figures 5.5, 5.6, and 5.7 shows that, as the separation between N and SN distributions increases, the predicted ROC curve rises more rapidly and departs from the positive diagonal of the graph by a greater amount. In all three cases, it is seen that, as the criterion is lowered, the predicted point on the ROC curve becomes higher.

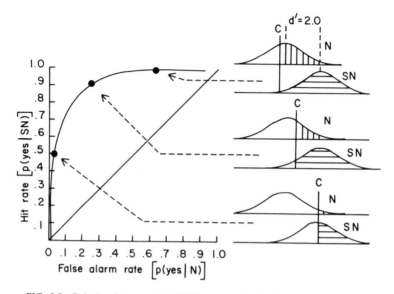

FIG. 5.5. Relation between the ROC curve and the theoretical noise and signal-plus-noise distributions. Variation in the observer's criterion results in different points along the ROC curve. The hit rate is equal to the proportion of the area of the signal-plus-noise distribution that is above criterion. The false alarm rate is equal to the proportion of the area of the noise distribution that is above criterion.

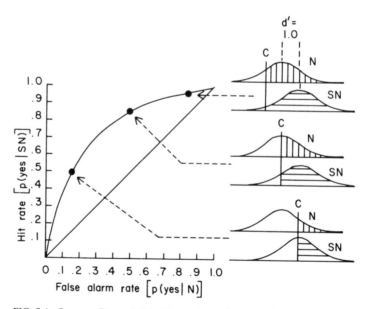

FIG. 5.6. Same as Figure 5.5 but the noise and signal-plus-noise distributions are closer together.

114

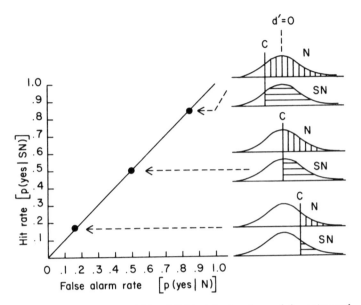

FIG. 5.7. Same as Figures 5.5 and 5.6 but the locations of the noise and signal-plus-noise distributions are identical.

The shape of the ROC curve is a function of the way the areas under the N and SN distributions above the criterion change when the location of the criterion is changed. When N and SN distributions are identical, as in Figure 5.7, lowering the criterion increases the area above criterion by exactly the same amount in the N and SN distributions, and the resulting ROC curve is linear with a slope of 1.0. When the two distributions are separated, as in Figures 5.5 and 5.6, lowering the criterion from high to moderate changes the area above criterion more rapidly for the SN than for the N distribution, and consequently, the lower section of the ROC curve rises at a rapid rate with slopes greater than 1.0. Lowering the criterion from moderate to low, on the other hand, changes the area above the criterion less rapidly for the SN than for the N distribution, and although the ROC curve continues to rise, it does so at a diminished rate with slopes less than 1.0.

It is important to understand that the ROC curves presented in Figures 5.5, 5.6, and 5.7 are predicted from TSD. Testing the validity of TSD requires that ROC curves determined in experiments in which observers detect signals be compared with the ROC curves predicted from the theory. To obtain an ROC curve, the observer is presented with a random series of trials that either contain or do not contain a signal. On each trial, the observer must report the presence or absence of the signal. At various stages of the experiment, the observer is induced to change the location of the criterion. This criterion change can be accomplished in many ways, including changing the proportion of trials containing a signal, or changing the payoff for correct responses and the punishment for errors. Hit and false alarm rates are recorded for each criterion set by the observer. The ROC curve is obtained when the hit rates are plotted as a function of the false alarm rates. Thus, each data point on an ROC curve represents the hit and false alarm rates obtained for a single criterion of the observer. Many experiments designed in this manner have been conducted, and, generally, the shapes of the ROC curves obtained in the laboratory are in close agreement with those predicted from TSD. Because TSD has been supported so well by experimental research, most psychophysicists accept the theory, and many have used it to solve the old problem of obtaining pure measurements of an observer's sensitivity to stimuli uninfluenced by the location of the criterion.

MEASURING SENSITIVITY

In the classical psychophysical experiment, the results expressed as thresholds were a function of both stimulus detectability and the location of the observer's criterion. Thus, as a measure of sensitivity to stimuli, the threshold may be hopelessly contaminated by changes in the observer's criterion. Such contamination can lead to faulty conclusions about the results of an experiment. For example, there have been cases in which investigators incorrectly attributed large changes in thresholds to changes in the sensitivity of sensory processes. In fact, as revealed by subsequent experimentation, only the criterion had changed. As seen in Figure 4.16, psychometric functions obtained by the method of constant stimuli can be substantially influenced by changing the proportion of trials on which the signal was presented. When the proportion of signal trials was increased, the proportion of "yes" responses increased at all intensities of the signal. The increase in the proportion of "yes" responses can be attributed to a lowering of the observer's decision criterion. One consequence of this increase in the proportion of "yes" responses is a shift in the position of the psychometric function such that the estimated *absolute threshold*, defined as the intensity of a signal that is detectable 50% of the time, is substantially lowered. The threshold, estimated from the psychometric function, becomes a biased estimate of sensitivity insofar as performance in the task is influenced by the location of the observer's criterion, as well as by sensitivity level. Figure 5.8 illustrates the possible confounding effects of criterion location on threshold estimation. The psychometric functions on the top of the figure illustrate a case in which observer A and observer B, having the same sensitivity and decision

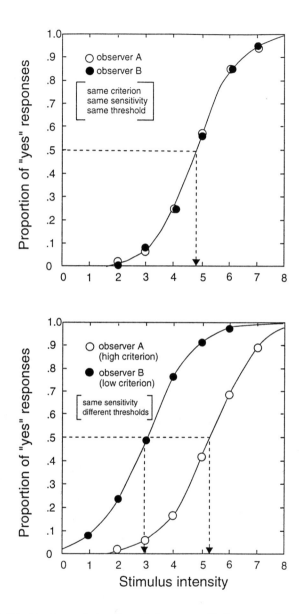

FIG. 5.8. Psychometric functions of observers with the same criterion and sensitivity (top) and psychometric functions of observers with different criteria and the same sensitivity (bottom).

criterion, have the same estimated threshold. In the bottom of the figure, the estimated threshold of observer B is lower than that of observer A because, although the observers have the same sensitivity, observer B has a lower criterion than does observer A.

TSD and its associated methodology afford a means of independently measuring the observer's sensitivity and criterion location. The theory proposes that d', a measure of detectability, is equal to the difference between the means of the SN and N distributions ($M_{SN} - M_N$) divided by the standard deviation of the N distribution (σ_N):

$$d' = \frac{M_{SN} - M_N}{\sigma_N}. \tag{5.3}$$

Because the location of the SN distribution in relation to that of the N distribution is entirely a function of stimulus intensity and properties of the sensory system, d' is a pure index of stimulus detectability that is uncontaminated by the location of the observer's criterion.

But how can this theoretical concept of signal detectability be measured? Since different d' values predict different ROC curves, the value of d' in a particular situation can be ascertained by determining on which member of the family of ROC curves an observer's response probabilities fall. A family of ROC curves corresponding to d' values ranging from 0 to 3.0 is seen in Figure 5.9. Because only a limited number of curves are usually presented in such a graph, it is best to use them when only approximate values of d' are needed. Fortunately, simple methods are available for the determination of exact values of d'.

The value of d' can be quickly computed from the experimentally determined values of the false alarm and hit rates. The proportion of false alarms, when subtracted from 1.0 and converted to a z score through Table A of the appendix, gives Z_N, the location of the criterion on the abscissa of the noise distribution. These operations are summarized below and are illustrated in Figure 5.10.

$$1.0 - p(\text{false alarms}) \rightarrow Z_N \tag{5.4}$$

The location of the criterion on the abscissa of the signal-plus-noise distribution, Z_{SN}, is found by subtracting the hit rate from 1.0 and converting this p value to a z score. These operations are summarized below and are illustrated in Figure 5.10.

$$1.0 - p(\text{hit}) \rightarrow Z_{SN} \tag{5.5}$$

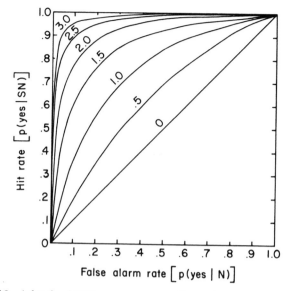

FIG. 5.9. A family of ROC curves corresponding to d' values ranging from 0 to 3.0.

To obtain d', Z_{SN} is subtracted[2] from Z_N.

$$d' = Z_N - Z_{SN} \qquad\qquad (5.6)$$

In the example in Figure 5.10, 1.0 minus the false alarm rate of .02 (i.e., .98) gives the proportion of the area under the noise distribution below the criterion. Converting .98 to a z score yields a Z_N value of 2.05, which represents the location of the criterion on the abscissa of the noise distribution. The hit rate of .35 subtracted from 1.0 (i.e., .65) gives the proportion of the area under the signal-plus-noise distribution below the criterion. When .65 is converted to a z score, Z_{SN} is found to be .39. This value represents the location of the criterion on the abscissa of the signal-plus-noise distribution. To find d', the Z_{SN} value of .39 is subtracted from the Z_N value of 2.05 to yield a d' value of 1.66. This value of 1.66 is the number of z-score units between the mean of the noise distribution and the mean of the signal-plus-noise distribution.

---

[2]An alternative, and frequently used method for calculating d', is to use the formula d' = Z (hit) − Z (false alarm). Although the same result is obtained with this method and the one specified above, I prefer teaching the concept of d' in terms of Z_N and Z_{SN} rather than Z (false alarm) and Z (hit), because Z_{SN} and Z_N specify the location of the observer's criterion in terms of z-score units on the abscissa of the SN and N distributions, respectively (see Fig. 5.10).

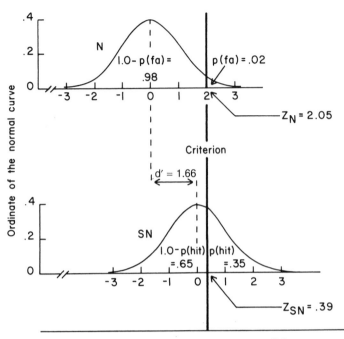

Magnitude of sensory observation (X)

FIG. 5.10. Distributions of noise and signal plus noise expressed in z scores. The location of the criterion on the noise distribution is found by subtracting the false alarm rate from 1.0 and converting this value to a z score. The location of the criterion on the signal-plus-noise distribution is found by subtracting the hit rate from 1.0 and converting this value to a z score. The value of d', a measure of the observer's sensitivity to the signal, is found by subtracting Z_{SN} from Z_N ($d' = Z_N - Z_{SN}$).

The d' values for each data point on the ROC curves of Figures 5.5, 5.6, and 5.7 can be determined by the method just described. When these calculations are performed, we find that d' will be 2.0 for each point on the ROC curve in Figure 5.5, 1.0 for each point on the curve in Figure 5.6, and .00 for each point on the curve in Figure 5.7. It should be clear that, for a particular separation of the noise and signal-plus-noise distributions, the value of d' will remain constant for all possible criterion positions. Thus, an ROC curve is a description of performance changes that are accounted for by a constant d' and a continuously variable criterion.

It has been experimentally demonstrated for both visual stimuli (Swets, Tanner, & Birdsall, 1955) and auditory stimuli (Tanner, Swets, & Green, 1956) that d', as a measure of sensitivity, is not contaminated by the effects of variables which shift an observer's response criterion. Furthermore, d' values, unlike the different threshold values obtained through the use of the various classical psychophysical methods, remain relatively invariant when measured by different experimental procedures (Swets, 1959; Tanner & Swets, 1954).

Once the correct ROC curve has been determined, the location of the observer's criterion, β, can be determined by observing exactly where on the ROC curve the point is located. If the point is near the bottom of the ROC curve where the slope is great, the criterion is high; if the point is near the top of the curve where the slope is slight, the criterion is low. The exact value of β is equal to the slope of the ROC curve at a particular point.

To reiterate, β is a value of the likelihood ratio. It is the ratio of the ordinate of the SN distribution at the criterion to the ordinate of the N distribution at the criterion, as follows:

$$\beta = \frac{\text{ordinate of SN distribution at criterion}}{\text{ordinate of N distribution at criterion}}. \tag{5.7}$$

Ordinate values (O) of the normal distribution curve for various p values and z-score values are found in Table A in the appendix. Figure 5.2 illustrates that moving the criterion to the right increases the value of β, and moving it to the left decreases β. A low value of β represents a lax criterion where the observer will be liberal about reporting signals, while a high value of β represents a strict criterion where the observer will be conservative about reporting signals.

The value of β can be calculated from a pair of hit and false alarm rates. The ordinate of the N distribution at criterion can be estimated as the ordinate value given in Table A that corresponds to 1.0 minus the false alarm rate. Likewise, the ordinate of the SN distribution at criterion is obtained by converting 1.0 minus the hit rate into the ordinate value on the normal distribution curve. For example, ordinate values for a false alarm rate of .20 and a hit rate of .85 are .2801 and .2333, respectively:

$$\beta = \frac{.233}{.280} = .83.$$

The techniques of computing d' and β equip investigators who wish to study the effects of a particular variable with a means of testing whether the effects of that variable are on detectability or on the location of the criterion. They have only to observe whether systematic changes in the variable result in different points along a single ROC curve or points located on different ROC curves. The values of d' and β can also be calculated for various experimental conditions. In some experiments, manipulation of an independent variable has led to changes in both β and d'.

RESPONSE BIAS

Response bias is a tendency of the observer, determined by factors other than signal intensity, to favor one response over another. The sensitivity measure, d', depends on stimulus parameters but remains constant when the situation dictates that one response should be made more frequently than another. Thus, d' is independent of response bias. Up to this point we have described how response bias can be measured through the calculation of β. Calculating β from the hit and false alarm rates, although providing a useful description of the location of the observer's criterion in terms of a likelihood ratio, is not the only feasible way to describe response bias. An alternative index of response bias is C (for criterion), which is defined as

$$C = 0.5 [Z_{SN} + Z_N].$$ (5.8)

When the false alarm rate and the miss rate are equal, the hit rate and correct rejection rate will also be equal and the value of C will be zero. For example, as illustrated in Figure 5.11, when both the false alarm and miss rate is 0.1 and the hit rate and correct ejection rate is .9, the value of Z_N is $(1.0 - 0.1) \rightarrow Z_N = 1.28$, while the value of Z_{SN} was $(1.0 - 0.9) \rightarrow Z_{SN} = -1.28$. Thus, the value of C is .5(−1.28 + 1.28) = 0.0. It should also be kept in mind that C is zero at the point where the N and SN distributions cross. This point, illustrated in Figure 5.11, is regarded as the point at which the observer's responses are neither biased toward "yes" responses nor toward "no" responses. Because the area of the SN distribution above the criterion is exactly equal to the area of the N distribution below the criterion the hit and correct rejection rates are exactly equal. Likewise, because the area of the SN distribution below the criterion is equal to the area of the N distribution above the criterion the miss and false alarm rates are equal. Indicative of the absence of response bias in this situation in which the value of C is zero, the total number of "yes" responses (hits plus false alarms) will be the same as the total number of "no" responses (misses plus correct rejections). Negative values of C, on the other hand, would reflect a bias toward frequent "yes" responses and positive values of C would reflect a bias toward frequent "no" responses. It should be recognized that C, because it is computed from Z_N and Z_{SN}, is the number of standard deviation units (z-score units) that the criterion is above or below the zero bias point where the N and SN distributions cross. A convenient feature of expressing the criterion in this way is that both the sensitivity measure, d', and the criterion are expressed in the common units of z scores of the two distributions. In the present example, we can say that the means of the N and SN distributions are separated

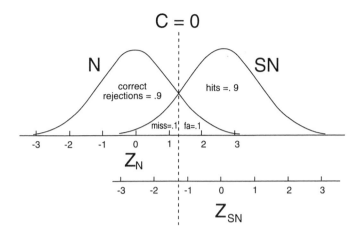

FIG. 5.11. The determination of C from Z_N and Z_{SN}. In this example, C = 0, the point where the N and SN distributions cross.

by 2.56 z-score units ($d' = Z_N - Z_{SN} = 1.28 - -1.28 = 2.56$), while the location of the criterion in z-score units from the point at which the N and SN distributions cross is 0.0 ($C = .5 [Z_{SN} + Z_N = .5[-1.28 + 1.28] = 0$).

In addition to β and C, a third measure of response bias is C'. While β is the value of the likelihood ratio at the criterion, and C is the distance of the criterion in z-score units from the crossing point of the N and SN distributions, C' represents the value of C as a proportion of sensitivity distance (d'). The value of C' can be calculated as

$$C' = C/d' = .5[Z_{SN} + Z_N] / [Z_N - Z_{SN}].   (5.9)$$

The answer to the question of which index of response bias is better depends on the degree to which each of the three measures, β, C, and C', are independent of changes in sensitivity. It has been demonstrated that neither β or C' is statistically independent of d', whereas C is (Macmillan & Creelman, 1991). Furthermore, the range of C does not depend on d', whereas the range of β and C' does (Banks, 1970; Ingham, 1970). When d' is large, the range of C' is small while the range of β is large. When d' is small, the opposite is true. In situations where both the sensitivity and criterion of the observer change as experimental conditions change, C is the only measure of response bias that can be interpreted without knowledge of d' (Snodgrass & Corwin, 1988; Macmillan & Creelman, 1990; Macmillan & Creelman, 1991).

The three measures of response bias are simply related. If d' and one of the bias measures is known, it is easy to calculate the other two. The value of C' is obtained by dividing C by d', while multiplying C by d'

yields log β. Taking the antilog of log β where log β is the natural rather than common log of β yields β. It is important to carefully consider the results obtained with different bias measures because, in some circumstances, they may each lead to different conclusions about the experimental results.

PROBLEMS

5.1. Assume that the variance of the N and SN distributions are equal. Plot ROC curves on proportion coordinates for a d' of .8 and for a d' of 1.6. Plot at least 5 points on each curve. Use the equation $d' = Z_N - Z_{SN}$ to solve the problem.

5.2. Assuming that N and SN distributions are normal with equal variance, calculate the values d', β, C, and C' for the hit and false alarm rates found in the table below.

Observer	False Alarm Rate	Hit Rate
1	.18	.84
2	.38	.96
3	.42	.69
4	.30	.48
5	.70	.98

5.3. An observer performed a signal detection task in which he was paid $2.00 for each correct response and was charged $1.00 for each error. Calculate $β_{opt}$ when $p(S)$ is .30 and when $p(S)$ is .70.

5.4. An observer performed a signal detection task in which she was paid $2.00 for each hit, and $1.00 for each correct reject. Each miss and each false alarm cost her $1.50 and 50 cents respectively. The value of $p(s)$ was .50. Calculate the value of $β_{opt}$.

6

Further Considerations of TSD

In Chapter 5, the basic characteristics of TSD were described. TSD was seen to be a powerful model for conceptualizing what observers do when they make decisions about the presence or absence of signals. According to the model, a sensory event arising from the presentation of a signal is fundamentally no different than one that arises from noise. There is no threshold to divide sensory events into those that are suprathreshold and those that are subthreshold, and there are no distinguishing characteristics that would enable the observers to identify the event as resulting from noise or, alternatively, from signal added to noise. Instead the observer experiences sensory events that vary in magnitude along a single continuum. The problem with which the observer is confronted is to decide whether a particular sensory event originated from the distribution of noise or from that of signal plus noise. According to the model, the problem is solved when the observer evaluates sensory events relative to the position of a decision criterion. The decision rule is that if the magnitude of the sensory event is greater than the value of the criterion, a signal is reported and if it is below this value it is not. The position of the criterion relative to the location of the noise and signal-plus-noise distributions is determined by practical considerations such as the probability of the signal being presented and the costs and values of the decision outcomes. The position of the criterion, as well as the detectability of the signal, specified as the d' distance between the means of the noise and signal-plus-noise distributions, can be inferred from experimental data by determining the observer's hit rate and false alarm rate in the detection situation. One of the greatest strengths of this approach in psychophysics is that it provides the investigator with separate and independent measures of the location of the criterion and signal detectability. In classical psychophysics, this was not possible, but instead thresholds, as detectability measures, were often contaminated by response bias resulting from the unaccounted for location of the criterion. Thus, TSD represents a substantial improvement in psychophysical methodology.

In this chapter we consider how the assumptions of TSD are tested and how the results of these tests affect the measurement of signal detectability.

TESTING THE ASSUMPTIONS OF THE THEORY OF SIGNAL DETECTION

The form of the ROC curve predicted from TSD can be more easily subjected to experimental tests if the hit rates and false alarm rates obtained in an experiment are plotted on the ROC curve as z scores. In such a graph, Z_{SN} is plotted as a function of Z_N. If the N and SN distributions are normal in form and also have equal variances, the ROC curves should be linear with a slope of 1.0 when z scores for 1.0 – p(hit) are plotted against z scores for 1.0 – p(false alarms). It is conventional to plot the negative Z_{SN} values above and the positive Z_{SN} values below the zero point on the ordinate, and to plot the negative Z_N values to the right of and the positive Z_N values to the left of the zero point on the abscissa.[1] Figure 6.1 illustrates that when the N and SN distributions have the form of the normal curve and have equal variances, shifting the criterion by a particular z-score distance on the N distribution results in exactly the same shift of the criterion in z-score units on the SN distribution.

The linearity prediction follows from the assumption that the N and SN distributions are normal in form. The slope of 1.0 indicates that the variances of the N and SN distributions are equal. The prediction from TSD is that ROC curves plotted as z scores should be linear with a slope of 1.0, as in Figure 6.1. It is not difficult to determine whether or not experimental results confirm the theory. The standard procedure is to determine the best-fitting straight line for the data plotted as z scores. If the data points do not significantly deviate from the function, the assumption of normal distribution is supported. If the slope of the function does not significantly deviate from 1.0, the equal variance assumption is supported.

---

[1]When Z (hit) and Z (false alarm) are plotted rather than Z_{SN} and Z_N, the positive Z (hit) values are plotted above and the negative Z (hit) values below the zero point on the ordinate, and the positive Z (false alarm) values are plotted to the right and the negative Z (false alarm) values to the left of the zero point on the abscissa.

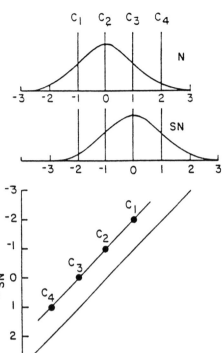

FIG. 6.1. Distributions of noise and signal plus noise expressed in z scores. The values of Z_N for the four criteria are determined by converting $(1.0 -$ false alarm rate) into z scores. The values of Z_{SN} for the four criteria are determined by converting $(1.0 -$ hit rate) into z scores. When Z_{SN} is plotted as a function of Z_N, a linear ROC curve with a slope of 1.0 indicates that the noise and signal-plus-noise distributions are normal in form and have equal standard deviations.

Empirically obtained ROC curves plotted as Z_{SN} and Z_N scores are almost always linear, and consequently, the hypothesis that the N and SN distributions are normal distributions has attained general acceptance. This kind of analysis of detection data, however, has also revealed that the assumption that the N and SN distributions have equal variances is often not true. The slope of the ROC curve is frequently found to be less than 1.0. This result is usually explained by assuming that the variance is greater for the SN than for the N distribution. A more general statement of this assumption is that the variance of the SN distribution increases as the mean of the distribution increases.

Figure 6.2 shows an ROC curve for an observer in an experiment on the detection of auditory signals (Tanner et al., 1956). Because the ROC curve was asymmetrical, the assumption was made that the standard deviation of the SN distribution (σ_{SN}) was greater than the standard deviation of the N distribution (σ_N). The deviation of the results of this experiment from the equal variance of N and SN distributions can be seen more clearly when the data are plotted as Z_{SN} and Z_N (Figure 6.3). If it is assumed that both N and SN distributions are of normal form,

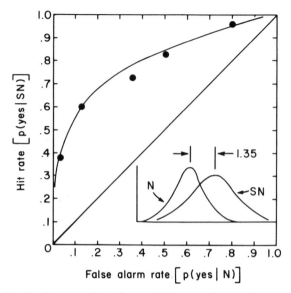

FIG. 6.2. Receiver-operating characteristic curve for an observer in an experiment on the detection of auditory signals. The asymmetrical ROC curve is consistent with the hypothesis that the noise and signal-plus-noise distributions are normal in form but have unequal variances. (From Tanner, Swets, & Green, 1956).

then the reciprocal of the slope of the ROC curve is equal to σ_{SN}/σ_N. The slope of the ROC curve for observer 1 is 1.0, and therefore the N and SN distributions have the same variance since $\sigma_{SN}/\sigma_N = 1.0$. The slope of the ROC curve for observer 2 is .75, and σ_{SN} is greater than σ_N since the reciprocal of .75, the value of σ_{SN}/σ_N, is 1.33.

Figure 6.4 illustrates the basis of Equation (6.1).

$$\frac{\sigma_{SN}}{\sigma_N} = \frac{1.0}{\text{slope of } z \text{ score ROC curve}} \tag{6.1}$$

In the problem illustrated in Figure 6.4, the standard deviation of the SN distribution is twice as large as the standard deviation of the N distribution. For example, when the criterion is changed from C_1 to C_2, its location on the N distribution is changed by 1.0 z-score unit, from $Z_N = 2.0$ to $Z_N = 1.0$, but its location on the SN distribution changes by only .5 z-score units, from $Z_{SN} = .5$ to $Z_{SN} = 0.0$. Examination of the ROC curve and the N and SN distributions in Figure 6.4 indicates that for every 1.0 unit change in the value of Z_N there is a .5 change in Z_{SN}. In other words, the slope of the ROC curve is .5. Thus, the value of $\sigma_{SN}/\sigma_N = 1/.5 = 2.0$.

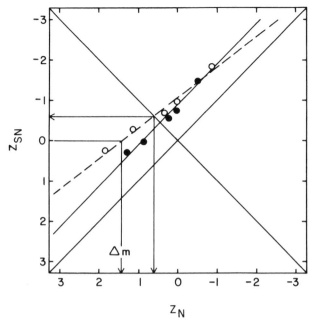

FIG. 6.3. Receiver-operating characteristic curves plotted in Z_N and Z_{SN} units from an experiment on the detection of auditory signals. The open points are for the observer whose data are plotted in Figure 6.2. The filled points are for another observer. (From Tanner, Swets, & Green, 1956.)

In cases when the variance of the SN distribution is greater than that of the N distribution, the symbol Δm, rather than d', is sometimes used to denote the difference between the means of normal N and normal SN distributions. Thus, the quantities d' and Δm are symbols for the same measures of signal detectability applied to the cases of equal and unequal variances, respectively.

Note in Figure 6.3, however, that for observer 2 the value of d', conventionally determined as the value of the difference between Z_{SN} and Z_N, is not constant along the ROC curve. In cases where the ROC curve slope is less than 1.0, Δm may be used as the measure of detectability. The value of Δm is equal to the absolute difference between Z_{SN} and Z_N at a point where Z_{SN} is equal to 0. Since we start with the mean of the SN distribution [$Z_{SN} = 0$ and $p(yes \mid SN) = .5$] and determine the corresponding Z_N value, the value of Δm is expressed in the standard deviation units of the N distribution (σ_N). In the Tanner et al. (1956) experiment, Δm for observer 2 was 1.35. Notice that for observer 1 the value of d' is .85 at all points on the ROC curve.

A measure of signal detectability that is sometimes used instead of Δm is d_e'. The value of d_e' is the absolute difference between Z_N and Z_{SN} at a

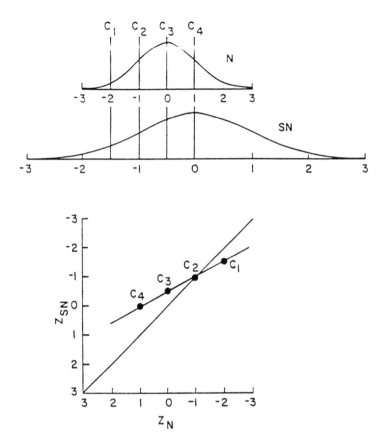

FIG. 6.4. Distributions of noise and signal plus noise expressed in z scores. In this example, the standard deviations of the signal-plus-noise distribution is twice as large as the standard deviation of the noise distribution. When Z_{SN} is plotted as a function of Z_N, the function is linear, indicating that the two distributions are normal in form. The fact that the slope of the ROC curve is less than 1.0 indicates that the standard deviation of the signal-plus-noise distribution is greater than the standard deviation of the noise distribution. The fact that the slope is .5 indicates that the standard deviation of the signal-plus-noise distribution is exactly twice as large as the standard deviation of the noise distribution.

point on the ROC curve where it crosses the diagonal with negative slope. The negative diagonal is drawn as a line of –1.0 slope that passes through the origin of the graph (point where Z_N and Z_{SN} are both zero). The primary benefit of using this measure is that it gives equal weight to σ_N and σ_{SN}. In the present example, the value of d_e' for observer 2 is 1.23.

A third measure of signal detectability used when the variances of the N and SN distributions are unequal is d_a. As with d_e', the measure d_a

specifies signal detectability in terms of units that represent the average of the standard deviations of the N and SN distributions. In both cases, signal detectability is the number of standard deviation units separating the means of the N and SN distributions when the standard deviation is the average of those of these two distributions. These measures contrast with d' and Δm that, in both cases, specify signal detectability in terms of the distance between the means of the N and SN distributions expressed as the number of standard deviation units of the N distribution. The difference between d'_e and d_a is in the way in which the size of the standard deviations of the N and SN distributions are averaged. In the case of d'_e, the detectability of the signal is expressed in terms of the arithmetic average of the standard deviations of the two distributions. On the other hand, d_a expresses signal detectability in terms of the root-mean-square (rms) average of the standard deviation of the N and SN distributions. The root-mean-square standard deviation is equal to the square root of the mean of the squared standard deviations of N and SN. To calculate d_a, the slope and intercept of the ROC curve must be determined. This information is provided by determining the best fitting straight line of the ROC curve plotted on Z_N and Z_{SN} coordinates. The slope (s) of the ROC curve tells us that the standard deviation of the N distribution is S times as large as that of the SN distribution. Thus, we can set the standard deviation of the N distribution to s and that of the SN distribution to 1.0. The standard deviation used for calculation of d_a is $\sqrt{0.5(1 + s^2)}$, the rms average of the standard deviations of the N and SN distributions. The slope of the ROC curve of observer 2 was .75 and therefore in this example the standard deviation used to determine d_a is $\sqrt{0.5(1 + s^2)} = \sqrt{0.5(1 + .75^2)} =$ .88. The value of d_a is found by dividing the absolute value of the intercept (b) of the z-score ROC curve by the value of the rms average standard deviation:

$$d_a = b/ \sqrt{0.5(1 + s^2)} \qquad (6.2)$$

In the case of observer 2 the absolute intercept value is 1.0 (intercept = −1.0) and thus

$$d_a = {}^{1.0}\!/_{.88} = 1.14 \ .$$

The final measure of signal detectability to be described is $p(A)$, the proportion of the area of the entire graph that lies beneath the ROC curve. Illustrated in Figure 6.5 is a case in which the value of $p(A)$ is .75. It can also be seen from Figure 6.5 that $p(A)$ can vary from 0.50 to 1.0. When the observer's performance is at the level of chance, $p(A)$ will be 0.5 because the hit rate will be the same as the false alarm rate at all locations along the

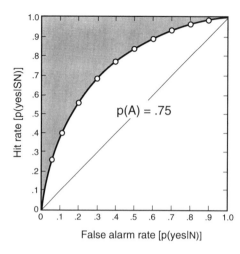

FIG. 6.5. Illustration of $p(A)$ as a measure of sensitivity. In this example $p(A)$ is .75. The positive diagonal represents chance level performance where the value of $p(A)$ would be .5.

positive diagonal, and the proportion of the area below the diagonal will be 0.5. On the other hand, when the observer's performance is perfect, and $p(A)$ is 1.0, the ROC curve is a function with the hit rate being 1.0 for all values of the false alarm rate. It should be clear that when $p(A)$ is 1.0 the entire graph lies beneath the ROC curve. Intermediate values of $p(A)$ between .5 and 1.0 represent performance that is better than chance but less than perfect. There are two features of $p(A)$ that make it a highly useful measure of signal detectability. First, $p(A)$ is defined without regard to underlying distributions. For example, to correctly interpret the value of $p(A)$, no assumption has to be made that the N and SN distributions are normal and have equal variances as is the case with d'. The calculation of $p(A)$ eliminates the necessity of curve- fitting required for the other measures just described. Instead, one simply connects the ROC points by straight lines and measures the area under the ROC by counting blocks on the graph paper. A more accurate procedure, however, is to fit a straight line to the z-score ROC curve and determine A_z, the area under the ROC curve fitted to the data points. The frequent use of this procedure is justified by the fact that z-score ROC curves are fitted well by straight lines (Swets, 1988). Both $p(A)$ and A_z represent the area under the ROC curve where the proportion of hits is plotted as a function of the proportion of false alarms. Determining A_z requires the calculation of $z(A) = s(\Delta m)/\sqrt{1 + s^2}$, where s is the slope of the z-score ROC curve and Δm is just defined. The value of $z(A)$ is expressed in z-score units and can be converted to A_z, the proportion of the area under the ROC curve, by converting this z score to a proportion through Table A. In the example of observer 2, $z(A) = .75(1.35)/\sqrt{1 + .75^2} = .81$. By converting this z-score value to a proportion, through the use of Table A, we find that the value of A_z is .79.

The second noteworthy positive feature of the area under the ROC curve as a measure of sensitivity is that it is equivalent to p(c), the proportion correct in a two-alternative forced-choice task (described in chap. 5) in which the observer is required to report in which of two observation intervals the signal was presented.

A summary of the sensitivity measures computed for observer 2 is seen in Figure 6.6. It can be seen that Δm, d'_e, and d_a represent the difference between the means of the N and SN distributions expressed in different units. In Δm, the unit is the standard deviation of the N distribution. In d'_e, the unit is the arithmetic average of the N and SN standard deviations, and in d_a it is the root mean square average of the N and SN standard deviations. On the other hand, A_z, rather than expressing sensitivity in terms of the difference between the means of the N and SN distributions, expresses it as the proportion of the area under the ROC curve.

With the exception of d', the ROC curve must be determined to calculate a measure of signal detectability. This requirement for calculating Δm, d'_e, d_a, and A_z would be very time-consuming if an entire experiment on the effects of signal probability or payoff had to be conducted in order to obtain data points for the ROC curve. Fortunately, the confidence rating procedure discussed in the next chapter provides an exceptionally eco-

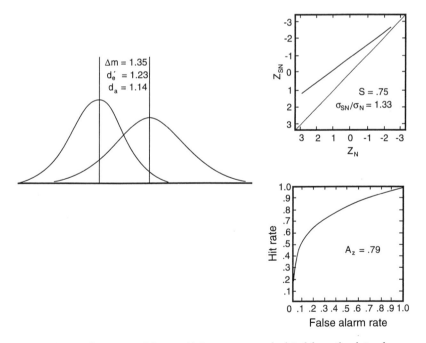

FIG. 6.6. Summary of the sensitivity measures calculated from the data of observer 2 of Tanner, Swets, and Green (1956).

nomical method for obtaining the data needed to determine the ROC curve. The use of a computer program (see Swets & Pickett, 1982) greatly facilitates the determination of the best fitting ROC curve and the area below it (A_z). The program also gives estimates of Δm, d_e', and d_a.

One virtue of TSD made apparent by the previous discussion of the ROC curve is that the theory is experimentally testable. Precise, quantitative predictions of what should happen in the detection situation under a variety of conditions can be made from the theory. Experimental results that do not correspond to predicted results have served as a basis for modifying the quantitative statements of the theory. Furthermore, the range of predictions from TSD is comprehensive and extends far beyond the limited confines of earlier psychophysical theories which dealt exclusively with sensory processes. Experimental data continue to accumulate rapidly in support of TSD. The use of detectability measures such as d', Δm, d_e', d_a, and $p(A)$, and of criterion measures such as β, C, and C' to separate the observer's sensitivity from the location of his decision criterion therefore becomes increasingly justifiable.

LOW THRESHOLD THEORY

We have seen that high threshold theory predicts ROC curves which are not consistent with experimental data. The theory of signal detection, an alternative theory consistent with empirically determined ROC curves, was then discussed. In TSD, the concept of sensory threshold, so central to classical psychophysics, is rejected in favor of an adjustable decision criterion. In fairness to threshold theory, however, it should be pointed out that one version of the threshold concept predicts ROC curves that fit the data nearly as well as the predictions from TSD. In this threshold theory, the threshold is assumed to be much lower, located slightly above the mean of the N distribution, than that of classical threshold theory. The theory was originally described by Swets et al. (1955, 1961). In *low threshold theory*, some of the false alarms on catch trials are due to an observation being above threshold, while others are due to guessing when the observation is below threshold. It should be recalled that all false alarms on catch trials were attributed to guessing in classical theory. The shape of the ROC curve predicted from low threshold theory is seen in Figure 6.7. The curved shape of the ROC curve up to $p(\text{yes} \mid N)$ of about .50 is assumed to be due, as it would be in TSD, to a progressive lowering of the observer's decision criterion and would result in an increase in the proportion of hits and false alarms. Beyond this point, the function is linear because the criterion is lower than the threshold, which at this point would begin to determine the observer's decisions. For observations below threshold, response bias changes the guessing rate and, therefore,

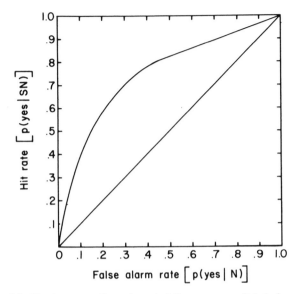

FIG. 6.7. Receiver-operating characteristic curve predicted from low threshold theory.

this upper branch of the ROC curve must be linear. Thus, the linear segment of the curve and the linear curve of classical threshold theory are both attributed to changes in the guessing rate.

Luce (1963) proposed another version of low threshold theory. In Luce's theory, the threshold is assumed to exist somewhere between the middle and the upper end of the noise distribution. During a sensory observation, an observer is in the *detect state* if the observation exceeds threshold and in the *nondetect state* if the observation is below threshold. As in other threshold theories, observations below threshold are assumed to be indiscriminable. But in this theory, observations above threshold are also assumed to be indiscriminable from one another. Thus, for the purpose of detecting signals, observers can discriminate between two kinds of sensory events—those that put them into the detect state and those that put them into the nondetect state. The response one makes in either state may be biased by nonsensory factors. One may say yes when in the nondetect state or say no when in the detect state. Manipulating variables such as payoff and signal probability changes the observers' response bias when they are in either one of the two possible detection states. The ROC curve predicted from Luce's theory is two straight lines (Figure 6.8) for several different signal strengths. This ROC curve is sometimes found to fit detection data as well as the ROC curves predicted from signal detection theory.

Krantz (1969) has reviewed the problem of obtaining experimental data that provide an adequate test of low threshold theory. Although low

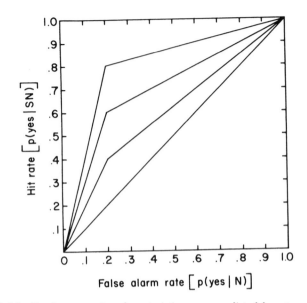

FIG. 6.8. Receiver-operating characteristic curves predicted from two-state
theory.

threshold theory is consistent with some available experimental data, the
threshold that is postulated cannot be measured by classical psychophysical methods. Furthermore, without a threshold concept, signal detection
theory has accounted for a great deal of the psychophysical data on
detection behavior. These data provide compelling evidence that if thresholds do exist, they are almost always lower than the observer's decision
criterion and, consequently, seldom influence detection behavior.

It is important to realize that the threshold concept, at least as it is
used in threshold theory, represents a barrier separating sensory states
inside the observer. These *observer thresholds*, which are inferred from the
analysis of detection judgments, primarily through examination of the
forms of ROC curves, are not to be confused with psychophysical *energy
thresholds* measured by various psychophysical methods. Krantz (1969)
made a sharp distinction between observer thresholds and energy thresholds. He stated that it is possible that both observer and energy thresholds
exist, that neither type of threshold exists, or that only one of the two
types of threshold exists. We have seen that the evidence for observer
thresholds is equivocal. What can be said about energy thresholds?

The best evidence for energy thresholds comes from studies which
illustrate that an observer's performance is the same when a weak stimulus
is presented as when no stimulus is presented, unless the weak stimulus is
above some critical value. Data from an experiment by Gescheider et al.
(1971) illustrate an energy threshold for the detection of a 60-Hz vibration

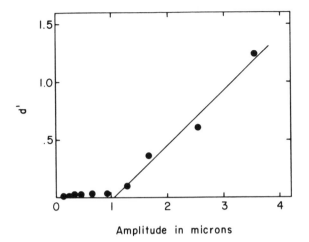

FIG. 6.9.   The relation between d' and signal amplitude for detecting 60-Hz vibration on the fingertip. The data indicate an energy threshold corresponding to a signal amplitude of 1.0-µm peak-to-peak displacement of the stimulator. (From Gescheider, Wright, Weber, & Barton, 1971.)

on the fingertip. Data plotted in Figure 6.9 illustrate that d' was near 0 for all stimulus strengths less than 1-µm peak-to-peak displacement of the vibrator contactor. These data, though indicative of an energy threshold, are not inconsistent with TSD. They do not necessarily imply the existence of an observer threshold. Unlike the observer threshold concept, the energy threshold is not tied to the assumption that there is a boundary on the continuum of sensory magnitude below which events cannot be discriminated and above which events can be discriminated. In the context of TSD, an energy threshold simply implies that as stimulus intensity is increased above zero, a critical intensity value must be exceeded before the mean of the SN distribution becomes greater than the mean of the N distribution. The use of d', or some other TSD measure of signal detectability, as a performance measure for determining energy thresholds is an advisable procedure. Under such conditions, the value of the threshold will not be contaminated by variations in the observer's judgment criterion. The threshold is defined as the point on the stimulus scale where the observer's d' first becomes greater than zero.

Vendrik and Eijkman (1968) found that the probability of detecting mechanical and electrical stimuli on the skin does not change until a certain stimulus strength is exceeded. The perception of warmth and cold, on the other hand, showed a linear increasing function throughout the entire range of stimulus intensities. Vendrik and Eijkman concluded that the temperature sensory system does not have a measurable threshold, while both the tactile system and the system stimulated by electrical current do have energy thresholds.

The hypothesis that the sense of touch has an energy threshold has gained strong support from studies in which it has been possible to record neural activity from cutaneous nerve fibers of humans. By inserting a microelectrode through the skin and into a nerve fiber innervating the hand, Vallbo and Johansson (1976) were able to record action potentials from single nerve fibers while applying various tactile stimuli to the observer's hand. Nerve fibers responsive to changes in mechanical stimulation were found never to be spontaneously active in the absence of stimulation, but rather to become active only when the stimulus was above some intensity level. Thus, with regard to their capacity to generate action potentials, single cutaneous mechanoreceptors have thresholds. Furthermore, Vallbo and Johansson found that these neural thresholds determined the observer's psychophysical threshold. Specifically, on all occasions in which the stimulus was strong enough to produce a single action potential on the nerve fiber, the observer reported feeling the stimulus, while on all occasions in which the stimulus was too weak to produce an action potential, the observer reported feeling nothing. This finding that human observers can reliably detect a single nerve impulse in a single cutaneous nerve fiber, in addition to demonstrating the remarkable sensitivity of the tactile system, provides strong support for a psychophysical threshold hypothesis. The observer's response did not depend on the location of a decision criterion, but instead it depended entirely on whether or not the stimulus was strong enough to produce a single action potential.

Additional support for the threshold hypothesis comes from the psychophysical experiments of Hamer (1979) in which observers detected vibrotactile stimuli in the presence and in the absence of background stimuli. Thresholds for detecting a 300-msec vibration on the thenar eminence of the hand were measured. On some trials, the test stimulus was presented alone; on other trials, it was presented in the middle of a 700-msec background stimulus. The intensity of the background was systematically varied from well below to well above the observer's threshold. The effect of the background stimulus was specified as the difference between the test stimulus thresholds measured in the presence and in the absence of the background. As seen in Figure 6.10, the effect of background stimulation depended upon its intensity. When the background stimulus was more than 10 dB above threshold, it had the effect of elevating the threshold of the test stimulus. This threshold elevation was proportional to the intensity of the background stimulus. The surprising finding of this study was that when the intensity of the background stimulus was below threshold, it had the effect of lowering, rather than elevating, the threshold for detecting the test stimulus. To account for this apparent enhancement in sensitivity, Hamer hypothesized that, for the test stimulus to be detected, its intensity must exceed a threshold in the receptor for generating action potentials. Under these conditions, the background stimulus, if its intensity is below

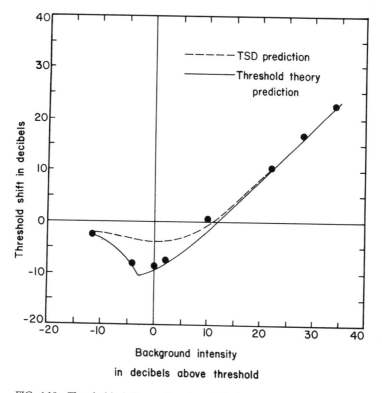

FIG. 6.10. Threshold shift as a function of background intensity. (From Hamer, 1979.)

threshold, could act as a stimulus pedestal by decreasing the intensity of the test stimulus needed to exceed the receptor's threshold. For example, if the background stimulus is only slightly below threshold, adding a very weak test stimulus may be sufficient to exceed threshold. A very weak background, on the other hand, would be of little benefit, and to be detected, the added test stimulus would have to be nearly as intense as when presented alone. It can be seen in Figure 6.10 that the experimental results are in close agreement with predictions from the threshold theory, but differ substantially from the predictions of TSD.

STATUS OF THE THRESHOLD CONCEPT

A few definite statements can be made about the present status of the threshold concept. It can be said with confidence that if there is an observer threshold, it is not the high threshold of classical theory but a much lower threshold located somewhere near the mean of the noise distribution. Since the observer's criterion would usually be higher than this threshold, their judgments of signals would be based on whether a sensory observation is above or below criterion rather than above or below threshold. The results of hundreds of experiments have indicated that TSD is basically correct as a model of detection behavior. Further experimentation is needed, however, to determine whether TSD and low threshold theory will have to be combined to account for all the data of detection experiments. Regardless of the outcome of this particular research problem, it can be said that the usefulness of the *empirical threshold* concept is not in question.

The fundamental nature of the threshold concept becomes apparent when we distinguish among three types of thresholds—observer thresholds, energy thresholds, and empirical thresholds. As we have already seen in our discussion of observer thresholds and energy thresholds, observer thresholds occur only when it is possible to demonstrate that the observer's nervous system is capable of being in two different states—the subthreshold state (nondetect state), or the suprathreshold (detect state), whereas energy thresholds occur only when it can be demonstrated that the observer's performance is the same in the presence of as in the absence of a weak signal. When neither an observer threshold nor an energy threshold can be demonstrated, an empirical threshold, nevertheless, may be defined as the intensity of the signal needed to produce some specified level of performance by the observer. Because this type of threshold represents the signal intensity required for the observer to achieve a designated performance level above chance but below perfection, such as correctly responding 75% of the time in a two-alternative forced choice situation, empirical thresholds are sometimes called *statistical thresholds*. The three threshold concepts, observer, energy, and empirical, are illustrated in Figure 6.11. In both a and b, the solid line indicates no energy threshold. When the signal is presented, no matter how weak, performance increases above the level observed in the absence of the signal (when its intensity is zero). In both a and b, the dashed line indicates an energy threshold because the intensity of the signal must be at the same threshold level for performance to be above that seen when no signal is presented. In a, there is an observer threshold, and the probability of the observer being in the above threshold state (i.e., the detect state) is plotted as a function of signal intensity. In b, there is no observer threshold and therefore a measure of signal detectability, in this case d', is plotted. In each of these four possible conditions, observer threshold without energy threshold, observer threshold with energy threshold, energy threshold without observer threshold, and no energy or observer threshold, an empirical threshold can be established as the signal intensity needed to achieve some arbitrarily designated level of the observer's performance. Thus, the empirical threshold becomes a highly useful measure of sensitivity whether or not observer and energy thresh-

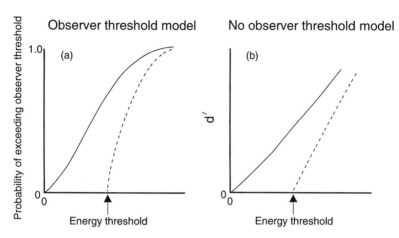

FIG. 6.11. Illustration of situations in which there is an observer threshold (a) and there is no observer threshold (b). The dashed lines in both a and b indicate the existence of energy thresholds, whereas the solid line indicates their absence.

olds exist. In fact, our present understanding of sensory systems would not be possible if it were not for the thousands of experimental studies on empirical thresholds conducted since Fechner outlined his psychophysical methods in 1860. The chief limitation of the early measurements of empirical thresholds as measures of sensitivity is that they may have been affected by the observer's decision criterion. In more recent times, through the use of TSD methodology, empirical thresholds have become free from the effects of the observer's criterion and thus have provided highly useful unbiased measures of sensitivity.

PROBLEMS

6.1. An observer was induced to set his criterion at six different levels during six different experimental sessions. Plot an ROC curve on Z_N and Z_{SN} coordinates. Draw the best-fitting straight line by eye. Calculate the values of Δm, d_e', d_a, and A_z.

Criterion Level	Hit Rate	False Alarm Rate
1	.99	.94
2	.96	.84
3	.94	.58
4	.84	.27
5	.58	.12
6	.42	.02

7

Procedures of TSD

The procedures of TSD are designed to provide the psychophysicist with data in the form of response proportions that can be readily converted into the theoretical constructs of sensitivity, criterion, distribution variance, and distribution shape. TSD can be tested by comparing the values of the constructs predicted from the theory with those that are derived from response proportion data. In those circumstances where the data support the applicability of TSD, the theory can be used to solve many empirical problems. The situation in which a variable is found to have a large effect on response proportion is illustrative. By converting response proportion data into theoretical terms such as d', A_z, C, and β, an investigator can determine whether the effect was due to changes in the observer's sensitivity, criterion, or both sensitivity and criterion. Today, there are several basic procedures of TSD used to solve such problems in psychophysics.

SOME BASIC PSYCHOPHYSICAL PROCEDURES OF TSD

The Yes–No Procedure

With the *yes–no procedure* observers are given a long series of trials, usually more than 300 in a session, in which they must judge the presence or absence of a signal. Some proportion of the trials is SN, and the remaining proportion is N. At the start of the session, the observer is usually told what the proportion of SN trials will be, and what the costs and values associated with the various decision outcomes will be. In many experiments, an observation interval is designated on each trial by the presentation of a light, a sound, or some other cue during which SN or N alone is presented in the sensory modality under consideration. In a study on auditory detection, for example, a light of one-second duration might be presented every five seconds. The observer must judge as quickly as possible whether or not a tone was presented during the period of time when the light was on.

An ROC curve for a single signal strength can be plotted if the proportions of hits and false alarms are obtained for several criterion locations. Generally, payoff contingencies and signal probability are kept constant for an experimental session, so that the observer's criterion will remain stable for the session. Data for different criterion levels are often obtained by changing signal probability or payoff contingencies for different sessions. The ROC curve in Figure 7.1 was obtained by Tanner et al. (1956) in an experiment on the detection of tones against a background of white noise. Signal probability was either .10, .30, .50, .70, or .90. Each data point on the ROC curve was obtained by using one of these values for a block of 600 trials. As expected, the data points ordered themselves

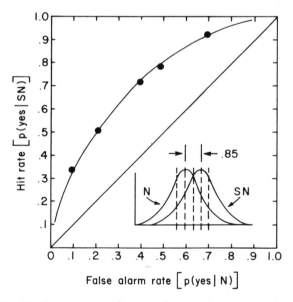

FIG. 7.1. Receiver-operating characteristic curve from an experiment on the detection of auditory signals. Data points were obtained by varying the probability of signal occurrence. The theoretical noise and signal-plus-noise distributions with five criterion locations are shown in the insert. (From Tanner, Swets, & Green, 1956.)

on the ROC curve according to signal probability. The ROC curve fitted to the data is the theoretical curve for normal N and SN distributions of equal variance. The theoretical N and SN distributions are shown as an insert in the figure. The value of d' was .85, and dashed lines in the insert indicate the location of the five criteria that the observer employed for the five signal probabilities.

In the second part of the experiment, the same observer was again induced by variation of payoff conditions to vary his criterion for detecting the same stimulus. Signal probability was .50, and the payoff varied from being relatively high for correct responses on N trials to being relatively high for correct responses on SN trials. The data points on the ROC curve (Figure 7.2) ordered themselves as expected. When the payoff for being correct on N trials was relatively high, the values of $p(\text{yes} \mid N)$ and $p(\text{yes} \mid SN)$ were low, and when the payoff for being correct on SN trials was relatively high, $p(\text{yes} \mid N)$ and $p(\text{yes} \mid SN)$ were high. It is significant that the same ROC curve fits the data from both parts of the experiment. Because the physical stimulus was the same in both parts of the experiment, the shape and locations of the N and SN distributions did not

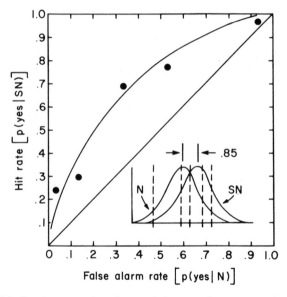

FIG. 7.2. Receiver-operating characteristic curve from an experiment on the detection of auditory signals. Data points were obtained by varying payoff conditions. The theoretical noise and signal-plus-noise distributions with five criterion locations are shown in the insert. (From Green & Swets, 1966. Reprinted from D. M. Green and J. A. Swets, *Signal Detection Theory and Psychophysics*. Copyright © 1966 by John Wiley & Sons, Inc.)

change. Thus, in spite of the fact that large variations in the observer's criterion were produced by two distinct procedures, measurements of sensitivity remained stable under all conditions.

When a single session has been conducted, and the proportions of hits and false alarms are available for only a single criterion location, the value of d' and β can be estimated from the data, though an ROC curve cannot be plotted. The difference between Z_N and Z_{SN} will yield an estimate of d'. The value of β can be obtained by dividing the ordinate value on the normal curve corresponding to Z_{SN} by the ordinate value corresponding to Z_N. If the proportion of hits is .84 and the proportion of false alarms .50, the value of d' would be 1.0, and the value of β would be .243/.399 = .61.

The procedure outlined above was used in an experiment to determine the effects of an auditory stimulus on the detection of a tactile signal applied to the fingertip (Gescheider, Barton, Bruce, Goldberg, & Greenspan, 1969). An attempt was made to measure both the detectability of a tactile stimulus and the location of the observer's criterion when the auditory stimulus was set at various intensity levels. The observer was required to decide whether or not a stimulus had been presented in an observation interval. Over a series of such trials, a random half of the observation intervals contained a tactile signal, while the other half contained no signal. Both the value of d' and the value of β were estimated from the proportions of yes responses made on the signal and on the nonsignal trials. At two different tactile signal intensities, d' was found to decrease slightly when β increased as a function of the auditory stimulus intensity (Figure 7.3). Thus, the disruptive effect of intense auditory stimulation on tactile signal detection performance is primarily due to the observer setting a relatively high criterion.

When ROC curves are not available to check the validity of the normal distribution and equal variance assumptions, measures of sensitivity not requiring these assumptions are often used. One such nonparametric measure of sensitivity, termed A', has been proposed by Pollack and Norman (1964). The formula for calculating A' is

$$A' = \frac{1}{2} + \frac{[p(\text{hits}) - p(\text{false alarms})]\,[1 + p(\text{hits}) - p(\text{false alarms})]}{[4p(\text{hits})]\,[1 - p(\text{false alarms})]}. \quad (7.1)$$

In the example above where $p(\text{hits})$ was .84 and $p(\text{false alarms})$ was .50 the formula would yield:

$$A' = \frac{1}{2} + \frac{(.84 - .50)\,(1 + .84 - .50)}{(4 \times .84)\,(1 - .50)} = .77.$$

The Forced Choice Procedure

An excellent technique for obtaining a measure of the observer's sensitivity which is uncontaminated by fluctuations in criterion is the *forced-choice procedure*. On a particular trial, two or more observation intervals are presented, and it is the observer's task to report which observation interval contained a signal. The assumption is made that, in the absence of response bias toward one or more of the observation intervals, the observer chooses the observation interval containing the largest sensory observation. Since the observer's criterion is not a factor in such a judgment, the proportion of correct responses, $p(c)$, can be used as a measure of sensitivity. The value of $p(c)$ will be underestimated when response bias toward one of the observation intervals exists. Procedures for correcting the $p(c)$ obtained when response bias exists are found in Green and Swets (1966).

Experimentally determined $p(c)$ values can be converted to the d' measure of sensitivity. The calculations have been provided by Hacker and Ratcliff (1979) and are found in Table B of the Appendix for various numbers of alternatives in the forced-choice task. For each value of $p(c)$, there is a corresponding value of d' given for each number of alternative observation intervals (n). For example, when $p(c)$ is .75, in a two-alterna-

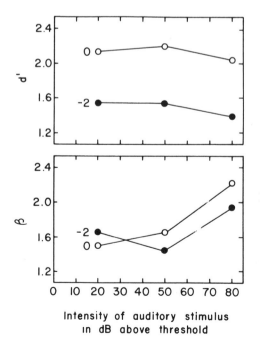

FIG. 7.3. The values of d' and β for the detection of a tactile signal change as a function of the intensity of a simultaneous auditory stimulus. The results are shown for two tactile signal intensities. (From Gescheider, Barton, Bruce, Goldberg, & Greenspan, 1969. Copyright 1969 by the American Psychological Association. Reprinted by permission.)

tive forced choice (2AFC) task in which the observer must choose which of two observation intervals contains the signal, the value of d' is .95. It can be seen that as the number of observation intervals increases, d' increases for a constant value of $p(c)$. For example, when $p(c)$ is .75 the values of d' for 2AFC, 4AFC, and 6 AFC tasks are .95, 1.68, and 1.97, respectively. This result can be understood by considering the fact that performance at the level of random chance, when the observer simply guessed on each trial, decreases as the number of observation intervals increases. As seen in Table B, chance performance, in which d' is equal to zero, for 2 AFC, 4AFC, and 10AFC tasks is .5, .25, and .1, respectively. Thus, a $p(c)$ value of .75 indicates a substantially higher level of signal detectability when there is a large number, rather than just two, alternatives. Converting $p(c)$ to d' has the advantage of providing the investigator with a sensitivity measure that can be compared across experiments in which the number of alternatives in forced-choice tasks was not the same. The results can also easily be compared with d' values obtained with other methods such as the yes–no and confidence rating procedures.

When comparisons of results obtained with forced-choice and yes–no methods are made, it is the forced-choice procedure that yields the better performance. At intensity levels of the signal where the yes–no procedure yields chance performance the observer's decisions in the forced-choice procedure are often somewhat above chance, indicating that, in the first case, the signal could not be discriminated from noise but in the second it could. Indeed, observers using the forced-choice method will often report that they could not detect the signal in any observation interval (a yes–no judgment) but, at the same time, will consistently perform above chance in selecting the interval containing the signal. The reason for the superior performance of the forced-choice procedure arises from the statistical properties of a situation in which the observer is presented with a random observation from the noise distribution and a random observation from the signal-plus-noise distribution on every trial. This is to be contrasted with the yes–no procedures in which a single observation randomly selected from either the noise distribution or the signal-plus-noise distribution is presented on each trial. The greater amount of information provided in the forced choice situation yields superior performance.

In some experiments, instead of determining how $p(c)$ changes as a function of changes in the stimulus, it is desirable to determine stimuli that produce a constant $p(c)$. For example, a two-interval forced choice procedure could be used to determine the intensity of light of various wavelengths that can be correctly detected 75% of the time.

Zwislocki, Maire, Feldman, and Rubin (1957) were the first to combine the forced-choice method with the Békésy threshold tracking method. As in the forced-choice method, *forced-choice tracking* requires the observer to

choose which observation interval contained the stimulus. In the Zwislocki et al. (1957) study, listeners had to choose which of two observation
intervals marked by flashes of light contained a tone presented to the
observer through earphones. After each error, the intensity of the tone
was increased by 2.0 dB; and after three correct responses (not necessarily
consecutive), the intensity was decreased by 2.0 dB. In this way, $p(c)$ was
held constant at .75. Other values of $p(c)$ could have been used by simply
changing the number of correct and/or incorrect responses required to
change the intensity of the stimulus. Each time the intensity of the tone
changed, the value was recorded on a graphic recorder. Thus, the intensity
of a tone that was correctly detected 75% of the time was tracked over
the duration of the experiment. Figure 7.4 shows a typical tracking record.
Sensitivity expressed in terms of attenuation of the tone corresponding
to a $p(c)$ rate of .75 was found to improve as the session progressed. The
results suggest that inexperienced observers require a considerable
amount of practice to learn to attend to weak tones that are barely
discriminable from internal noise generated within their own nervous
systems. Tracing rapid changes in the observer's sensitivity would probably be impossible with the relatively time-consuming yes–no procedure
in which an entire session might be required to obtain a single measure
of sensitivity derived from one ROC curve. It should be clear that the
strength of the forced-choice tracking method is its freedom from the
influences of the observer's criterion and its efficiency.

Forced-choice procedures are used to measure difference thresholds as
well as absolute thresholds. In a two-alternative forced-choice situation, a
standard stimulus could be randomly presented in one of the two observation intervals and a comparison stimulus presented in the other. The

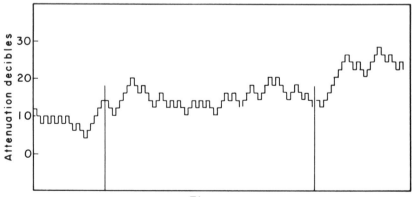

FIG. 7.4.   Forced-choice tracking record. (From Zwislocki, Maire, Feldman,
& Rubin, 1957.)

observer would then perform the task of choosing the observation interval containing the comparison stimulus. The difference threshold would be calculated as the measured difference between the standard stimulus and the comparison stimulus when the observer's performance had reached some specified level such as $p(c) = .75$. For example, the difference in the amplitude (ΔA) of two vibrotactile stimuli applied to the hand needed for discrimination at a $p(c)$ level of .75 was measured as a function of the age of the observers (Gescheider, Edwards, Lackner, Bolanowski, and Verrillo, 1996). In this study it was found that, although the absolute threshold of observers over the age of 65 years were much higher than those of college students, the relative intensity difference thresholds for the two groups, expressed as $\Delta A/A$, were the same. The results are plotted in Figure 7.5. The mean absolute thresholds of the young and old groups were .05 μm and .56 μm, respectively. Thus, absolute thresholds were more than 10 times higher in the elderly than in the young observers. The relative difference thresholds, however, are seen to be nearly the same for the two groups at all but the weakest intensity of the standard stimulus. Thus, in both groups the amplitude of vibration had to be increased by a proportion of approximately 0.2 to be noticed.

Confidence Rating Procedure

Often, it is desirable to obtain an ROC curve from data in a single session within which signal probability and payoff contingencies are fixed. The *confidence rating method* is very economical, since data for several points

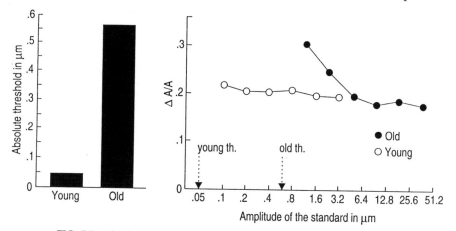

FIG. 7.5. Absolute and relative difference thresholds for young and old observers. The absolute thresholds of the two groups are indicated on the left graph and the values of $\Delta A/A$ on the right. The absolute thresholds of the two groups are also marked on the DL graph. (From Gescheider, Edwards, Lackner, Bolanowski, & Verrillo, 1996.)

on an ROC curve can be obtained for a single experimental condition by having the observer make a confidence rating for each yes–no judgment. For example, the observer might be instructed to say "five" if sure a signal was presented, "four" if fairly sure a signal was presented, "three" if not sure, "two" if fairly sure a signal was not presented, and "one" if sure a signal was not presented. It is assumed that to make the ratings, the observer sets up n minus 1 criteria along the sensory continuum to delineate rating categories (Figure 7.6). The number of criteria in Figure 7.6 is one less than the number of categories. In this particular example, "five" is given to observations that are equal to or greater than C_4, "four" to observations that are equal to or greater than C_3 but less than C_4, "three" to observations equal to or greater than C_2 but less than C_3, "two" to observations equal to or greater than C_1 but less than C_2, and "one" to observations that are less than C_1.

During the experiment, the proportion of responses for each of the rating categories for the SN trials and for the N trials are determined. Hypothetical data are shown in Table 7.1. The bottom part of the table lists the calculated hit and false alarm rates that would occur if the observer were induced to set a yes–no decision criterion at each of the four criterion points defined by the five rating categories. For the C_4 criterion, the estimated hit rate of .15 corresponds to the proportion of "five" responses given on SN trials, and the estimated false alarm rate of .03 corresponds to the proportion of "five" responses on N trials. For the C_3 criterion, the estimated hit rate of .55 is the proportion of "four" responses plus the proportion of "five" responses for the SN trials. This combination of proportions includes all of the SN observations above C_3. For the same reason, the estimated false alarm rate of .19 for C_3 is the proportion of "four" responses plus the proportion of "five" responses for the N trials. The estimated hit rate of .88 for C_2 is the summation of proportions of "five," "four," and "three" responses on SN trials, while the estimated false alarm rate of .57 for C_2 is the summation of proportions of "five," "four," and "three" responses on N trials. Finally, the estimated hit rate of .99 for C_1 is the summation of proportions of "five," "four," "three," and "two" responses for SN trials, and the estimated false alarm rate of .91 for C_1 is the summation of proportions of "five," "four," "three," and "two" responses for N trials. Each of the four pairs of hit and false alarm proportions that results from this procedure provides a point for the ROC curve in Figure 7.6.

Gescheider, Wright, and Polak (1971) used the confidence rating method for examining the effects of the observer's expectation of signal strength on detection behavior. The ROC curve in Figure 7.7 was obtained for the detection of a 2.8 –μm amplitude vibration on the fingertip. The open points were obtained when the observer was expecting weak signals,

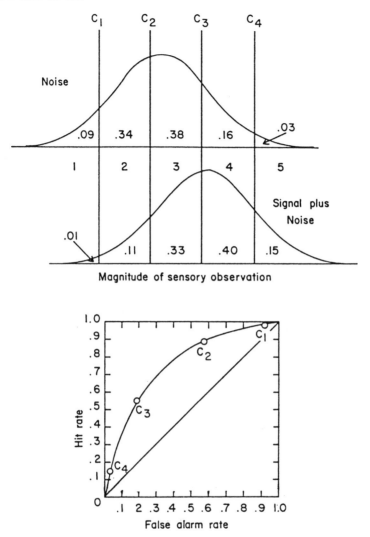

FIG. 7.6. A representation of how an observer might set up four criteria along the sensory magnitude dimension for the purpose of using the confidence rating method for detecting signals. The ROC curve is obtained experimentally from the observer's confidence ratings.

while the filled points were obtained when he was expecting strong signals. The results suggest that signal detectability was apparently not affected by changes in signal strength expectancy, since the data for both conditions could be fitted by a single ROC curve. However, it is also evident that when the observer was expecting weak signals, he set a lower criterion than when he was expecting strong ones.

TABLE 7.1
Determination of an ROC Curve by the Confidence Rating Procedure

	Confidence rating				
	1	2	3	4	5
SN	.01	.11	.33	.40	.15
N	.09	.34	.38	.16	.03
		C_1	C_2	C_3	C_4
SN		1.00	.99	.88	.55	.15
N		1.00	.91	.57	.19	.03

Because sufficient data can be quickly obtained for constructing an ROC curve by the confidence rating procedure, its use can provide a convenient means of testing the hypotheses of normality of N and SN distributions and equal variance of N and SN distributions. When Z_{SN} is plotted against Z_N, a linear ROC curve is consistent with the normality of distributions assumption, and a slope of 1.0 is consistent with the equal variance assumption. When the ROC curve is linear but the slope is not 1.0, the value of σ_{SN}/σ_N can be obtained by calculating the reciprocal of the slope of the function.

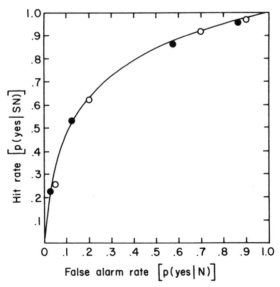

FIG. 7.7. Receiver-operating characteristic curves for the detection of 60-Hz vibration of the fingertip when observers were expecting weak signals (open points) and when they were expecting strong signals (filled points). (From Gescheider, Wright, & Polak, 1971.)

When the slope of the z-score ROC curve has a value of 1.0, any point on the curve provides the same estimate of signal detectability. In this case, obtaining confidence ratings is unnecessary because the entire ROC curve can be inferred from a single point obtained from the yes–no procedure. On the other hand, if before the experiment is conducted, the slope of the ROC curve is unknown, it is important that it be determined. The most efficient way to obtain this slope is to use the confidence rating method—a procedure that will yield measures of signal detectability, and response bias, as well as providing the investigator with the slope of the ROC curve. It has been estimated that the slopes of ROC curves, in a wide variety of tasks, vary from about 0.5 to 2.0 (Swets, 1986; Swets & Pickett, 1982). Because of this variability in slopes, Macmillan and Creel- man (1990) recommended that ROC curves should always be determined in a signal detection experiment. Confidence rating is the most efficient procedure for determining ROC curves and, thus, the procedure should be incorporated into any experiment in which the slope of the ROC curve is unknown and where measures of response bias and signal detectability are affected by this slope.

The validity of confidence rating data is supplied by the finding that the yes–no procedure and the rating procedure generally yield very simi- lar values of signal detectability (Green & Swets, 1966; Markowitz & Swets, 1967). The values of d' obtained from the yes–no procedure and the rating procedure in the study of vibrotactile sensitivity by Gescheider et al. (1971) were plotted against signal amplitude (Figure 7.8). The open and filled points represent d' values obtained from the yes–no procedure when the observer's criterion was low and high, respectively. The squares are d' values from the rating procedure. The correspondence of values obtained with the two methods is remarkable. An important aspect of this study was the finding of an energy threshold of approximately 1.0 μm. This threshold was independent of the method of measurement and was not contaminated by the effects of the observer's criterion as deter- mined by expectations of strong or weak signals. Thus, it appears that TSD methodology provides a powerful technique for determining energy thresholds which are valid measures of sensitivity.

The Same–Different Procedure

With the *same–different* procedure, each trial consists of the presentation of two stimuli that are either the same or different. The observer's task is to report whether the two stimuli were the same or different on each trial. If the observer is being tested for his ability to discriminate S_A from S_B there are four possible stimulus pairs that can be presented on a particular trial: $(S_A S_A)$, $(S_B S_B)$, $(S_A S_B)$ and $(S_B S_A)$. The correct response is "same" for the first

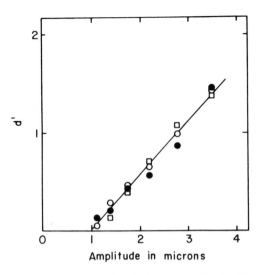

FIG. 7.8. The relation between d' and vibration amplitude. The open and filled points represent d' values obtained from the yes–no procedure when the observer's criterion was low and high, respectively. The squares are d' values from the rating procedure. (From Gescheider, Wright, & Polak, 1971.)

two stimulus pairs and "different" for the last two. The advantage of this method is that the observer does not have to be able to articulate or even be aware of the ways in which the stimuli actually differ. Instead, the observer needs only to report whether a pair of stimuli differ.

This becomes particularly important when the relevant stimulus cues are unknown, as in discriminating differences among complex speech sounds (e.g., Elliot, 1986) or when the experimenter may have difficulty describing the stimulus differences to the observer, as in wine tasting. The same–different procedure is very useful in such situations because the observer can use whatever cues are useful in discriminating between two stimuli. The objective is not to determine the specific cue or cues used by the observer but instead simply to determine the discriminability of the stimuli. If discriminability is zero, the proportion of trials on which the observer reports a difference will be the same on trials where the two stimuli are the same as on the trials where they are different. When the discriminability of the two stimuli is greater than zero, the proportion of "difference" responses is greater on trials where there is a stimulus difference than on trials where there is not.

Table 7.2 contains hypothetical results in which the same–different procedure is used to measure an observer's ability to discriminate between stimulus A and stimulus B. In this hypothetical example, the stimuli in the pair, S_A and S_B, were different on 100 trials and on 100 trials they were the same. On a random half of the trials where the stimuli were different

TABLE 7.2
Hypothetical Results for the Same–Different Procedure

| | Response | | Number |
Stimulus pair	"different"	"same"	of Trials
$(S_A S_B)$ or $(S_B S_A)$	75	25	100
$(S_A S_A)$ or $(S_B S_B)$	15	85	100

the order of presentation was S_A followed by S_B and on the other trials it was S_B followed by S_A. On the trials where the two stimuli were the same, a random half of the trials consisted of two presentations of S_A and on the other half of the trials S_B was presented twice. The hit rate is simply the proportion of "different" responses that occur when there is a stimulus difference. In our example, the hit rate is $^{75}/_{100} = .75$. The false alarm rate is the proportion of "different" responses when there is no stimulus difference, which in our example is equal to $^{15}/_{100} = .15$. The sensitivity measure, d', is often computed from the hit and false alarm rates. In the same–different procedure, the value of d' specifies the difference between the means of S_A and S_B distributions in z-score units of the normal distributions. These distributions are analogous to the N and SN distributions of the signal detection situation in that they are normal distributions of sensory observations but, in this case, both distributions are generated by two stimuli.

The determination of d' is complicated by the fact that its calculation is dependent on the decision rule one assumes the observer uses when making decisions about whether two stimuli use the same or different. More specifically, the calculation procedures associated with each assumed decision rule are different, yielding different values of d' from the same experimentally determined hit and false alarm rates. For example, if one assumes that the observer's decision rule is based on an independent-observation strategy (Noreen, 1981), in which the observer compares the independent experience produced by each stimulus with a criterion and calls two things different only if each falls on a different side of the criterion, the value of d', when the hit rate was .75 and the false alarm rate was .15, would be 2.45. On the other hand, for these same hit and false alarm rates, d' would be 2.99 if the decision rule is based on a differencing strategy (Sorkin, 1962), in which a difference is reported when the absolute difference between two sensory observations exceeds some criterion. Tables for converting hit and false alarm rates to d' for both the independent-observation strategy and the differencing strategy are available (Macmillan & Creelman, 1991).

Macmillan and Creelman (1991) suggested that it is appropriate to assume the independent-observation strategy when the observer is presented with only two stimuli to be discriminated, as in the example presented in Table 7.2. They also recommended that the differencing strategy be assumed when several pairs of different stimuli such as (S_AS_B), (S_BS_C), and (S_CS_D) are presented within a series of trials. Table 7.3 defines conditions and provides hypothetical results for these stimulus pairs. By calculating the proportions of "different" responses when there was a stimulus difference and when there was none it would be possible to compute the hit and false alarm rates for each of the three stimulus pairs. For the stimulus pair (S_AS_B) or (S_BS_A), the hit and false alarm rates were .75 and .15, respectively, and d′ was 2.99; for the stimulus pair (S_BS_C) or (S_CS_B), the hit and false alarm rates were .85 and .20, respectively, and d′ was 3.28; and for the stimulus pair (S_CS_D) or (S_DS_C), the hit and false alarm rates were .80 and .15, respectively, and d′ was 3.23. These d′ values were determined from Table A 5.4 in Macmillan and Creelman (1991). Recently, statistical procedures have been developed for empirically distinguishing the actual decision rule used by the observer in the same–different procedure (Dai, Versfeld, & Green, 1996).

The same–different procedure can be used to measure a difference threshold. In this case one of the two stimuli would be a fixed standard stimulus and the other would be the comparison stimulus. On some trials, the standard and comparison stimuli would be presented and on other trials, the two stimuli would be the same—either two standard stimuli or two comparison stimuli. In each of these stimulus pairs, the observer would indicate whether the two stimuli were the same or different. The value of d′ would be computed from hit rates and false alarm rates. This procedure would be employed using several values of the comparison stimulus but the same value of the standard stimulus. From the results, it would be possible to determine the difference threshold by calculating the difference between the measured values of the standard stimulus and the comparison stimulus when the observer's performance attained some specified level, such as that resulting in a d′ of 1.0.

TABLE 7.3
Hypothetical Results for the Same–Different Procedure

| | Response | | Number |
Stimulus pair	"different"	"same"	of Trials
(S_AS_B) or (S_BS_A)	75	25	100
(S_AS_A) or (S_BS_B)	15	85	100
(S_BS_C) or (S_CS_B)	85	15	100
(S_BS_B) or (S_CS_C)	20	80	100
(S_CS_D) or (S_DS_C)	80	20	100
(S_CS_C) or S_DS_D)	15	85	100

Recall from the discussion of the confidence rating procedure that this method is the most efficient means of obtaining an ROC curve, and that the ROC curve provides valuable information about the underlying events within the observer determining his or her decisions. By combining the confidence rating procedure with the same–different procedure, it is possible to obtain ROC curves for the discrimination of stimulus differences. Irwin, Stillman, Hautus, and Huddleston (1993) took this approach in measuring how well two concentrations of a commercially available orange drink, Refresh, could be discriminated. Samples of Refresh were presented in pairs. The pairs consisted of two weaker concentrations, two stronger concentrations, or one weaker and one stronger concentration presented in two different orders. Thus, on a particular trial the probability of the two concentrations being the same or different was 0.5. After sipping and spitting out each sample of a pair, the observers rated their confidence that the samples were the same concentrations by calling out a number from "one" (certain different) to "six" (certain same). Hit rates and false alarm rates were determined from the results by the method described in our discussion of the confidence rating procedure. The ROC curve seen in Figure 7.9 was constructed from these hit and false alarm rates. The asymmetric form of the ROC curve suggested to the investigators that a differencing strategy had been used by the observers in which differences were reported when the difference between the perceived intensities of the two samples in a pair exceeded a criterion. The differencing strategy predicts an ROC curve that is asymmetrical about the negative diagonal of the ROC graph, whereas the independent-observation strategy predicts a symmetrical ROC curve. It is clear from Figure 7.9 that it is possible to reject the independent-observation hypothesis for the conditions of this taste experiment. The ROC curve is clearly asymmetrical. Further support for the hypothesis that observers use a differencing strategy in the same–different procedure came from a hearing

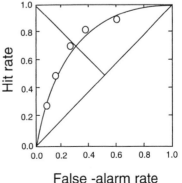

FIG. 7.9. ROC curve for the same–difference procedure. The smooth curve is the best-fitting ROC curve predicted from the differencing model. (From Irwin, Stillman, Hautus, & Huddleston, 1993.)

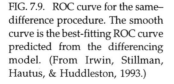

False -alarm rate

experiment in which ROC curves were constructed from confidence ratings of same–different judgments of the intensity of 1000-Hz tones (Hautus, Irwin, & Sutherland, 1994). As in taste discrimination, the ROC curve for hearing was found to be asymmetrical, again supporting the hypothesis that the observer used a differencing, rather than an independent-observation, strategy. These two experiments demonstrate the feasibility and utility of obtaining ROC curves in the same–difference task.

The Oddity Procedure

As is true of the same–different procedure, the *oddity procedure* provides a means of measuring the observer's ability to discriminate between different stimuli. In this task there are three or more observation intervals. One stimulus is presented in all but one of the observation intervals and the other stimulus is presented in the remaining interval. The observer's task is to select the interval containing the odd stimulus. As with the same–different procedure, observers are free to make the discrimination on whatever basis they choose rather than on a basis prescribed by the experimenter. Performance is specified as the proportion of correct responses that can then be converted to the d' sensitivity measure.

Let us consider an example in which we choose the oddity procedure with three observation intervals to measure the observer's ability to discriminate between two taste stimuli, Pepsi and Coke. On a random half of the trials, Coke would be the odd stimulus and on the remaining trials, Pepsi would be. The position of the odd stimulus would be randomized from trial to trial. With three observation intervals, chance performance would correspond to a $p(c)$ value of .33 and in this circumstance d', as the measure of discriminability would be 0.0. The value of d' will increase as $p(c)$ increases beyond the chance level of .33 and approaches 1.0. For example, in discriminating Pepsi from Coke, if the $p(c)$ values for three observers were .4, .6, and .8, the corresponding d' values would be .88, 1.98, and 3.18, respectively. It should be kept in mind that d' obtained with the oddity procedure, as with any method, represents the distance in z-score units between the means of two distributions of internal events. In this particular example, d' is the distance between the means of the distributions of taste events generated by Pepsi and Coke. A table for converting $p(c)$ values obtained with the three-alternative oddity procedure to d' values is found in Macmillan and Creelman (1991). The oddity procedure can also be used with more than three intervals and tables are available for easily converting $p(c)$ values to d' values (Versfeld, Dai, & Green, 1996) for cases of 3, 4, and 5 observation intervals.

The oddity procedure could be adapted to measuring difference thresholds. On some trials, all but one observation interval would contain the standard stimulus and the remaining interval would contain the comparison stimulus, whereas on other trials, all intervals but one would contain the comparison stimulus and the remaining interval would contain the standard stimulus. The observer would perform the task of choosing the interval containing the odd stimulus and the value of $p(c)$ would be computed. This procedure would be employed using several values of the comparison stimulus but the same value of the standard stimulus. The difference threshold would then be specified as the difference between the measured values of the standard stimulus and the comparison stimulus when the observer's performance attained some specified level such as that indicating a d' value of 1.0.

ADAPTIVE METHODS FOR MEASURING THRESHOLDS

We have seen that TSD provides procedures for measuring signal detectability at varied levels of signal intensity. In the experimental situation, a measure of signal detectability such as d' or A_z, computed from the observer's performance in a signal detection task, is the dependent variable that typically is observed to change as the experimenter manipulates the level of the independent variable—signal intensity. From these experiments, we are able to determine functional relationships between the intensity of a signal and its detectability. Given the existence of a functional relationship between a measure of signal detectability and signal intensity, it is possible to experimentally proceed in the opposite direction, in which the intensity of the signal, or rather its detectability, becomes the dependent variable. In these experiments, the fundamental goal is to determine the intensity of the signal corresponding to a fixed level of signal detectability. The measured signal intensity corresponding to some fixed designated performance level of the observer is an empirical threshold. As we saw in chapter 6, the measurement of empirical thresholds provides valuable information concerning the sensitivity of a sensory system, without necessarily implying the existence of either energy thresholds or observer thresholds.

In order to measure an empirical threshold, the experimenter must decide what signal intensities should be used in the experiment. It should be clear that choosing signals that are all greatly above or greatly below the detectability level designated to correspond to threshold will provide little information leading to an accurate estimation of the threshold. Recalling our discussion in chapter 3 of the method of constant stimuli and illustrated in Figure 3.1, the threshold of 12.3 could be estimated by presenting a series of stimuli ranging in intensity from 4 to 20 units. Had the threshold not been contained within this range, the experiment would have failed. Historically, such failures were avoided by conducting preliminary testing or by referring to published normative results to aid in choosing an appropriate set of signals to be used in an experiment. Such an approach is far from optimally efficient and consequently the adaptive methods for measuring threshold have evolved.

In all adaptive procedures, the intensity of a signal presented on a particular trial is determined by the observer's performance in detecting signals presented on prior trials. One of the early applications of this principle was seen in chapter 3 in our discussion of the threshold tracking method developed by Békésy (1947) to measure auditory thresholds. Recall that, in this method, the intensity of a tone is continuously decreased over time, as long as the observer indicates hearing it by pressing a switch. When the tone eventually becomes inaudible the observer releases the switch, whereupon the tone is continuously increased until it can again be detected. At this point, the switch is pressed by the observer causing the intensity of the tone to decrease. The observer continues in this manner until performance becomes stable for some specified period of time. Threshold is estimated by averaging the tone intensities corresponding to reversals in the observer's responses. The strength of the method is the efficient presentation of only stimuli near the observer's threshold. The major weakness of this particular adaptive procedure is that, as with other classical psychophysical procedures developed prior to the advent of TSD, measured thresholds may be biased by the location of the observer's response criterion. Although the potential bias inherent in using this method is not so great as to invalidate its use in clinical diagnoses of hearing loss, the method is not recommended for use in experimental research in which highly accurate measurements of thresholds are required. Fortunately, several highly efficient adaptive methods that control for the effects of the observer's criterion are now available for measuring thresholds.

Forced-Choice Tracking

The first adaptive method to adequately control for the observer's criterion was forced-choice tracking developed by Zwislocki, Maire, Feldman, and Rubin (1957). This was already described in discussing the forced-choice procedure. The forced-choice aspect of the procedure greatly reduces or eliminates the possibility that threshold measurements will be contaminated by the observer's criterion. The adaptive aspect of the procedure involves rules for changing the intensity of the signal presented in one or the other of two observation intervals. Specifically stated, the rule governing changes in signal intensity is that each error made by the observer in choosing which interval contained the signal causes an increase in the intensity of the signal presented on the next trial, while every three correct responses (not necessarily consecutive) causes a decrease in signal intensity on the subsequent trial. Under these conditions, the intensity of the signal, being linked to the observer's performance, eventually stabilizes at a threshold value needed for the observer to choose correctly 75% of the time.

Macmillan and Creelman (1991) pointed out that to define an adaptive procedure, the experimenters must answer four separate questions: "(1) what results should lead to a decision to end testing at the current level and shift to a new one? (2) when the stimulus level is to be changed, to what level should it be changed? (3) when does an experimental run end? (4) how should an estimate of threshold be calculated?" (p. 190). The characteristics of the various adaptive procedures now available depend on the answers given to each of these four questions. For example, in forced-choice tracking, (a) the intensity of the signal is increased by one step when an error is made and decreased one step when three correct responses (not necessarily consecutive) are made, (b) the size of the stimulus change is always the same when increasing and decreasing the signal level, (c) the experimental run ends when the stimulus level remains within a specified narrow range for some specified number of responses (usually 20–30 responses), and (d) the value of the threshold is taken as the average signal level within the period of stable tracking.

Up-Down Transformed Response (UDTR) Method

A method similar to forced-choice tracking is the *up-down transformed response* (UDTR) method developed by Wetherill and Levitt (1965) and further described by Levitt (1971). In this method, the sequence of correct and incorrect responses at the current signal level is compared, after each trial, to a list of possible patterns. Some patterns demand an increase in signal strength, whereas others demand a decrease. When there is a match between the observer's pattern of responses and one of the patterns on the list, the signal intensity is changed appropriately and a new record of responses is started that, on each trial, will again be compared to the list. If there is no match, another trial is presented at the same signal intensity. A frequently used UDTR rule applied in two-alternative forced-choice testing has been that each incorrect response leads to a more intense signal, whereas a sequence of two correct responses leads to a decrease. This rule aims at determining the signal intensity that results in 71% correct responding. Other rules have been applied to measure thresholds corresponding to performance levels other than the 71% correct responding level. For example, the threshold for choosing correctly 84% of the time can be determined by the rule that the signal is decreased after four successive correct responses and that it is increased after a single incorrect response. Threshold is generally computed in UDTR as the average signal intensity over a period of stable responding at the targeted performance level (71% and 84% in the examples just discussed).

In both forced-choice tracking and UDTR, the size of the increases and decreases in signal intensity remains constant over the experimental run. The choice of step size and initial signal level is generally determined by what worked best in the past. There can be problems with this procedure if the chosen starting point is well above or well below threshold, in which case the method becomes inefficient because a great number of adjustments requiring a large number of responses will be needed to bring the signal intensity into the intensity region of the threshold. There can also be problems if the chosen step size in signal intensity is too small or too large. The step size may be so small as to make no substantial difference in the observer's performance when the signal intensity is changed by one step. In this case, many more steps and, consequently, many more responses would be required to arrive at threshold than if a larger step had been used. On the other hand, if the step size is too large, correct and incorrect responses may result in swings in signal intensity from levels well below to levels well above threshold, with very few, if any, signal presentations at the threshold level. Under these conditions, the accuracy of threshold estimations would be compromised.

Parameter Estimation by Sequential Testing (PEST)

To combat some of the difficulties of accurately and efficiently measuring thresholds when inappropriate starting level and step size in signal intensity have been chosen, Taylor and Creelman (1967) developed a procedure called *parameter estimation by sequential testing*, now known widely as PEST. In PEST, the step size starts out large at the beginning of a run and generally becomes smaller as the run proceeds and threshold is approached. Specifically, (1) with each reversal in which the signal strength is changed in the opposite direction from the previous step, the step size is reduced by half until (2) a minimum step size is reached wherein step size remains constant. On the other hand, (3) when there is no reversal, but instead the program calls for a change in signal strength in the same direction as the last, the step size remains the same for the first two such steps but (4) the third step in the same direction requires a doubled step size as does each successive step in the same direction until a reversal occurs with the stipulation that the maximum step size is limited to a certain number of times that of the minimum step size. One exception to these rules is that (5) if a reversal follows a doubling of step size, then three steps of the same size, instead of two, can be taken before a doubling of step size is required.

The PEST rules just described are illustrated in the tracking record presented in Figure 7.10. The graph shows the sequence of signal intensity changes associated with each of the five rules. The numbers on the graph refer to the rule numbers just stated. The threshold is reached when a specified number of responses are made when the step size is within the range of the minimal size.

Maximum-Likelihood Methods

It should be clear from examination of Figure 7.10 that, as with other adaptive procedures, changes in signal intensity in PEST depend on the past history of responding within the run. However, in PEST, as in forced-choice tracking and UDTR, the history of responding that determines changes in signal intensity is limited to no more than a few responses before the change is made. In a class of procedures called *maximum-likelihood methods*, the intensity of the signal presented on each trial is determined by a statistical estimation of the observer's threshold, which is made from all of the results obtained from the beginning of the run. This estimation determines whether the intensity on the next trial will be increased or decreased. If the signal intensity on the prior trial is below the estimated threshold, it will be increased on the next trial, but if it is above the estimated threshold its intensity will be decreased. After each trial, a new estimation of the threshold is calculated and the signal intensity is adjusted accordingly. As the run proceeds, the estimations of

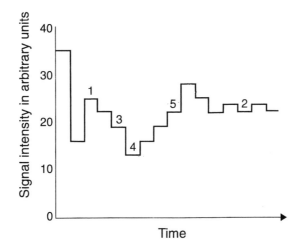

FIG. 7.10. Tracking record illustrating each of the five PEST rules.

threshold tend to become increasingly more accurate because they are based on increasingly large amounts of information accumulated since the start of the run, and consequently the intensity of the signal presented to the observer tends to more closely approximate the threshold level. When the estimated threshold eventually becomes stable, changing little from trial to trial, the run is terminated and the value of the signal corresponding to the estimated threshold is recorded.

The statistical technique of maximum-likelihood estimation assumes that the underlying psychometric function describing changes in the observer's performance as a function of changes in signal intensity has a specific form. For example, in a two-alternative forced-choice task, the function describing how the proportion of correct responses increased from a chance level of .5 to 1.0 as signal strength increases could be assumed to be a Gaussian (the cumulative normal distribution), logistic, Weibull, or some other function.

The maximum-likelihood estimation determines the position along the signal intensity axis and the slope of the psychometric function that has the highest probability of accounting for the available data. From this estimated psychometric function, the threshold, defined as the value of signal associated with a specified level of performance of the observer (e.g., 75% correct responding), is calculated and the intensity of the signal to be presented on the next trial is adjusted accordingly. Because the best-fitting psychometric function with its estimation of the threshold is recalculated after every trial in the run, it can be used to determine the intensity of the signal to be presented on the next run. Two widely used maximum-likelihood methods assume different forms of the psychometric function. Pentland's *best PEST* assumed the psychometric function to be logistic (Lieberman & Pentland, 1982; Pentland, 1980), whereas Watson and Pelli's *QUEST* (1983) assumed the Weibull function. Because the functions have similar forms, the estimated thresholds determined by the two methods are not greatly different. In both cases, however, the computations are complicated enough to require the use of a sufficiently powerful online computer to accomplish them. In laboratories where such methods are used, the procedures are entirely automated so that the experimenter has only to start the run and wait until the observer has made enough responses to provide an acceptably accurate estimation of the threshold.

In all adaptive psychophysical methods, it is desirable to minimize the variability of the threshold estimates. In this way fewer threshold estimates are necessary to achieve an accurate estimation of the observer's true average threshold. As we have seen, a strength of the adaptive methods is their efficiency in determining accurate estimates of threshold. It has been further demonstrated that the efficiency of these procedures can be enhanced by the correct choice of the performance level chosen to define threshold. For example, Laming and Marsh (1988) and Watson and Pelli (1983), using the maximum-likelihood procedure, suggested that to minimize variability between threshold estimates, thresholds should be defined by a point relatively high on the psychometric function. In a two-alternative forced-choice task, for example, threshold variability is minimized when threshold is defined as the stimulus intensity that is correctly detected 84% to 94% of the time (Green, 1990). Unfortunately, for many years, thresholds have usually been tracked at performance levels between 71% (e.g., UDTR) and 75% (two-alternative forced-choice tracking) rather than at the optimal level. The consequence of choosing performance levels for threshold that are not optimal in minimizing variability of threshold measurement is that an increased number of measurements are needed to maintain precision. Thus, if efficiency is of great concern, as would be the case in situations in which many thresholds must be measured in a short period of time, it is recommended that, when using adaptive procedures such as those just described, threshold be defined in terms of performance levels of the observer that minimize variability of measurements.

In conclusion, the adaptive methods for measuring thresholds are efficient and accurate and are, therefore, highly recommended for experimental work in which precise measurements are required. Although precision of measurement may be less critical in diagnosing disorders, the efficiency of the adaptive methods makes them well suited for use in the clinic as well as in the research laboratory.

PROBLEMS

7.1. The table below contains the numbers of judgments of each of five categories of confidence in detecting the *presence or absence of a signal*. From these data, derive proportions of hits and false alarms corresponding to four criterion levels and plot them as an ROC curve.

Categories

	sure no signal	fairly sure no signal	not sure	fairly sure signal	sure signal
SN	2	12	46	116	24
N	30	68	68	32	2

8

Some Applications of TSD

The theory of signal detection has provided refined measures of the capacity of human observers to detect sensory stimuli. But in addition, by incorporating aspects of decision making, the theory provides many connections between psychophysics and other areas of psychology. Advances in psychophysical methodology are no longer restricted in their usefulness to the study of sensory thresholds, but instead may provide powerful techniques for studying how people make decisions about environmental events in general. For example, TSD has been useful in studying decision processes ranging from how clinicians diagnose illness from a set of symptoms to how people decide whether or not they have seen a person's face before. The research described below is but a small sample of the many applications of TSD to problems of determining how people make decisions.

Recognition Memory

The continuity–noncontinuity issue has a long history in several areas of psychology besides the study of sensory processes. The essential question, however, is always the same: do psychological processes change on a continuum, or do they change in discrete steps? For years, psychologists have been concerned with the problem of whether learning is an all-or-none or a continuous process. Does the learning curve represent a number of small discrete increments in learning, or does it represent a gradual and continuous change in the amount learned? A closely related problem arises in the study of recognition memory. To be recognized, must a stimulus exceed some threshold below which memory strength is zero, or must the stimulus exceed a criterion on a memory-strength continuum?

In a recognition-memory test, an observer is first exposed to a series of stimulus items such as words, nonsense syllables, or visual nonsense forms. Subsequently, the observer is exposed to a series of stimulus items, some of which are old items from the earlier series and some of which are new items. The observer is required to report "old" or "new" for each presentation of an item. Reporting "old" for an old stimulus is a hit, while a false alarm is reporting "old" for a new stimulus. Reporting "new" for a new item is a correct rejection, while reporting "new" for an old item is a miss.

In the TSD model of recognition memory, each item, whether old or new, is assumed to be located on a continuum of memory strength. Variability in memory strength for different items is assumed to form two overlapping normal distributions on the memory-strength continuum (Figure 8.1). The distributions for new and old items are analogous to the N and SN distributions of the detection situation. According to the TSD analysis, the observer will report "new" if the memory strength of the item is below a criterion but will report "old" if the memory strength is above the criterion. The experiment might be repeated several times with different sets of items. By inducing the observer to change the criterion for each new experiment, several pairs of hit and false alarm proportions can be obtained and plotted as an ROC curve. If the TSD analysis is correct and memory strength varies on a continuum, the ROC curve, called a *memory operating characteristic* (MOC) curve, should be curvilinear when plotted as proportions and linear when plotted as z scores.

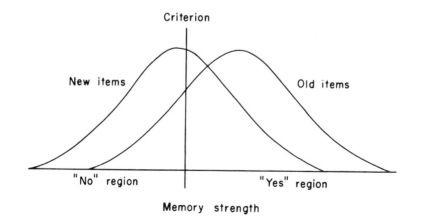

FIG. 8.1. Distributions of memory strength for new and old items. The criterion indicates the memory strength below which the observer will report "new" and above which he will report "old."

In the noncontinuity model of recognition memory, it is postulated that an item either has a suprathreshold memory strength which always results in a recognition response or is below the recognition threshold and results in a recognition response only when the observer guesses. This model of recognition memory is exactly analogous to the high threshold theory of detection. The threshold is assumed to be unaffected by changes in the observer's expectations and motivation. From the threshold model, the MOC curve is predicted to be linear when plotted as proportions. The prediction that the proportion of hits will be a linear function of the proportion of false alarms follows from the assumption that all old items above threshold will be recognized, while the new items will never be above threshold and, therefore, will never be recognized. Accordingly, the false alarm proportion is defined as the rate at which the observer will guess "old" when an item is below threshold and he is in the nonrecognition state. The hit rate is equal to the proportion of old items above threshold plus the proportion of old items below threshold multiplied by the false alarm rate. When conditions are altered to induce the observer to change the rate of guessing old items, the proportion of false alarms and hits will increase. A review of the discussion of Equation (4.4) will reveal that the logic behind the prediction of a linear ROC curve for detection and a linear MOC curve for recognition memory is exactly the same.

The general finding has been that MOC curves are curvilinear rather than linear when plotted as proportions (see Banks, 1970, and Lockhart & Murdock, 1970, for reviews of the experimental findings). Thus, a model with a high recognition threshold located above the mean of the new item distribution appears to be untenable, while the data are consistent with the TSD model. A mathematically precise statement of a TSD model of memory, in which old and new items are assumed to vary in memory strength along a continuum, has been developed by Wickelgren and Norman (1966).

The demonstration that TSD provides a good description of recognition memory led to an important methodological advance in this field of research. It is now possible to use any of the three basic psychophysical procedures of TSD to determine whether factors such as age, brain damage, and drugs known to influence recognition performance do so through changes in a person's ability to discriminate old from new items or through changes in the decision criterion. For example, Abel (1971) found that marijuana taken after presentation of a list of words impaired the ability of subjects to discriminate old from new words presented during a recognition test. At the same time, the drug also had the effect of inducing the subjects to lower their decision criteria, an effect indicated by an increase in the false alarm rate. Thus, marijuana seems to make people both less cautious about reporting events they think they have previously experienced and at the same time reduces their ability to discriminate between new and previously experienced events.

Although a drug like marijuana may induce subjects to set low decision criteria, depression may cause them to set high criteria. The tendency for depressed patients to be conservative and set high criteria on recognition memory tests was shown by Miller and Lewis (1977). These investigators were interested in investigating losses in recognition memory observed in both elderly depressed patients and patients with senile dementia, since both disorders are associated with impairments in memory. A TSD procedure was used in their study to determine whether recognition of geometric designs is impaired in these patients. Groups of elderly depressed patients, senile patients, and normal people were presented with 20 different geometric designs followed by 140 presentations of some new designs and some of the previously seen designs. The proportion of correct recognitions of previously seen designs and the proportion of incorrect recognitions of new designs constituted the hit and false alarm rates, respectively. The outcome of the experiment was that the values of d' were substantially lower for senile than for normal subjects, while depressed patients, although having no loss in sensitivity as measured by d', set their decision criteria much higher than did the normal subjects. This finding indicates that memory loss in elderly depressed and senile patients may occur for very different reasons. Senile patients seem to have actual memory impairment, while depressed patients, perhaps due to a general lack of confidence, are simply excessively conservative about reporting previously experienced events. Miller and Lewis proposed that using TSD procedures in measuring the recognition memory of senile and elderly depressed mental patients could improve the accuracy of diagnosis.

The results of Brooks (1974) show that the impaired recognition memory in patients with brain damage caused by head trauma is different from that observed in the study by Miller and Lewis on senile and depressed patients. Brooks found that patients with brain damage had both lower d' measures of sensitivity and a higher decision criterion. Perhaps brain damaged individuals were cautious about reporting recognition of a previously experienced event because they were aware of their deficiencies in memory. Efforts to help these patients lower their decision criteria may improve their recognition memory, since actual impairment may be aggravated by their conservative decision strategy.

Pain

Pain, the unpleasant experience primarily associated with tissue damage, has been a topic of psychophysics for many years. Insofar as it is a sensory experience elicited by a stimulus, pain, like visual, auditory, tactile, and other sensory experiences elicited by stimuli, should be subject to psychophysical analysis. It is, therefore, somewhat surprising that in our understanding of sensory systems, pain lags far behind. One of the reasons for the relatively slow rate of progress in the psychophysics of pain is that pain is not simply a sensory experience elicited by a stimulus. In fact, it is often impossible to accurately predict the psychophysical response of pain from information about the stimulus. For example, different individuals may react very differently to the same stimulus—some reporting that it is excruciating, while others reporting that it is only mildly distressing or not painful at all. The wide range of reactions to noxious stimuli may be attributed to the fact that pain is both a sensory and an emotional experience. Added to the sensory experience initiated by activity in sensory neurons are associated ideas, expectations, and past learning. The magnitude of the experience of pain will be greatly affected by a person's interpretation of the sensory input to the brain. A chronic mild pain sensation of unknown cause may become associated with fear of death from cancer and, as a result, be transformed into unbearable suffering. On the other hand, upon discovery that these fears are unfounded, the pain may subside.

The discovery that pain has both a sensory and emotional component has led to many questions about which component is affected by factors known to influence judgments of pain. For example, do analgesic drugs reduce pain through attenuation of sensory input, by regulation of emotional arousal, or by some combination of the two? For those investigators who have attempted to analyze the complex phenomenon of pain into its fundamental components, methods of TSD have recently been found to be very helpful. Through the use of these methods, it is now possible to determine whether factors known to influence pain do so by changing the sensitivity of the sensory component or by changing the decision criterion.

Clark (1969) was the first investigator to exploit the advantages of TSD for research on pain. For many years, it had been known that patients who take a placebo will often report their pain has subsided. Clark measured the effect of a placebo on the perception of pain produced by radiant heating of the skin. Observers were given a placebo and strong suggestions about its analgesic effects. They were then required to make judgments of the amount of pain experienced when five stimuli ranging from weak to strong were presented. The results were compared with those obtained when no placebo was given. TSD analysis indicated that the ability of the observer to discriminate among the stimuli of different intensities was not affected by the placebo, although the placebo did have the effect of inducing the observer to increase his decision criterion. Thus, although fewer reports of intense pain were recorded after the placebo, the observer's sensitivity to pain was not altered. Perhaps observers gave fewer pain responses after the placebo, because they thought that fewer such responses were expected of them.

Chapman and Feather (1973) found that the tranquilizer diazepam acted like a placebo, having no significant effects on the discriminability of painful stimuli. On the other hand, nitrous oxide, a commonly used anesthetic gas, was found to reduce discriminability, as measured by d', of different levels of painful radiant heat stimulation of the skin, as well as to induce observers to increase their decision criteria. Furthermore, Chapman, Gehrig, and Wilson (1975) found that the discriminability of various levels of electrical stimulation of the tooth pulp was decreased by acupuncture and also by nitrous oxide. It may be of some practical significance that the pain-reducing effects of these treatments were substantially greater for mildly painful than for very painful stimuli. Finally, the work of Clark and Mehl (1971) suggests that our ability to discriminate the intensity of painful stimuli declines with age. Elderly people tend to set higher criteria for reporting pain, as indicated by their unwillingness to frequently report that stimuli are painful.

Diagnostic Testing

Few decisions are more important than those made in clinical diagnosis, yet clinical judgments are often inaccurate. Recently, TSD methodology has been used to study how clinicians made their judgments of the presence or absence of disease. Lusted (1971), for example, has reported on the application of TSD to x-ray diagnosis of pulmonary tuberculosis and breast cancer. The reason for concern in this area is the fact that, in mass screening programs, radiologists have been found to overlook 30% of the positive tuberculosis films, and that specialists disagreed with their own diagnosis 20% of the time. Lusted reviewed results of studies in which observers viewing known positive and negative x-ray plates had to report the presence or absence of disease. The hit and false alarm rates calculated from the results permitted calculations of d' values. It was found that direct observation of the plates resulted in higher d' values than TV viewing of images. It was significant that performance has been found to increase with practice for a number of diagnostic detection tasks, including tactile detection of lumps in the breast (Adams, Hall, Penny-packer, Goldstein, Hench, Madden, Stein, & Catania, 1976), as well as detection of disease from observation of x-ray plates.

Computerized tomography (CT) and radionuclide (RN) scans have been employed in the detection of brain lesions. TSD methods have been used to evaluate the relative accuracy of these two diagnostic procedures (Swets, Pickett, Whitehead, Getty, Schnur, Swets, & Freeman, 1979). Twelve radiologists, 6 CT specialists, and 6 RN specialists interpreted CT

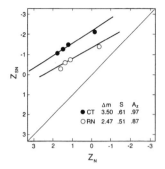

FIG. 8.2. ROC curves for the detection of brain lesions by computerized tomography (CT) and radionuclide (RN) scans. Hit and false alarm rates are expressed as Z_{SN} and Z_N, respectively. (From Swets, Pickett, Whitehead, Getty, Schnur, Swets, & Freeman, 1979.)

and RN images of 136 patients. Some of the patients were known to have brain lesions and some were known not to have lesions. A confidence rating procedure in which the radiologists rated the confidence of their judgments on a 5-point scale was used to construct ROC curves for each diagnostic procedure. The method of deriving the ROC curve from such ratings was essentially the same as that described earlier in this chapter. The z-score ROC curves are plotted in Figure 8.2 and the values of Δm, A_z, and the slope (s) of the functions are indicated in the insert. It is clear that the accuracy of diagnosing brain lesions in this study was higher for CT than for RN imaging methods. In Figure 8.3, the results are also plotted as proportions of hits and false alarms instead of Z_{SN} and Z_N.

Recall that the measure A_z refers to the area under the ROC curve plotted on proportion coordinates. It is clear from examination of Figure 8.3 that this area is greater for CT than for RN imaging. It is also clear from examination of the ROC curves that the hit and false alarm rates that occur in diagnosis using both methods are highly influenced by the radiologists decision criterion. If the radiologist were to set a low criterion, there would be a high rate of detecting brain lesions when they exist in patients but there would also be a high rate of false alarms for patients without lesions. On the other hand, setting a high criterion, although reducing the false alarm rate, would have the negative consequence of reducing the hit rate.

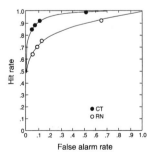

FIG. 8.3. ROC curves for the detection of brain lesions by computerized tomography (CT) and radionuclide (RN) scans. Based on the same data used to construct the z-score ROC curves of Figure 8.2. (From Swets, Pickett, Whitehead, Getty, Schnur, Swets, & Freeman, 1979.)

Swets (1992) pointed out that the optimal criterion in high stakes diagnostics depends on both probability of occurrence of the signal (in medical diagnosis, the signal is the presence of disease), the probability of occurrence of noise (in medical diagnosis, this is the absence of disease), the benefits of correctly detecting disease, the benefits of correctly detecting the absence of disease, the costs of falsely detecting disease when none exists, and the costs of missing the presence of disease when it exists. For example, for a fixed set of benefits and costs, the optimal criterion is relatively high when the probability of the presence of the disease is low. As Swets pointed out, such might be the case when using the test broadly for screening individuals from a nonsymptomatic population. In contrast, if the same test were to be given in a medical referral center, with a much higher probability that the tested individuals would have the disease, the optimal criterion would be lower. With this lenient criterion the false alarms can be tolerated because the number of disease free cases is relatively small.

When the probability of the presence of disease is constant, the location of the criterion will be greatly influenced by the benefits of correctly detecting the presence of disease or of correctly identifying its absence and the costs of falsely identifying disease when none exists or of missing disease when it does exist. For example, a high criterion might be set when the surgical procedure undertaken for a disease has high risks and a low chance of curing the disease. The high criterion in this situation is appropriate because of the potentially high costs associated with false alarms and the low benefits associated with hits. On the other hand, if the cost associated with false alarms is low (e.g., having to take an antibiotic for 10 days for a falsely diagnosed bacterial infection) and the benefit of correctly detecting the infection is high (e.g., treating the infection to prevent a potentially life threatening condition from developing) the criterion should be low for deciding that the patient has the disease. The importance, in clinical diagnosis, of setting the optimal criterion that will maximize positive outcomes and minimize negative outcomes should be clear. It should also be clear from this discussion that clinical information supporting a positive diagnosis varies along a continuum and that this information could arise from either of two probability distributions— one in which disease is present (SN distribution) and one in which it is not (N distribution). The greater the accuracy of the diagnostic test, the greater will be the separation of these two distributions. Thus, clinical diagnosis rarely involves black or white situations in which there is a threshold for a test result which, when exceeded, indicates that the patient has the disease and which, when not exceeded, indicates the absence of the disease. Thus, in sensory psychophysics as well as in medical diagnosis, all-or-none thresholds are rare, whereas situations in which an observation can arise from either noise or signal added to noise appears to be the norm.

Swets (1992) argued for the direct applicability of TSD to problems such as HIV testing and material testing of airplanes. He pointed out that little has been done to apply principles of TSD in these areas despite the high national visibility and priority of these diagnostic problems. Given the probability of occurrence of the events under consideration and the cost and values of the various decision outcomes, what is the optimal criterion for deciding that a person is HIV positive or that an aircraft has a crack in its metal structure? What is the accuracy of the tests that are used? How can the results of different tests be combined to improve accuracy, and what affect does this have on the optimal criterion? How can people be trained to most effectively process the information supplied by the tests? What is the best way to standardize diagnostic procedures to uniformly provide optimal outcomes? These are the kinds of questions that could be answered by applying TSD principles to diagnostic decision making in areas such as HIV testing and the inspection of aircraft for structural defects. The need for such an approach can be illustrated by a TSD analysis, reported by Swets (1992), of the performance of technicians whose job it was to detect metal fatigue in airplanes. In the study reported by Swets, 148 metal specimens, some with and some without flaws, were taken to 17 U.S. Air Force bases where they were inspected by 121 technicians using ultrasound and 133 technicians using an eddy-current technique. The performance of each technician, specified as a hit rate and a false alarm rate, was represented as a single point on an ROC graph. Figures 8.4 and 8.5 show the results for ultrasound and eddy-current methods, respectively. It is clear that the performance of the technicians, with respect to accuracy (how far the point is above the positive diagonal where performance would be at the level of random chance), and the

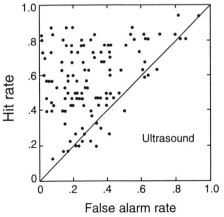

FIG. 8.4. ROC points for 121 technicians inspecting metal specimens for cracks with an ultrasound method. (From Swets, 1992.) Reprinted with permission.

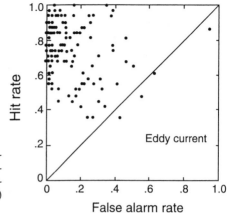

FIG. 8.5. ROC points for 133 technicians inspecting metal specimens for cracks with an eddy-current method. (From Swets, 1992.)
Reprinted with permission.

position of the criterion (whether data points tend to be located in the
lower-left, middle, or upper-right parts of the graph) was about as variable
as it could be. For ultrasound, hit and false alarm rates varied from near
0.0 to near 1.0. Some technicians adopted a high criterion and others
adopted a very low criterion. Performance was somewhat better for the
eddy-current method, where the hit rates tended to be higher and the
false alarm rates lower than those seen for the ultrasound method. As
with the ultrasound method, the location of the criterion varied greatly
among technicians, as did the accuracy of detecting flaws. The data points
of the most inaccurate technicians are near the positive diagonal and those
of the most accurate are located in the upper-left-hand corner of the graph
where the hit rate is high and the false alarm rate is low. The data points
of technicians with high criteria are located near the lower-left corners of
the graphs, while those with low criteria are located near the upper-right
corners. Thus, with both methods of detecting metal fatigue, no standards
have been established to ensure an optimal outcome. Swets (1992), however, pointed out that one hopeful sign is that the National Aeronautics
and Space Administration has begun to consider TSD analysis of cockpit
warning devices for engine malfunction, collision avoidance, ground
proximity, and wind-shear effects.

In conclusion, the goals of determining the optimal criterion and
accuracy of a diagnostic test have been shown to be applicable in a number
of important diagnostic fields. The costs of inappropriate criterion setting
in these situations would no doubt be very large. Swets (1988) argued for
the importance of convincing individuals in these fields of the benefits of
TSD analysis in determining the conditions necessary to produce optimal
diagnostic outcomes. He points out that diagnostic systems are used to
distinguish between "signals" and "noise" and, therefore, the ROC
analysis of TSD provides a precise and valid measure of diagnostic

accuracy. He argued that it is the only measure available that is uninfluenced by decision bias, and that it places the performance of diverse systems on a common and easily interpreted scale. For example, a measure such as the proportion of the area below the ROC curve, as determined by p(A) or A_z, can be used to assess and compare the accuracy of diagnosis in fields as different as medical imaging, materials testing, weather forecasting, information retrieval, polygraphic lie detection, and aptitude testing. In each of these examples there are two alternative environmental events. One event, the positive event, is what the diagnostic test is designed to detect, whereas the other, the negative event, includes all other conditions in which the positive event is absent. Thus, the positive event is the signal and the negative event is the noise. Specifically, a patient either does or does not have a brain lesion. The airplane either does or does not have a defect in its wing. It either will or will not snow on Christmas in Syracuse, NY. The article that you retrieved in your computer search is either relevant or not to the paper you are writing. A person given a polygraphic lie detection test is either guilty of the crime or is not. The high school student who is given an aptitude test either will or will not graduate from college. These events are independent of the diagnostic test, for they will occur whether the test is given or not. If the test is given, the diagnosis is either positive or negative. For example, the test may indicate the presence of a lesion (positive diagnosis) or the absence of a lesion (negative diagnosis). The two-by-two contingency table (Table 8.1) indicates the four possible diagnostic outcomes of any diagnostic test. The diagnosis is correct when the test either results in "true positive" or a "true negative." The diagnosis is incorrect when the test results in either a "false positive" or a "false negative." Data for evaluating a diagnostic system consists of the observed frequencies of the four possible outcomes of Table 8.1.

The diagnosis of personality disorders has also been studied by TSD methodology. Stenson, Kleinmuntz, and Scott (1975) examined the decision-making behavior of experienced clinicians, graduate students in clinical psychology, and undergraduate students in determining personality

TABLE 8.1
Four Possible Outcomes of a Diagnostic Test

		Event	
		Positive	*Negative*
Diagnosis	Positive	True Positive	False Positive
	Negative	False Negative	True Negative

disorders from observation of test results of the Minnesota Multiphasic Personality Inventory (MMPI). The MMPI consists of 10 basic scales, each of which is designed to assess the degree to which a patient suffers from a particular personality disorder. The 10 scales measure hypochondriasis, depression, hysteria, psychopathic deviation, masculinity–femininity, paranoia, psychasthenia, schizophrenia, hypomania, and social introversion. It has been found that the most effective diagnosis of personality disorder results from observation of the profile of results from the 10 scales rather than from searching for high scores on a single scale. Stenson, Kleinmuntz, and Scott required their observers to differentiate between 46 known abnormal MMPI profiles and 80 known normal profiles. Hit and false alarm rates were calculated, from which d' values were derived. The value of d' was found to be the same whether the observers were told that 30% or 70% of the patients had been hospitalized. Furthermore, when asked to sort the profiles according to whether or not patients needed hospitalization, the same d' values were obtained if the observers were told that hospitalization was costly and stigmatizing, or if they were told that the patients were dangerous to society. Thus, the use of TSD methodology could be very valuable in providing diagnostic information that is free of biasing factors such as knowledge of the consequences of the diagnosis.

Clinical diagnosis in some cases is based on the detection behavior of the patient, as well as on that of the clinician. In the field of audiology, for example, clinicians may attempt to detect hearing disorders by observing how well their patients detect auditory stimuli. From the audiogram, a graph of the difference between the patient's threshold and the normal threshold, the clinician may diagnose specific diseases of the auditory system. For example, the audiograms in Figure 8.6 suggest different disorders in the auditory systems of patients A and B. In the case of patient A, the threshold at any stimulus frequency is somewhat higher than normal, while the audiogram of patient B is normal at low frequencies but indicates elevated thresholds at high frequencies. The audiogram of patient A could have resulted from a problem in the conduction of sound through the outer ear and/or middle ear, while the audiogram of patient B suggests that the hearing loss may be the result of damage in the auditory nervous system.

Accurate diagnosis of hearing disorders depends on obtaining auditory thresholds that are not biased by the patient's decision criterion. For example, a patient with a very high decision criterion will have a high threshold measured by the method of limits, typically used in audiometric testing, and may be incorrectly diagnosed as having a hearing loss. It would be desirable, therefore, to use criterion-free TSD methods in audiometric testing when possible. The problem, however, is that most of these methods are too time-consuming to be used in clinical practice. Exceptions are the

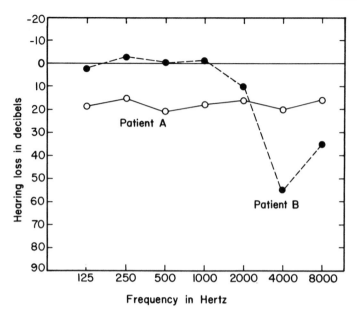

FIG. 8.6. Audiogram for two patients suffering from different types of hearing loss.

adaptive methods described earlier in chapter 7. These methods yield criterion-free threshold measurements and are efficient enough to use in clinical testing. Within a 1-hour session, thresholds for each ear could be measured by detecting each of the seven frequencies typically used in audiometric testing. However, because most commercially available audiometers are not designed for this type of testing, most audiologists, although aware of the importance of criterion-free testing, are still using the classical methods. We can anticipate that as they become available, new instruments for criterion-free testing will be used extensively, and that, as a result, the precision of diagnosis will be substantially improved.

Aggressive Behavior

In the social environment, an act is rewarded only when it occurs in the appropriate situation. For example, there is a time and place for telling a joke, making a sexual advance, or defending oneself. Thus, it is important for a socially adjusted individual to be able to discriminate appropriate from inappropriate situations when engaging in social behavior. Insofar as a social situation that is appropriate for a particular behavior can be thought of as a signal and inappropriate situations as noise, it should be possible to study discriminative capacities in social behavior with TSD techniques. In their research on aggressive behavior, Ulehla and Adams (1973) were the first to demonstrate that TSD techniques could serve as powerful tools for the study of social behavior. In this study, high school students made their responses on a questionnaire that included descriptions of situations in which an aggressive act would be justified, such as "standing up to a bully," and situations in which an aggressive act would not be justified, such as "roughing up a little guy you don't like." For each hypothetical situation, the subjects had to indicate whether or not they would expect positive consequences if they had performed the described act. The ability of the subjects to discriminate situations in which aggression was justified from situations in which it was not was measured by calculating d'. The proportions of times subjects reported that they expected positive consequences for aggressive behavior in situations in which aggression was justified and in situations in which aggression was not justified were taken as the hit and false alarm rates, respectively. The results yielded by detection analysis suggested that d' as a sensitivity index for the detection of appropriate situations for aggression may relate to important cultural and behavioral variables. The values of d' were different for different ethnic groups. The highest d' values were found for Anglo, the lowest for Black, and intermediate values for Hispanic students. This ordering is consistent with the hypothesis that the more advantaged students would be more sensitive to widely accepted cultural norms for appropriate aggressive behavior. It was also found that students judged by teachers to be deviantly aggressive in their behavior at school had substantially lower d' values than nonaggressive students. Perhaps with regard to aggressive behavior, deviantly aggressive students have failed to learn the norms of society.

Within our social environment we encounter a wide variety of situations. Some situations signal that certain behaviors are appropriate. Presumably, these signals are established through social learning, in which specific acts are rewarded only when they occur in specific situations. In an orderly social system, individuals are highly sensitive to these signals and act accordingly. If a subgroup is not sensitive to, or ignores, the signals that regulate the behavior of the majority group, its members are more likely to violate social norms established by the majority, and consequently to be ostracized by the broader community. The methods of TSD offer a quantitative approach to the study of such problems.

CONCLUDING STATEMENT ON THE THEORY
OF SIGNAL DETECTION

The theory of signal detection has been a major advancement in experimental psychology. Along with the work of S. S. Stevens on psychophysical scaling, it has been responsible for recent intense interest in psychophysics. The discovery that human observers behave in ways closely paralleling statistical decision theory when detecting signals immersed in noisy back-grounds is not evidence that observer thresholds do not exist, however. Experimental data clearly indicate that when observers are placed in a situation in which there is an N distribution and an SN distribution they behave as if they are testing a statistical hypothesis. When they are presented with a sensory observation, they try to decide from which distribution it came. An observer will tend to choose one distribution over the other depending on such circumstances as costs and values of decision outcomes and signal probability. Behavior in such noisy situations does not appear to be governed by an all-or-none threshold: instead, decisions appear to be determined by the location of the adjustable decision criterion.

But what can we say of the observer's behavior in situations where noise is absent or greatly reduced? S. S. Stevens (1961b) suggested that TSD applies to noisy situations where the threshold is obscured. He claimed that when noise is absent, the all-or-none step function of the threshold will emerge. Accordingly, Stevens (1961b) suggested that

> We should continue to explore the fertile and heuristic domain of detection theory (because signals often do in fact occur in noise), and we should study methods for reducing the noise in our experiments on differential sensitivity in order to see how the nervous system operates on pure signals, unobscured by noise. A complete suppression of noise may not be possible, of course, but a sufficient reduction may be achieved to allow a quantal step function to manifest itself in the action of the sensory system. (p. 808)

Stevens compared this basic problem in psychophysics to the problem of the nature of electricity:

> When, after years of effort, R. A. Millikan finally succeeded in suppressing enough sources of noise in his oil drop experiment, he was able to show that the charge on the electron is not normally distributed as some evidence had suggested, but has a fixed, all-or-none value. (p. 808)

We have seen that a theory of a high threshold near the upper end of the N distribution is not consistent with experimental data. We have also seen that there are no experiments which prove definitively that thresh-olds do not exist at some point relatively low in the N distribution. Furthermore, there are no clear-cut data that disprove the neural quantum theory of the difference threshold. Perhaps further experimentation will reveal that some combination of the postulates of TSD and low threshold theory will best account for the facts of signal detection behavior. Or perhaps the prediction by Urban (1930) of a new psychophysics without the threshold concept as its cornerstone will be confirmed.

The finding in recent years, and one supporting Urban's point of view, is that almost all sensory neurons exhibit spontaneous activity in the form of neural responses in the absence of stimulation. For example, single fibers of the optic nerve, auditory nerve, and many cutaneous nerve fibers show substantial amounts of neural activity in the form of fairly high firing rates of action potentials when no stimulus is present. The pervasiveness of such noise in the nervous system suggests that, in nearly all situations, observers must judge the presence or absence of signals against an ever-present background of neural noise. Because action potentials are fundamentally the same whether they are generated spontaneously or through presentation of an external stimulus, the observer, in the detection task, when making an observation of neural activity is provided with no clue as to its origin. In such situations where, at any point in time, a sample of neural activity may be stimulus generated or spontaneous, the observer's performance is most rationally governed by the decision rule to report a signal only when the sensory observation is above some criterion level and to report its absence when the observation is below that level.

Because the noise may exceed the criterion on some occasions and on others the signal added to the noise may fall below the criterion, the observer's responses are not perfectly correlated with the cause of the sensory observation. Instead, the observer's behavior is governed by the magnitude of the sensory observation resulting from a sample of neural activity that varies along a single underlying continuum. Thus, the observer's responses fail to differentiate between different internal states. Reporting "yes" may represent the correct detection of the signal or it may represent a false alarm. Reporting "no" may represent the correct rejection of the signal and therefore the correct identification of noise or it may, alternatively, represent a miss of the signal.

In threshold theory, on the other hand, "yes" and "no" responses are purported to differentiate between suprathreshold and subthreshold states of the observer's nervous system. For example, in the high threshold theory discussed in chapter 4, the observer is assumed to always report the signal when it is above threshold and to report the signal when it is below threshold only when guessing. According to the model, experimental measurement of subthreshold and suprathreshold states can be specified as a threshold value, after correcting the observer's responses for guessing. Because threshold theories and their associated methodologies promise to provide a means of accessing internal states from observations of overt behavior they have historically had great appeal (Macmillan & Creelman, 1991). According to TSD, however, there are no subthreshold and suprathreshold states, but instead sensory observations, whether caused by an external signal or by internal noise, that exist on a single continuum. Although such a single state model may lack the appeal of threshold models that hold out the promise of providing techniques to measure different internal states of the observer, TSD has been found consistently to account for the results of detection experiments with no reference to internal thresholds within the observer.

Because the single state model of TSD is parsimonious and accounts well for most of the data of a wide variety of detection situations ranging from detection of sensory stimulation in vision, hearing, pain, touch, and so on, to tumor detection in medical diagnosis, it has, in recent years, been widely accepted over multistate threshold models. It should be pointed out that although this may be the present state of affairs within the field of psychophysics, future research may reveal some conditions under which the threshold concept is applicable. However, given the omnipresent existence of internally generated noise in the nervous system, it would seem that to follow Stevens' recommendation to reduce external noise by carefully controlling and measuring the stimulus, although well taken as advice on how to properly conduct psychophysical experiments, will never reveal that observer thresholds widely exist.

9

The Measurement of Sensory Attributes and Discrimination Scales

Most of the early work in psychophysics was concerned with the problem of measuring absolute and differential sensitivity for the various sense modalities under a variety of stimulus conditions. Little attempt was made to measure directly such sensory attributes as loudness, brightness, pain, warmth, pressure, pitch, hue, and perceived duration.

Although the investigation of sensitivity by measuring absolute and difference thresholds provides valuable information about the senses, it does not in itself give a complete picture of a sensory system. If the input to a sensory system is the physical stimulus and the output is sensation, then all measurements in classical psychophysics were made on the input side of the system. Absolute and difference thresholds are not stated in sensation units but in units of stimulus energy at points where output can just be detected or where changes in outputs are just discriminable. An analogous situation is an engineer testing the sensitivity of a photo cell or sound level meter where certain changes in the output of the device are measured as a function of input changes. The absolute sensitivity of the device might be measured by determining the smallest amount of energy that will yield a meter reading. Differential sensitivity could be measured by determining the smallest changes in energy required to change the meter reading. Such measurements on the electronic device are useful, but obviously incomplete until the output of the device has also been measured and related to the input. If the device were a photo cell, we would complete the set of measurements by determining the output in voltage or current as a function of energy input.

Psychophysical scaling of sensory attributes is a necessary part of sensory psychology because sensation changes do not usually stand in a one-to-one relationship with changes in the stimulus. The exact relationships between sensations and stimuli must therefore be determined experimentally. If the intensity of a sound is doubled, its loudness is increased by a barely perceptible amount. To discover how loudness increases with stimulus intensity, we must be able to measure both stimulus intensity and psychological loudness. Techniques of physics are employed to measure the energy in the stimulus, and psychophysical procedures have been refined in the past 40 years for measuring such sensory attributes as loudness, pitch, brightness, hue, pain, touch, warmth, cold, taste, and smell. Through the use of these procedures, numbers can be assigned to sensation magnitudes. A psychophysical relationship called a *psychophysical magnitude function* is established when the magnitude of a sensory attribute is plotted against corresponding physical values of the stimulus.

The form of the psychophysical magnitude function for a particular sense modality and a particular set of stimulus conditions may tell us something about the transmission of information through the sensory nervous system. For example, if we know how observers' judgments of the intensity of their sensations change as stimulus intensity changes, we may be able to make inferences about how receptor mechanisms transduce stimulus energy into neural impulses, how neural impulses code information about properties of the stimulus, and how judgmental processes in the central nervous system work. Besides their usefulness in understanding the operation of sensory systems, psychophysical magnitude functions have also been used for practical purposes. Knowing that to double loudness requires sound energy to be increased by about ten times, rather than by two, has been extremely useful to designers of auditory communications systems. With this sort of information, various signals can be specified in terms of their psychological loudness as well as in terms of their physical intensity. Psychological magnitude functions have also been useful in solving problems in illumination engineering, the measurement of clinical pain, and the quantification of taste and smell in the food industry.

Psychophysical magnitude functions can be determined only when both the stimulus and the sensory response to the stimulus can be measured. As early as 1860, Fechner recognized this problem. His proposal that sensation magnitude increases with the logarithm of stimulus intensity implies measurement of both stimulus and response terms. Fechner believed that sensations could not be directly measured. He derived measures of sensory magnitude from measurements of difference thresholds. Because all jnd's are minimal increments in sensation necessary for discrimination, Fechner assumed that they must be psychologically equal. Having established the jnd as a unit of sensory magnitude, it was logical for Fechner to propose that sensation magnitude could be measured by counting the number of jnd's that a stimulus is above absolute threshold. The psychophysical magnitude function is the number of jnd's above absolute threshold as a function of stimulus intensity.

When it is not possible to measure and to control the physical characteristics of the stimulus, psychophysical magnitude functions cannot be obtained. Nevertheless, many of the psychophysical scaling methods have been used to measure psychological responses to stimuli so complex that it is impossible to specify their relevant physical properties. Notable in this regard was the work of L. L. Thurstone, who was the first psychologist to develop methods of measuring sensory experience where properties of physical stimuli cannot be specified. Like Fechner, Thurstone also proposed that sensation could be measured only indirectly through measurement of stimulus discrimination. In 1927, he proposed the *law of comparative judgment* as a mathematical model for the analysis of paired comparison judgments. From the proportion of times one stimulus is judged to be greater than another stimulus with respect to some attribute, the psychological scale values for the two stimuli can be calculated. Stimuli that are frequently confused with one another are thus assumed to be psychologically similar, and stimuli that are infrequently confused are assumed to be psychologically different. Thurstone's method has been used to quantify numerous psychological qualities, such as the experience of esthetic worth produced by works of art, for which there are no specifiable stimulus properties. His work was a major advance because it was the first attempt to extend the boundaries of psychophysics beyond the investigation of sensory systems. Much of this work is discussed in Thurstone's book, *The Measurement of Values* (1959).

The distinction has been made between *indirect scaling* and *direct scaling* of sensory magnitude. The attempts of Fechner and Thurstone to measure sensation through measurement of discrimination represent indirect scaling: The measurements are derived from data on how well observers can tell one stimulus from another, rather than from their direct judgments of the sensation magnitudes. Experiments using direct scaling convert observers' judgments of their sensations directly into measurements of sensory magnitude. If an observer must tell how much brighter one light is than another, he judges the sensory magnitude of the two lights. Furthermore, his responses directly provide the experimenter with a measurement of the two brightnesses. If, for example, the observer reported that light *A* was three times as bright as light *B*, measurement might be achieved by assigning a number to the brightness of light *A* that is three times as large as the number assigned to the brightness of light *B*. An important assumption is made that the observer can follow the instructions of the experiment and make the required quantitative judgments. If the observer is successful, the psychological scale follows directly from the observer's judgments. Although there are many techniques for direct scaling of sensory magnitude, the direct *ratio scaling* methods have been most useful in facilitating our understanding of sensation. Although ratio scaling was introduced as early as 1888 when Merkel asked observers to adjust a stimulus to produce a sensation twice as great as that of another stimulus, it was not until the early 1950s that investigators began to refine these techniques. It was the persistent efforts of S. S. Stevens and his fellow workers over a period of more than 20 years that resulted in dozens of ratio scales for sensory magnitude. These scales include psychophysical magnitude functions for brightness, loudness, cutaneous sensations, taste, and smell. Stevens' solution to the problem of direct ratio scaling of sensation was simply to present stimuli to observers and ask them to assign numbers to them which seemed to correspond to their sensations. The use of this method, now known as *magnitude estimation*, resulted in Stevens' proposal of a new law to replace Fechner's logarithmic law. Stevens' power law is based upon the finding that magnitude estimations for a variety of sensory dimensions increase in proportion to the stimulus intensity raised to a power. The size of the power exponent to which stimulus intensity is raised in order to predict magnitude estimations changes depending on sensory modality and stimulus conditions. The power law has become one of the best established empirical relations in psychology.

Chapter 9 consists of a general description of the various indirect and direct psychophysical scaling procedures followed by a more specific description of scales based on the observer's ability to discriminate among stimuli. In each case, the object is to obtain numerical measures of sensory magnitude. In that psychophysical scaling is a part of the more general problem of measurement in science, measurement theory becomes important in evaluating the various scaling procedures. Thus, a brief discussion of measurement theory precedes the description of psychophysical scaling methods.

MEASUREMENT SCALES

The concept of measurement is basic to an understanding of the various methods devised to quantify sensory attributes. Measurement is the assigning of numbers by rules to represent properties of objects or events. The numbers, as symbols of properties in the world of objects and events, can be manipulated in accordance with the rules of mathematics. If the properties of the number system reflect the properties of objects or events, new information about the measured properties may be revealed from such symbolic manipulations.

It is often the case that, for a particular measurement scale, the properties of the number system only partially reflect the properties of objects or events. In these cases, the operations that can be performed legitimately on the numbers and the conclusions that can be drawn about differences among these numbers are restricted, and define four basic types of measurement scales: *nominal, ordinal, interval*, and *ratio*. These scales represent different degrees of correspondence between the number system and the property systems of objects or events. The essential properties of the number system to be considered when determining which of these types of measurement scale is in use are *identity, order, interval*, and *origin*.

Each symbol in the number system is different and therefore has a unique identity. Like any set of symbols, the number system can be used for classification or identification purposes. Thus, different numbers are assigned to different players on an athletic team. The numbers do not imply anything about the degree of any properties the players may possess, but are simply labels to allow us to identify individuals. Such nominal scales do not use numbers quantitatively and, therefore, cannot provide a means of measurement.

In the number system, the numbers are arranged in an ordered sequence so that different numbers have a greater-than–less-than relation between them. An *ordinal scale* is a set of measurements in which the amount of a property of objects or events can be ranked. The rank number represents the scale value for each measurement. Some property of athletic performance is measured on an ordinal scale when first, second, third, fourth, and fifth place are awarded to contestants. Only the property of order in the number system can be applied to ordinal scale measurements. Two numbers, one being larger than the other, *only* signify greater than–less than relations between measured properties. It is obvious that, on the basis of rankings alone, we cannot conclude that the difference in performance between Rank 1 and Rank 2 is necessarily the same as the difference in performance between Rank 3 and Rank 4 (interval); nor that Rank 4 represents twice as proficient a performance as Rank 2 (origin).

Intervals between numbers are ordered in the number system. The difference between any pair of numbers is greater than, equal to, or less than the difference between any other pair of numbers. If an *interval scale* has been achieved, the intervals between the scale values represent differences or distances between amounts of the property measured. The temperature scale is often cited as an instance of an interval scale because the difference between two scale values can be meaningfully compared with the difference between two other scale values. For example, the difference between 40° and 60° is equal to the difference between 70° and 90° as measured physically by a thermometer. This 20° difference in temperature is twice as large as the 10° difference between 100° and 110°, but half as large as the 40° difference between 90° and 130°. Thus, in an interval scale, the size of the differences between numbers, as well as their ordinal relation, has meaning.

The number system has an origin represented by "zero." A particular number can be said to be so many times greater than or less than another number with respect to zero. In the number system, 10 is twice 5 and half of 20. A *ratio scale*, as well as having the properties of order and distance, has a natural origin to represent zero amount of a property. In these scales, the ratios of the scale values have meaning. For example, a 50-lb ball and a 25-lb ball stand in a 2-to-1 ratio on the property of weight. This kind of statement cannot be made about scale values on an interval scale, where the zero point is arbitrary and does not represent zero amount of the property. Zero degrees on the centigrade or Fahrenheit temperature scales do not represent zero amounts of heat, and thus 100° cannot be said to be twice the temperature of 50°. The Kelvin scale of temperature, however, is a ratio scale, since zero degrees Kelvin represents absolute zero where no heat exists. Ratio scales are highly desirable achievements because they have all three basic properties of the number system and therefore afford greatest opportunity to use the number system as a model of the measured property. It is for these reasons that many of the psychological scaling techniques were designed to construct ratio scales of sensory attributes.

The concept of *invariance* is based on the distinction among nominal, ordinal, interval, and ratio scales. The numbers used in a specific situation are a limited set of numbers drawn from an infinitely large set of numbers. The numbers may be altered in certain ways without changing their significance. If the numbers are changed, and their significance remains the same, the transformation is said to leave the scale *invariant*. S. S. Stevens (1951) has classified measurement scales in terms of the nature of the numerical transformations that can be performed upon scale values while leaving the structure of the scale undistorted. The more precise the type of measurement scale (nominal scales being the least and ratio scales the most precise), the more restricted are the transformations that can be applied to a scale, while leaving it invariant.

In a nominal scale, the numbers are merely symbols for distinguishing one thing from another. A nominal scale remains intact when any number is substituted for any other number. As long as the transformation is public, no meaning is lost when two athletes exchange numbers. The only property of the number system that is relevant in this case is that each symbol in the number system has a separate identity that can be used to signify different objects or events. Since amounts in a nominal scale are not considered, the size of the number is not important. The scale is invariant to any transformation as long as no two things are assigned the same number.

The construction of an ordinal scale requires the application of the rule that numbers must be arranged so that their rank order corresponds to the rank order of the property being measured. This rule permits much freedom in the selection of specific numbers as scale values. In an ordinal scale, the only properties of the number system that are important are the identity and the order of the numbers. The differences and ratios among numbers are irrelevant. Thus, an ordinal scale is invariant to any transformation that preserves the rank order of the scale values. These transformations are called monotonic transformations and are illustrated in Fig. 9.1. The essential feature of these transformations is that, because the function does not change direction, the rank order of transformed values is the same as the rank order of the original scale values.

Interval scale measurement requires numbers to be assigned to properties in such a way that the differences among numbers reflect the differences among properties in the real world. In an interval scale, the relative difference among scale values is unaffected by any linear transformation of the form $X' = aX + b$, where X is the original scale value and X' is the transformed scale value (Figure 9.1). In other words, a measurement, which has yielded a set of scale values X, can be converted to a new scale X' by multiplying each X value by the constant a and adding the constant b. The transformed results retain the same meaning as the original scale values. The value of the multiplier constant a determines the arbitrary size of the scale unit, and the value of the additive constant b determines the arbitrary location of the zero point on the scale. An example of such a transformation is the conversion of temperature from the centigrade to the Fahrenheit scale by the equation $F = 32 + 1.8C$. When properties are measured on an interval scale, any nonlinear transformation will violate the structure of the scale by destroying the correspondence of the differences among scale values and the differences among proper-

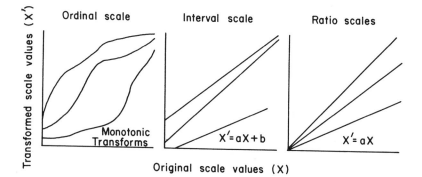

FIG. 9.1. Examples of transformations of scale values that leave the scale invariant.

ties in the real world. The critical property of an interval scale is that the ratios of differences are invariant across permissible transformations. If a ratio scale has been achieved, the nature of the invariance transformation is restricted to linear transformations of the form $X' = aX$ (Figure 9.1). The origin is fixed at absolute zero; therefore, unlike interval scales, a constant cannot be added to scale values. However, the size of the unit of a ratio scale is arbitrary, and scale values may therefore be multiplied by a constant. For example, one can convert the unit of length from feet to inches by applying the transformation, inches = feet × 12. Only transformations of this form leave invariant the ratios between scale values, and therefore, they are the only permissible transformations of ratio scales. The critical property of a ratio scale is that the ratios of scale values are invariant across permissible transformations.

A summary of the characteristics of nominal, ordinal, interval, and ratio scales is found in Table 9.1. It is important for an investigator to know the type of scale his measurements constitute. Without such knowledge, serious errors are likely to arise from the use of inappropriate statistical analysis and other inappropriate calculations performed on the numbers. Incorrect conclusions are often made from an experiment in which the scale of measurement is not as high on the hierarchy as the investigator had assumed. In psychophysics, the various scaling methods were devised to obtain quantitative data on an observer's responses to stimuli. In most cases, attempts have been made to construct either interval or ratio scales of sensation from such data. The procedures used

TABLE 9.1
Four Scales of Measurement[a]

Scale	Operations performed	Permissible transformations	Some appropriate statistics
Nominal	Identify and classify	Substitution of any number for any other number	Number of cases Mode Contingency correlation
Ordinal	Rank order	Any change that preserves order	Median Percentiles Rank-order correlation
Interval	Find distances or differences	Multiplication by a constant Addition of a constant	Mean Standard deviation Product–moment correlation
Ratio	Find ratios, fractions, or multiples	Multiplication by a constant	Geometric mean Percent variability

[a]After S. S. Stevens (1975). (Reprinted from S. S. Stevens, *Psychophysics: Introduction to Its Perceptual, Neural and Social Prospects.* Copyright © 1975 by John Wiley & Sons, Inc. Reprinted by permission of John Wiley & Sons, Inc.)

to scale sensation should be critically evaluated in relation to the type of measurement scale that is claimed.

PSYCHOPHYSICAL SCALES

The methods of constructing and validating scales of sensory attributes must be considered before dealing with the use of such scales in psychological measurement problems. The loudness scale, for example, has been used to specify the subjective loudness of sounds in a variety of experimental and practical situations, but it is important to begin with a discussion of how such scales are developed.

According to S. S. Stevens (1960), the methods for constructing psychological scales can be classified into three types: confusion scaling, partition scaling, and ratio scaling. Each is designed to generate a numerical scale of sensory magnitude, although each requires a different kind of perceptual response from the observer. *Confusion scaling* requires an observer to make discriminative responses between stimuli that are slightly different physically. Confusion scales of sensation are based on indirect scaling procedures in which sensory magnitudes of stimuli are inferred from measures of stimulus discriminability. The observer's task is to report whether the sensation produced by one stimulus is greater than or less than the sensation produced by another stimulus. Discriminability is taken as the measure of how different one sensation magnitude is from another. Successful confusion scaling results in an interval measurement scale, since discrimination data indicate the differences but not the ratios among sensation magnitudes. In more recent times these scales have come to be called *discrimination scales*. Fechner was the first to employ a form of this method in his construction of a psychological scale from difference thresholds. Thurstone later proposed a method for constructing a scale from data obtained by paired comparison procedures where each stimulus is compared with all other stimuli. *Partition scales* are obtained by direct scaling procedures in which the observer must make direct judgments of the psychological differences among stimuli. The resulting scales are interval scales because they measure the differences among sensations. The observer must attend to several stimuli along the physical continuum and partition them into a limited number of categories. Instructions are given to perform this task so that the categories are separated by psychologically equal intervals. For example, before the development of photometry, astronomers judged the apparent brightness of stars on a scale from 1 to 6; 1 stood for the brightest star and 6 for the dimmest. Judgments were made so that the psychological difference between category 1 and category 2 was the same as the distance between category 2 and category 3 and the same as the distance between all other successive pairs of categories. *Ratio scaling* of sensations relies on the ability of the observer to make direct judgments of the ratio relationships between the magnitudes of sensations. The observer might be required to tell when two loudnesses stand in a 2-to-1 ratio. If the observer is able to perform this task, we have a basis for measuring sensations on a ratio scale. Since the observer has indicated that one loudness is twice as great as another, we may assign to the sensations any pair of numbers that stand in a ratio of 2 to 1. The actual units, whether 2 and 1, 4 and 2, 20 and 10, or 2000 and 1000, are arbitrary, as they are in physical measurement. Length, weight, and sensory magnitude, if they are measured on ratio scales, can be specified in units of any size, as long as the ratios between scale values are maintained as the size of the unit is changed.

Discrimination Scales

Discrimination scaling methods are designed to construct interval scales of psychological attributes indirectly from the discrimination responses of the observer. They are based upon the principle that the difference between the psychological magnitudes of two stimuli increases as a function of the observer's ability to discriminate between them.

DL Scales

Fechner's law ($\psi = k \log \phi$) requires the assumption that DL's are equal increments in sensation magnitude at all levels of stimulus intensity. This assumption, combined with the assumption of the correctness of Weber's statement that the size of the DL in physical units is proportional to stimulus intensity, permitted the mathematical derivation of Fechner's law. As pointed out previously, the Weber fraction is not constant over the entire range of stimulus intensities. The interesting possibility remains, however, that a valid psychophysical scale might still be established from DL's if the size of the DL as a function of stimulus intensity is obtained experimentally rather than by calculation from Weber's law. If the assumption is made that DL's are equal sensation magnitude increments, a scale can be derived by adding up DL's along the stimulus dimension (Falmagne, 1971, 1974, 1985; Luce & Galanter, 1963).

Any one of the psychophysical methods outlined in chapter 2 can be used to determine the DL for each of several values along the stimulus dimension. The results of such an experiment are plotted on a graph such as Figure 9.2, and a smooth curve is fitted to the data points. The absolute

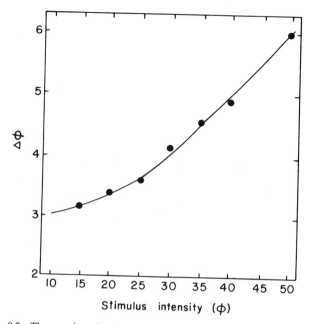

FIG. 9.2. The results of a hypothetical experiment in which Δφ was determined for seven values of stimulus intensity. The curve is extrapolated down to an absolute threshold of 10 units.

threshold in stimulus units is 10, and the size of the first DL above threshold obtained from Figure 9.2 is 3. This value is added to the value of the absolute threshold (10 + 3 = 13) to obtain the stimulus value one jnd above absolute threshold. The stimulus at absolute threshold is considered as the zero point on the scale of sensation, and the stimulus intensity of 13, being one jnd above this zero point, is regarded as capable of producing a sensation magnitude of one unit. The stimulus value producing a sensation magnitude of two units is obtained by discovering the stimulus that is two jnd's above absolute threshold. From Figure 9.2, it is determined that 3.1 is the size of the DL for a stimulus intensity of 13. The DL value of 3.1 is added to 13 to yield a stimulus intensity of 16.1, which represents a stimulus value two jnd's above absolute threshold. The results of this calculation procedure are summarized in Figure 9.3 for the first six jnd's. Starting at the absolute threshold value of 10, the stimulus intensity of each successive stimulus increases by a value equal to Δφ. These values of φ, equal to 10, 13, 16.1, 19.3, 22.6, 26.1, and 29.9 correspond to 0, 1, 2, 3, 4, 5, and 6 jnd's above absolute threshold, respectively. This procedure of successively summating jnd's and relating them to corresponding stimulus values results in a psychophysical function such as that shown in Figure 9.4.

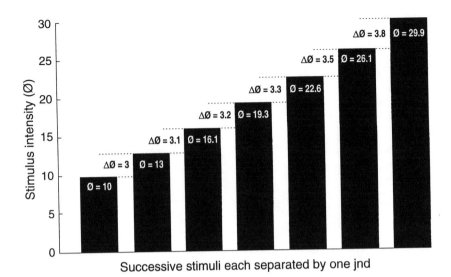

FIG. 9.3. Illustration of a series of stimulus intensities in which successive stimuli are separated by one jnd.

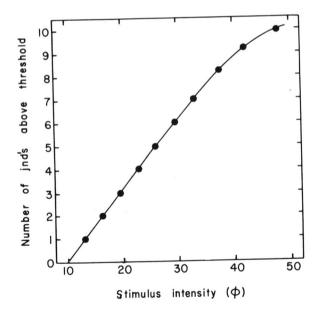

FIG. 9.4. A psychophysical scale produced by summation of jnd's above absolute threshold. The scale is derived from the Δφ function of Figure 9.2.

An example of a DL scale is the *dol scale* for the perception of pain determined by Hardy, Wolff, and Goodell (1947). Pain was produced by focusing radiant heat from a powerful lamp on the forehead of the observer for a time period of 3 sec. The absolute threshold was determined by increasing the intensity of radiation until a stimulus presentation resulted in a feeling of warmth followed by a sharp pain just before the end of the 3-sec exposure. The time between trials was long enough to allow for the dissipation of heat from the skin. The absolute threshold was 220 mcal (millicalories)/sec/cm², and the most intense stimulus that could be tolerated without damage to the observer was 480 mcal/sec/cm². Between these two values were found 21 jnd's for detecting increments in the sensory magnitude of pain. The dol scale for pain illustrated in Figure 9.5 is based on the cumulative number of pain jnd's as a function of stimulus intensity. The *dol* is the unit of measurement for pain, and one dol is equal to two jnd's.

DL scales have been extremely useful to researchers who find it convenient to specify differences among stimuli in terms of the number of discriminable steps rather than in physical units. Often, measures of response (e.g., those obtained in some conditioning situations or in reaction-time experiments) have been found to be meaningfully related to properties of the stimulus only when these properties are expressed in terms of number of jnd's. Even if these scales were proven to be invalid as measurements of sensation magnitude, they do appear to measure accurately the important property of the number of discriminable steps between stimuli.

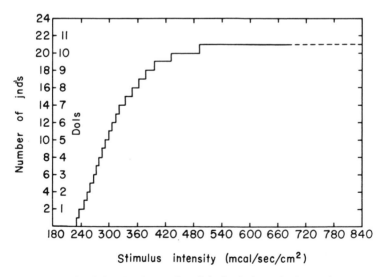

FIG. 9.5. The dol scale of pain. One dol of pain intensity is equal to two successive jnd's. (From Hardy, Wolff, & Goodell, 1947.)

The DL and the Slope of the Sensation Magnitude Function

If one makes the assumption, as did Fechner and others who have constructed DL scales, that all jnd's represent equal changes in sensation magnitude, then it follows that the size of the DL must be inversely related to the slope of the sensation magnitude function. This concept is illustrated in Figure 9.6 where sensation magnitude, as determined by counting the number of jnd's above absolute threshold, is plotted as a function of stimulus intensity. Each increment in sensation magnitude is constant because jnd's are assumed to be constant changes in sensation magnitude that correspond to DL's. It can be seen by comparing the upper and lower graphs of Figure 9.6 that the sensation magnitude function with the steeper slope is associated with smaller DL's. For example, the size of the fourth DL above absolute threshold was 17.0 when the slope was shallow and only 7.0 when it was steep. Experimental results fail to confirm the Fechnerian hypothesis that the size of the DL is inversely related to the rate of growth of sensation magnitude.

Hellman, Scharf, Teghtsoonian, and Teghtsoonian (1987), for example, measured DL's for discriminating changes in the intensity of 1000-Hz tones

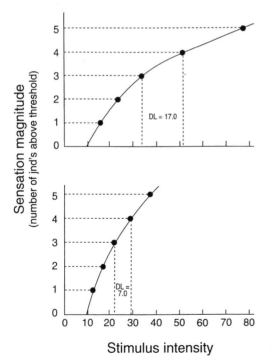

FIG. 9.6. Hypothetical sensation magnitude functions with different slopes and their possible relation to the size of the DL according to the Fechnerian idea that all jnd's represent equal changes in sensation magnitude.

presented against a background of narrow-band and wide-band noise and found them to be unrelated to the slopes of the loudness functions. They measured the rate of growth of loudness using a loudness-matching procedure. The observer adjusted the intensity of a 1000-Hz tone presented in the quiet and a 1000-Hz tone presented in noise so that they sounded equally loud. This procedure was used for a wide range of sound intensities. The results for wide-band and narrow-band noise are presented in Figure 9.7. Although the rate of growth of loudness, measured by the loudness-matching procedure was greater when tones were heard in a background of narrow-band than in a background of wide-band noise, the size of the DL was the same at the point where the two loudness level functions crossed (see figure insert). At this point on the loudness level function, the slopes are different yet the tone presented in narrow-band noise and the tone presented in wide-band noise had the same intensity and also the same perceived loudness. These results support the hypothesis that the size of the DL is independent of the slope of the sensation magnitude function. This hypothesis, one that clearly contradicts the Fechnerian assumption that all jnd's are subjectively equal, was first proposed by Zwislocki and

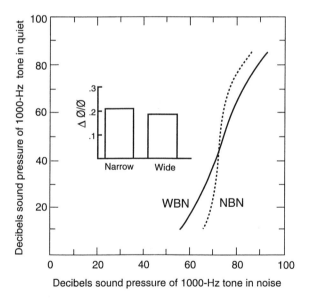

FIG. 9.7. Growth of loudness of a 1000-Hz tone presented against a background of narrow-band or wide-band noise. At the point where the two curves cross, the intensities and loudnesses of the tones presented with narrow-band and wide-band noise were the same as were the measured DL's, yet the slopes of the sensation magnitude functions differed. (From Hellman, Scharf, Teghtsoonian, & Teghtsoonian, 1987.)

Jordan (1986). The hypothesis arose out of the observation that the size of the DL for stimuli presented to an ear with cochlear impairment, where the growth of loudness with intensity is abnormally rapid, is the same as the DL for stimuli of equal perceived loudness presented to the normal ear of the patient. The principle that the size of the intensity DL is independent of the slope of the sensation magnitude function has been found to generalize across sensory modalities. For example, it has been found that although the slopes of vibrotactile sensation magnitude functions are greatly affected by the presence of background masking stimulation, the intensity DL, at any particular level of sensation magnitude, is not (Gescheider, Bolanowski, Zwislocki, Hall, & Mascia, 1994).

Paired Comparison Scales

Fechner conceived the idea that a psychophysical experiment could be conducted in which an observer makes judgments on a psychological dimension having no obvious physical correlate. In his book on the experimental study of esthetics (1876), he suggested that the pleasantness of two objects could be studied by having observers choose the object which was more pleasant. The first experimental study in which this method was employed was an investigation of color preferences by Cohn (1894). A theoretical analysis of the data provided by the method came in 1927, when Thurstone published his paper on the law of comparative judgment as applied to paired comparison judgments.

As in the measurement of DL's, the observer's task in the method of paired comparison is to discriminate between two stimuli, but the logic of scale construction for the method of paired comparison is considerably more elaborate. Both techniques of psychological scaling, however, are based on the notion that the proportion of times stimulus A will be judged greater than stimulus B is determined by the degree to which sensation A and sensation B differ. Having assumed this link between judgments of stimuli and their concurrent sensations, Fechner further assumed that the DL's along a given psychological continuum represent equal changes in sensation; this statistical assumption was justified by the fact that each DL was derived from a standard result—a 75% frequency of the judgment that two stimuli were different. In psychological scaling by the method of paired comparison, the use of p values is not restricted to .75.

If, in a large number of comparative judgments, the proportion of times an observer judges stimulus B greater than stimulus A is only .55, then the average sensation magnitudes elicited by the two stimuli must be only slightly different with respect to the attribute under study. If, however, the proportion of times stimulus C is judged greater than stimulus A is .95, one can safely assume that the presentation of stimulus C results in a considerably greater average perceptual response than the presentation of stimulus *A*. Thus, if the average sensation magnitudes produced by two stimuli differ by only a small amount, judgments of the stimuli will be confused, and the value of *p* will be close to .50. But, if the average sensation magnitudes are very different, the confusion is much less, and the value of *p* approaches 1.00. That this idea might serve as a basis for scaling psychological attributes was recognized by Thorndike (1910), who was interested in developing a scale of excellence of handwriting. Thorndike thought it reasonable to transform the *p* value associated with comparing two handwriting samples to a *z* score. The *z* score was considered as the number of psychological scale units separating the perceptual judgments of excellence elicited by the two stimuli.

The reason for using *z* scores rather than *p* values as psychological scale units is clarified by examining the work of Thurstone (1927). He developed fully this method of scaling by providing us with a mathematical model for deriving scale values from comparative judgment proportions. In Thurstone's terms, the application of a stimulus to the organism's sensory receptors results in a *discriminal process* (sensory process) which has some value on the *psychological continuum*. Because of momentary fluctuations of the organism, repeated applications of the same stimulus to sense receptors does not usually result in exactly the same sensation. Thus, for Thurstone, a stimulus was capable of producing a range of discriminal processes along the psychological continuum. It was assumed that such variation formed a normal distribution on the psychological continuum, the standard deviation of which was called the *discriminal dispersion*. The psychological scale value of the discriminal process associated with the stimulus was taken as the mean on the frequency distribution.

But how can one obtain this distribution on the psychological continuum so that the average discriminal process (i.e., the scale value of the discriminal process) can be found for a certain stimulus? Thurstone felt that the value of the discriminal process could not be directly reported by the observer but had to be obtained indirectly by consideration of the *p* values associated with the observer's comparative judgment of pairs of stimuli. For example, if it is known that stimulus *A* and stimulus *B* produce pairs of discriminal process distributions with means separated by a certain amount on the psychological continuum (Figure 9.8), the observer would be expected to judge stimulus *B* as greater than stimulus *A* some specific proportion of the time. Therefore, in a particular scaling problem, the *p* value is obtained from comparative judgments of stimulus *A* and stimulus *B*; by then working through the equations of the theory, the separation of the means of the discriminal process distributions on the psychological continuum can be calculated.

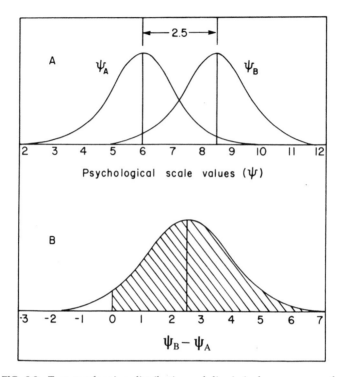

FIG. 9.8. Two overlapping distributions of discriminal processes on the psychological continuum resulting from the repeated presentation of two different stimuli (A) and the resulting distribution of differences between two discriminal processes produced by repeated presentation of the two stimuli (B).

Thurstone's logic of psychological scale construction based on discrimination data is somewhat similar to the way TSD has been applied to detection data. In both cases, theoretical probability distributions on a psychological continuum are inferred from judgmental response proportions. The differences between the means of the distributions, expressed in standard deviation units, are used to quantify mental processes in both cases. In TSD, the difference between the means of the N and SN distributions specifies stimulus detectability (d'), and in Thurstone's model, the difference between the means of two distributions of discriminal processes specifies the difference on the psychological continuum between the sensations for two stimuli. In the language of TSD, the problems of TSD are with N and SN distributions, while those of Thurstone's model are with several SN distributions.

The symbol ψ will be used to signify the discriminal process (sensory magnitude) elicited by a particular stimulus. The size of ψ, of course, must be measured in psychological units. The scaling problem is to discover the average ψ values corresponding to a number of values of the physical stimulus. Suppose that S_A and S_B are stimuli for overlapping normal distributions of ψ_A and ψ_B on the psychological continuum and that an average ψ_A value of 6.0 and an average ψ_B value of 8.5 have been determined by Thurstone's method (Figure 9.8). For the purpose of understanding Thurstone's model, let us examine how the proportion of times S_B would be judged greater than S_A could be predicted from these average psychological scale values for ψ_B and ψ_A. Thurstone's model assumes that, when S_A and S_B are presented together for comparison, the one resulting in the greater ψ value will be reported as the greater stimulus. The size of the difference between the two discriminal processes for a single presentation of S_A and S_B, $\psi_B - \psi_A$, is called a *discriminal difference*. When a large number of trials is given, there will be variation of both ψ_A and ψ_B; consequently, the discriminal difference will vary from trial to trial. Variation of the discriminal difference can be represented as a normal distribution on the psychological continuum (Figure 9.8). On trials when $\psi_B - \psi_A$ is greater than zero, S_B will be judged greater than S_A, and on trials when $\psi_B - \psi_A$ is less than zero, S_A will be judged greater than S_B. The mean of this distribution of differences will correspond to the difference between the means of the ψ_A and ψ_B distributions. This correspondence occurs because the difference between the means of two distributions is equal to the mean of a set of differences between pairs of scores that are selected randomly, one from each distribution.

The formula for computing the standard deviation of differences between pairs of numbers is applied to this problem to determine the standard deviation of the $\psi_B - \psi_A$ values:

$$\sigma_{\psi_B - \psi_A} = \sqrt{\sigma_{\psi_A}^2 + \sigma_{\psi_B}^2 - 2r_{\psi_A \psi_B} \sigma_{\psi_A} \sigma_{\psi_B}} , \qquad (9.1)$$

where σ_{ψ_A} and σ_{ψ_B} are the standard deviations of the distributions of ψ_A and ψ_B, respectively, and $r_{\psi_A \psi_B}$ is the correlation between momentary pairs of ψ_A and ψ_B values. The value of $r_{\psi_A \psi_B}$ indicates the extent to which a sample from the ψ_B distribution and a sample from the ψ_A distribution tend to be interdependent. If, in sampling a pair of ψ_B and ψ_A values from their distributions, it is possible to predict ψ_B from ψ_A, or ψ_A from ψ_B, then the value of $r_{\psi_A \psi_B}$ would be high.

In Figure 9.8B the shaded area to the right of the zero point corresponds to the proportion of times that ψ_B is greater than ψ_A. This zero point can now be converted to a z score by the standard z-score formula:

$$z = \frac{X - M}{\sigma} , \qquad (9.2)$$

where X is a particular score, M is the mean of the set of scores, and σ is the standard deviation of the set of scores. In this problem, $0 - 2.5$ must be divided by $\sigma_{\psi_B - \psi_A}$:

$$z_{BA} = \frac{0 - M_{\psi_B - \psi_A}}{\sigma_{\psi_B - \psi_A}}. \tag{9.3}$$

Using a conversion table relating z values to p values, this z score could be converted directly to the proportion of times ψ_B should exceed ψ_A.

The easiest way to obtain $\sigma_{\psi_B - \psi_A}$ is to make a few simplifying assumptions about $r_{\psi_A \psi_B}$ and σ_{ψ_A} and σ_{ψ_B}. One assumption often made is that the values of ψ_A and ψ_B are independent; that is, on trials where ψ_A is high, there is no systematic tendency for ψ_B also to be high or vice versa. Under these circumstances, the term $r_{\psi_A \psi_B}$ in Equation (9.1) becomes zero and may be eliminated. In some experiments, the assumption can also be made that σ_{ψ_A} and σ_{ψ_B} are equal. The value of σ_{ψ_A} and σ_{ψ_B} can then be set at any arbitrary value which will determine the unit of measurement of the psychological scale. For convenience, 1.0 is usually employed. The formula for calculating $\sigma_{\psi_B - \psi_A}$ is now simplified to

$$\sigma_{\psi_B - \psi_A} = \sqrt{1 + 1}. \tag{9.4}$$

The zero point on the $\psi_B - \psi_A$ distribution therefore corresponds to a z score of $-2.5/1.41 = -1.77$ under these two assumptions. A table of the normal curve reveals that a z score of -1.77 has a proportion of .96 of the normal distribution above it. In our scaling problem, .96 is the proportion of times that ψ_B is greater than ψ_A and is therefore the proportion of times S_B will be judged greater than S_A.

To facilitate understanding of Thurstone's scaling model, our illustration started with knowledge of the scale values $\overline{\psi}_A$ and $\overline{\psi}_B$ (means of ψ_A and ψ_B distributions), and the p values for comparative judgments of S_A and S_B were derived from the model. In actual practice, the p values for comparative judgments of S_A and S_B are determined experimentally, and it is the scale values of $\overline{\psi}_A$ and $\overline{\psi}_B$ that are derived. The difference between $\overline{\psi}_B$ and $\overline{\psi}_A$ can be calculated by converting the proportion of times S_B is judged greater than S_A to a z score and multiplying by $\sigma_{\psi_B - \psi_A}$:

$$\overline{\psi}_B - \overline{\psi}_A = z_{BA}\, \sigma_{\psi_B - \psi_A}. \tag{9.5}$$

In our present example, .96 is converted to a z score of 1.77. The product of 1.77 and 1.41 (the value of $\sigma_{\psi_B - \psi_A}$) is 2.5 (the value of $\overline{\psi}_B - \overline{\psi}_A$).

Since the relationships between $\sigma_{\psi_B - \psi_A}$ and the discriminal dispersions and the correlation factor for the two stimuli is known from Equation (9.1), Thurstone's complete *law of comparative judgment* can be written as

$$\overline{\Psi}_B - \overline{\Psi}_A = z_{BA}\sqrt{\sigma_{\Psi_A}^2 + \sigma_{\Psi_B}^2 - 2r_{\Psi_A\Psi_B}\sigma_{\Psi_A}\sigma_{\Psi_B}} . \qquad (9.6)$$

The separation on the psychological continuum between $\overline{\Psi}_B$ and $\overline{\Psi}_A$ can be calculated by converting the experimentally obtained proportion $p_{S_B - S_A}$ to a z score, obtaining measures of the terms under the radical, and solving the equation. The terms under the radical cannot be measured experimentally; therefore, the values they receive are determined by assumptions or are estimated from experimental data. Thurstone outlined the following five "cases" as different ways of applying the law of comparative judgment:

Case I. The law is applied in its complete form as stated in Equation (9.6), and the unknown terms must be estimated from the data. In Case I, repeated judgments are made by a single observer.

Case II. As in Case I, the law is applied in its complete form, but many observers make single judgments on the pair of stimuli.

Case III. An assumption is made that there is no correlation between ψ_A and ψ_B over a large number of judgments. The term $r_{\Psi_A\Psi_B}$ is assigned a value of zero and therefore dropped from the equation. The law becomes

$$\overline{\Psi}_B - \overline{\Psi}_A = z_{BA}\sqrt{\sigma_{\Psi_A}^2 + \sigma_{\Psi_B}^2} . \qquad (9.7)$$

The discriminal dispersions are estimated from experimental data.

Case IV. The discriminal dispersions are assumed to be approximately equal, but their values still must be estimated.

Case V. The simplest solution of all is provided by making the additional assumption that the discriminal dispersions are equal. If we arbitrarily give each discriminal dispersion a value of one, the law reduces to

$$\overline{\Psi}_B - \overline{\Psi}_A = z_{BA}\sqrt{2} . \qquad (9.8)$$

It was this form of the law that was used above in illustrating the major details of Thurstone's model.

The particular solution of the law used in deriving scale values is completely dependent upon the circumstances of each particular scaling problem. Fortunately, there are ways of evaluating the adequacy of the assumptions and estimations made when using one of Thurstone's cases (Guilford, 1954; Torgerson, 1958).

TABLE 9.2
Derivation of Differences Among Scale Values by Applying
the Law of Comparative Judgment to Paired Comparison Data

Comparisons	p values for standard stimulus judged greater than comparison stimulus	z	$\psi_C - \psi$ $= z \sqrt{2}$
$S_C - S_A$	.90	1.28	1.80
$S_C - S_B$	.65	.39	.55
$S_C - S_D$	.30	−.53	−.75
$S_C - S_E$	.15	− 1.04	−1.47

When the law of comparative judgment is applied to an actual scaling problem, scale values must be determined for the discriminal processes associated with several values of the stimulus. For example, one might be interested in finding the psychological scale for the values of S_A, S_B, S_C, S_D, and S_E. The simplest procedure might be to use one of the stimuli, such as S_C, as a standard stimulus for comparison with the four other stimuli. The hypothetical outcome of such an experiment is presented in Table 9.2. From the results of several comparative judgments of each stimulus pair ($S_C - S_A$, $S_C - S_B$, $S_C - S_D$, $S_C - S_E$), p values were calculated and subsequently converted to z scores. Using Thurstone's Case V, the scale value separations between each stimulus and the standard stimulus S_C were computed by Equation (9.8). The scale value of $\overline{\psi}_C$ is arbitrary, and Table 9.3 shows the results when $\overline{\psi}_C$ was given a value of zero. If one wishes to convert all scale values to positive numbers, the number which yields a value of zero when added to the lowest negative number is added to all scale values. In our example, a constant of 1.80 was added to all $\overline{\psi}$ values. Since the placement of the zero point is completely arbitrary, the method results in an interval scale of measurement.

The *method of paired comparison* is the method most frequently employed to collect data for constructing psychological scales based upon comparative judgments. It represents an elaboration of the method discussed above, where one stimulus in a series serves as a standard for comparison with the other stimuli in the series. In the method of paired comparison, however, the observer is required to make comparative judgments for all possible

TABLE 9.3
Final Scale Values Derived from the Law of Comparative Judgment

	Scale values				
	$\overline{\psi}_A$	$\overline{\psi}_B$	$\overline{\psi}_C$	$\overline{\psi}_D$	$\overline{\psi}_E$
$\overline{\psi}_C = 0$	− 1.80	−.55	.00	.75	1.47
$\overline{\psi}_A = 0$	.00	1.25	1.80	2.55	3.27

TABLE 9.4
Proportions Obtained by Using the Method of Paired Comparison

	S_A	S_B	S_C	S_D	S_E
S_A	—	$p_{A>B}$	$p_{A>C}$	$p_{A>D}$	$p_{A>E}$
S_B	$p_{B>A}$	—	$p_{B>C}$	$p_{B>D}$	$p_{B>E}$
S_C	$p_{C>A}$	$p_{C>B}$	—	$p_{C>D}$	$p_{C>E}$
S_D	$p_{D>A}$	$p_{D>B}$	$p_{D>C}$	—	$p_{D>E}$
S_E	$p_{E>A}$	$p_{E>B}$	$p_{E>C}$	$p_{E>D}$	—

pairs of stimuli. This situation can be regarded as one in which each stimulus serves as the standard in a series of comparative judgments with the other stimuli. The treatment of the results is basically the same as that used when only one of the stimuli serves as the standard stimulus. The p values are first computed for each pair of stimuli and then placed in a proportion matrix such as Table 9.4. Each row of the table gives the p values for comparative judgments when each of the stimuli served as the standard. In this example, five separate sets of psychological scale values can be generated by converting the p values to z scores and applying the appropriate version of the law of comparative judgment. In other words, for each of five stimuli, five independent estimates of the distances between $\overline{\psi}$ values can be computed (Table 9.5). The final $\overline{\psi}$ values assigned to the stimulus is the average of these five distances between $\overline{\psi}$ values.

Since the law of comparative judgment provides a model for converting observed proportions of a paired comparison experiment into scale values, it should be possible to reverse the procedure and calculate proportions from the scale values. The proportions calculated from the final scale value obtained by paired comparison can be compared with those originally obtained in the experiment. If there is a close correspondence between the proportions predicted from the model for a particular set of final scale values and the proportions obtained experimentally, the applicability of the model is supported. For example, $p_{A>B}$ can be predicted from the difference between the final scale values of $\overline{\psi}_A$ and $\overline{\psi}_B$. Using

TABLE 9.5
Scale Value Differences Obtained by
Using the Method of Paired Comparison

	S_A	S_B	S_C	S_D	S_E	Mean
S_A	—	$\overline{\psi}_A-\overline{\psi}_B$	$\overline{\psi}_A-\overline{\psi}_C$	$\overline{\psi}_A-\overline{\psi}_D$	$\overline{\psi}_A-\overline{\psi}_E$	$\overline{\psi}_A$
S_B	$\overline{\psi}_B-\overline{\psi}_A$	—	$\overline{\psi}_B-\overline{\psi}_C$	$\overline{\psi}_B-\overline{\psi}_D$	$\overline{\psi}_B-\overline{\psi}_E$	$\overline{\psi}_B$
S_C	$\overline{\psi}_C-\overline{\psi}_A$	$\overline{\psi}_C-\overline{\psi}_B$	—	$\overline{\psi}_C-\overline{\psi}_D$	$\overline{\psi}_C-\overline{\psi}_E$	$\overline{\psi}_C$
S_D	$\overline{\psi}_D-\overline{\psi}_A$	$\overline{\psi}_D-\overline{\psi}_B$	$\overline{\psi}_D-\overline{\psi}_C$	—	$\overline{\psi}_D-\overline{\psi}_E$	$\overline{\psi}_D$
S_E	$\overline{\psi}_E-\overline{\psi}_A$	$\overline{\psi}_E-\overline{\psi}_B$	$\overline{\psi}_E-\overline{\psi}_C$	$\overline{\psi}_E-\overline{\psi}_D$	—	$\overline{\psi}_E$

the law of comparative judgment, we can solve for Z_{AB}, which is then converted to the predicted $p_{A>B}$ by referring to the table of the normal distribution. For example, if Thurstone's Case V had been assumed in deriving the scale values, then z_{AB} would be calculated from Equation (9.8). This procedure would be repeated for all possible p values, and a table with a format similar to that of Table 9.4 would be filled in.

The model can be tested by determining how well the predicted proportions correspond to those obtained experimentally. A procedure used frequently is to calculate the average absolute deviation between the predicted and obtained proportions. If the average absolute deviation is small, we can conclude that the model fits the data. The overall differences between the predicted and the observed proportions can be tested for statistical significance by using a goodness-of-fit test such as chi square. A statistically significant chi square would indicate that the predicted and obtained proportions differed by more than would reasonably be expected by chance and thus that one or more of the assumptions of the model must be incorrect (see Torgerson, 1958).

PROBLEMS

9.1. For ordinal, interval, and ratio scales, illustrate the concept of invariance by constructing a graph in which transformed measurements are plotted against original measurements. The graph should show the most radical mathematical transformations that can be performed on the data and that leave the scale invariant.

9.2. Listed here are stimulus intensity values and corresponding DL values. Plot a graph of the DL as a function of intensity. Draw a smooth curve by eye that best fits the data points. From this curve, determine the relationship between the number of jnd's above absolute threshold and stimulus intensity. Assume that the value of the absolute threshold is 10.

Stimulus Intensity

	10	20	30	40	50	60
DL	1.0	1.5	2.2	3.5	5.0	7.5

9.3. Using Thurstone's Case V, derive scale values for stimuli A, B, C, D, and E from the proportions determined by the method of paired comparison. Set up a table of p values, a table of z values, and derive the scale values.

Comparison	A > B	A > C	A > D	A > E	B > C	B > D	B > E	C > D	C > E	D > E
Proportion	.58	.72	.90	.97	.64	.84	.95	.77	.89	.71

10

Partition Scales

Partition scaling methods are designed to construct interval scales of psychological attributes directly from the judgments of the observers. In these methods, the observer is required to partition the psychological continuum into equal sensory intervals. To accomplish this objective, two main kinds of method, *equisection scaling* and *category scaling*, have been developed.

EQUISECTION SCALES

Equisection is a method which, as its name implies, requires observers to section the psychological continuum into equal *sense distances*. The psychological difference between two brightnesses, two loudnesses, or two sweetnesses are examples of sense distances. The observer's task is to report whether the sense distance between sensations A and B is less than, greater than, or equal to the sense distance between sensations C and D. The experimental problem is to discover the stimuli corresponding to a series of sensations separated by equal sense distances.

Bisection, the earliest version of the equisection approach to psychological scaling, was used by Plateau in the 1850s (Plateau, 1872). In this method, two stimuli are presented for inspection; the observer is then asked to choose a third stimulus of intermediate value, so that the sense distance between the two end stimuli is divided exactly in half—thus resulting in two sense distances of equal size defined by three stimulus values. Plateau, for example, had artists paint a gray that was midway between black and white. The term equisection is generally reserved for the extension of this procedure to situations where the observer sections off, not just two, but several equal intervals on the psychological continuum. Typically, the procedure is one in which the observer is asked to choose a limited number of stimuli (e.g., five from a large stimulus assortment) that produce sensations equidistant on the psychological continuum. The ends of the continuum are defined to the observer by the presentation of the lowest and highest stimulus values. The lightness of grays has been scaled by Munsell, Sloan, and Godlove (1933) using such a procedure. Observers chose a series of gray surfaces so that the psychological continuum of lightness, starting with black and ending with white, was divided into eight psychologically equal steps.

There are two somewhat different techniques for extracting estimations of a series of equal sense distances from an observer. The observer may be presented with the two end stimuli and asked to choose n minus 1 stimuli to create n equal sense distances. This procedure is called a *simultaneous solution*, because all of the scale values are estimated at once by the observer. The procedure is illustrated in Figure 10.1. The observer

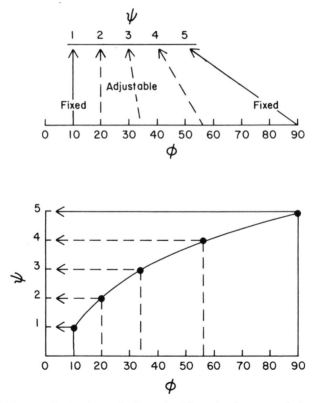

FIG. 10.1. Equisection scale determined by a simultaneous solution.

first asked to notice the sensory difference between fixed stimulus intensities of 10 and 90. Then, the observer is asked to adjust the intensities of three stimuli so that this sensory difference is divided into four psychologically equal increments. In analyzing the results, values of 1 and 5 have been assigned to sensations produced by the fixed stimuli of 10 and 90, respectively. Values of 2, 3, and 4 have been assigned to the sensations produced by the three stimuli adjusted by the observer. Thus, in the psychological domain, sensory magnitude is numerically represented by the equal increment series of 1, 2, 3, 4, and 5. On the other hand, the intensities in the stimulus domain corresponding to these equal increments in sensation were found, through the observer's judgments, to be 10, 20, 34, 56, and 90. The equisection scale is plotted in the lower part of Figure 10.1. An alternative to the simultaneous solution is the *progressive solution*, which requires an observer on a particular trial to choose only one stimulus bisecting a sensory distance. By progressively bisecting sense distances into smaller and smaller sense distances, the desired number of successive equal sense intervals is obtained. If four equal intervals were desired, for example, the interval between the two end stimuli would be bisected first, and the two resulting equal intervals would be subsequently bisected, first one and then the other. The simultaneous solution and the progressive solution are illustrated schematically in Figure 10.2.

The assigning of numbers to the sensory continuum to form an interval scale of a given attribute is relatively simple. Since the equisection experiment yields a series of stimulus values corresponding to a series of sensations that change in equal psychological increments, any number series that increases in equal steps (1, 2, 3, . . . , n, etc.) can be assigned as scale values to the sensations. A psychophysical magnitude function

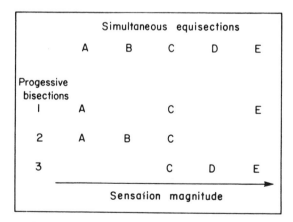

FIG. 10.2. Sensations that are separated by equal sense distances as determined by simultaneous and progressive solutions.

may be constructed by plotting psychological scale values against stimulus values.

S. S. Stevens and Volkmann (1940) have constructed a psychological scale of auditory pitch by the method of equisection. The basic procedures of their experiment provide a meaningful illustration of the application of this method. The purpose of the investigation was to determine the relationship between psychological pitch and pure tone frequency from 40 to 12,000 Hz. On different occasions, observers were required to section into four psychologically equal intervals each of three overlapping frequency ranges (40–1000 Hz, 200–6500 Hz, and 3000–12,000 Hz). For each of these three frequency ranges, the end stimuli were of fixed frequency, and the observer had to adjust the frequency of three variable stimuli to create four psychologically equal increments in pitch. Ten observers made each of these three equisection judgments five times. Table 10.1 shows the average frequency settings made by the observers for the three frequency ranges.

For each of the frequency ranges, a series of numbers representing amounts of pitch was assigned to the five frequencies judged equidistant with respect to pitch. The only requirement for an interval scale of pitch is that equal increments in pitch be designated by equal increments in the number system. Therefore, the five successive frequencies obtained by equisection of a particular frequency range were assigned five successive numbers increasing by steps of one and representing five equal increments in pitch. Pitch values plotted against stimulus frequency for each of the three frequency ranges are seen in Figure 10.3. Smooth curves fitted to the data points yield the three psychological magnitude functions.

The objective of the experiment, however, was to construct, not three, but one psychophysical function covering the entire stimulus frequency range of 40–12,000 Hz. The three psychophysical functions for the overlapping frequency ranges had to be combined to form a single psychophysical function covering the entire frequency range. To solve this problem, Stevens and Volkmann employed graphical methods that involved much trial and error. The same result is achieved by a more systematic procedure suggested by Torgerson (1958). The procedure converts the

TABLE 10.1
Results Obtained by Observers Who Equisectioned Each of Three
Frequency Ranges into Four Equal Intervals of Psychological Pitch

Frequency ranges (Hz)	Stimulus frequency defining intervals				
40–1000	40	161	404	693	1000
200–6500	200	867	2022	3393	6500
3000–12,000	3000	4109	5526	7743	12,000

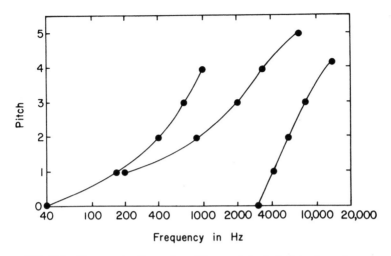

FIG. 10.3.   Three equisection scales of the psychological pitch of pure tones for three overlapping frequency ranges. (From Stevens & Volkmann, 1940.)

scale values of stimuli in the lower and upper frequency ranges into scale units of the middle frequency range, resulting in one homogeneous scale and a single psychophysical function. In Figure 10.4, the scale values assigned the frequencies 200, 404, 693, 867, and 1000 Hz in the middle (M) range are plotted against the scale values for these frequencies in the lower (L) range. The scale values of these stimuli for the middle and lower frequency ranges were read from the psychophysical magnitude functions of Figure 10.3. A straight line fitted to the data points gave the equation

$$M = 0.4L + 0.56.$$

The scale values for *any* frequency in the lower range can be converted to the units of the middle range by this equation. For example, the scale value for 40 Hz is $0.4 \times 0.0 + .56 = .56$. The scale value for 161 Hz is $0.4 \times 1.0 + .56 = .96$. For 404 Hz, the scale value is $0.4 \times 2.0 + .56 = 1.36$. For 693 Hz, the scale value is $0.4 \times 3.0 + .56 = 1.76$; for 1000 Hz, it is $0.4 \times 4.0 + .56 = 2.16$. The same procedure was applied to the scale values of frequencies common to the middle and upper (U) frequency ranges (3000, 3393, 4109, 5526, and 6500 Hz) and the equation

$$M = 0.5U + 3.8$$

was determined from Figure 10.5. From this equation, the scale values for *any* frequency in the upper range can be converted to units of the middle frequency range. For 3000 Hz, the value is $0.5 \times 0.0 + 3.8 = 3.8$; for 3393 Hz,

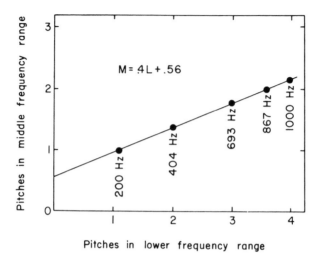

Pitches in lower frequency range

FIG. 10.4. Psychological pitch for stimuli presented in the context of the middle frequency range plotted against the psychological pitch of the same stimuli presented in the context of the lower frequency range. The linearity of the function indicates that the observers' judgments were internally consistent. The equation is used to convert the scale values of stimuli in the lower range into the units of the scale for the middle frequency range. (From Torgerson, 1958. Reprinted from W. S. Torgerson, *Theory and Methods of Scaling*. Copyright © 1958 by John Wiley & Sons, Inc.)

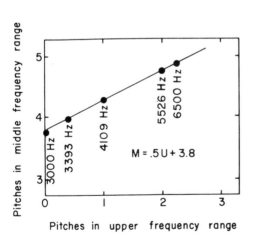

Pitches in upper frequency range

FIG. 10.5. Psychological pitch for stimuli presented in the context of the middle frequency range plotted against the psychological pitch of the same stimuli presented in the context of the upper frequency range. The linearity of the function indicates that the observers' judgments were internally consistent. The equation is used to convert the scale values of stimuli in the upper range into the units of the scale for the middle frequency range. (From Torgerson, 1958. Reprinted from W. S. Torgerson, *Theory and Methods of Scaling*. Copyright © 1958 by John Wiley & Sons, Inc.)

it is $0.5 \times 1.0 + 3.8 = 4.3$; for 4199 Hz, it is $0.5 \times 2.0 + 3.8 = 4.8$; for 5526 Hz, it is $0.5 \times 3.0 + 3.8 = 5.3$; and for 6500 Hz, the scale value is $0.5 \times 4.0 + 3.8 = 5.8$.

In the Stevens and Volkmann study (1940), the conversion of all scale values to a common unit resulted in a single scale of psychological pitch for all 15 stimulus frequencies in Table 10.1. The final psychophysical function covering the entire stimulus frequency range is presented in Figure 10.6. The squares, circles, and triangles on the function represent average scale values for stimuli in the lower, middle, and upper frequency ranges, respectively.

Application of the method of equisection, however, does not demand the use of overlapping stimulus ranges requiring separate scalings. In many experiments, observers have simply been asked to section into n equal sense distances the entire stimulus range. When the stimulus range is extensive, as it is for the frequency of auditory stimuli, however, judgments may be more accurate when the number of equal sense distances estimated is small, covering a limited stimulus range. Furthermore, the independent scaling of stimuli in different situations or stimulus contexts provides a valuable opportunity to validate scale values. If the observer's judgments of stimuli produce a valid psychological scale, then they must be independent of the particular stimulus context within which they are made. In this case, scale values of stimuli obtained in one stimulus context will be linearly related to the scale values of these stimuli obtained

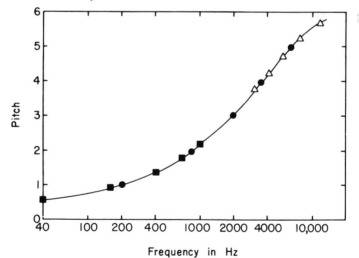

Frequency in Hz

FIG. 10.6. The final pitch scale for frequencies from 40 to 12,000 Hz. The squares, circles, and triangles represent data obtained from the lower, middle, and upper frequency ranges, respectively. (From Torgerson, 1958; based on the data of S. S. Stevens & Volkmann, 1940.) (Reprinted from W. S. Torgerson, *Theory and Methods of Scaling*. Copyright © 1958 by John Wiley & Sons, Inc.)

in some other stimulus context. As described earlier, a valid interval scale of measurement is invariant to linear transformations. Figures 10.4 and 10.5 show that the pitch scale meets this particular requirement for validity. Scale values of stimuli in the lower frequency range that were also in the middle range were linearly related, as were scale values of stimuli that were common to upper and middle ranges.

CATEGORY SCALES

Methods of category scaling, like those of equisection scaling, are designed to measure sensory attributes on an equal interval scale. If the scaling is successful, the end product in both cases is a partitioning of the perceptual continuum into several psychologically equal intervals—the boundaries of which are identified by specific stimuli. Category and equisection scaling techniques, though similar in rationale, require the observer to perform somewhat different tasks. The observer's task under the equisection method is to choose from a large stimulus sample the stimuli that result in a specified number of perceptually equal sense distances. In category scaling, the observer is presented with a large number of stimuli and told to assign all of them to a specified number of categories. The number of categories is usually somewhere between 3 and 20. Categories are usually specified to the observer either as numbers (such as 1, 2, and 3) or as adjectives (such as low, medium, and high).

The method of *equal-appearing intervals* is the simplest version of category scaling. In the use of this method, it is assumed that observers are capable of keeping the intervals between category boundaries psychologically equal as they assign stimuli to the various categories. Under this assumption, the experimenter treats the category values assigned to a particular stimulus as interval-scale values.

Accurate estimations of psychological scale values require a fairly large number of judgments of a particular stimulus. Replication of judgments can be achieved by having many observers judge each stimulus once, or by having one observer judge each stimulus many times. In the most powerful form of replication, several observers judge each stimulus several times.

For a particular stimulus, the psychological scale value of the sensory attribute under investigation is taken as the average (mean or median) category value assigned to the stimulus. The form of the psychophysical magnitude function is revealed when the average category value is plotted against values of the stimulus. Table 10.2 contains hypothetical data for an experiment using five categories and ten stimulus values. The cells of the table contain the numerical frequency with which observers assigned

TABLE 10.2
Frequency with Which Each Stimulus Is Judged in
Each Category in a Hypothetical Experiment

Stimuli	Categories					Median scale value
	1	2	3	4	5	
10	38	46	16	0	0	1.76
15	12	42	32	14	0	2.40
20	4	28	38	22	8	2.97
25	0	18	36	32	14	3.39
30	0	12	30	35	23	3.73
35	0	6	24	38	32	4.03
40	0	0	22	40	38	4.20
45	0	0	18	32	50	4.50
50	0	0	12	31	57	4.62
55	0	0	9	29	62	4.69

a particular stimulus to a particular category. The median scale values computed for each stimulus value are presented in the far left column. The psychophysical magnitude function is seen in Figure 10.7. The form of this curve is typical of psychophysical magnitude functions obtained by category scaling techniques.

Category scales constructed by the method of equal-appearing intervals have frequently been found to have a serious defect. If the category judgment of the observer is determined solely by the sensation magnitude on the psychological continuum produced by some stimulus, the judgment should be completely independent of the values of other stimuli presented on other trials. The scale values for a particular stimulus, however, are often found to be dependent on the values of other stimuli used in the experiment. This contaminating effect results from a strong tendency for observers to assign the stimuli to categories in such a way that all categories are used about equally often. Thus, the particular spacing of the stimuli on the physical continuum may greatly influence the shape of the psychophysical function. The typical negatively accelerated curvature of the function obtained by the method tends to be exaggerated when a cluster of low intensity stimuli with a few high intensity stimuli are used. The stimuli at the low end of the physical continuum are distributed over all but a few of the highest categories, and the intense stimuli are assigned to the remaining one or two categories. The psychological scale value separation is exaggerated between low intensity stimuli, and the separation between high intensity stimuli is minimized; consequently, the psychophysical function becomes very negatively accelerated. Likewise, because of the tendency to distribute the stimuli

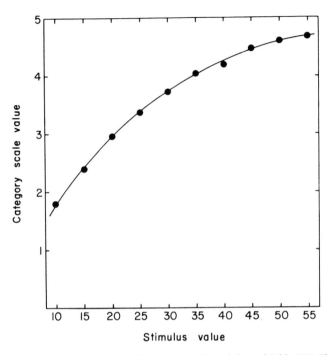

FIG. 10.7. Category scale based on the hypothetical data of Table 10.2. The median category rating is plotted for each stimulus value.

evenly over categories, the curvature of the function is reduced when a cluster of stimuli near the high end of the stimulus continuum with only a few low intensity stimuli is used.

The effects of the spacing of stimuli are illustrated in Figure 10.8. In this hypothetical example, when the stimulus values were clustered near the low end of the stimulus range, the curvature of the function was very negatively accelerating, whereas the function was almost linear when the stimuli were clustered near the high end.

Parducci (1965, 1974) developed a model to describe biases that observers have in the use of categories in category scaling. According to Parducci's *range-frequency model*, the distribution of the observer's category responses depends on both the stimulus range and on the frequency with which various stimuli are presented. Specifically, observers tend to divide the stimulus range into equal intervals over which they distribute their response categories. According to this principle, all of the categories would be used whether the stimulus range was narrow or wide. The effects of changes in the size of the stimulus range on the observer's category judgments is illustrated in Figure 10.9, where it is seen that a steeper scale results when the stimulus range is narrow than when it is

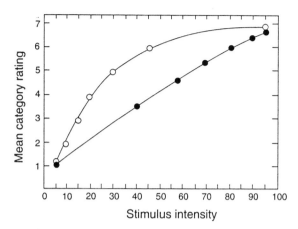

FIG. 10.8. The effects of stimulus spacing on the form of the category scale. Data points are hypothetical.

wide. This occurs because observers tend to distribute their response categories over the entire stimulus range. Secondly, observers tend to use the categories equally often. Because of this second principle, the frequency with which various stimuli are presented will influence the average category rating given to a particular stimulus. The effects of changing the relative frequency of presentation of different stimuli are seen in Figure 10.10. When the frequency distribution of stimulus presentation is positively skewed with the weak stimuli being most frequently presented, the resulting category scale is negatively accelerated. This occurs because observers tend to make the different category responses equally often,

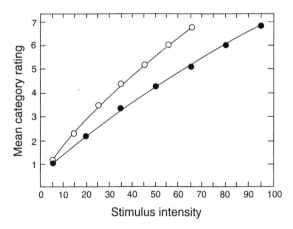

FIG. 10.9. Effects of the size of the stimulus range on the form of the category scale. Data are hypothetical.

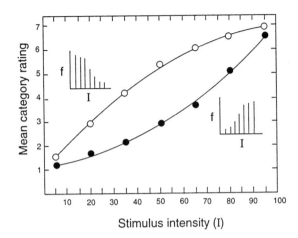

Stimulus intensity (I)

FIG. 10.10. Effects of the relative frequency of presentation of different stimuli on the form of the category scale. Data are hypothetical.

distributing them widely over the frequently presented weak stimuli with the highest categories reserved for the strongest stimuli. When the frequency distribution of stimulus presentations is negatively skewed with strong stimuli being most frequently presented, the resulting scale may be positively accelerated. This is because most of the categories are distributed over the frequently presented strong stimuli with the lowest categories reserved for the rarely presented weak stimuli.

Thus, category scales of the same stimuli scaled in the context of different stimulus distributions are not linearly related. Since a valid interval scale is invariant to linear transformations and distorted by any nonlinear transformation, the nonlinearity between category scales of the same stimuli suggests that their usefulness is very limited. Unless distortion due to stimulus distribution effects is eliminated, category scales must be regarded as ordinal scales at best.

S. S. Stevens and Galanter (1957) proposed that an iterative procedure could be used to obtain category scales free of the distorting influences of the observer's tendency to use all of the categories equally often. The observer is assumed to expect the series of stimuli to be arranged so that categories appear equally often. At the onset of an experiment, the stimulus spacing is arbitrary, and a scale is constructed based on the category judgments of a group of observers. This scale is the first approximation to the uncontaminated scale. On the basis of this scaling, a new series of stimuli is chosen with the stimuli separated by equal distances on the first psychological scale. This stimulus spacing is used in the construction of a second scale (second approximation to the uncontaminated scale) using a new group of observers. From the second scale, a new stimulus spacing, with stimuli separated by equal distances on the second psychological scale, is derived, and a third group of observers is used in the construction of a third approximation of the uncontaminated scale. This procedure is repeated until successive scales do not differ, indicating that an uncontaminated scale has been achieved by neutralizing the effects of the observer's expectations about the stimulus spacing.

Perhaps the oldest category scale of sensation is the scale of stellar magnitude, invented by the Greek astronomer Hipparchus over 2000 years ago. The purpose of the scale was to quantify the brightness of stars. The numbers 1 through 6 were used to indicate various perceived brightnesses. The number 1 was assigned to those stars that looked brightest and 6 to the faintest. Between the extremes, the numbers 2, 3, 4, and 5 were assigned to stars of decreasing brightness. Until the invention of photometers for measuring the physical intensity of stellar light, the psychological scale of stellar magnitude was used extensively by astronomers. To the delight of Fechner, the relationship between category judgments of stellar magnitude and the physical intensity of light from the stars was found to be approximately logarithmic. The psychophysical magnitude function of Figure 10.11 represents the average relative light intensity values for stars that were assigned to each of the six categories. The light intensity values were derived by S. S. Stevens (1975) from the data provided by Jastrow in 1887.

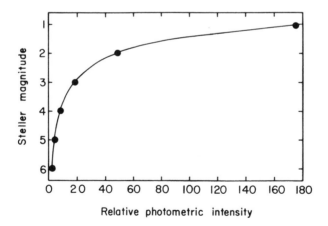

Relative photometric intensity

FIG. 10.11. Category scale of stellar magnitude. The scale indicates how the judgments of early astronomers are related to the photometric intensity of starlight. The relationship is approximately logarithmic. (From S. S. Stevens, 1975; based on data from Jastrow, 1887.) (Reprinted from S. S. Stevens, *Psychophysics: Introduction to Its Perceptual, Neural and Social Prospects.* Copyright © 1975 by John Wiley & Sons, Inc.)

Astronomers no longer depend on visual estimations of stellar magnitude. However, photometric measurements are now converted to the stellar magnitude scale which has been corrected to be a perfect logarithmic function of light intensity. Thus, the astronomer's scale of star brightness came to be in perfect agreement with Fechner's law.

Verbally Labeled Category Scales

A category scaling procedure that is now frequently used requires that the observer be given a verbal label for each of the numerical categories. The verbal labels provide "landmarks" and "anchors" that help the observer to make reliable judgments (Borg & Borg, 1994). Borg (1970), for example, developed a scale of perceived exertion called the *ratings of perceived exertion* (RPE scale), in which verbal labels are applied to perceived exertion experienced in exercise such as riding on a stationary bicycle under varied work loads. In a recent version of the scale, the highest number on the RPE scale is 20 and is associated by the verbal label of "maximal exertion." The lowest number on the scale is 6 and is associated with the label of "no exertion at all." Labels for levels of exertion between no exertion and maximal exertion were assigned to specific numbers between 6 and 20, with spacing carefully selected so that the numerical scale values assigned by the observer were linearly related to the work loads for exercise as measured on the bicycle ergometer (Figure 10.12). Observers in any exercise situation in which it was desirable to measure perceived exertion would simply be told to report 6 for no exertion, 7 or 8 for extremely light exertion, 9 for very light exertion, 11

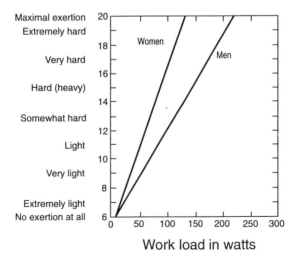

Work load in watts

FIG. 10.12.   The Borg scale of ratings of perceived exertion (RPE scale).

for light exertion, 13 for somewhat hard exertion, 15 for hard (heavy) exertion, 17 for very hard exertion, 19 for extremely hard exertion and 20 for maximal exertion. It has been found that the category numbers given by observers are linearly related to their heart rates and oxygen consumption as well as to work load. The RPE scale has been used in regulating exercise levels of patients with cardiovascular and pulmonary diseases and in training athletes. The scale has also been recommended for healthy people who are in an exercise program to maintain fitness. Another application of the RPE scale is the measurement of perceived effort associated with performing various tasks required in a job such as different kinds of industrial work. A major advantage that verbally labeled category scales have, as opposed to unlabeled category scales, is that, relatively high agreement can be established across individual observers. For example, the experience of maximal exertion is something that individuals have in common, providing a common anchor in the use of the number 20 in the RPE scale.

The results of another experiment in which the categories in category scaling were defined by verbal labels is seen in Figure 10.13 (Bolanowski, Gescheider, & Sutton, 1995). In this study, the intensity of pain induced by the use of various mouth rinses was assessed during 30 seconds of mouthrinsing and for 195 seconds following the rinse. Testing was conducted with nine commercially available mouthrinses containing various amounts of alcohol (Clear Choice, 0.0%; Plax, 7.5%; Viadent, 10.0%; Cepacol, 14.0%; Scope Peppermint, 16.6%; Scope, 18.9%; Cool Mint Listerine, 21.6%; and Listerine, 26.9%). The purpose of the study was to test the hypothesis that pain associated with the use of some of these products is related to their alcohol content. Pain ratings were made on a scale containing seven categories presented through a paper-and-pencil questionnaire, in which 0 was assigned for no pain; 1 for very weak pain; 2 for weak pain; 3 for moderate pain; 4 for strong pain; 5 for very strong pain; and 6 for intolerable pain. During the 30-second rinse, ratings were made every 5 seconds. After the rinse, the observer expectorated, but continued to make ratings during a 195-second recovery period. It is clear from the results presented in Figure 10.13 that pain rating increased with increasing ethanol concentration, with the maximum amount of pain experienced just before expectoration of a particular mouthrinse. Ratings of very weak pain were associated with Clear Choice and Plax with 0% at 7.5% ethanol, and ratings of strong pain were obtained for Listerine containing 26.9% ethanol. As can be seen in Figure 10.13, the general trend for all of the products was for the pain ratings to increase rapidly during the rinse until expectoration and then to decrease gradually after expectoration. The results of this study serve as an illustration of how category scaling with verbal labels can be successfully used in evaluating commercial products.

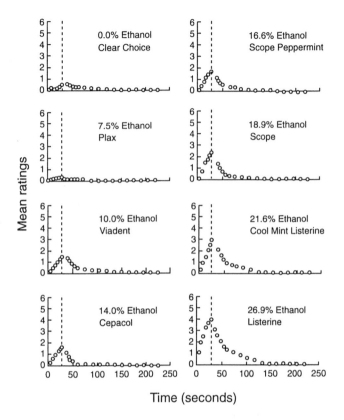

Time (seconds)

FIG. 10.13. Category ratings of pain induced by mouth rinsing with nine commercially available products containing various amounts of alcohol. Each graph shows pain ratings for a particular product plotted as a function of time since the start of the rinse until expectoration (dashed line) and time after expectoration. (From Bolanowski, Gescheider, & Sutton, 1995.)

In addition to producing reliable results, the use of verbally labeled categories in category scaling seems to reduce the susceptibility of the category scale to some of the potentially biasing effect of stimulus spacing (Ellermeier, Westphal, & Heidenfelder, 1991). One such biasing effect is the tendency of observers to use the same range of categories for a set of stimuli presented in both low and high ranges of intensities. Ellermeier, Westphal, and Heidenfelder (1991) determined whether this tendency would occur in the category rating of pain induced by pressure applied to the finger. The high range of pressures consisted of 750, 940, 1190, and 1500 kPa and the low range was 600, 750, 940, and 1190 kPa. The observer was instructed to rate the pain by first determining into which of the following categories it fell: very slight pain, slight pain, medium pain, severe pain, and very severe pain. After choosing a verbal category, the observer was then required to fine-tune the rating, using a 50-point category scale, by giving a numerical value without the category. The number ranges within categories were: very slight pain (1–10), slight pain (11–20), medium pain (21–30), severe pain (31–40), and very severe pain (41–50). The results presented in Figure 10.14 show that, using this scaling procedure, observers did not show the biasing tendency of using the same range of category judgments for both the low and the high stimulus ranges. Instead they tended to give category judgments that reflected the absolute levels of the stimuli presented. The procedure used in this study was derived from the work of Heller (1985), who attempted to specify the conditions under which observers make category judgments based on the *Bezugs system* (reference frame) of their experiences in everyday life rather than on the context of the other stimuli presented in the testing session. The Bezugs system is based on everyday experiences with the stimulus dimension and, as a result, categories of everyday language are naturally formed. For example, because of our experiences with pain accumulated over our lives, we all have concepts of what constitutes very slight pain, slight pain, medium pain, severe pain, and very severe pain. With these experiences as our reference frame, it should be possible to make category judgments of stimuli presented in the laboratory independent of each other. This is because the reference frame for making judgments comes not from the context of stimuli presented in the testing session but, instead, from the context of accumulated experi-

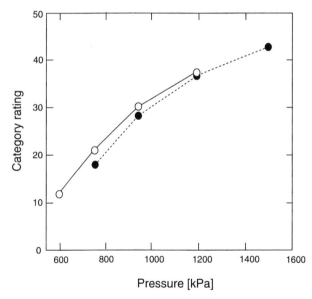

FIG. 10.14. Category ratings of pain as a function of pressure applied to the fingertip for stimuli in a low range and stimuli in an overlapping higher range of intensities. (From Ellermeier, Westphal, & Heidenfelder, 1991.)

ences outside of the laboratory. If observers are given only numbers as categories, with no verbal labels, they tend to use the numbers to categorize stimuli in a testing session relative to each other rather than to categorize them within the broader reference frame of experiences outside, as well as inside, the laboratory.

Although verbally labeled category scaling procedures, by encouraging observers to categorize stimuli according to an external frame of reference, may avoid bias due to the particular stimulus values chosen for use in the testing session, they introduce another major problem into the situation. The problem is that the form of the psychophysical magnitude function constructed from the category scaling experiment may be influenced by the arbitrary choice, by the experimenter, of the numbers to which the various verbal labels are assigned. Figure 10.15 illustrates the possible distorting effects the choice of numbers for verbal labels can have. Two pain scales are plotted based on hypothetical results in which the numbers associated with verbal categories were arithmetically (very slight pain, 5; slight pain, 15; moderate pain, 25; severe pain, 35; very severe pain, 45) or logarithmically (very slight pain, 3; slight pain, 6; moderate pain, 12; severe pain, 24; very severe pain, 48) distributed over the five verbal categories. The left and right ordinates of the graph apply to the arithmetic and logarithmic distributions, respectively. It is clear that the numbers assigned to the verbally labeled categories greatly affects the form of the pain scale. This could be a potential source of bias in this type of psychophysical scaling. Thus, it is important in using verbally labeled category scales, that the assignment of numbers to verbal categories not be arbitrary but, instead, be based on well-developed rationale.

INTEGRATION PSYCHOPHYSICS

In addition to the study of how perceptions relate to stimuli, category scales are used extensively to study how perceptions relate to one another. In this approach, referred to by Anderson (1992) as *integration psycho-*

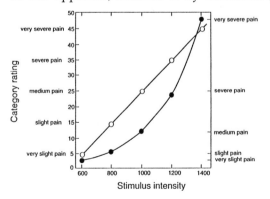

FIG. 10.15. Hypothetical results for verbally labeled category scales of pain in which the numbers assigned to the verbal labels affect the form of the scale. This could be a potential source of bias in verbally labeled category scales.

physics, the focus is on how separate perceptions combine, such as when the taste and smell of a fine wine combine to produce the perceptual experience we might refer to as its exquisite flavor.

Consider how integration psychophysics might be applied to answering questions about relations among pain sensations induced by simultaneous noxious stimulation of different sites on the skin. Pain will be experienced if we apply heat at approximately 43° C to the tip of the index finger. The same is true if we apply the heat to the tip of the middle finger. It would be interesting to know if simultaneous pains on the two fingers would combine to produce a pain different from that on either of the fingers alone. If the pains on the two fingers are integrated to produce a new level of pain, it would be important to know the integration rule by which this occurs. Is the total pain equal to the sum, the average, or the product of the separate levels of pain experienced on the two fingertips. Anderson (1970) developed an approach called *functional measurement* to answer such questions about the cognitive algebra of perceptual processes. Within this framework (discussed more extensively in chap. 12), Anderson (1992) advocated the use of 20-point category scales because they reveal that the integration of perceptions obey simple, theoretically interesting, algebraic rules. In fact, Anderson (1992) argued that the validity of these scales is supported by the finding that when they are used to explore perceptual integration, the scales reveal that the process obeys simple and meaningful rules of cognitive algebra. For example, if the pain rating for stimulation of two fingertips were found to be equal to the sum of the pain ratings for stimulation of each fingertip separately the proposed integration rule would be one of simple additivity. It would be concluded that total pain is equal to the summation of the two component pains, and that the category scale for pain must have been valid for such a simple integration rule to be revealed. This approach to validating scales seems to be founded on the belief that the laws of nature in the psychological, as well as in the physical, domain, are fundamentally simple.

In psychophysical scaling, the concept of *scale validity* refers to the question of whether the scale values derived from the scaling procedure are linearly related to the internal psychological process under investigation. In category scaling, the question of validity is one of whether observers are capable of assigning category numbers to their perceptual experience in such a way that the numbers are linearly related to the magnitudes of their experiences. In other words, a valid scale is one in which the numbers of the scale reflect the magnitudes of the psychological process being measured. In functional measurement, validity defined in this way, is obtained when the cognitive algebra revealed by the experiment obeys simple rules that are also theoretically interesting. According to Anderson (1992), the 20-point category scale must be valid because its use frequently reveals that the integration of psychological processes frequently obeys simple empirical laws.

To further illustrate this point, let us consider in more detail the experimental procedures that might be used and a set of hypothetical results that might be obtained in the experiment on painful stimulation of the fingertips. The two variables of this experiment, intensity of stimulations (5 levels) and number of fingers stimulated (1 or 2) could be combined, as prescribed by functional measurement, in a factorial design to form 10 independent stimulus conditions. Observers would be required to make category scale ratings on a 20-point pain scale, with 1 being the least pain and 20 being the most pain they could imagine experiencing. Each observer would make several category ratings of the pain experienced under each of the 10 conditions. The category ratings made within a condition would be averaged and the results plotted on a graph as illustrated in Figure 10.16. The interesting feature of the results, from the perspective of function measurement, is that the category rating scale for two fingers is higher and parallel to the scale for one finger. Assuming that the category scale is valid, the results suggest that, at every intensity level, noxious stimulation of two fingers adds a constant amount of pain to the pain experienced when only one finger is stimulated. When the results of such factorially designed experiments exhibit parallelism, as in our hypothetical results, it is often concluded that the experiment reveals simultaneously that the cognitive algebra is simple addition and the category scale is valid. Thus, as just stated, the validity of the scale is

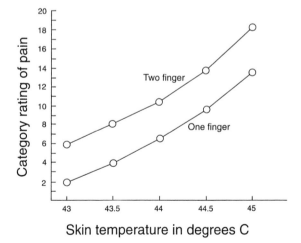

FIG. 10.16. Hypothetical results for category scales of pain when either one or two fingers are stimulated by heat.

determined by whether the scaling experiment reveals simple empirical laws. A problem arises with this approach when the results of a particular experiment can be explained by more than one proposed cognitive algebraic law. For example, in the present hypothetical example, the same results could be explained by a theory in which pains add to produce total pain and the category scale is valid, or alternatively by a model in which the category scale is nonlinear and, thus, not valid, and pains multiply to produce total pain (see chapter 14 for further discussion of this issue).

Although such problems of scale validation may at times arise, functional measurement has served as a very powerful method, within integration psychophysics, for studying how perceptions relate to one another. The approach has not been confined to studies in which category scales are used, but instead has been used with a variety of scaling methods, including ratio scaling methods described in chapters 11 and 12. Thus, although functional measurement had its origins in category scaling, the logic of the approach is independent of the scaling method.

ESTIMATION OF SENSORY DIFFERENCES

It is possible to construct psychophysical scales from the observer's judgments of sensory differences between stimuli. The observer might be required to give a numerical estimation of sensory intervals, or simply to say whether one sensory interval, resulting from the presentation of stimulus S_A and stimulus S_B, is greater than or less than the sensory interval resulting from the presentation of stimulus S_C and stimulus S_D. The objective is to determine a rank ordering of sensory differences among a series of stimulus pairs in which the values of the pairs are located all along the stimulus continuum of interest. Mathematical procedures called *nonmetric scaling* have been developed for converting a rank order of sensory differences into an interval scale of sensory magnitude. Thus, by knowing the rank order of sensory differences and the corresponding stimulus pairs, it is possible to establish a psychophysical magnitude function describing the relationship between the magnitude of a sensory attribute and the corresponding physical values of the stimulus (Shepard, 1966). For this to be possible, the rank ordering of the intervals must exhibit certain properties (Marks & Algom, in press). One of these properties is weak transitivity of the ordering as illustrated in Figure 10.17 where it can be seen that if $S_A S_B \geq S_B S_C$ and $S_B S_C \geq S_C S_D$, then $S_A S_B \geq S_C S_D$.

The other property, monotonicity, is illustrated in Figure 10.18 where it is seen that if $S_A S_B \geq S_D S_E$ and $S_B S_C \geq S_E S_F$, then $S_A S_C \geq S_D S_{SF}$. The results

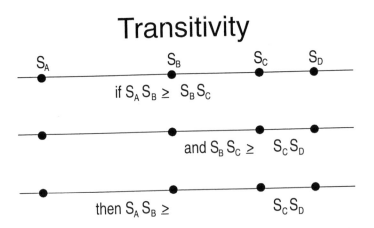

FIG. 10.17. Illustration of transitivity of intervals required in nonmetric scaling.

obtained by this method indicate that sensation magnitude increases as a power function of stimulus intensity in which the exponents of the functions are smaller than those obtained with ratio scaling methods (see chapters 11 and 13 for discussions of ratio scaling methods and power functions, respectively). Much of the work using this method has been focused on the problem of constructing scales of loudness in which loudness, the sensation magnitude of a sound, is functionally related to the sound's intensity (Algom & Marks, 1984; Dawson, 1971; Parker & Schneider, 1974; Popper, Parker, & Galanter, 1986; Schneider, 1980; Schneider, Parker, & Stein, 1974; Schneider, Parker, Valenti, Farrell, & Kanow, 1978). The scale plotted in Figure 10.19 from the study of Schneider, Parker, and Stein (1974) illustrates a typical loudness scale obtained by the method of nonmetric scaling of sensory differences.

Monotonicity

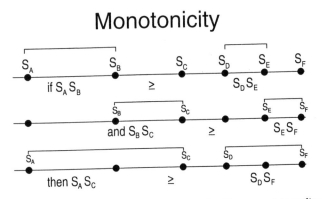

FIG. 10.18. Illustration of monotonicity required in nonmetric scaling.

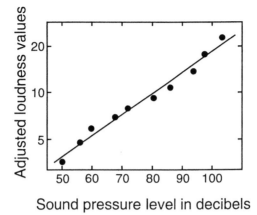

Sound pressure level in decibels

FIG. 10.19. Loudness scale constructed from nonmetric scaling. (From Schneider, Parker, & Stein, 1974.)

PROBLEMS

10.1. The method of equisection was used to establish a scale of brightness. An observer looked at light A and light E. Light A and light E had intensities of 5 and 60, respectively. The observer was instructed to adjust the intensity of light C so that the difference in psychological brightness between light A and light C was equal to the difference in brightness between light C and light E. The observer set light C at 22 units. The observer then set light B to 11 units in an attempt to bisect the difference in brightness between lights A and C. Finally, in bisecting the brightness difference between light C and E, the observer set the intensity of light D to 38 units. Construct a brightness scale in which psychological units of brightness are plotted against stimulus intensity.

10.2. In the following table is a set of data from an experiment in which observers made category ratings of stimuli of varied intensity. The table contains the number of times each category was used for each stimulus intensity. Calculate the mean-scale value for each stimulus and plot the results.

	Categories						
Stimuli	*1*	*2*	*3*	*4*	*5*	*6*	*7*
5	85	12	3				
10	2	8	70	16	4		
15			3	14	65	13	5
20				5	10	60	25
25				1	14	45	40
30				2	10	8	70
35					2	8	90
40					1	3	96

11

Psychophysical Ratio Scaling

Measurement of physical properties on ratio scales has always been a highly desirable achievement, since these scales can contain the characteristics of order, distance, and origin while retaining maximal correspondence with the number system. Methods for constructing ratio scales of sensation have been used extensively in the past 35 years. However, as far back as 1888, Merkel was interested in finding the stimulus that doubled sensation. Merkel had observers adjust a variable stimulus so that its sensation was twice as great as the sensation produced by a fixed stimulus. A similar procedure used by Fullerton and Cattell (1892) required observers to adjust a stimulus to produce a sensation that was some fraction or multiple of the sensation produced by a standard stimulus. These procedures result in ratio scales of sensation when the ratio of one sensation magnitude to another can be specified. It was not until the 1930s, when acoustical engineers became concerned with the problem of numerically specifying psychological loudness, that psychologists became interested in ratio measurements of sensation.

The practical problem of measuring loudness arose out of an obvious failure of Fechner's law. Acoustical engineers had assumed the validity of Fechner's law and adopted the decibel scale, which is a logarithmic scale of sound energy. It was hoped that, with this new scale, sounds could be specified in numbers reflecting the magnitude of the sensations they produced. It soon became apparent, however, that a sound of 60 dB was much more than twice as loud as a sound of 30 dB. It was through the development of special techniques for measuring loudness that psychophysics was supplied with the several ratio scaling methods subsequently used with success in the construction of scales of literally dozens of perceptual dimensions.

The methods of *ratio production, ratio estimation, magnitude estimation,* and *magnitude production* require observers to make judgments of the ratio between the magnitudes of two sensations. The observer's proficiency in performing this task determines the validity of a sensory scale constructed by any one of these methods. Fortunately, there are tests of internal consistency for evaluating an observer's performance on such a task. The construction of a psychophysical scale for a particular sensory attribute requires knowledge of the ratios between sensations at several points along the sensory dimension. If an experiment has provided this information and has withstood tests of internal consistency, one has a basis for assigning to sensations numbers that represent a ratio scale of measurement.

RATIO PRODUCTION

In the use of the method of *ratio production,* often called fractionation, the observer is required to adjust a variable stimulus while observing a standard stimulus. The two sensations are adjusted to a prescribed ratio (e.g., ¼, ⅓, ½). This method was used in several studies of psychological loudness that were summarized by Churcher (1935) for the purpose of developing measures of the sensation magnitude of industrial noise. Based on Churcher's work, S. S. Stevens (1936) produced the original loudness scale called the *sone* scale. Several procedures were employed to find stimulus values that resulted in sensation loudnesses standing in a 2-to-1 ratio. In one procedure, observers listened to a tone of a certain fixed intensity level and were required to adjust the intensity of another tone until it was exactly half as loud as the stimulus of fixed intensity. The intensity levels in physical units for the two stimuli were recorded, and the procedure was repeated for several stimulus intensities.

A second procedure was based on the assumption that a tone will be perceived as exactly twice as loud when presented to both equally sensitive ears (binaural stimulation) as when presented to only one ear (monaural stimulation). To find stimulus intensities that produce loud-nesses in a 2-to-1 ratio, the observers were required to adjust the intensity of a monaural tone to match the loudness of a binaural tone of fixed intensity. If this monaural stimulus were applied binaurally, it should have a loudness exactly twice that of the binaural stimulus of fixed intensity. The results obtained using this method were in close agreement with those obtained by the half-judgment method, a finding which lends support to the validity of both methods.

To construct a measurement scale of the attribute loudness, a unit of measurement called the sone was established by defining one sone as the loudness of a 1000-Hz tone at 40 dB above absolute threshold (Stevens,

1936). A scale value of 2 sones of loudness was assigned to a stimulus intensity of 47 dB, since this stimulus produced a sound judged twice as loud as the sound of the 40-dB tone. Likewise, a stimulus intensity of 55 dB was given a loudness value of 4 sones because it was judged to be exactly twice as loud as the 47-dB tone. In this stepwise fashion, loudness values were assigned to intensities from 40 dB to 120 dB. For loudnesses less than 1 sone, the stimulus judged exactly half as loud as the 40-dB stimulus was determined (34 dB) and given a loudness value of .50 sones, and the stimulus judged half as loud as 34 dB was determined (28 dB) and was given a loudness of .25 sones, and so on down the scale.

Figure 11.1 represents the psychophysical magnitude function for loudness where loudness in sones is plotted against stimulus intensity in decibels. Fechner's theoretical statement that sensation intensity is proportional to the logarithm of stimulus intensity is not supported by the shape of this empirically determined loudness function. A straight-line relationship between loudness and decibels (a logarithmic scale of sound energy) is predicted from Fechner's law. However, the psychophysical function is positively accelerated, rather than linear, when loudness is plotted against decibels.

Many scales of sensation intensity have been constructed by the method of ratio production. There are, for example, scales of brightness, loudness, weight, taste, smell, apparent duration, pain, touch, and vibration, to

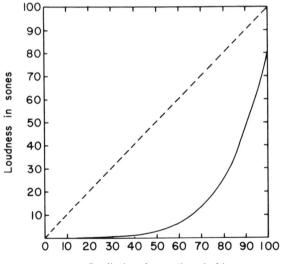

FIG. 11.1. Loudness of a 1000-Hz tone in sones as a function of stimulus intensity in decibels above absolute threshold. The relationship deviates greatly from the straight-line predicted from Fechner's law. (From S. S. Stevens, 1936. Copyright by the American Psychological Association. Reprinted by permission.)

name only a few. The forms of the various psychophysical functions relating values of the scaled sensation to values of the stimulus are often quite different. For example, apparent duration has been found to be linearly related to actual time (Gescheider, 1967; Gregg, 1951; Ross & Katchmer, 1951), while apparent weight increases as a positively accelerated function of physical weight (Harper & Stevens, 1948), and loudness and brightness increase as negatively accelerated functions of sound energy and light energy, respectively (Hanes, 1949a, 1949b; Stevens, 1936). One form of the psychophysical function conspicuously absent from the large compilation of scales constructed by this method is the logarithmic relationship predicted from Fechner's law.

The application of the ratio production method requires that a stimulus be continuously variable over the range of stimuli used in the experiment. Stimulus variation in small steps may be sufficient to fulfill this requirement, for under such conditions, the stimulus can be manipulated with respect to a fixed standard stimulus until the observer is satisfied that the two sensations stand in exactly the ratio prescribed by the experimenter.

One of the psychophysical methods described in chapter 3 is usually employed to obtain an estimation of the stimulus which, when paired with a standard stimulus, results in the prescribed sensation ratio. If the method of adjustment is used, the observer or experimenter may manipulate the variable stimulus until the observer is satisfied that it is psychologically set at some prescribed fraction of the standard stimulus. When the method of constant stimuli is used, the observer is required to indicate whether a particular setting of the comparison stimulus is psychologically greater or less than some prescribed fraction of the standard stimulus. If the method of limits is used, the variable stimulus is changed progressively in steps until the observer indicates that the sensation is just noticeably greater than the prescribed fraction of the standard stimulus, or until he indicates that the sensation is just noticeably smaller than the prescribed fraction. With both the method of constant stimuli and the method of limits, the stimulus value analogous to the point of subjective equality is taken as the estimation of the stimulus value corresponding to the prescribed sensory ratio.

The prescribed ratio most frequently employed in experiments has been ½, presumably because halving judgments seems to be easier than making judgments of larger ratios. Many investigators, however, have used more than one ratio within the same experiment to evaluate the validity of scale values. For example, from a scale based on halving-judgment data, one should be able to predict with reasonable accuracy the values of pairs of stimuli judged to result in sensation ratios of ⅓, ¼, ¹⁄₁₀, and so on. It seems advisable to at least use both the ratio and its complement for the construction of any scale using the ratio production method. In using a 2-to-1 ratio, observers would be required to make both halving judgments and doubling judgments. Using such a balanced procedure provides a validity check on the observer's judgments. Furthermore, when the scale obtained with a particular fraction differs from that obtained with the complement fraction, averaging the two scales often eliminates the biasing effects due to the use of the two fractions chosen for the experiment.

No set rule can be stated for deciding on the number of standard stimulus values to be used in a given experiment. Torgerson (1958) has, however, suggested that at least seven standard stimuli distributed over the range of the attribute to be scaled should be employed. It is important that enough values be used so that a smooth curve can accurately be fitted to the ratio judgments plotted against standard stimulus values. An example of such a curve is shown in Figure 11.2, where the value of the stimulus judged half as intense as a standard stimulus is plotted against eight values of the standard stimulus. Each point on the curve represents an average (such as the arithmetic mean, geometric mean, or median) of several judgments either of the same observer or of different observers.

As a test of the validity of the results, data from both halving and doubling judgment procedures have been included in this graph, and it

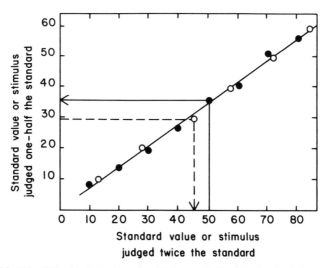

FIG. 11.2. Stimulus intensity judged to be one half of the standard stimulus as a function of the value of the standard stimulus. The filled points are based on halving judgments, and the open circles are based on doubling judgments. In order to make the data from the two kinds of judgment directly comparable, the observer's half judgments are plotted on the ordinate, but his doubling judgments are plotted on the abscissa. Hypothetical data.

can be seen that judgments made by the two procedures are in close agreement. Fitting a smooth curve to these data points provides a means of estimating the stimulus that would be judged half as great as any stimulus value within the range of values used in the experiment.

To generate the psychophysical magnitude function, a scale unit must first be established. The unit is specified when any positive number is assigned to any one of the stimulus values. The particular number and stimulus value used to establish the unit may be completely arbitrary, but in some cases they have been determined by practical considerations such as making a scale comparable to another scale. In our example using hypothetical data, 800 is arbitrarily assigned to the sensation produced by a stimulus value of 40, and the first point is entered on the psychophysical function of Figure 11.3. From the half-judgment function (Figure 11.2), it is seen that a stimulus of 28.5 is judged to be psychologically half that of the stimulus of 40. Since a stimulus of 40 has a psychological scale value of 800, a psychological scale value of 400 must be assigned to the 28.5 stimulus in establishing the second point on the psychophysical magnitude function. The half-judgment function is again examined to determine the stimulus value judged to produce a sensation magnitude half as great as that produced by the 28.5 stimulus. This is seen to be a stimulus value of 20.0, which is assigned a psychological scale value of

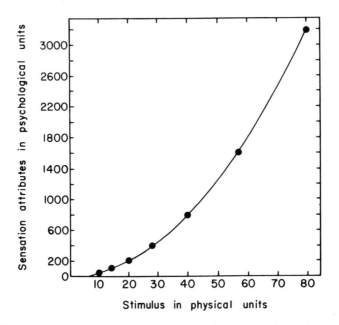

FIG. 11.3. Psychophysical magnitude function based on the half-judgment function of Figure 11.2.

200, since the stimulus value of 28.5 has been given a psychological scale value of 400. Thus, a third point on the psychophysical magnitude function is established. Working further down the scale, a stimulus of 14.0 is assigned a psychological scale value of 100, since the half-judgment function revealed that this stimulus was judged as psychologically half as great as the stimulus of 20. The fourth point of the psychophysical function is plotted. Finally, by the same procedure the lowest point on the psychophysical function is established at a stimulus value of 10 and a psychological scale value of 50.

In our hypothetical example, psychological scale values for stimuli above 40 may also be obtained by referring to the half-judgment function. However, the procedure is slightly different than that used for stimuli smaller than 40. If we locate 40 on the ordinate of the half-judgment graph in Figure 11.2, we find the stimulus judged as having a sensation magnitude twice that of the 40 stimulus by referring to the half-judgment curve and locating the corresponding stimulus value on the abscissa, which is seen to be 57. Since a stimulus value of 40 has a psychological scale value of 800, the stimulus value of 57 is given a scale value of 1600, and another point is plotted on the psychophysical magnitude function. Similarly, the half-judgment function reveals that a stimulus value of 80 results in a sensory magnitude twice that of the 57 stimulus. The stimulus of 80 is therefore given a scale value of 3200. The points on the psychophysical magnitude function are connected by a smooth curve. From this graph, the sensation magnitude for any stimulus within the range used in the experiment can be estimated.

RATIO ESTIMATION

The method of *ratio estimation* is closely related to the method of ratio production. Instead of adjusting two stimuli so that sensations are in a prescribed ratio, however, the observer's task in ratio estimation is to respond to two stimuli by estimating the apparent ratio between them. This method has proved very useful as one means of testing the validity of scales constructed by ratio production. For example, a reexamination of the ratio production in Figure 11.3 reveals that many predictions could be made about an observer's estimations of the apparent ratios between pairs of stimuli. Stimuli of 20 and 40 units produce sensations of 200 and 800, respectively; therefore, the prediction can be made that an observer will estimate the apparent ratio of these two stimuli to be ¼. If the observer were then asked to repeat the procedure for stimuli of 20 and 80 units, his predicted response would be ¹⁄₁₆. When observers are required to make estimations of the apparent ratios for several pairs of stimuli along the

stimulus dimension, the degree of correspondence between results predicted from the ratio production scale and the obtained results serves as a
check on the validity of both methods. In general, psychophysical scales
constructed by ratio estimation and ratio production methods are in close
agreement.

Today, ratio production and ratio estimation methods are not frequently used because they have been found to be particularly sensitive
to stimulus context effects. Garner (1954) demonstrated that changing
such factors as the stimulus range from which the observer had to choose
greatly influenced the observer's fractionation judgments. However, such
errors can be minimized in a carefully controlled experiment. For example,
Engen and Tulunay (1956) found that practiced observers are much less
affected by context effects than are inexperienced ones.

MAGNITUDE ESTIMATION

The method of psychophysical ratio scaling most frequently used in
current investigations is the method of *magnitude estimation*. The observer
in a magnitude estimation experiment is required to make direct
numerical estimations of the sensory magnitudes produced by various
stimuli. S. S. Stevens, whose name is most closely associated with this
method, conducted early experiments using magnitude estimation to
study brightness and loudness (1953, 1955). According to Stevens: "It all
started from a friendly argument with a colleague who said 'You seem
to maintain that each loudness has a number and that if someone sounded
a tone I should be able to tell him the number.' I replied, 'That's an
interesting idea. Let's try it' " (S. S. Stevens, 1956, p. 2).

Stevens (1958) described two main ways of applying the magnitude
estimation technique to a scaling problem. In one, the observer is
presented with a standard stimulus and told that the sensation it produces
has a certain numerical value (modulus), such as 10. On subsequent trials,
other stimuli are presented, and the observer assigns numbers to his
sensations relative to the value of the modulus. The observer is instructed
to make his judgments reflect how many times greater one sensation is
than another (the ratio between the two sensations). If a stimulus seemed
to have twice the apparent magnitude of the modulus, the observer would
say 20; if it had half the apparent magnitude, he would say 5. The data
from several observers may be combined by calculating the median or
geometric mean of the judgments for each stimulus value. The arithmetic
mean is seldom used because its value may be greatly affected by a few
unrepresentative high judgments.

In the other version of the method, the modulus is not defined by the
experimenter. The stimuli are randomly presented to the observer, who
assigns numbers to his sensations in proportion to their magnitudes. Since

the observer is readily able to establish his own modulus, psychophysical scales with or without an experimenter-defined modulus are in close agreement. Instructions to the observer may be modeled after the following example provided by S. S. Stevens (1975):

> You will be presented with a series of stimuli in irregular order. Your task is to tell how intense they seem by assigning numbers to them. Call the first stimulus any number that seems appropriate to you. Then assign successive numbers in such a way that they reflect your subjective impression. There is no limit to the range of numbers that you may use. You may use whole numbers, decimals, or fractions. Try to make each number match the intensity as you perceive it. (p. 30)

Most investigators feel it is better to permit the observer to choose his own modulus than to designate one for him. In either variation of the method, the average of the numbers assigned to a particular stimulus is the psychological scale value for that stimulus. The psychophysical magnitude function, then, is simply the average magnitude estimation plotted as a function of some property of the stimulus. It has been recommended that when no modulus is designated, the data of the different observers can be combined by computing the geometric mean for each stimulus value (see S. S. Stevens, 1971a). The equation for the geometric mean is:

$$\text{Geo Mean} = \text{antilog of } \frac{\Sigma \log X}{N}, \qquad (11.1)$$

where X is a score value and N is the number of scores.

During an experimental session, between 10 and 20 stimuli should be presented in irregular order. The order of stimulus values should be different for each observer. Stevens (1971a) suggests that one or two judgments should be obtained from each observer. No extensive training on the task is necessary, and, therefore, all the data for a single observer can be obtained in one or two sessions. In most circumstances, because judgments can be obtained relatively rapidly, magnitude estimation provides a valuable method for extensive experiments which vary several parameters of the stimulus.

Such an experiment was conducted by J. C. Stevens and Marks (1971). A description of their experiment will serve as an illustration of how the method of magnitude estimation has been used to investigate complex problems of sensory information processing. J. C. Stevens and Marks were primarily interested in spatial summation in the perception of warmth. Before they conducted their experiment, it was known that spatial summation extends over several hundred square centimeters of skin surface for the detection of warmth at absolute threshold. In determining absolute

thresholds for warmth, Kenshalo, Decker, and Hamilton (1967), for example, found a near-perfect inverse relationship between stimulus intensity and the size of the stimulus. As the area of the stimulus was made
smaller, the required increase in temperature needed to barely detect a
sensation of warmth increased. In fact, to arouse a threshold sensation, a
constant value of stimulation equal to the product of intensity and area
was necessary. Thus, the critical factor which determines whether or not
warmth is felt is not just intensity (energy per unit area), but the total
heat input to the skin. This experiment demonstrated that the sensory
system for warmth is capable of integrating stimulation over large areas
of the skin.

J. C. Stevens and Marks were interested in the relationship between
intensity and area for warmth sensations above threshold. The method
of magnitude estimation provided a means of quantifying warmth sensations for stimuli of various intensities above threshold and various areal
extents. Stimuli were applied to the skin of the back or the forehead by
the heat from a 1000-watt (W) projector lamp. Radiant intensity was varied
by regulating the voltage of the lamp. By means of a timer that operated
a shutter located between the lamp and the skin, the experimenter applied
the radiation to the skin for precisely 3 sec. The areal extent of radiation
was varied by placing aluminum masks of various sizes between the lamp
and the skin. During a session, a stimulus was presented to the observer
once every 30 sec. Each of 18 observers made two magnitude estimations
of each stimulus. Observers were instructed to judge how warm each
stimulus felt by assigning numbers to stand for the amount of apparent
warmth. No fixed standard stimulus or modulus were used.

The data in Figure 11.4 are the geometric means of the magnitude
estimations of the 18 observers for stimuli applied to the forehead. The
family of curves plotted on double logarithmic axes are psychophysical
magnitude functions for stimuli of various sizes. Spatial summation is
indicated by the higher magnitude estimation for larger areas of stimulation for any particular stimulus intensity. The amount of summation,
however, is not constant for all levels of stimulus intensity. The amount
of spatial summation is relatively small at high stimulus intensities. It can
be seen in Figure 11.4 that the area of the stimulus has a diminishing
effect on the judgments of warmth as stimulus intensity increases. In fact,
extrapolation of the functions for different areas of stimulation indicates
that at an irradiance of 800 mW/cm^2 the amount of spatial summation
should become zero. It is significant that at approximately 800 mW/cm^2
the sensation changes from warmth to pricking pain, and the pain threshold has been found lacking in spatial summation (Greene & Hardy, 1958).
In a subsequent experiment, Marks and J. C. Stevens (1973), using a wider

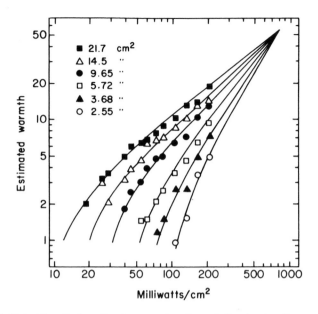

FIG. 11.4. Magnitude estimation as a function of stimulus irradiance on the forehead. The parameter is areal extent of stimulation. (From J. C. Stevens & Marks, 1971.)

range of stimulus intensity values, were able to obtain magnitude estimation data for different areas of stimulation that converged on the pain threshold as stimulus intensity increased.

In order to further evaluate the amount of spatial summation of warmth at different stimulus intensities, J. C. Stevens and Marks determined from the data of Figure 11.4 the combinations of intensity and area necessary to keep warmth at some particular level. The results are plotted in Figure 11.5 as equal warmth contours for seven levels of apparent warmth. It can be seen from Figure 11.4 that when judged warmth was 55, the stimulus intensity was 800 mW/cm² for all areas of the stimulus. This relationship is indicated in Figure 11.5 as a horizontal line at 55 for intensity as a function of area. In order to keep the sensation of warmth constant at a value of 55, no compensating reduction in intensity is necessary as area is increased. Thus, the sensory system, when operating at this high level, is unable to take advantage of increases in stimulus area. On the other hand, at the lowest warmth levels there is nearly perfect spatial summation, as indicated by the inverse relationship between intensity and area. Each of the parallel dashed lines in Figure 11.5 represents the predicted slope for complete spatial summation. For all points along one of these lines, the products of intensity and area are

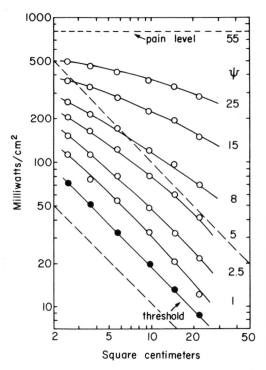

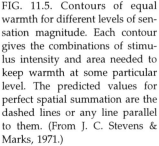

FIG. 11.5. Contours of equal warmth for different levels of sensation magnitude. Each contour gives the combinations of stimulus intensity and area needed to keep warmth at some particular level. The predicted values for perfect spatial summation are the dashed lines or any line parallel to them. (From J. C. Stevens & Marks, 1971.)

constant. By reducing irradiance as area is increased, the total amount of irradiance is kept constant. It can be seen from the psychophysical data that there is a gradual progression from nearly complete summation to no summation as the intensity of the warmth sensation approaches the threshold for pain.

If the pain threshold determines the point of convergence of the psychophysical functions, changing the pain threshold should change the convergence point. The pain threshold is increased by reducing the duration of the radiant stimulus. When Marks and J. C. Stevens (1973) used a .5-sec stimulus, rather than the 3.0-sec stimulus used in the earlier study, they found that the psychophysical magnitude functions converged at the higher value of 2300 mW/cm². The new convergence point is in reasonable agreement with the higher pain threshold. Thus, the appearance of pain seems to correspond to the complete loss of spatial summation in the warmth sense.

Marks (1974a) has pointed out that spatial summation of warmth is important for the regulation of body temperature. Since body temperature is determined by the total irradiance over large body areas, it is to the advantage of the organism to also sense warmth in this way. On the other hand, tissue damage due to burning is more dependent on the absolute temperature of the skin than on the size of the heated area. In this case, it is to the organism's advantage to feel pain at critical intensity levels that are independent of the areal extent of stimulation.

The discussion of experiments on the sense of warmth and pain serves as an example of how the magnitude estimation procedure has been used to investigate the complex problems of how a sensory system functions. The method has become one of our most valuable tools for the study of sensory processes. The use of the technique has not been restricted to the study of the senses, however. In fact, the simplicity of the method makes it applicable to the scaling of any psychological attribute. Attributes as different as the brightness of a light and the psychological worth of money have yielded to measurement through the use of magnitude estimation. In addition, the method has been found to be a valuable tool in certain clinical cases involving problems ranging from pain, fear, and drugs to medical decision making (Grossberg & Grant, 1978). A brief review of some of this research illustrates the usefulness of magnitude estimation in solving practical problems.

Some Practical Applications of Magnitude Estimation

Hilgard (1969) has used magnitude estimation to evaluate the analgesic effects of hypnosis. Pain, in varying amounts, was produced by varying the temperature and exposure duration of cold water into which an observer's hand was placed or by varying how long a tourniquet was applied to the arm. Magnitude estimations of pain were reliably related to stimulus intensity, and under some circumstances, magnitude estimations of pain were lowered by hypnosis. Hilgard's enthusiasm for the use of magnitude estimation to study pain is illustrated by his defense of the procedure to those investigators who favor more "objective" physiological measures over "subjective" verbal reports.

> I emphasize these findings as a reply to those who would degrade the subject's statements as being "merely" verbal reports, as though some sort of physiological response would be sounder. I wish to assert flatly that there is no physiological measure of pain which is either as discriminating of fine differences in stimulus conditions, as reliable upon repetition, or as lawfully related to changed conditions as the subject's verbal report. (Hilgard, 1969, p. 107)

Today, magnitude estimation procedures are frequently used to measure clinical pain as well as experimentally induced pain (see Rollman, 1992). These procedures are very useful in assessing both chronic and acute clinical pain. The results are often important in making medical decisions ranging from what type and how much of an analgesic drug to use to relieve pain to whether surgery is performed.

The assets of magnitude estimation are further illustrated in application of the procedure to the measurement of emotional experience. Before the development of magnitude estimation procedures, the assessment of fear and other emotional states typically relied on category scales in which the intensity of experiences were rated on a scale from 1 to 5, 1 to 7, or over some other limited range of numbers. At best, such a procedure has provided clinicians with an ordinal scale of a patient's emotional experiences. Because the intensity of experiences may vary over a wider range than the limited range of numerical values provided in category scaling, it is much better not to restrict the range of categories, but instead to allow the patient to use any numbers that seem appropriate to describe the intensity of their experiences. This simple modification of the category rating method yields magnitude estimation. Such magnitude estimation measurements have been found to be systematically related to various physiological indicants of emotion. For example, Frankenhaeuser, Sterky, and Järpe (1962) found a positive relationship between magnitude estimation of stress and epinephrine secretion following varying levels of gravitational stress produced in a human centrifuge. Similar close relationships between magnitude estimations of stress and physiological responses were found for psychological stress produced by the Stroop Color–Word Interference Test (Frankenhaeuser, Fröberg, Hagdahl, Rissler, Björkvall, & Wolff, 1967).

Another clinical application of magnitude estimation to the measurement of emotion is seen in the treatment of phobias. Phobias have been treated successfully by techniques of behavior modification such as systematic desensitization, in which the patient imagines scenes that vary in closeness to the feared object. For example, a patient with a fear of flying might be asked to imagine sitting in an airplane on the ground or sitting in an airplane in the air. The amount of fear elicited by the second image should be considerably greater than that elicited by the first. Wolpe (1963) has shown that the amount of fear elicited by such images and the subsequent decline during therapy can be successfully measured by magnitude estimations. Furthermore, Tryon (1977) has shown that magnitude estimation is superior to other scaling procedures in the measurement of fear elicited by imagined scenes.

The emotional stress produced by various life events has also been measured by magnitude estimation. Holmes and Rahe (1967) had their subjects make magnitude estimations of the intensity and length of time necessary to accommodate to each of 43 life events (e.g., death of a spouse, retirement, son or daughter leaving home, marriage, etc.). The resulting scale values, called *life change units*, varied from 11 to 100. Minor violations of the law received a scale value of 11, while death of spouse received

100. The scale values from some of the other life events were: divorce—73, marital separation—65, marriage—50, fired at work—47, marital reconciliation—45, retirement—45, death of a close friend—37, change to a different line of work—36, trouble with in-laws—29, outstanding personal achievement—28, change in residence—20, vacation—13. Knowing scale values for stressful life events provides the clinician with a technique for specifying the total magnitude of stressful life events experienced by a patient within a particular time period. The patient indicates which life events were experienced in a specified period and the scale values for these events are added to get a total score in life change units. Rahe, Romo, Bennett, and Siltanen (1974) have found in 275 survivors of heart attacks and 22 cases of abrupt coronary death, that there was often marked elevation in the magnitude of total life changes during the 6 months prior to the heart attack. Thus, this technique provides a way to quantify a risk factor in coronary prone individuals.

Another clinical application of magnitude estimation comes from the research by Ekman, Frankenhaeuser, Goldberg, Hagdahl, and Myrstern (1964) on the perception of states of intoxication as a function of amount of alcohol in the blood of observers. In this study, magnitude estimations of drunkenness were in close agreement with blood alcohol concentrations. This finding may be helpful in attempts to train heavy drinkers to monitor their own blood alcohol level, so that they can stop drinking before they become unable to do so.

Finally, magnitude estimation has been helpful in establishing the reliability of diagnosis of the severity of mental disorders in psychotic patients (Stone, 1968). In this study, psychiatrists made magnitude estimations of the severity of mental disorders in a large group of psychotic patients. Magnitude estimations of the severity of pathology were found to be reliably related to other measures of pathology such as length of stay in the hospital, IQ scores, and a psychoticism score. This demonstration suggests that clinical judgments using magnitude estimation may improve the accuracy of psychiatric diagnosis, which in the past has been notoriously unreliable.

Magnitude estimation is currently one of the most frequently used psychophysical scaling methods. Each year there are many articles published on the application of magnitude estimation to the scaling of sensory and nonsensory stimuli. Because the method is extremely efficient, permitting quick acquisition of large amounts of data, it is ideal for use in experiments requiring the scaling of a large number of stimuli. In contrast, psychophysical scaling using the older methods of Fechner and Thurstone, while theoretically interesting, require so much time for determining the discriminability of stimuli as to be impractical for most scaling problems. Magnitude estimation is also superior to category scaling, since category scaling, although efficient, usually results in measurement no better than an ordinal scale.

MAGNITUDE PRODUCTION

Magnitude production is the inverse of magnitude estimation. The experimenter tells the observer the numerical value of some sensory magnitude and then requires him to adjust a stimulus to produce it. It is essential in the use of this method for the stimulus to be continuously variable over the stimulus range used in the experiment. The psychophysical magnitude function is constructed by plotting the prescribed sensation magnitude values against the average setting of the stimulus. Magnitude production can also be put to use as a valuable method of testing the validity of scales constructed by magnitude estimation. Close agreement between magnitude production and magnitude estimation scale values constitutes one source of evidence supporting the validity of the scale.

S. S. Stevens (1958) has suggested that the use of magnitude production and magnitude estimation procedures in the same scaling experiment might be a way to offset any systematic errors inherent in either method. This idea is based on the assumption that systematic errors inherent in magnitude estimation and magnitude production are on the average equal in size but opposite in sign. One systematic error which tends to affect psychophysical judgments is a regression of the observer's judgments toward the mean of his or her judgments. This tendency is called the *regression bias*, in which observers are conservative in their judgments. In other words, the observers are reluctant to make extremely low or extremely high judgments even though they may be correct in terms of their perceptions. Consequently, their magnitude estimations may not be low enough for the weak stimuli or high enough for the strong stimuli. Likewise, in magnitude production they may fail to adjust the stimulus to a low enough value when asked to produce a particular weak sensation magnitude or to a high enough value when asked to produce a particular strong sensation. In the case of magnitude estimation, the effect reduces the slope of the psychophysical function, while in magnitude production, the effect increases its slope.

The results of an experiment by S. S. Stevens and Guirao (1962) shown in Figure 11.6 illustrate the regression effect in magnitude estimation and magnitude production for judgments of the loudness of a 1000-Hz tone. Each data point is the geometric mean of two magnitude estimations or two magnitude productions by each of ten observers. Because of the regression effect, magnitude production resulted in a steeper function than magnitude estimation. It is generally assumed that the unbiased function lies somewhere between the two functions; therefore, it is con-

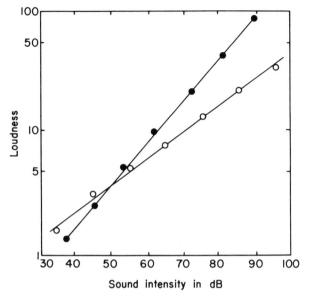

FIG. 11.6. Loudness of a 1000-Hz tone as determined by magnitude estimation (open circles) and magnitude production (filled circles). (From S. S. Stevens & Guirao, 1962.)

sidered advisable to combine them by some procedure. The resulting function should be a better estimate of the unbiased function than either the magnitude estimation function or the magnitude production function.

A procedure for combining the functions for magnitude estimation and magnitude production has been described by Hellman and Zwislocki (1963), who were interested in establishing an unbiased psychophysical magnitude function for the loudness of a 1000-Hz tone. Essentially, it consists of geometrically averaging the two psychophysical functions. The procedure has been called the *method of numerical magnitude balance*.

Loudness functions were obtained by Hellman and Zwislocki (1968) for three pure tone frequencies. Each loudness function seen in Figure 11.7 was obtained by the method of numerical magnitude balance. It is significant that the growth of loudness with intensity is more rapid for the low frequency tones than for the 1000-Hz tone. At low intensity levels, the frequency of the stimulus has a relatively large effect on loudness, but the effect of frequency diminishes as intensity increases. The results are in agreement with the way the equal loudness contours reported by Robinson and Dadson (1956) changed shape at different intensity levels (see Figure 3.11). The relatively flat contours at high intensity levels indicate that loudness can be kept constant with only slight adjustment of intensity as frequency is changed. In contrast, at low intensity levels, intensity must be greatly increased for low frequencies if loudness is to be kept the same for

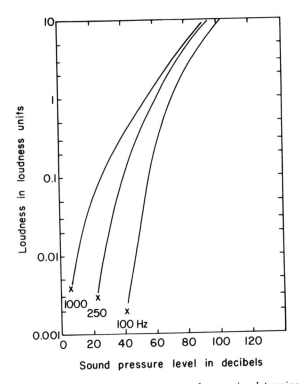

FIG. 11.7. Loudness scales for three pure tone frequencies determined by the method of numerical magnitude balance. (From Hellman & Zwislocki, 1968.)

all frequencies. Each equal loudness contour was obtained by having observers adjust the intensity of a tone of some frequency so that its loudness was the same as that of a 1000-Hz tone of fixed intensity.

Although the procedures of numerical magnitude balance and sensation magnitude matching represent two extremely different tasks for the observer, the results from the two procedures are essentially the same. Such agreement between measurements obtained by diverse methods constitutes strong support for their validity. For this reason, it is advisable to design experiments whenever possible that will yield one set of measurements with one method that predict the outcome of a second set of measurements made with a different method.

ABSOLUTE MAGNITUDE ESTIMATION

An absolute scale is a restricted case of a ratio scale in which the scale values cannot be transformed in any way. In nonabsolute ratio scales, the unit of measurement is arbitrary and can be changed by multiplying all scale values by a constant. The length of tables, for example, can be measured in feet or in inches. Transforming the measurements from feet to inches by multiplying them by 12 does not violate the structure of the scale. The ratios of measurements of the different tables remain invariant, and only the unit of measurement changes. In absolute scaling, on the other hand, the unit of measurement is not arbitrary and therefore cannot be changed. Counting objects is an example of an absolute scale. In scaling numerosity, we ordinarily do not permit any transformation of the scale values. In other words, it is customary to count by ones.

It has been argued by Hellman and Zwislocki (1961) that observers use absolute judgments rather than ratio judgments when making magnitude estimations of sensation magnitude. When no modulus is designated, different groups of observers, free to assign any numbers that match impressions of loudness, were in remarkable agreement on the absolute values of numbers assigned to stimuli (Zwislocki & Goodman, 1980).

The data in Figure 11.8 are median magnitude estimations of the loudness of a 1000-Hz tone. Observers were instructed to assign numbers

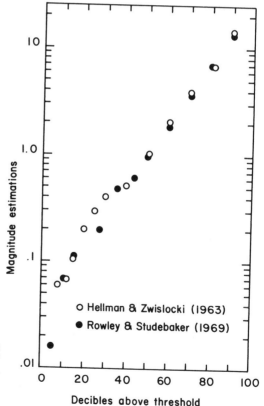

FIG. 11.8. Absolute magnitude estimations of the loudness of tones from two separate experiments. (From Zwislocki & Goodman, 1980.)

250

to loudness. The open circles on Figure 11.8 represent the median judgments of nine observers in a study by Hellman and Zwislocki (1963), and the closed circles are median judgments of ten observers from Rowley and Studebaker (1969). It is clear that, on the average, both groups of observers assigned approximately the same numbers to the same sound intensities and, presumably, to the same loudnesses. In addition, Zwislocki and Goodman (1980) found that observers' judgments of a particular stimulus were independent of the values of other stimuli used in the experiment. These findings clearly support the hypothesis that observers made absolute rather than ratio judgments of sensation magnitude.

The tendency to make absolute judgments of sensation magnitude may be acquired at an early age. Zwislocki and Goodman (1980) found that the magnitude estimations of lengths of lines given by adults and 5–6-year-old children were the same. The results are shown in Figure 11.9. The filled circles are the data of six children who perceived a 2.8-cm line as their first stimulus, and the unfilled circles are the data of six children who started with a 53.5-cm line. The crosses are the data of the adults. The judgments of children and adults are essentially the same for all but the shortest lines. The adults assigned fractional numbers to the shortest

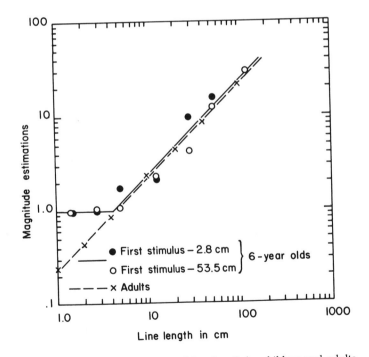

FIG. 11.9. Magnitude estimation of line length by children and adults. (From Zwislocki & Goodman, 1980.)

lines, but the children, not knowing fractions, had to use the number 1 for these stimuli. Because the shortest lines appeared shorter than a longer line to which they had already assigned 1, the children often hesitated and considered giving 0 as their answer, but ultimately they chose 1. It would seem that the unit of measurement in sensation magnitude judgments is fixed at an early age. Zwislocki and Goodman point out that when children learn numbers, they do not learn them at first as abstractions but by counting objects. Thus, the first associations of numbers are with the impressions of numerosity, and since numerosity is an absolute scale, judgments of sensory impressions may also be on an absolute scale. Evidence for absolute scaling of sensation magnitude supports the hypothesis that observers in the scaling experiment match their subjective impressions of the size of numbers to their subjective impressions of sensory stimuli. Presumably, the observer's subjective impressions of the size of numbers is an absolute scale fixed at an early age by experiences of counting. For example, a stimulus that is judged to be moderately intense would be assigned a number that the observer regarded as being moderately large. What is regarded as a moderately large number is determined by the early experiences of the observer in counting objects.

If observers make absolute rather than ratio judgments of sensory magnitude, it becomes very important never to use a standard stimulus with an assigned subjective value (modulus). Such a procedure would have the effect of forcing the observers to use numbers that did not match their impressions of the sensation magnitude of stimuli. It should be obvious that this could result in serious biasing effects that could render the psychophysical scale meaningless.

The consequences of using a standard for magnitude estimations of the loudness of 1000-Hz tones were investigated by Hellman and Zwislocki (1961). Loudness scales presented in Figures 11.10 and 11.11 were obtained when a standard stimulus, with a subjective value of 10, was 40, 80, or 90 dB above absolute threshold. The observers estimated the loudnesses of tones presented to both ears through earphones. They were instructed to judge the loudness of tones of varied intensity, and all judgments were to be made relative to a loudness of 10 arbitrarily assigned to the standard stimulus. If the observers had been able to make ratio judgments of loudness, the intensity of the standard stimulus would have had no effect on the form of the loudness scale, other than shifting all magnitude estimations by a constant ratio. Ratio scaling would have produced a vertical shift of the entire curve by a constant distance when magnitude estimations were plotted on a logarithmic axis. Under these conditions, the ratios of the magnitude estimation values for various stimuli would remain the same even though changing the standard stimulus would force the observer to assign higher or lower numbers.

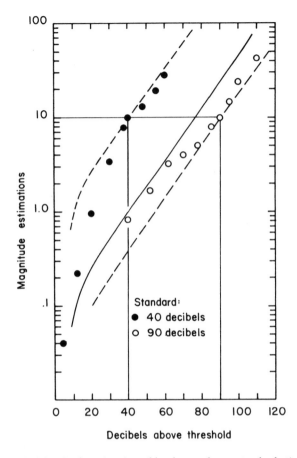

FIG. 11.10. Magnitude estimation of loudness when a standard stimulus of 40 or 90 dB was assigned a subjective value of 10. (Data from Hellman & Zwislocki, 1961.)

It can be seen in Figure 11.10 that when the standard stimulus was 40 and was 90 dB above threshold, the resulting loudness scales were not parallel over the entire range of stimulus intensities. Only within the restricted range near the value of the standard were the curves parallel. The solid curve is the binaural loudness scale derived from absolute magnitude estimation (Zwislocki & Goodman, 1980). The dashed curves are parallel to the absolute magnitude estimation curve. It is evident from examination of Figure 11.10 that when a standard is used, magnitude estimations of stimuli distant from the value of the standard tend to converge on the curve derived from absolute scaling. The finding that the loudness scales obtained with 40- and 90-dB standards are reasonably parallel within the intensity range of the standard suggests that within

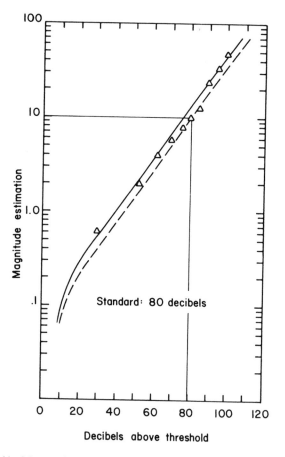

FIG. 11.11. Magnitude estimation of loudness when the standard stimulus of 80 dB was assigned a subjective value of 10. (Data from Hellman & Zwislocki, 1961.)

this limited range, observers are capable of making ratio judgments of sensation magnitude. Outside this range, their responses tend to drift toward what may be interpreted as a natural absolute scale.

The standard stimulus seems to bias the psychophysical scale only when the experimenter has arbitrarily assigned to it a subjective value different from that which the observer would assign in absolute scaling. When observers made absolute magnitude estimations of loudness, a tone of 76 dB was assigned a value of 10. It can be seen in Figure 11.11 that using a standard stimulus of 80 dB, and assigning to it a subjective loudness value of 10, yielded almost the same loudness scale that resulted from absolute scaling. Since the 80-dB tone has an absolute subjective loudness value near 10, the subjective value assigned by the experimenter and by the observer are almost in agreement, and, consequently, the use of the standard has a minimal biasing effect on the scale. Presumably, using a 76-dB standard stimulus with a subjective value of 10 would have totally eliminated this bias. Under these circumstances, the subjective value assigned by the experimenter and by observers in absolute magnitude estimation would be identical.

The hypothesis that observers have a strong tendency to assign numbers to sensations on a natural absolute scale is also suggested by the work of Ward (1973), who had observers make magnitude estimations of the loudness of 1000-Hz tones. At the start of an experimental session, the observer was presented with a standard stimulus at 56 dB above threshold, and was told that this tone had a subjective value of 10. This and other stimuli were presented many times throughout the session, but no further statements were made by the experimenter of the subjective value of the standard stimulus. By the end of the session, the average value assigned to the standard by the observers was not 10, but instead was 2.08. Zwislocki and Goodman (1980) have pointed out that 2.08 is almost exactly what observers assign to this stimulus by absolute magnitude estimation. It appears that unless observers are repeatedly reminded of the arbitrary subjective value of a standard stimulus, they will eventually use their own natural numbers.

Because of the potential biasing effects of a standard stimulus, it is recommended that magnitude estimation should not be done with a standard. Instead, the method of absolute magnitude estimation should be used. In the use of this method, it is important that observers be properly instructed in how to match their impressions of the magnitude of numbers to the magnitude of sensations. The instructions below are a generalized version adapted from those used by Zwislocki and Goodman (1980) for the judgment of line lengths.

> In this experiment we would like to find out how intense various stimuli appear to you. For this purpose, I am going to present a series of stimuli to you one at a time. Your task will be to assign a number to every stimulus in such a way that your impression of how large the number is matches your impression of how intense the stimulus is. We all have impressions of how large various numbers are, and impressions of how intense various stimuli are. I would like you to assign a number to each stimulus so that your impression of the size of the number matches your impression of the intensity of the stimulus. You may use any positive numbers that appear appropriate to you—whole numbers, decimals, or fractions. Do not worry about running out of numbers—there will always be a smaller number than the smallest you use and a larger one than the largest you use. Do not worry about numbers you assigned to preceding stimuli. Do you have any questions?

Using instructions such as these, Verrillo (1983) recently examined the stability of absolute magnitude estimations of the lengths of lines. Observers, after having made judgments of the lengths of lines, were called back to the laboratory after either a 1- or 2-year period and were required to repeat the procedure. The absolute values of the numbers given by the observers during this second testing session were in remarkable agreement with the values given during the first session. This stability of absolute magnitude estimations did not seem to result from a memory of numbers assigned during the first session. After the second testing, when asked whether they had remembered their previous responses from the first testing session, only one observer answered in the affirmative.

Zwislocki and Goodman (1980) describe how absolute scaling procedures can be employed for magnitude production, as well as for magnitude estimation. In absolute magnitude production, the observer is presented with numbers and is asked to adjust the intensity of the stimulus so that the impression of sensation magnitude matches the impression of the size of the number. The scale of loudness produced by absolute magnitude production was nearly identical to the one produced by absolute magnitude estimation with a different group of observers. This finding constitutes strong support for the hypothesis that the observer is capable of making matches between impressions of number size and sensation magnitude on an absolute basis.

Although research on absolute scaling shows that different groups of observers produce nearly equal scales, the results of individual observers within a group may differ by as much as a factor of ten. This variability in judgments within a group of observers implies that if people use absolute scales, the scale units may differ substantially among individuals. Nevertheless, the units show a sufficient central tendency, so that mean scales for groups of about 10 observers are in close agreement.

Zwislocki and Goodman point out that because the average absolute scales for different groups agree and are little influenced by contextual variables such as the order and range of stimuli presented, they should have widespread validity. "For example, loudness of noise scaled at some location in New York City on one group of people should be roughly comparable with the loudness of noise scaled at some location in Los Angeles by a different group of people" (Zwislocki and Goodman, 1980, p. 38).

CONTEXTUAL EFFECTS

The Effects of Other Stimuli Presented in the Test Session

The judgment, by an observer, of the sensory magnitude of a stimulus has been found to be strongly influenced by the context within which the stimulus is presented. For example, if a stimulus is presented after the presentation of several weaker stimuli, it is often judged to be more intense than had it been presented after the presentation of several stronger stimuli. The results of such an experiment are seen in Figure 11.12 (Gescheider, Bolanowski, & Verrillo, 1992; Gescheider & Hughson, 1991). Average magnitude estimations of the loudnesses of 1000-Hz tones are plotted as a function of intensity expressed in decibels above threshold. In separate experiments using absolute magnitude estimation and conventional magnitude estimation instructions, observers, in separate sessions, judged the loudness of tones presented within either a low (10–60 decibels above threshold) or high (40–90 decibels above threshold) range. For both methods of magnitude estimation, the judgments of stimuli common to the two ranges (40, 50, and 60 decibels above threshold) were judged higher when presented within the context of the low, rather than within the context of the high range of intensities. As was also found in other studies, the size of the context effect differed greatly from observer to observer (Marks, Szczesiul, & Ohlott, 1986). The judgments of some observers were entirely unaffected by stimulus context whereas those of others were greatly affected. It is also noteworthy that context had a greater affect on conventional magnitude estimation judgments than on

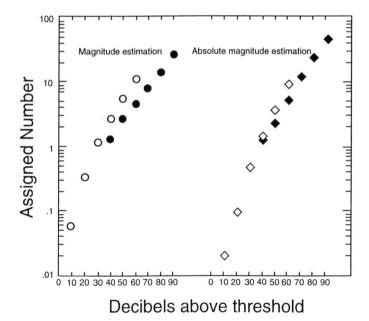

Decibels above threshold

FIG. 11.12. Magnitude estimation of the loudness of tones presented within the context of a low or a high intensity range. (Absolute magnitude estimation data from Gescheider & Hughson, 1991; magnitude estimation data from Gescheider, Bolanowski, & Verrillo, 1992.)

absolute magnitude estimation judgments. The smaller effects of context in absolute magnitude estimation may be due to the explicit instructions given to the observer that the judgment of a stimulus should be made without regard for judgments made of prior stimuli (see instructions for absolute magnitude estimation). However, even though observers were instructed to ignore prior stimuli when judging the sensation magnitude of a stimulus, absolute magnitude estimations were affected somewhat by stimulus context.

The fact that stimulus context affects judgments of sensation magnitude raises two important questions: what is the mechanism for context effects, and what are the implications of context effects for the validity of psychophysical scaling procedures? The answer to the first question may help provide the answer to the second. For example, one proposed explanation of context effects is that they are due to response bias in which observers tend to use the same range of numbers in magnitude estimation, regardless of the position of the stimulus range (Foley, Cross, & O'Reilly, 1990; Mellers, 1983; Poulton, 1979). An extreme case of the concept is illustrated in Figure 11.13. In this hypothetical set of data, the observer gave exactly the same set of six magnitude estimations to the six stimuli in the high range (40, 50, 60, 70, 80, and 90 dB) as was given to the low range (10, 20, 30, 40, 50, and 60 dB). According to the response bias hypothesis, although the sensation magnitudes of stimuli common to the two ranges (40, 50, and 60 dB) are uninfluenced by stimulus context, the observer's judgments are and, thus, the psychophysical scales for the two stimulus ranges are invalid. The observer's judgments of the stimuli with

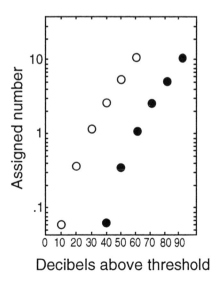

FIG. 11.13. Hypothetical data on magnitude estimation of the loudness of tones presented within the context of a low or a high intensity range.

Decibels above threshold

intensities of 40, 50, and 60 dB are influenced more by their positions within the stimulus range than by their sensation magnitudes. Because context effects are so pervasive in psychophysical scaling, the proponents of the response bias hypothesis tend to have serious doubts about the possibility of ever constructing valid psychophysical scales.

An alternative hypothesis to account for the effects of context in psychophysical scaling is that context, rather than exerting its effects through response bias, affects perception, which then, in turn, determines the observer's judgments (Algom & Marks, 1990; Helson, 1964; Marks, 1992; Parker & Schneider, 1994; Schneider & Parker, 1990; Ward, 1990). According to this hypothesis, context effects do not threaten the validity of psychophysical scaling procedures because it is not the process of judgment (e.g., in the case of magnitude estimation, the assigning of numbers to sensation magnitudes) that is affected by context, but instead it is the sensation magnitudes of stimuli that are affected. Context affects perception not judgment. In the experiment just described (Figure 11.12) by Gescheider and Hughson (1991) on the scaling of loudness, the 40-, 50-, and 60-dB tones were assigned larger numbers when heard in the context of weaker sounds than when heard in the context of more intense sounds because, in the first instance, they were heard as louder than in the second. According to this point of view, perceptions of stimuli are relative. A baseball may be perceived as very large relative to a marble but very small relative to a beach ball. Although a 10-story building would be perceived as very tall in Clinton, NY, it would be perceived as very small in midtown Manhattan. Several years ago, my friend's medium-size dog appeared to shrink in size over a period of about a year as my large dog attained his full growth. The context effects described thus far are examples of *contrast effects*, where the perceived magnitude of a stimulus is greater if presented with weaker than with stronger stimuli.

Perceptual contrast effects were explained some years ago by Helson's (1948, 1959, 1964) *adaptation level theory*. According to Helson, a stimulus is perceived and judged within a frame of reference determined by the values of other stimuli present in the situation and by the recent stimulus history of the observer. The observer's perceptions and subsequent judgments of sensory magnitude are determined by the adaptation level established by the frame of reference. The adaptation level determines the level of stimulation that is perceived as having a medium value. It is whether a stimulus is above or below the adaptation level that determines whether it is perceived as relatively strong or weak. Thus, all stimuli are judged relative to an adaptation level that can change from one situation to the next. In our present example of loudness scaling, the presentation of tones within the low range (10–60 decibels above threshold) established a lower adaptation level in the observer than did the presentation of tones within the high range (40–90 decibels above threshold). Consequently the 40-, 50-, and 60-dB tones of the low range were perceived as louder than the same tones presented in the high range.

Sequential Effects

We have just seen that an observer's judgment of the sensation magnitude of a particular stimulus can be influenced by the stimulus context provided by the presentation of other stimuli within the testing session. The effect, as just illustrated, is often one of contrast in which the judged sensation magnitude of the stimulus is greater when the other stimuli presented in the testing session are weaker than the stimulus than when they are stronger.

It has also been found that the observer's judgment of the sensation magnitude of a particular stimulus will vary from trial to trial within a testing session. Variation in the numerical response given by the observer can be substantial in some circumstances, with magnitude estimations varying by a factor of 2:1. These variations are sometimes random from trial-to-trial and can be attributed to random variation in either the sensory system or the observer's judgments. On the other hand, trial to trial variations in the observer's judgments of the sensory magnitude of a particular stimulus are sometimes systematically related to the values of stimuli presented, and responses made, on the previous few trials (Cross, 1973; Jesteadt, Luce, & Green, 1977; Luce & Green, 1974; Ward, 1973). Such sequential effects have generally been found to exhibit *assimilation*. In assimilation, the observer's magnitude estimation of a particular stimulus tends to be greater when the stimulus follows the presentation of a stronger stimulus than when it follows the presentation of a weaker stimulus. Such assimilative sequential context effects are opposite in direction to the contrast effects described earlier. Contrast and assimilation are illustrated in Figure 11.14. A contrast effect is seen when the response to stimulus S_F is greater when all other stimuli are weaker than S_F, than when all other stimuli are stronger than S_F. Assimilation is seen when the response to stimulus S_F is greater immediately following a response to a more intense stimulus, S_J, than immediately following a response to the weaker stimulus, S_B. In assimilation, the response to the stimulus is drawn in the direction of the response to the previous stimulus. In contrast effects, the response to the stimulus is drawn in the direction opposite to responses given to other stimuli.

Although sequential effects are almost always found to exhibit assimilation, Ward (1990) argued that these effects actually contain both an

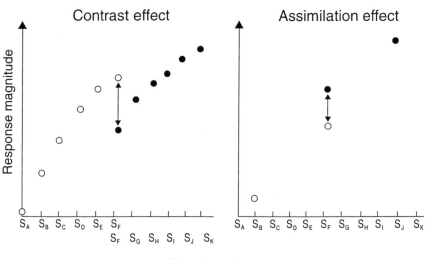

FIG. 11.14. Illustration of contrast and assimilation effects.

assimilative component and a contrastive component. The assimilative component is thought to depend on the size of the response given on previous trials, whereas the contrastive component depends on the intensities of stimuli presented on the previous trials. For example, if the stimulus was more intense on the previous trial than on the current trial, the perceptual contrast effect would cause the observer to have a tendency to judge the sensation magnitude of the current stimulus to be low. But, at the same time, because the magnitude estimation given to the intense previous stimulus was high, the process of assimilation would operate to cause the observer to give a high magnitude estimation to the current stimulus. The net effect of these two opposing tendencies is generally one in which assimilation dominates over contrast and, therefore, the response to the current stimulus is usually larger when preceded by a strong than by a weak stimulus. It was pointed out by DeCarlo (1992, 1994) that inferring contrast from the results of a psychophysical scaling experiment depends on the particular quantitative model used to analyze the data. The use of one model with its unique set of assumptions may lead to the conclusion that contrast is a component of sequential effects, whereas another model with different assumptions may not. DeCarlo (1994) made an important point that the size of assimilative sequential effects depends on the instructions to the observer. Thus, if assimilative effects are regarded as a contaminating influence on the observer's judgments of sensation magnitude, it will be important in future research to determine which instructions minimize such effects.

Stimulus Range

The size of the stimulus range employed within an experimental session may have a large effect on judgments of sensation magnitude. In general, it has been found that the slope of the psychophysical magnitude function increases as the stimulus range, defined as the ratio of the largest to the smallest stimulus in the series, decreases (Foley, Cross, Foley, & Reeder, 1983; Frederiksen, 1975; Montgomery, 1975; Teghtsoonian, 1973; Teghtsoonian & Teghtsoonian, 1978). This is because observers have a tendency to use the same response range for different stimulus ranges. This tendency has been identified by Poulton (1979) as the *stimulus-range equalizing bias*. Examination of the actual response ranges used by observers reveals that this tendency does not completely dominate their behavior. In fact as the stimulus range is decreased, a corresponding decrease in the response range is generally seen. Results on magnitude estimation of loudness are seen in Figure 11.15 for a wide (20–80 dB) and narrow (35–65 dB) range of stimulus intensities (Gescheider & Hughson, 1991). The dashed line is the psychophysical magnitude function predicted from the hypothesis that, when the stimulus range is changed from wide to narrow, the observer's judgments are determined entirely by the stimulus-range equalizing bias. It is clear that, although the psychophysical magnitude function became steeper when the stimulus range was decreased, it did not become as steep as predicted from the hypothesis that the observer's response range remains constant as the width of the stimulus range is changed. Moreover, it has been found that large changes in the slope of the psychophysical magnitude function only occur when the stimulus

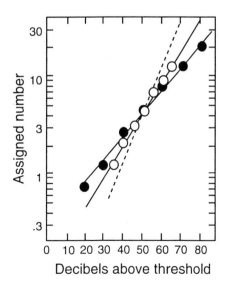

FIG. 11.15. Magnitude estimation of the loudness of tones presented within a wider or narrow range of stimulus intensities. (From Gescheider & Hughson, 1991.)

range becomes very small (Teghtsoonian, 1973; Teghtsoonian & Teght-soonian, 1978).

Although one interpretation of the stimulus range effect is that it reflects response bias of the observer and, therefore, renders the psychophysical magnitude function invalid, another is that it results from changes in the observer's perceptions of the sensory magnitudes of the stimuli. In our example, when the stimulus range became narrow, the stimuli at the upper end of this range would be perceived as more intense than the same stimuli within the wider range. Also, the stimuli at the lower end of the narrow range would be perceived as less intense than the same stimuli within the wider range. If the stimulus range affects perception rather than response bias, then magnitude estimation could be a valid way of examining this phenomenon. There is considerable recent evidence to support the perceptual magnitude over the response bias hypothesis (Algom & Marks, 1990; Parker & Schneider, 1994; Schneider & Parker, 1990).

PROBLEMS

11.1. On separate unlined 5 × 7 cards, draw circles with diameters of .25, .50, 1.00, 1.50, 2.00, 2.50, 3.50, and 4.50 inches. Present the circles in a random order to an observer and on each presentation require her to make a magnitude estimation of circle size. Use the instructions for absolute magnitude estimation on page 254. Repeat this procedure under similar viewing conditions for 10 observers. Plot the geometric mean of the judgments of circle size as a function of the area of the circle.

11.2. The following results were obtained in an experiment using ratio production:

	Stimulus Value							
	10	20	30	40	50	60	70	80
Stimulus judged $X\frac{1}{2}$	8	9	10	12	17	20	30	39
Stimulus judged $X2$	21	62	69	80				

Were the observer's $X\frac{1}{2}$ judgments consistent with his $X2$ judgments? From these results, construct a psychophysical magnitude function. Assign a psychological scale value of 300 to the stimulus value of 80.

11.3. The following data were obtained by numerical magnitude balance.

Magnitude Estimation		Magnitude Production	
Stimulus	Numerical Estimation	Stimulus Setting	Numerical Value
10	20	12	10
20	30	18	20
30	38	22	30
40	44	27	40
50	49	40	50
60	52	54	60

Plot the results in the correct way, and draw a curve that is an estimation of an unbiased scale. What is the nature of the bias that one attempts to correct through this method?

12

Evaluation of Ratio Scaling Methods

DO RATIO SCALING METHODS MEASURE
SENSATION MAGNITUDE?

In the methods of magnitude estimation and magnitude production, numerical estimations of sensation magnitude are obtained for a series of stimuli of varied intensity. The objective of the experiment is to establish precisely the functional relationship between stimulus intensity and sensation intensity. To accomplish this objective, valid measurements must be made of both stimulus and sensation intensity. It is important that the validity of both stimulus measurements and psychophysical judgments of sensation intensity be experimentally demonstrated. This has traditionally taken the form of demonstrations of additivity and transitivity of measurements.

Additivity

Techniques of physical measurement, when correctly used, generally produce valid measurements of the stimulus. It has been the tradition in physical science that any new method of measurement, in order to become widely accepted, must withstand vigorous tests of its validity. One test of validity requires that the measurements produced by a new method be in agreement with those produced by another method that is known to be valid. If a method with established validity does not already exist, other procedures must be used to test the validity of the new method. One such test is to evaluate the *additivity* of the measurements produced

264

by the method. For example, to establish a valid scale of weight, it is sufficient to demonstrate that the sum of the weights of two objects measured separately is equal to the weight of the two objects when measured together.

As in validating physical measurements, the validity of sensation magnitude measurements depends upon the successful demonstration that either the measurements are in agreement with known valid measurements, or they are additive. Since there is no wide agreement on which psychophysical scales of sensation magnitude are valid, most tests of the validity of new psychophysical scales have been attempts to demonstrate additivity of measurements. Some of the most systematic attempts have been made by Anderson (1970, 1974) for interval scaling and by Marks (1978b, 1978c; 1979a, 1979b) and Zwislocki (1983) for ratio scaling.

Without tests of additivity, the validity of an observer's numerical estimates of sensory magnitude is highly questionable, and therefore the estimates should not be treated as mathematical entities. For example, we must be critical when an investigator claims that because an observer gave a numerical judgment of the loudness of a 70-dB tone that was twice as great as his estimate of the loudness of a 60-dB tone, the 70-dB tone has twice the sensation magnitude of the 60-dB tone. How do we *really* know that the observer experienced the 70-dB tone to be twice as loud as the 60-dB tone? We can be sure of the validity of this conclusion only if it can be demonstrated that loudness estimates are additive. For example, two tones of widely different frequencies, when presented together, should have a total loudness equal to the sum of the individual loudnesses of the two tones.

Additivity of loudness judgments was first suggested by Fletcher and Munson (1933), but was more rigorously tested later by Zwislocki, Ketkar, Cannon, and Nodar (1974), who found evidence for loudness additivity when two equally loud tones, widely separated in frequency, were presented in rapid succession. It was found that observers adjusted a matching stimulus 10 dB higher when matching its loudness to the overall loudness of the pair of tones than when matching its loudness to that of either one of the tones presented alone. This difference of 10 dB in the intensity of the matching stimulus corresponds exactly to a doubling of loudness on the loudness scale determined by magnitude estimation. Thus, when two equally loud tones are presented together, they are judged to be twice as loud as either tone alone. This finding strongly supports the hypothesis that numerical judgments of loudness obtained by the magnitude estimation procedure pass the validity test of additivity. It appears that observers are capable of accurately assigning numbers to loudness.

Further support for this hypothesis comes from an experiment by Zwislocki (1983), who required observers to make magnitude estimations of the loudness of two brief tones separated by only 50 msec. The first tone had a frequency of 4000 Hz, and the second tone was 1000 Hz. Based on loudness scales determined by magnitude estimation of the two tones presented individually, it was possible to adjust the intensity of the first tone so that its estimated loudness was either the same as, half that, or twice that of the second tone. If loudness sums linearly, and if observers are capable of accurately estimating loudness, then the magnitude estimations of the tone pairs should be equal to the sum of the magnitude estimations of the individual tones. In general, this prediction was confirmed. For example, if the two tones when presented individually were judged to be equal in loudness, the pair of tones was estimated to be twice as loud as the individual components. If when presented individually the 4000-Hz tone of the pair was estimated to be half as loud as the 1000-Hz tone, the tone pair was judged to be 1.5 times as loud as the 1000-Hz tone alone. In other words, the estimated loudness of the tone pair was equal to the sum of the estimated loudnesses of the individual tones. This additivity of loudness estimations was also observed when the 4000-Hz tone was judged to be twice as loud as the 1000-Hz tone. In this case, the magnitude estimations of the tone pair were approximately three times as large as those of the 1000-Hz tone alone.

To further illustrate how the assumption of additivity of sensation magnitude estimations has been tested, the model of loudness summation is presented in Figure 12.1. In this presentation of the model, there are three stages. In the first stage, the auditory system converts stimulus energy to psychological loudness. This transformation is made separately for each component of a complex sound as long as the components of the sound are sufficiently different in frequency. Loudness is a negatively accelerated function of sound energy. This relationship is illustrated for the perception of sound X or sound Y. The total loudness of a complex sound is determined in the second stage. Total loudness is assumed to be the sum of the loudnesses of the components of a complex sound. In our example, when sound X and sound Y are presented together, the total loudness, L, is the sum of the loudnesses produced by stimulus X and stimulus Y, L_x and L_y. In the third stage, total loudness of the sound is converted into numerical values, which are reported by the observer as magnitude estimations. This stage comes into play only when people are asked to act as observers and give numerical estimates of loudness. According to the model, observers are capable of making accurate numerical estimates of their sensations of loudness. Thus, the conversion between loudness and magnitude estimations is linear.

Predictions from the model for the magnitude estimation of single tones and pairs of tones are seen in Figure 12.1. If sound X and sound Y each receive the same numerical estimate, the estimation of loudness

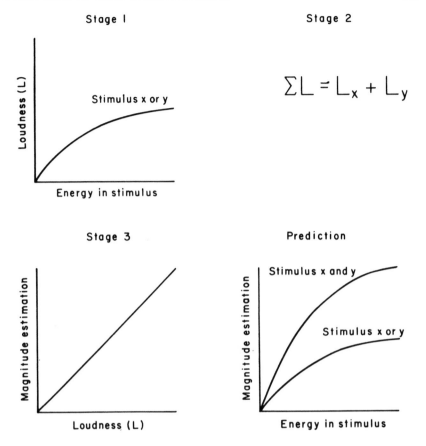

FIG. 12.1. Model of loudness summation.

should be twice this value when the two sounds are presented together. It can also be seen that if the intensities of sounds X and Y are adjusted so that one sound is twice as loud as the other, the total loudness of the pair of sounds should be three times that of the weaker sound and 1.5 times that of the more intense sound. These predictions were confirmed in Zwislocki's experiment (1983).

Research on the binaural summation of loudness also supports this model. When a sound is presented to both ears, it sounds louder than when it is presented only to one ear. Hellman and Zwislocki (1963), using the method of numerical magnitude balance, derived a loudness scale for binaural hearing that was double the scale for monaural hearing. From examination of the binaural and monaural loudness scales in Figure 12.2, it is seen that, at any intensity level, loudness judgments are doubled when the sound is presented to two ears rather than to just one. It seems

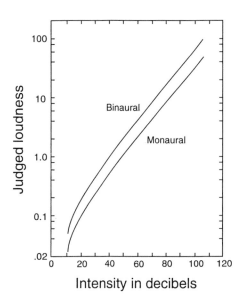

FIG. 12.2. Loudness functions for monaural and binaural listening. Binaural loudness summation is illustrated by the fact that the loudness during binaural stimulation was always twice that which obtained during monaural stimulation, regardless of intensity level. (From Gulick, Gescheider, & Frisina, 1989.)

that the two ears summate their loudnesses for a particular stimulus to produce the total loudness of the stimulus. This hypothesis was further tested by Marks (1978b), who had observers magnitude estimate the loudness of tones of equal or unequal intensities to the two ears. The results of this experiment are consistent with the hypothesis that total loudness is the linear sum of the loudnesses of the individual left-ear and right-ear components. These results and those of Zwislocki (1983) on the magnitude estimation of single tones and pairs of tones also support the hypothesis that ratio scaling methods can be used to measure the magnitude of sensations.

The additivity of sensation magnitude measurements obtained by magnitude estimation has also been demonstrated in vision and in touch. With a ganzfeld in which the entire field of vision of the eye is exposed to light of uniform intensity, Bolanowski (1987), using absolute magnitude estimation, demonstrated perfect binocular brightness summation. Under these conditions it was found that at all levels of light intensity the magnitude estimations of brightness were twice as high when two eyes were stimulated at the same intensity level than when only one eye was stimulated. These results are seen in Figure 12.3. The results are consistent with the hypothesis that the perceived brightness in a binocular ganzfeld is the sum of the brightnesses of the two monocular ganzfelds. Important to our discussion of the validity of psychophysical scales of sensation magnitude, is the finding that the measurements of perceived brightness exhibited additivity. Assuming that binocular brightness is the sum of two monocular brightnesses, the brightness scales are valid because when

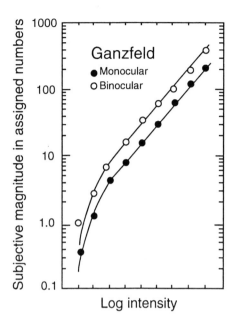

FIG. 12.3. Magnitude estimation of brightness in a monocular and in a binocular ganzfeld. (From Bolanowski, 1987.)

the scale values obtained for two monocular ganzfelds were added together a value is obtained which is the same as the scale value obtained for the binocular ganzfeld.

Using tactile stimuli, Marks (1979a) reported similar results for an experiment in which observers made magnitude estimations of the sensation magnitudes of vibrations of the hand. In this experiment, it was found that the sum of the numerical values of magnitude estimations of separately presented stimuli was equal to the magnitude estimation given when both stimuli were applied together. Thus, as in hearing and vision, psychophysical scale values obtained for the sense of touch exhibit additivity.

Are all observers capable of giving magnitude estimations that are proportional to their sensations? Zwislocki (1983) argued that although the averaged data for a group of subjects indicate that magnitude estimations are proportional to sensation magnitude, the responses of individual observers may deviate from this ideal. This argument was based upon the finding that some observers did not show perfect summation in their judgments of loudness. Magnitude estimations of the total loudness of the pair of tones were, in some cases, more than the value predicted, and in other cases, less than the values predicted for perfect summation. If we can assume that the mechanism for loudness summation in stage 2 of the model works perfectly in all observers, then the remaining mechanism—the transformation of loudness to magnitude estimations in stage 3—must be nonlinear for those observers whose magnitude estimations were not additive. If it is assumed that a loudness summation in stage 2 is linear, it is possible to determine, for individual observers, the nonlinear transformation in stage 3 that was responsible for the lack of additivity of the magnitude estimations. Using this approach, Zwislocki (1983) determined that magnitude estimations and psychological loudness for individual observers were related by power functions with exponents that varied from .83 to 1.33 with a mean of 1.08. A power function with an exponent of 1.0 is a linear function. Thus, the averaged data indicate that observers are capable of accurately assigning numbers to sensation magnitude, but an analysis of the results of individuals indicates that some observers deviate slightly from this ideal.

Zwislocki (1983) also obtained data from these same observers on the estimation of lengths of lines. The averaged data in this experiment, as well as those of many earlier experiments, indicate that magnitude estimation of length is proportional to line length. The results could be described by a power function with an exponent of approximately 1.0. It is now widely accepted that the sensory experience of line length is directly proportional to actual length. It is particularly significant that in Zwislocki's experiment, the results of individual observers sometimes deviated from this ideal power exponent of 1.0 for magnitude estimation of length and the actual line length. In every case, the exponent for the estimation of line length was almost identical to the theoretical exponents calculated for the relationship between magnitude estimation responses and the sensation of loudness. Thus, some observers seem to make systematic errors in assigning numbers to the intensity of their sensations, which carry over from one sensory modality to another. These errors in the use of numbers mean that an observer's magnitude estimations will fail to accurately indicate her sensations. Fortunately, the errors in assigning numbers to sensations are small in most observers, and since they are symmetrically distributed around perfect performance, they tend to average out when the responses of several observers are averaged.

It is highly recommended that a measure of distortion in the use of numbers in ratio scaling experiments be determined for each observer. For example, if the functional relationship between the observer's magnitude estimations and sensation magnitude is known, it would be possible to correct inaccurate magnitude estimations of stimulus intensity. Figure 12.4 illustrates how such a correction could be made for an observer's judgment of loudness. Each magnitude estimation is converted into units of sensation magnitude (Figure 12.4a), and these corrected magnitude estimation values are plotted as in Figure 12.4b. A convenient way to experimentally determine the relationship between magnitude estimation and sensation magnitude (Figure 12.4a) is to have each observer make magnitude estimations of line length. Since it is a reasonable assumption that the sensation magnitude of line length is directly pro-

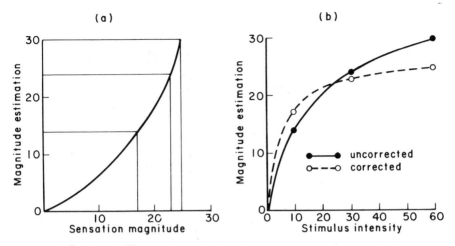

FIG. 12.4. Conversion of magnitude estimations into sensation magnitude units.

portional to actual line length, any deviation in an observer's magnitude estimation from direct proportionality with line length is a reflection of distortions in the use of numbers. The graph of magnitude estimation of length as a function of line length can be used for correcting magnitude estimations of other dimensions of stimulus intensity such as sound or light intensity. Implicit in this procedure is the assumption that distortions in the use of numbers are the same for all stimulus dimensions. Another good reason for having observers estimate the length of lines before estimating other stimulus dimensions is that practice in estimating line lengths often eliminates these troublesome response biases of magnitude estimation (Zwislocki, 1983).

Transitivity

Experiments in which the method of absolute magnitude estimation was used support the validity of the resulting psychophysical scales through their demonstration of the transitivity of scale values. *Transitivity* is the requirement that if a set of measurements is valid, then if a = b and a = c, it must be true that b = c. This concept from measurement theory can be applied to psychophysical as well as physical measurement. If observers assign numbers to their sensations on an absolute scale, then stimuli in two different modalities are equal in sensation magnitude when the stimuli are given the same number in magnitude estimation. It should, therefore, be possible to demonstrate the transitivity of scales by predicting the absolute values of cross-modality matches. The prediction is that stimuli from the two modalities that have been assigned the same number in magnitude estimation experiments will be judged to be psychologically equal in cross-modality matching in which the observer directly compares the two stimuli and reports whether they are equal in sensation magnitude.

In an experiment on the transitivity of absolute magnitude estimations, Collins and Gescheider (1989) required observers to match their impressions of number size to their impressions of line length and to the loudness of 1000-Hz tones. In the second phase of the experiment, the same observers were required to match their impressions of line length to the perceived loudness of the tones. The results of one observer are seen in Figure 12.5. The psychophysical scales for subjective line length and loudness, in which magnitude estimations are plotted as a function of stimulus intensity, are

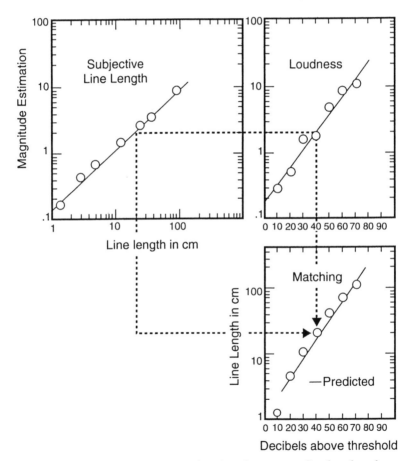

FIG. 12.5. Magnitude estimation functions for apparent line length and loudness (top left and right) and the obtained (open circles, lower right) as predicted (line, lower right) cross-modality matching functions.

presented in the upper two graphs of the figure. The lines represent the best fitting functions for each scale. The line of the cross-modality matching function in the lower right graph was predicted from the subjective line length and loudness functions. It is clear that the actual matches, as indicated by the data points, are in agreement with the predicted cross-modality function. The dashed lines in the figure illustrate the prediction of a single point on the cross-modality matching function where a magnitude estimation value of 2.0 corresponds to a line length of 20 cm and a tone of 40 dB above threshold. The fact that this and all other cross-modality matching values are predicted accurately from the magnitude estimation scales of subjective line length and loudness supports the hypothesis that the scales are valid. The transitivity of magnitude estimation scales demonstrated in this experiment has also been demonstrated in studies of vibration of the skin and loudness (Bolanowski, Zwislocki, & Gescheider, 1991), the loudness of tones of different frequencies (Hellman, 1976), the loudness of tones in the presence and in the absence of noise (Hellman & Zwislocki, 1964), and the subjective magnitude of vibrotactile stimuli of different frequencies (Verrillo, Fraioli, & Smith, 1969). In all of these studies, values of psychophysical matches of the sensation magnitude of qualitatively different stimuli were accurately predicted from magnitude estimation judgments. The important point is that when two qualitatively different stimuli had the same sensation magnitude scale values determined through magnitude estimation, they were judged in a psychophysical matching experiment to be equal in sensation magnitude. In all of these experiments, the procedure was to (a) determine the magnitude estimation function for each sensory dimension; (b) determine from the magnitude estimation functions, the predicted psychophysical matching function in which each point on the function defines two stimulus values, one from one sensory dimension and one from the other, which produce the same magnitude estimation numbers; and (c) measure stimulus values, one from each dimension, that are judged by the observer, in a matching task, to be equal in sensation magnitude.

PSYCHOPHYSICAL, PSYCHOLOGICAL, AND SENSORY RESPONSE LAWS

In psychophysical scaling experiments, sensory responses of the observer are recorded for a number of different values of the stimulus. For example, magnitude estimations of loudness might be recorded when a sound is presented to an observer at several different intensity levels. The relationship between the sensory response and the value of the stimulus provides a basis for formulating three types of law: (1) *psychophysical laws*, (2) *psychological laws*, and (3) *sensory response laws*. Each law consists of theoretical explanations for the results of the scaling experiment. The discovery of these laws is a primary objective of the psychophysicist. The laws consist of fundamental principles describing how sensations relate to environmental stimuli (psychophysical law), how sensations relate to one another (psychological law), and how sensations relate to sensory responses (sensory response law).

Psychophysical Laws

Psychophysical laws describe the relationship between stimulus and sensation. Over a century ago, Fechner proposed that the magnitude of sensation increases with the logarithm of stimulus intensity, and more recently S. S. Stevens (1957) hypothesized that sensation magnitude is proportional to stimulus intensity raised to a power. Since the time of Fechner, the discovery of psychophysical laws has been central to psychophysics. Measurement of both stimulus and sensation are necessary in formulating psychophysical laws. Although measurement of the stimulus has improved as methods in physics and engineering have been developed for measuring environmental energies, the measurement of sensation remains a difficult problem. Because sensations are subjective events, we cannot directly observe and measure them in others. We must infer their existence and magnitude from observable behavior such as magnitude estimations. Consequently, the validity of a psychophysical law is dependent on accurate inference of sensation magnitude from observable sensory responses. When the sensory responses of observers are an accurate reflection of their sensations, then formulating a valid psychophysical law simply requires a statement of the relationship between sensory responses and the stimuli that provoked them. The problem is that it is usually not known whether sensory responses obtained through a particular scaling method accurately reflect the observer's sensations.

For this reason, the assumption made by Stevens that the judgments of observers were proportional to sensation magnitude has been challenged (e.g., Anderson, 1970; Birnbaum, 1982; Shepard, 1981). Shepard (1981) argued that there are major limitations in the use of magnitude estimation and that Stevens' (1975) contention that assigned numbers in magnitude estimation were directly proportional to sensation magnitude is logically flawed. The problem is illustrated in Figure 12.6. The limitations of the method become apparent only when the investigator interprets the experimentally determined functional relationship (f_3) between stimulus (ϕ) and response (R),

$$R = f_3(\phi), \tag{12.1}$$

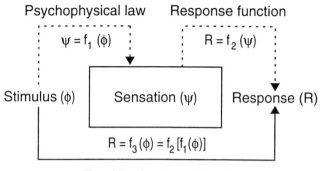

FIG. 12.6. Relations among the psychophysical law, the response function, and the empirically determined stimulus–response function.

to be the *stimulus transformation function* (psychophysical law), describing the functional relationship (f_1) between the intervening variable, sensation magnitude (φ), and the stimulus

$$\varphi = f_1(\phi). \tag{12.2}$$

Shepard pointed out that this formulation is incomplete. He indicated that we must also consider a second transformation, the *response transformation* (sensory-response law), which determines the final response. This second transformation is the functional relationship (f_2) between the response and the intervening variable, sensation magnitude (φ). The first transformation between the stimulus and sensation, $\varphi = f_1(\phi)$, being followed by the second transformation

$$R = f_2(\varphi), \tag{12.3}$$

results in the experimentally observed relationship, $R = f_3(\phi)$, between stimulus and response.

Shepard pointed out that, because the intervening variable, φ, is not itself observable, the equation for R must be written as

$$R = f_3(\phi) = f_2[f_1(\phi)] \tag{12.4}$$

in which Equation 12.2 does not explicitly appear. Unless one of the two component functions of f_3 (i.e., f_1 or f_2) is known, it is impossible to determine the other by knowledge of the experimentally determined f_3. According to Shepard, the conclusion drawn by Stevens from magnitude estimation data that f_1 is a power function, depends on the assumption that instructions to the observer have ensured that f_2 is a linear function with zero intercept of the form

$$R = a\varphi. \tag{12.5}$$

Shepard pointed out that the grounds for Stevens' assumption that instructions would have exactly this effect were never adequately explained. The general concept of a two-stage theory of magnitude estimation in which the first stage is sensory and the second is cognitive, involving processes of judgment, has its origin in the early work of Attneave (1962), and Curtis, Attneave, and Harrington (1968). According to this theory, the observer's response results from a two-stage process in which the stimulus first produces a sensation and, following this, the sensation results in a judgment response. It is important to keep in mind that if we, in psychophysics, are primarily interested in the first of these two stages, we must take into account the second when making inferences from observed relations between the stimulus and the observer's response.

Sensory Response Laws

The problem of inferring a psychophysical law from sensory responses measured in an experiment, as discussed above, is illustrated in Figure 12.7. When sensory responses and their physical stimuli are measured in a psychophysical experiment, the relationship that emerges describes how the sensory response changes as a function of changes in the stimulus (top of Figure 12.7). But the goal of the experiment is to determine the relationship between the sensation and stimulus. To derive this relationship from the experimentally determined relationship between sensory response and stimulus, one needs to know a third relationship—the relationship between sensory response and sensation, often referred to as the *sensory response law*. Some investigators have simply assumed that the relationship between the sensory response and sensation is linear. This assumption is illustrated in the lower right of Figure 12.7. When this assumption is correct, the sensory response provides a direct measure of sensation, and, consequently, the experimentally measured relationship between sensory response and stimulus (top of Figure 12.7) reveals the relationship between sensation and stimulus. For example, consider the results of a scaling experiment illustrated in the top left of Figure 12.8. These results are predicted from the psychophysical law plotted in the lower right of the figure. (Note that the ordinate of this function is presented horizontally rather than in its usual vertical orientation.) By using the sensory response law, sensation magnitudes are transformed to sensory responses. This process is illustrated for one intensity of the stimulus. From the psychophysical law, the stimulus is converted to

EXPERIMENTAL RESULTS

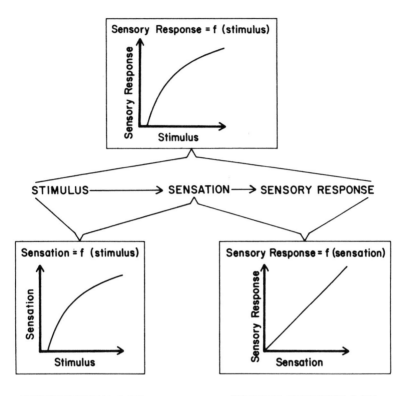

FIG. 12.7. Illustration of two-stage theory of sensory scaling in which the psychophysical law and the sensory response law intervene to determine the observed relationship between sensory responses and stimulus intensity.

sensation magnitude, which then, through the sensory response law, is converted to a sensory response. The sensory response, with its corresponding stimulus, is plotted as a predicted point in the graph of experimental results. By following the arrows from the psychophysical law to the experimental results, the conversion of the stimulus to sensory magnitude and the conversion of sensory magnitude to the sensory response are seen for one intensity of the stimulus. The predicted curve for the experimental results is generated by repeating this procedure for all values of the stimulus. Since the sensory response law is linear, the predicted experimental curve and the psychophysical law are identical. On the other hand, Figure 12.9 illustrates how experimental results and the psychophysical law will always differ when the sensory response law is nonlinear. Zwislocki's (1983) work on magnitude estimation of the

GOVERNORS STATE UNIVERSITY
UNIVERSITY PARK
IL 60466

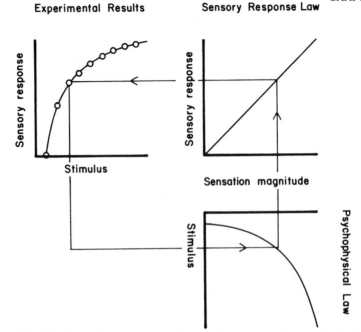

FIG. 12.8. According to two-stage theory of sensory scaling, a stimulus produces a sensation of a particular magnitude, which in turn produces a sensory response of a particular magnitude. In this example, the sensory response law is linear, and therefore, the experimental results and the psychophysical law are identical relationships.

loudness of tones and the length of lines seems to indicate that, for some observers but not others, sensations and sensory responses are linearly related.

In psychophysical scaling, it is essential that the investigator attempt to discover this basic relationship between sensation magnitude and the observer's sensory response. This relationship or sensory response law is of fundamental importance in discovering psychophysical laws of stimulus and sensation. Without knowledge of the sensory response law, the relationship between the sensory response and the stimulus can be accounted for by an infinite variety of combinations of proposed psychophysical and sensory response laws. Figure 12.10 shows how different combinations A, B, and C of psychophysical laws and sensory response laws can predict the same experimental results. In this example, the prediction is made that a stimulus will produce the same sensory response with each combination of psychophysical and sensory response laws. If we knew which of the three sensory response laws was correct, we would also know which psychophysical law was correct. We are fundamentally interested in the psychophysical law, but to derive it from experimental results we must know the sensory response law. This

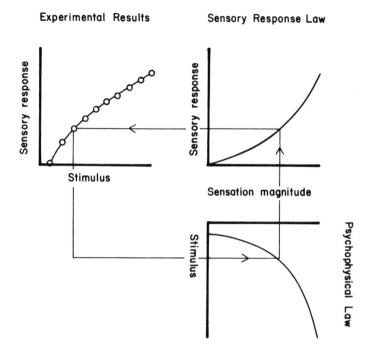

FIG. 12.9. Two-stage theory of sensory scaling applied to a case in which the sensory response law is not linear. When the sensory response law is non-linear, the experimental results and the psychophysical law will always differ.

problem is particularly difficult to solve, since the sensory response law may change from situation to situation, from one scaling method to another, and even from observer to observer in the same situation in which the same scaling method is used.

Figure 12.11 illustrates how experimental results of two observers may be different even though the psychophysical law for each is the same. It should be clear that although the underlying relationship between stimulus and sensation (the psychophysical law) is the same for both observers, the relationships between sensory responses and stimulus intensity (the experimental results) are different. The situation can be conceptualized as two stages. In the first stage, the sensory system converts stimulus intensity into sensory magnitude. The psychophysical law is a mathematical description of this conversion and is illustrated in the lower right of Figure 12.11. In this example, the psychophysical law is identical for both observers. The conversion of stimulus energy to sensory magnitude is followed by a second stage in which the observer makes a sensory response, such as magnitude estimation, to the experienced sensory magnitude. It can be seen from the sensory response laws illustrated in Figure 12.11 that the sensory

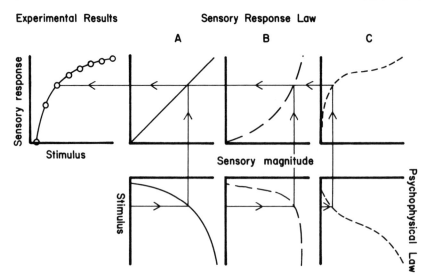

FIG. 12.10. Illustration of how the same experimental results are produced by three combinations (A, B, or C) of psychophysical and sensory response laws. It can be seen that the same stimulus results in different sensory magnitudes. However, as a result of different sensory response laws, the sensory response is the same in all three cases. The problem is to discover which combination of psychophysical law and sensory response law is correct.

responses of observer 1 are linearly related to sensory magnitude, but in the case of observer 2, sensory responses are nonlinearly related to sensory magnitude. As a consequence of this difference in the sensory response laws, the experimentally observed relationship between sensory responses and stimulus intensity is different for the two observers. Thus, differences in the relationship between observed sensory responses and stimulus intensity do not necessarily indicate differences in psychophysical laws among observers. Again, the importance of attempting to discover the sensory response laws of individual observers in scaling experiments must be emphasized. Only if we know the sensory response laws of an observer is it possible to deduce the psychophysical law from the experimental results. It can be seen from Figure 12.11 that if we know the sensory response laws of each observer, then it should be possible to convert experimental results to psychophysical laws. The sensory response laws of each observer are used to convert sensory responses to sensory magnitude. In this example, although the experimental results of the two observers are different, the psychophysical laws are the same. In other situations, the psychophysical laws of different observers may be different. In any case, to determine psychophysical laws from experimental results, we must know the sensory response laws of individual observers.

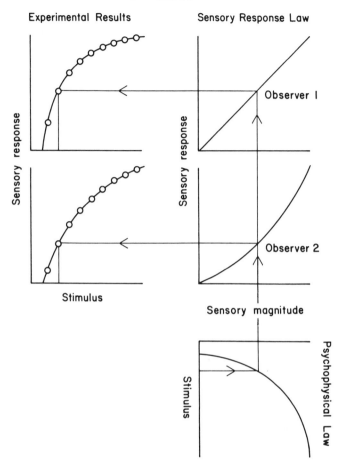

FIG. 12.11. Illustration of how different experimental results are produced from the same psychophysical law because observers have different sensory response laws.

Probably the best technique available for estimating sensory response laws is the psychophysical scaling of the perceived lengths of lines (Zwislocki, 1983). It is generally accepted that sensations of line length are proportional to physical line length. Average magnitude estimations of line length for 10 or more observers is consistently found to be linearly related to physical line length. When an individual observer's magnitude estimations are linearly related to line length, it is concluded that he is capable of accurately assigning numbers to sensations of length; that is, the sensory response law is linear. When an observer's magnitude estimations are nonlinearly related to line length, it is concluded that he is unable to accurately assign numbers to sensations of line length; that is, the sensory response law is nonlinear. However, the sensory response law can be established for each observer in an experiment on magnitude estimation of line length. These sensory response laws can be used to correct the magnitude estimations of other sensory dimensions such as loudness, brightness, pain, and so on. The technique is illustrated for one observer who made magnitude estimations of the loudness of tones and the apparent lengths of lines (Collins & Gescheider, 1989). Following the arrow in Figure 12.12, it can be seen how magnitude estimations of loudness can be converted to sensation magnitude (loudness). At each tone intensity, the magnitude estimation of loudness is converted to a line length that was given the same magnitude estimation as the tone. Assuming that the sensation magnitude of line length is proportional to actual line length, line length becomes the measure of sensation magnitude (in this case loudness). The second important assumption made when using this technique is that

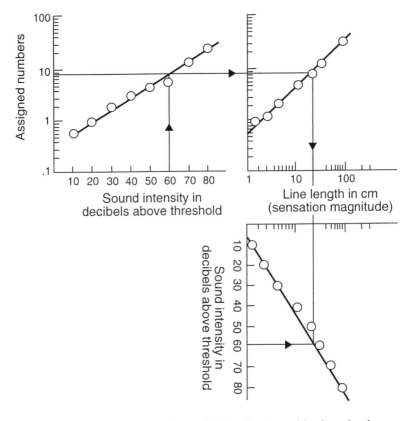

FIG. 12.12. The correction of magnitude estimations of loudness by the sensory response law estimated from magnitude estimations of the apparent length of lines. (From Collins & Gescheider, 1989.)

the way that an observer correctly or incorrectly uses numbers when magnitude estimating sensations on a particular sensory dimension will be the same on this dimension as it is for apparent line length. This assumption allows the investigator to use the apparent line length function of the observer as a standard calibration curve for converting magnitude estimations on any sensory dimension into units of sensation magnitude that are not contaminated by the inaccurate use of numbers.

A method that is being used with increasing frequency is the matching of apparent line length to the psychological magnitudes on the sensory dimension under consideration. Collins and Gescheider (1989) found essentially the same results for loudness scales measured by direct matching of apparent line length to loudness and loudness scales derived, as just described, from magnitude estimation of loudness and line length. The argument for avoiding magnitude estimation and instead matching the sensation magnitudes of line length to that of other dimensions, is that magnitude estimation requires observers to use numbers whereas line length matching does not. Also, in direct matching of line length, the data analysis is simplified. By plotting the line lengths that match the subjective magnitudes of stimuli, one has an estimation of the psychophysical law for the observer. The data points in Figure 12.12 for the corrected loudness function were, in fact, determined by direct matching of apparent line length to loudness. It is clear that the results obtained with the method of line length matching are in close agreement with those obtained by magnitude estimation of loudness corrected by the magnitude estimation of apparent line length. Because sensation magnitude scales obtained by line length matching are essentially the same as those determined from corrected magnitude estimation judgments, either method could be used with equal effectiveness and, therefore, practical consideration may govern which approach to take.

Individual Differences

It is generally agreed that the amount of variability in the psychophysical magnitude functions of individual observers far exceeds the variability of the underlying psychophysical process (Gescheider & Bolanowski, 1991). For example, the variability in the forms of the psychophysical magnitude functions for judgments of loudness is thought to be much greater than the variability of the underlying loudness functions. In other words, people differ far more in their judgmental responses (e.g., magnitude estimations) than they do in their actual perceptions. This being the case, it follows that the judgments of sensory magnitude in the scaling experiment are affected by both sensory and judgmental processes, and that both of these must contribute to the total variability in the results across individual observers.

If sensory and judgmental processes independently vary from observer to observer, then the total variability between observers must be greater for psychophysical magnitude functions, determined through judgments of observers, than for the underlying sensory functions of the observers. This contention has been supported by the finding that the variance of individual magnitude estimation functions for loudness is substantially reduced by correcting each of these functions for the idiosyncratic way an observer assigns numbers to sensations (Algom & Marks, 1984; Collins & Gescheider, 1989; Zwislocki, 1983).

Sensory Response Law and Line Length Calibration

In the study by Collins and Gescheider (1989), observers made absolute magnitude estimations of the loudnesses of tones of varied intensity and of the apparent lengths of lines. The apparent line length judgments were used to estimate the sensory response law for each observer. The left graph of Figure 12.13 shows the loudness judgments of 12 observers plotted as a function of sound pressure level in decibels above absolute threshold. The best fitting straight line was fitted to each observer's results. The graph on the right contains the functions of the left graph after each has been corrected for the sensory response law of the observer. Thus, using the logic discussed in the previous section, an attempt was made to estimate each observer's psychophysical law for loudness perception by converting

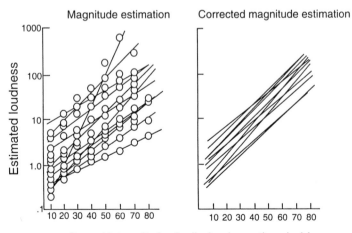

FIG. 12.13. Magnitude estimation of loudness by individual observers before correction for the sensory response law estimated from each observer's judgments of apparent line length (left graph) and after correction (right graph). (From Collins & Gescheider, 1989.)

sensory responses (loudness judgments) to sensory magnitude (loudness) through the sensory response law as determined through the judgments of apparent line length. It is clear that the corrected functions on the right are much less variable than those on the left. Presumably, the large amount of variability in the experimental results is due to the fact that variability in judgments of loudness is affected by both variability in perceived loudness and variability in the ways different observers use numbers. The small amount of variability seen after correction of the results by the sensory response law was thought to be due to variability in how perceived loudness changes with sound intensity for different observers. It is clear that most of the variability in judged loudness was due to variability in the use of numbers. Indeed, in this study the calculated variance in the slopes of the magnitude estimation functions was 16 times higher than that of the corrected loudness functions.

Magnitude Matching

A similar approach to that of correcting individual magnitude estimation functions through line length judgments is that of *magnitude matching*, developed by Stevens and Marks (1980). Again, the goal is to eliminate the effects of the idiosyncratic ways in which individual observers assign numbers to their sensation magnitudes. If this goal is achieved, valid scales for individual observers can be constructed and comparisons made of the sensory processes of individuals. In magnitude matching, the objective is to have the observer judge the sensory magnitudes of stimuli from two different modalities, A and B, on a single, common scale. To this end, stimuli from the two modalities are presented within the same session, often alternating over trials from one modality to the other. One of the two modalities serves as the standard and the other as the test modality. By making the assumption that individuals or groups are alike in their perceptions of stimuli presented within the standard modality, it is possible to determine whether there are differences in perception of stimuli within the test modality.

Magnitude matching rests on the fundamental principle that to make valid comparisons of different groups or individual observers, their results must be measured on a common scale in which the unit is always the same. Consider a case in which one observer judges the loudness of a tone to be 20 while another observer judges its loudness to be 10. Is the loudness experienced by the first observer greater than that experienced by the second observer? If the judgments of the two observers were made on a common scale, the answer is yes, but if they were not, the answer is that you can't tell. In magnitude matching, an attempt would be made to put the results of these two observers on a common scale so that they could be meaningfully compared.

To illustrate the method, we turn to an experiment on the sense of taste (Marks, Stevens, Bartoshuk, Gent, Rifkin, & Stone, 1988). In this study, 18 tasters and 18 nontasters judged the sensation magnitudes of the tastes of various substances. Nontasters consist of about 30% of the population who have genetically determined high thresholds for detecting a class of bitter compounds such as PTC (phenylthiourea) and PROP (6-n-propylthiouracil). The standard modality, within which the sensory experiences of tasters and nontasters were assumed to be the same, was the perceived loudness of 1000-Hz tones. The test modality was taste and the taste stimuli were PROP and NaCl. In an experimental session, taste stimuli were alternated with tones and the observer was instructed to judge them, using magnitude estimation, on a common scale of sensation magnitude. Observers were instructed that the same number should be given to a sound and a taste if the loudness equaled the perceived taste intensity. The results presented in Figure 12.14 show clearly that the magnitude estimations of tasters and nontasters, after having been converted to a common scale, differed for the taste of PROP but did not for the taste of NaCl. For any concentration level, the bitter taste of PROP was judged to be more intense by tasters than nontasters, whereas the salty taste of NaCl was not different for the two groups. Converting the judgments of all of the observers to a common scale involved the following: (a) for each observer, the average of all of the loudness judgments (pooled over trials and intensities) was computed; (b) by dividing 10 by each observer's average judgment (10/average judgment), the multiplicative factor needed to bring each observer's average loudness judgment to 10 was determined; and (c) all the taste and loudness judgments of each observer were then multiplied by the multiplicative factor determined through steps 1 and 2. Thus, under the assumption that loudness is experienced in the same way by tasters and nontasters, the judgments of all of the observers were converted to a common scale based on

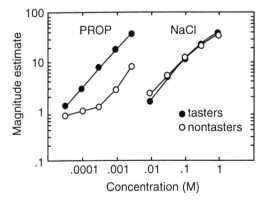

FIG. 12.14. Magnitude estimations for PROP and NaCl by tasters and nontasters after correction by magnitude matching. (From Marks et al., 1988.)

loudness judgments. After this procedure was performed, the corrected results were averaged and plotted as seen in Figure 12.14.

The method of magnitude matching has also been used to evaluate changes in the perception of suprathreshold taste stimuli (Bartoshuk, Rifkin, Marks, & Bars, 1986) and suprathreshold olfactory stimuli (Stevens, Plantinga, & Cain, 1982) that occur with aging. Thus, the method can be successfully used to demonstrate differences in the sensory magnitudes of stimuli experienced by old and young observers. In addition to the application of the method to problems of how clinical populations and aging populations of individuals may differ from those who are young and healthy, the method is useful in determining whether or not the sensory magnitudes experienced by an individual are different from the norm or different from those of another individual. Indeed, Marks (1991) demonstrated that differences in the results obtained by this method for individual observers are consistently observed over repeated testings.

Master Scaling

Berglund (1991) developed another procedure for dealing with individual differences called *master scaling* of sensory magnitude. Again, as in Zwislocki's line length calibration procedure and Stevens' and Marks' magnitude matching, the idea is to correct the data of individual observers or different groups of observers so their magnitude estimation judgments fall on a common scale. In this way, the judgments can be meaningfully compared. This method is particularly well suited for situations in which different observers make judgments of different target stimuli in real environmental situations. For example, suppose that we are interested in comparing the perceived loudness of traffic noise in downtown Manhattan with the industrial noise in a steel mill in Weirton, West Virginia. A group of pedestrians in Manhattan could be asked to make magnitude estimations of the loudness of the traffic sound and a group of steel workers in Weirton could be asked to do the same for industrial noise in the mill. Suppose that the average magnitude estimations for industrial noise and traffic noise were 12 and 4, respectively. Was the industrial noise louder than the traffic noise or not? Perhaps steel workers in Weirton tend to use larger numbers in magnitude estimation than do pedestrians in Manhattan and the loudness of industrial noise did not really differ from the loudness of traffic noise. The procedure of master scaling, if applied to this situation, would require that the magnitude estimations of the two groups be converted to a master scale, after which they would be compared and a legitimate conclusion made about whether the traffic noise and the industrial noise differed in loudness. The following steps would be taken in the construction and use of such a master scale: (a) a master scale would be constructed by having a group of observers make magnitude estimations of the loudness of bursts of noise of varied intensity, then, (b) the two groups of observers from Manhattan and Weirton would also make magnitude estimation judgments of the same noise bursts resulting in a *reference scale* for each group. At the same time, the group from Manhattan would also make judgments of the traffic noise *target stimulus* while the group from Weirton would make judgments of the industrial noise target stimulus, (c) equations would be determined for the best fitting function for the master scale and for each of the two reference scales, and (d) for both the Weirton and Manhattan loudness scales, an equation would be determined that would transform the reference loudness scale to the master scale. These equations would also be used to transform the Manhattan group's judgments of traffic noise and the Weirton group's judgments of industrial noise to the master scale, where they would then be compared on a common scale.

The procedure for converting judgments to a master scale is illustrated in Figure 12.15. Hypothetical magnitude estimations for the master scale and for the reference scales of the Manhattan and Weirton groups are plotted as a function of sound intensity in the left side of the figure. Equations describing the relationship between the numbers given in magnitude estimation (N) and sound intensity (I) are determined for the best fitting functions to the data obtained for the master scale ($N_m = f_2[I]$) and each of the two reference scales ($N_r = f_1[I]$ and $N_r = f_3[I]$). From the equations for the three magnitude estimation functions, it is possible to

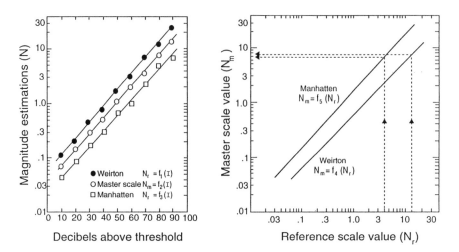

FIG. 12.15. Magnitude estimation of the loudness of noise by a reference group, a group of pedestrians in Manhattan, and a group of steel workers in Weirton (left graph). Magnitude estimations of the Manhattan and Weirton groups after converting the results to a master scale (right graph). (Hypothetical data.)

determine the relation between numbers given on the master scale and numbers on the reference scale. In the right side of the figure, the relationship between numbers on the master scale and numbers on the reference scale is indicated for each of the two groups. It can now be seen that when the magnitude estimations for industrial noise and traffic noise are converted to the master scale either graphical or through equations, $N_m = f_4(N_r)$ and $N_m = f_5(N_r)$, they no longer differ by a factor of three but, instead, hardly differ at all. Thus, had the difference in the ways that observers in the two groups use numbers not been taken into account through the master scale, we would have falsely concluded that industrial noise in the Weirton steel mill was substantially louder than traffic noise in Manhattan.

In the example just discussed, the results of two groups of observers have been converted to the master scale of comparison. The same procedure can be used for the judgments of individual observers.

The Category Ratio Scale

Borg (1982) was concerned with the problem of using psychophysical scaling procedures to measure individual differences in the experienced sensory magnitudes of stimuli. According to Borg, "If one subject calls the loudness of a certain sound '8' and another '20,' this does not necessarily mean that the person who says '20' perceives the sound to be louder than the one who says '8.' If, on the other hand, one says 'weak' and the other says 'loud' or 'strong,' we can be fairly sure that the first person perceives the sound to be weaker than the second one" (p. 28). According to Borg, ratio scaling procedures such as magnitude estimation yield information about the relative differences in the subjective impressions of stimuli, but provide no information about the absolute levels of such impressions. Consequently, it is not possible to meaningfully compare the absolute values of magnitude estimations of individual observers. Borg's solution to this problem has been to create a scaling procedure that has properties of both category and ratio scales—the *category ratio scale*. Borg initially designed the category ratio scale to measure perceived exertion during exercise, such as pedaling a stationary bicycle. He started with the assumptions that the experience of maximal exertion, although occurring at different work loads is the same for different individuals, and that the psychological range from minimal to maximal exertion is also the same for different individuals. Thus, all observers have a common scale of perceived exertion with a common anchor at the point of maximal exertion. It was also assumed that through association of descriptive adjectives (such as extremely strong, strong, moderate, weak, extremely weak, etc.) with various experiences of exertion, that similar perceived exertion described by a particular adjective would be experienced by different observers. For example, because maximal exertion is the same for different individuals, as is the psychological range from extremely weak to maximal exertion, states of exertion described as moderate should also be experienced as the same by different individuals. In constructing his category ratio scale Borg assigned numbers to a series of descriptive adjectives in such a way that the results obtained with his category ratio scale would be in essential agreement with those obtained with ratio-scaling methods such as magnitude estimation. The scale with its categories and associated numbers is presented here:

	Maximal
10	extremely strong (almost maximal)
9	
8	
7	very strong
6	
5	strong (heavy)
4	somewhat strong
3	moderate
2	weak (light)
1	very weak
0.5	extremely weak (just noticeable)
0	nothing at all

With this scale, individual differences are revealed in the different work loads that different individuals associate with a particular category. For example, in the hypothetical scales for observers A and B (seen in Figure 12.16), the experienced exertion of 3 designated as moderate exertion occurred with work loads of x and y for observers A and B, respectively. Thus, the two observers differ greatly in the work loads that were experienced as a moderate exertion of perceived effort. Likewise, if we compare the numerical value of the judged exertion experienced by each observer at a work load on the bicycle of y, we see that observer A experienced exertion at a level of 9 on the scale, a value associated with extremely strong exertion, whereas observer B experienced exertion at a moderate level of 3. Because the numerical values were assigned to the various categories so that the functions, such as those seen in Figure 12.16, agree with those obtained with magnitude estimation, Borg treats them as ratio scales. Thus, the exertion at level 9 experienced by observer A at work load y is three times that experienced by observer B at level 3 at the same work load. In such a case, it would appear that observer A is badly out of shape. Indeed, the scale can be used to assess the physical condition of individuals ranging from professional athletes to cardiac patients.

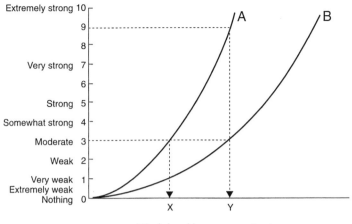

Work load in power output

FIG. 12.16. Hypothetical scale values for two observers obtained by category ratio scaling.

The category ratio scaling procedure of Borg and the magnitude matching procedure of Stevens and Marks, described earlier, have been compared for their ability to provide meaningful measures of individual differences (Marks, Borg, & Ljunggren, 1983). Both methods were found to be capable of measuring reliable differences among individual observers in their perceptions of exertion.

Borg (1982) argued that the same category ratio scale used for measurement of perceived exertion can be used for the measurement of sensation magnitude in other modalities. His argument was based on the assumption that the psychological ranges from minimal to maximal sensation for different modalities are the same. For example, according to this idea, the difference between minimal and intolerable pain is the same as the difference between a minimally audible sound and loudest sound that one can experience. Thus, although the stimulus ranges over which the observer experiences changes in sensation magnitude may be very different for the various sensory modalities, the range of sensation magnitude is always the same. This affords the opportunity to measure sensation magnitude on a common scale across different sensory modalities.

Psychological Laws

Psychophysical scaling methods have been used in attempts to discover psychological laws describing relationships among sensations. For example, magnitude estimation has been used to study the phenomenon of loudness summation. When several sounds are presented together, how do their loudnesses combine? Is the total loudness the sum of, the product of, or some other mathematical combination of the loudnesses of the separate sounds? Zwislocki (1983) found that magnitude estimations of the total loudness of a pair of tones were equal to the sum of magnitude estimations of the tones presented alone. The results of this experiment support the hypothesis that the psychological loudnesses of two tones combine additively to produce the total loudness of the tones when they are presented together (see Figure 12.1). Total loudness, L, is equal to the loudness of one tone, L_x, plus the loudness of the other tone, L_y.

$$L = L_x + L_y \qquad (12.6)$$

The equation above is an example of what Anderson (1977) has called a psychological law and what Marks (1974) has called a *psychosensory law*. In this type of law, the psychological magnitudes of stimuli are combined according to some rule of integration.

The relationships among the psychophysical law, the psychological law, and the sensory response law are illustrated in Figure 12.17. Individual sensations are related to stimuli by the psychophysical law. The integrated sensation is related to the individual sensations by the psychological law. Finally, the sensory response of the observer is related to the integrated sensation by the sensory response law. It is an important objective in psychophysical scaling to test hypotheses about the nature of these three types of law. The measurement of sensation magnitude, a major goal of psychophysics, can be accomplished only through knowledge of the underlying relationships between sensations and stimuli, among sensations, and between sensory responses and sensations.

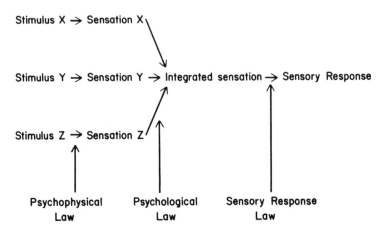

FIG. 12.17. Illustration of relationships among psychophysical laws, psychological laws, and sensory response laws.

In formulating psychological laws, discovery of sensory response laws is essential. Zwislocki's (1983) results on the magnitude estimation of loudness can be explained by a linear sensory response law and a psychological law stating that loudnesses combine by a linear summation rule. The results of individual observers who showed imperfect summation of sensory responses were accounted for by demonstrating that these observers had nonlinear sensory response laws. Thus, perfect loudness summation was also evident in these observers when their sensory responses were converted to psychological loudness through the use of their individual nonlinear sensory response laws. The individual sensory response law of each observer was estimated in a separate experiment on the judgment of line length. The significance of Zwislocki's study is the demonstration that psychological laws can be discovered using the method of magnitude estimation when the sensory response law for individual observers is known.

In studies of loudness summation, the integration of sensations produced by different stimuli is examined. The psychological law is a mathematical description of the integration process. Psychological laws can also describe how sensory attributes associated with a single stimulus relate to each other. For example, the loudness of a sound has been found to be lawfully related to two other sensory attributes of the sound. S. S. Stevens, Guirao, and Slawson (1965) found that magnitude estimations of the loudness (L) of a noise were proportional to the product of magnitude estimations of the volume (V) and the density (D) of the noise.

$$L = V \times D \qquad (12.7)$$

Volume refers to how large a sound seems. Volume, or the amount of space a sound seems to occupy, was found to increase as the sound intensity increased and sound frequency decreased. Density refers to the compactness of an auditory experience. A sound of high density is experienced as a large amount of sound concentrated into a particular amount of space. In contrast to volume estimations, density estimations were found to increase with increases in both sound intensity and frequency. The total loudness of the sound seems to be the amount of sound per unit area (density) times the total area of the auditory experience (volume).

Equation (12.7) is a theoretical model for explaining the results of the magnitude estimation experiments. It should be apparent that underlying this model is the assumed sensory response law that magnitude estimations are linearly related to sensation magnitude. Although the results of the magnitude estimation experiments are consistent with this model, other models could also account for the results. For example, the results would also be predicted when it is assumed that sensation magnitude is proportional to the log of magnitude estimations and that loudness is equal to volume plus density [Equation (12.8)].

$$L = V + D \qquad (12.8)$$

A sound that was estimated to have a volume of 10 and a density of 10 should be estimated to have a loudness of 100 (10 × 10 = 100). Taking the logarithm of these magnitude estimations of volume, density, and loudness yields a volume value of 1, a density value of 1, and a loudness value of 2. Thus, according to this model, loudness is proportional to volume plus density rather than volume times density.

Further research is needed to determine which, if either, of these two models provides the correct explanation of the magnitude estimation data on the volume, density, and loudness of sounds. However, Zwislocki's (1983) finding that, on the average, a group of observers is capable of giving magnitude estimations proportional to sensations of loudness supports the hypothesis that loudness is proportional to the product of volume and density.

PROBLEMS

12.1. Below are the magnitude estimations of line length and pain for an individual observer. Using the line-length results as an estimation of the sensory response law, correct the pain data for the observer's nonlinear use of numbers. Use the graphic method as illustrated in Figure 12.11, but plot the functions on arithmetic axes.

line length in cm	length estimation	noxious stimulus	pain estimation
1	2	10	2
10	12	15	3
20	20	20	5
30	23	25	8
40	27	30	12
50	29	35	16
60	31	40	25

12.2. Following, are magnitude estimation data obtained by the methods of magnitude matching for loudness and vibrotactile sensation magnitude on the foot for a group of normal observers and a group of patients with diabetic neuropathies. Plot the average loudness scales and the average vibrotactile scales for the two groups. Now, use the loudness data as the standard modality to correct the vibrotactile magnitude estimation data. Plot the results. Did the patients and normal observers differ in the perception of vibration?

Normal Observers

Sound intensity in dB	1	2	3	4	5	Vibration intensity in dB	1	2	3	4	5
10	0.4	0.1	1	0.5	2	5	0.1	0.2	0.1	1	0.3
20	0.8	0.2	4	1	4	10	0.3	0.3	0.2	2	0.5
30	2	0.4	8	4	6	15	0.6	0.6	0.5	4	1.2
40	4	1	15	7	10	20	1.3	1.5	1	7	2
50	10	2	20	15	20	25	3	3	3	13	3
60	20	5	30	28	35	30	5	6	7	20	6
70	40	10	40	60	70	35	9	10	13	30	11
80	90	25	80	100	110	40	17	21	22	60	20

Patients

Sound intensity in dB	1	2	3	4	5	Vibration intensity in dB	1	2	3	4	5
10	1	0.5	2	0.6	1.5	5	0	0	0	0	0
20	4	1	5	1	2.5	10	0.1	0.2	0.2	0.1	0.1
30	7	2	10	2	5	15	0.2	0.3	0.4	0.2	0.3
40	15	4	20	4	9	20	0.5	0.7	0.7	0.3	1
50	25	8	35	7	18	25	1	1.5	1.2	0.7	2
60	50	16	70	15	40	30	2	3	2	1.5	3
70	100	32	150	30	75	35	4	7	4	3	5
80	200	64	300	60	150	40	8	14	7	6	9

13

The Psychophysical Law

One of the fundamental issues in psychophysics concerns the form of the psychophysical law. The problem is that of discovering a simple equation which describes how the intensity of stimuli and our impressions of them are related. The solution of the problem would have far-reaching implications for scholars in a variety of fields. Certainly, the philosopher's concepts of epistemology and the psychologist's theories and research on information processing would be influenced by a psychophysical law. No doubt the neurophysiologist's search for the mechanisms by which the nervous system encodes environmental stimuli would be facilitated. Perhaps even some of the difficult problems confronting social scientists in their attempts to understand human behavior in social environments would become somewhat simplified by a psychophysical law. The law would probably have a variety of practical applications even in fields such as architectural design, communication systems design, the arts, medicine, and law.

One of the first efforts to formulate a psychophysical law was that of Daniel Bernoulli (1738). Bernoulli, a mathematician, was interested in the psychological worth of money. He proposed that people do not act on the basis of the actual value of money but on some psychological transformation of the actual value. It seemed to Bernoulli that the *utility* of money increases at a decreasing rate as the actual amount increases. A gain of one dollar is psychologically greater if you have only two dollars than if you have one hundred dollars. The economist would say that money exhibits a decreasing marginal utility. Bernoulli's specific proposal was that the utility of money increases as a function of the logarithm of the amount of money. Over 100 years later, Fechner proposed a logarithmic function for sensations and stimuli.

It is interesting that in a footnote to Bernoulli's paper he mentioned that a young mathematician named Gabriel Cramer had suggested in a letter a few years earlier that a power function may describe the relationship between utility and the amount of money (see S. S. Stevens, 1975). Both Cramer and Bernoulli thought that the utility of money increases at a diminishing rate as the amount of money increases, but their equations were different. Specifically, Cramer stated that utility grows with the square root of money; that is, utility is proportional to money raised to the power of .5.

According to S. S. Stevens (1975), Bernoulli's logarithmic function, which has had a large influence on those who theorize about utility, is incorrect, while Cramer's little-noticed power function is correct. Recent experiments in which people made various kinds of judgments on the value of money show that utility increases as a function of the amount of money raised to a power of approximately .45.

The first psychophysical law in psychology was that of G. T. Fechner. Fechner, like Bernoulli, proposed a logarithmic function. While in bed on the morning of October 22, 1850, Fechner was attempting to solve the problem of how the inner world of sensation is related to the outer world of stimuli, when it became clear to him that increasing a stimulus by a constant ratio should cause sensation to increase by a constant amount. For example, a temporal sequence of stimuli with intensities of 1, 2, 4, 8, and 16 should cause the sensation to increase in equal amounts with each successive presentation. Doubling the stimulus should always cause sensation to increase by the same increment. (The details of how Fechner derived his law were described in chapter 1.) The point to be made here is that there have been few principles in psychology that have been as important historically as Fechner's law: for over 100 years, the principle went relatively unchallenged. In fact, during this time the logarithmic law dominated psychophysics. It was so widely accepted that it led to biased judgments by scientists in a number of different fields. Investigators, using confusion and partition scaling methods, incorrectly identified logarithmic functions in their data; some neurophysiologists found logarithmic functions in data recorded electrically from receptors; and engineers developed a decibel scale with the belief that loudness increased with the logarithm of sound pressure level.

It was not until the mid-1950s that scientists began to seriously question the validity of Fechner's law. It started when S. S. Stevens, using ratio scaling methods, obtained psychophysical magnitude functions for brightness and loudness that did not even slightly resemble logarithmic functions (Stevens, 1953). Psychophysical judgments of both brightness and loudness were instead found to be proportional to the cube root of the energy in the stimulus. Stevens' discovery marked the start of what some scientists have called the "new psychophysics." The new psychophysics is characterized by the extensive use of methods for directly measuring sensation. Chief among these methods have been magnitude estimation and magnitude production.

STEVENS' POWER LAW

As a result of literally dozens of experiments on direct psychophysical scaling conducted in American and European laboratories, a new psychophysical law has emerged to take the place of Fechner's logarithmic law. S. S. Stevens (1957) proposed that the form of the relationship between sensation magnitude and stimulus intensity is a power function. This power law is stated as

$$\psi = k\phi^a, \tag{13.1}$$

where ψ is sensation magnitude, ϕ is stimulus intensity, k is an arbitrary constant determining the scale unit, and a is the power exponent which depends on the sensory modality and stimulus conditions. The value of the power function exponent determines the shape of the curve on a graph where ψ is plotted as a function of ϕ. For example, if the exponent is 1.0, the relationship is a straight line because the equation reduces to a statement that sensory magnitude is proportional to stimulus intensity. The relationship is positively accelerated when the exponent is greater than 1.0 and negatively accelerated when the exponent is less than 1.0. Recall that for Fechner's logarithmic law, the predicted psychophysical function was always negatively accelerated.

If the power law is correct, the scaling problem becomes the experimental determination of the exponent of the power function. The power function has a convenient feature of becoming a linear function with a slope equal to the value of the power exponent when a logarithmic transformation is performed on each side of the equation:

$$\log \psi = \log k + a \log \phi. \tag{13.2}$$

The exponent a of the power law for a particular set of experimental results can be found by plotting the logarithm of the psychological scale values ψ against the logarithm of the corresponding stimulus values ϕ and finding the slope of the straight line fitted to the points. This technique has also proved very useful in evaluating the closeness of fit of the power law to experimental data. Any systematic deviation of the data points from a straight line on a log–log graph is an indication that the psychophysical magnitude function is not a power function. If the psychophysical function of a particular experiment is a power function, the method of least squares

TABLE 13.1
Hypothetical Results from a Psychophysical Scaling Experiment

Stimulus Intensity	Log Stimulus Intensity	Psychological Scale Value	Log Psychological Scale Value
2	.301	.28	−.55
4	.602	.33	−.48
10	1.000	.68	−.17
20	1.301	1.00	0
40	1.602	1.40	.15
100	2.000	2.00	.30
200	2.301	2.51	.40
400	2.602	4.47	.65
1000	3.000	6.32	.80
2000	3.301	10.00	1.00
4000	3.602	15.90	1.20
10000	4.000	22.40	1.35

can be used to determine the constants log k and a in the power equation which best fit the data. In this application of the method of least squares, log ψ would be Y and log ϕ would be X [Equations (3.1) and (3.2)].

Table 13.1 contains hypothetical data from the kind of psychophysical scaling experiment in which the psychological scale values are obtained for stimuli of varied intensity. An example of such an experiment would be the magnitude estimation of the brightness of lights of varied intensity. When the scale values in Table 13.1 are plotted as a function of stimulus intensity, the resulting curve is negatively accelerated. Although the results in Figure 13.1 suggest that scale values are a power function of stimulus intensity,

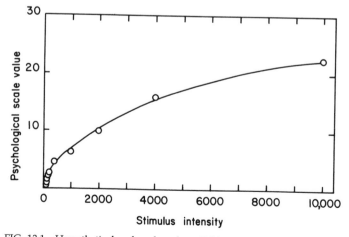

FIG. 13.1. Hypothetical scale values from Table 13.1 plotted as a function of stimulus intensity.

this hypothesis can be more precisely tested by plotting the logarithm of the psychological scale values against the logarithm of stimulus intensity. The logarithms of psychological scale values and the logarithms of stimulus intensity contained in Table 13.1 are plotted in Figure 13.2. It is clear that this logarithmic transformation of the data resulted in a linear function with a slope less than 1.0. The fact that the logarithm of the psychological scale values is a linear function of the logarithm of stimulus intensity indicates that the results can be described best by a power function. The fact that the slope of the function is less than 1.0 indicates that the exponent, a, of the power function is less than 1.0.

In this example, the exact value of a, the slope of the log-log magnitude estimation function, was .5. The Y-intercept of the graph, log k, is −.66. Thus, the equation that best describes the data is

Log psychological scale value = −.66 + .5 (log stimulus intensity).

Taking the antilog of each side of this equation results in the power function that best describes the data:

Psychological scale value = .22 (stimulus intensity)$^{.5}$.

In general, by plotting the logarithm of the psychological scale value against the logarithm of stimulus intensity, it is possible to test the hypothesis that a power function is a good description of a psychophysical magnitude function. If the points on the graph form a linear function, the hypothesis is supported. Furthermore, the slope of the graph gives the

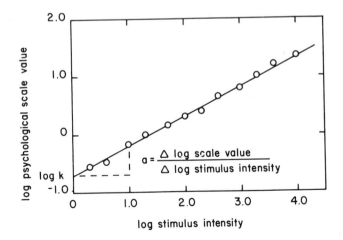

FIG. 13.2. Logarithm of hypothetical scale values from Table 13.1 plotted as a function of the logarithm of stimulus intensity.

value of a, the exponent of the power function, and the antilog of the intercept, log k, gives the value of the constant k.

Support for the power law comes from experiments on a large number of perceptual continua. The exponents of the power functions describing the relationship between sensation magnitude and stimulus magnitude are as small as .33 for brightness (J. C. Stevens & S. S. Stevens, 1963) and loudness (S. S. Stevens, 1955), and as large as 3.5 for electric shock on the fingertip (J. C. Stevens, Carton, & Shickman, 1958). Figures 13.3 and 13.4 show the psychophysical magnitude functions on log–log axes and on linear axes, respectively, for the brightness of a 5° target, the apparent length of lines, and electric shock of the fingertips. It can be seen that the sensation of electric current through the fingertips increases very rapidly with the stimulus intensity, whereas brightness grows very slowly as stimulus energy is increased. The apparent length of lines is directly proportional to actual length. Exponents of power functions of some representative perceptual continua are found in Table 13.2.

The values of exponents obtained for various sensory modalities are usually very dependent on stimulus conditions. For example, it can be seen in Table 13.2 that the exponent for brightness is .33 for a 5° target, .5 for a point source or a brief flash, and 1.0 for a point source briefly flashed. The exponent for the loudness of pure tones is slightly higher for the low frequencies than for midrange and high frequencies. The

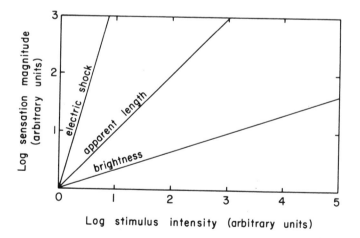

FIG. 13.3. Psychophysical magnitude functions for three perceptual continua. The linearity of the functions on double logarithmic coordinates indicates that sensation magnitude is a power function of stimulus intensity. The slope of the line corresponds to the exponent of the power function. The exponents for electric shock to the fingertips, line length, and the brightness of relatively large stimuli lasting about 1 sec are 3.5, 1.0, and .33, respectively.

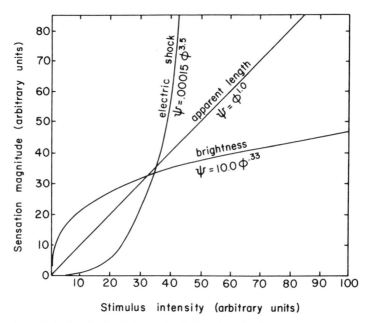

FIG. 13.4. Psychophysical magnitude functions for three perceptual continua plotted on linear coordinates. Each function is a power function. The form of the function is greatly influenced by the size of the exponent. An exponent of 1.0 corresponds to a linear function. An exponent less than 1.0 corresponds to a concave downward function, and an exponent greater than 1.0 corresponds to a concave upward function.

observer's state of sensory adaptation and the presence of masking stimuli had been found to alter the exponents for vision, audition, the cutaneous senses, and the chemical senses. In addition to their sensory modality and stimulus conditions, exponents are sometimes found to depend on specific experimental procedures. The exponents for taste, for example, are considerably higher when the substance is sipped in the mouth than when it is flowed over the tongue.

Much can be learned about a sensory system by studying the changes in the power function exponents as stimulus conditions are changed. In fact, in many scaling experiments today, stimulus variables in addition to intensity are systematically varied. For example, in the study of warmth by J. C. Stevens and Marks (1971) described in chapter 11, a great deal was learned about spatial summation of warmth sensations by studying how the power function exponents changed as the areal extent of a radiant stimulus changed.

Let us examine some of the actual data of some of the first experiments on magnitude estimation and the power law. In Figure 13.5 the results of experiments reported by S. S. Stevens (1961a) on loudness and

TABLE 13.2
Representative Exponents for Power Functions Relating
Sensory Magnitude to Stimulus Intensity[a]

Continuum	Measured exponent	Stimulus condition
Loudness	0.67	Sound pressure of 3000-Hz tone
Vibration	0.95	Amplitude of 60 Hz on finger
Vibration	0.6	Amplitude of 250 Hz on finger
Brightness	0.33	5° target in dark
Brightness	0.5	Point source
Brightness	0.5	Brief flash
Brightness	1.0	Point source briefly flashed
Lightness	1.2	Reflectance of gray papers
Visual length	1.0	Projected line
Visual area	0.7	Projected square
Redness (saturation)	1.7	Red–gray mixture
Taste	1.3	Sucrose
Taste	1.4	Salt
Taste	0.8	Saccharine
Smell	0.6	Heptane
Cold	1.0	Metal contact on arm
Warmth	1.6	Metal contact on arm
Warmth	1.3	Irradiation of skin, small area
Warmth	0.7	Irradiation of skin, large area
Discomfort, cold	1.7	Whole body irradiation
Discomfort, warm	0.7	Whole body irradiation
Thermal pain	1.0	Radiant heat on skin
Tactual roughness	1.5	Rubbing emery cloths
Tactual hardness	0.8	Squeezing rubber
Finger span	1.3	Thickness of blocks
Pressure on palm	1.1	Static force on skin
Muscle force	1.7	Static contractions
Heaviness	1.45	Lifted weights
Viscosity	0.42	Stirring silicone fluids
Electric shock	3.5	Current through fingers
Vocal effort	1.1	Vocal sound pressure
Angular acceleration	1.4	5-sec rotation
Duration	1.1	White noise stimuli

[a]After S. S. Stevens, 1975. (Reprinted from S. S. Stevens, *Psychophysics: Introduction to Its Perceptual, Neural and Social Prospects*. Copyright © 1975 by John Wiley & Sons, Inc. Reprinted by permission of John Wiley & Sons, Inc.)

brightness scaling are plotted. In the loudness experiment, each of 32 observers made two magnitude estimations of a 1000-Hz tone at each of several intensity levels. In the brightness experiment, each of 28 dark-adapted observers made two magnitude estimations at each stimulus level. The visual stimulus subtended an angle of about 5° and lasted about 3 sec. The magnitude estimation data in Figure 13.5 constitute compelling evidence that magnitude estimation of both loudness and brightness grow

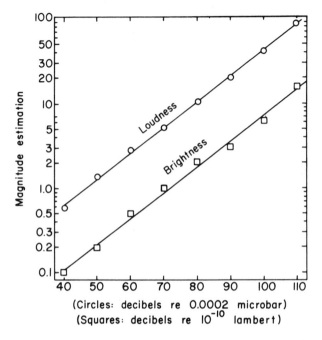

FIG. 13.5. Median magnitude estimations for loudness and brightness. (From S. S. Stevens, 1961a. Reprinted from *Sensory Communication*, W. A. Rosenblith, Editor, by permission of the M.I.T. Press, Cambridge, Massachusetts. Copyright © 1961 by the Massachusetts Institute of Technology.)

as a power function of stimulus energy. Furthermore, the exponents, as estimated from the slope of the curves, are approximately .33 in both cases. The loudness and brightness functions are directly comparable on the same graph, since in both cases stimulus energy is specified on the logarithmic scale of decibels. Increasing energy by 10 dB is equivalent to increasing it by a factor of 10 (i.e., 1 log unit):

$$N_{dB} = 10 \log \frac{E_1}{E_0}. \tag{13.3}$$

The number of decibels (N_{dB}) is equal to 10 times the logarithm of the ratio of a particular energy level (E_1) to an arbitrary reference energy level (E_0). Since it is advisable to specify stimulus energy on a common scale when psychophysical data on different sense modalities are compared, the decibel scale should be used whenever possible. Furthermore, in testing the psychophysical power law, a straight line is always predicted when log magnitude estimation is plotted against the logarithmic decibel scale.

Almost all of the psychophysical magnitude functions reported in support of the power law have been constructed by plotting the average magnitude estimation for a number of observers as a function of stimulus intensity. Psychologists for some years have been aware of the general problem of making inferences concerning the behavior of individuals from curves based on group data (e.g., Estes, 1956). Pradhan and Hoffman (1963) have suggested that the psychophysical power function is an artifact of the averaging of data from a number of observers. Based on an experiment in which observers made judgments of the apparent heaviness of weights, Pradhan and Hoffman proposed that individual observers seldom produce power functions but that when their data are combined by averaging, the power function inevitably emerges. Contrary to the results of Pradhan and Hoffman, J. C. Stevens and Guirao (1964) reported clear evidence that the power law applies to individual observers and that the psychophysical power function is in no way an artifact of averaging procedures. Magnitude production and estimation were combined by permitting the observers to adjust the intensity of an auditory stimulus to whatever level they liked and requiring them to report its apparent loudness. The observers were instructed to set the tone to different levels of loudness and to assign numbers to each of the loudnesses. They were told that they should make as many settings as they wanted and to cover a wide range of loudness. Eleven observers gave the results seen in Figure 13.6. The results indicate that power functions were obtained without averaging data from individual observers. In fact, power functions were obtained without even averaging the repeated judgments by individual observers. All judgments are plotted on the graph. Essentially, the same results were obtained for the perception of brightness by Marks and J. C. Stevens (1966), who repeated the procedure in an investigation of brightness psychophysical functions for individual observers.

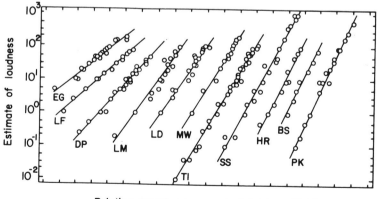

Relative sound pressure (subdivision = 20dB)

FIG. 13.6. Individual psychophysical magnitude functions obtained for each of 11 observers. Each data point represents a single judgment. (From J. C. Stevens & Guirao, 1964.)

The power law seems to apply without exception to any perceptual continuum which involves variations in sensory magnitude. Perceptual continua of sensory magnitude where observers are required to make judgments of "how much" (heaviness, brightness, loudness, etc.) have been termed *prothetic* by S. S. Stevens and Galanter (1957). Another class of perceptual continua in which sensations vary in quality and spatial location and observers make judgments of "what kind" and "where" (pitch, lateral position, etc.) has been labeled *metathetic* by Stevens and Galanter. Psychophysical scales of metathetic continua generally do not obey the power law.

Stevens and Galanter (1957) proposed that the two continua are mediated by different sorts of physiological processes. Prothetic continua are thought to be associated with additive neural processes, whereas metathetic continua are associated with substitutive neural processes. When sensations change in magnitude, an addition or subtraction of neural excitation occurs, but when sensations change in quality or spatial location, frequently one sort of neural excitation is substituted for another. For example, as pressure on the fingertip is made greater and sensations of pressure increase, the frequency of neural firing and the number of neural elements excited will increase. When the stimulus is moved to another finger, the location of the sensation and the mediating neural elements are changed. In light of this difference in underlying physiology of prothetic and metathetic continua, it is not surprising that they should yield different kinds of psychophysical magnitude functions.

During the last 35 years, dozens of investigators from laboratories in various parts of the world have confirmed the power law for prothetic continua. The power law has become one of the best established empirical relations in psychology. If the experiment is conducted with care, magnitude estimation will inevitably be found to increase as a power function of stimulus intensity. Because of the consistency of this experimental outcome, the psychophysical power function has, for most psychophysicists, attained the status of an empirical law.

In science, the significance of an empirical law is greatly enhanced if it can be derived from general principles. Mathematically, the power law has the simplicity of many of our basic natural laws. But are there any fundamental reasons why, in nature, sensation should increase with the power of the stimulus? The significance of the power law may lie in its implication that equal stimulus ratios produce equal sensation ratios. This principle is clearly suggested from psychophysical magnitude functions in which log magnitude estimation is linearly related to log stimulus intensity. If it is assumed that magnitude estimation data provide direct measurements of sensation magnitude, then it can be seen from a graph such as Figure 13.3 that changing the stimulus by some constant ratio (constant number of log units) will always change the sensation by some constant ratio (constant number of log units). For example, the power function for judgments of brightness with its exponent of .33 implies that brightness can always be doubled by increasing the intensity of light by 8 times. This relation is independent of the starting light intensity. For example, when the intensity of light is 1.0, the brightness is $1.0^{.33} = 1.0$, and when intensity is changed to 8.0, brightness is $8.0^{.33} = 2.0$.

Because the exponent is 3.5 for electric shock to the fingertips, an increase of only 22% in a stimulus of any intensity is sufficient to double sensation magnitude. For example, when the intensity of shock is 1.0, the sensation is $1.0^{3.5} = 1.0$; and when intensity is changed to 1.22, the sensation is $1.22^{3.5} = 2.0$. Between the extremes of brightness and electric shock, we find that it is possible to double apparent length with its exponent of 1.0 by simply doubling the actual length of the stimulus. These examples illustrate the principle that, when stimuli are changed by a constant ratio, the corresponding sensations also change by a constant ratio; however, the ratios in the two domains may be quite different.

CROSS-MODALITY COMPARISONS AND THE POWER LAW

A Test of Internal Consistency

The validity of the power law depends upon the observer's correct use of the number system in communicating the true magnitude of sensations. S. S. Stevens (1959a) has devised a technique for confirming the power law which does not require the observer to make numerical judgments. The observer's task is to equate the sensation magnitudes produced in two different modalities. For example, the observer might be asked to adjust the intensity of a vibration on his fingertip so that the sensory impression of vibration matches the loudness of a burst of noise. Such cross-modality matches are obtained at various levels of stimulus intensity. A graph called an *equal sensation function* is constructed showing the stimulus values of one modality plotted against those stimulus values of the other modality which result in judgments of equal sensory magnitude. Figure 13.7 is the equal sensation function for cutaneous vibration and sound.

The form of the equal sensation functions can be predicted from the psychophysical magnitude functions of each modality that are obtained by conventional ratio scaling techniques. If power functions are the correct equations for the two psychophysical magnitude functions, then the equal sensation function should also be a power function. Thus, the function should be linear when stimuli in both modalities are expressed in logarithmic units. If the equal sensation function is not a power function, one has reason to doubt the power law. Furthermore, when the exponents of the power function for the two modalities are known, a precise prediction of the slope of the equal sensation function can be made. The

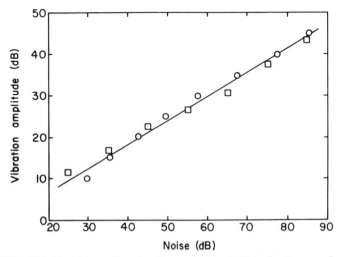

FIG. 13.7. Equal sensation functions relating 60-Hz vibration on the fingertip to the intensity of a band of noise. The circles represent adjustments of loudness to vibration, and the squares represent adjustments of vibration to match loudness. Both coordinates are logarithmic decibel scales. (From S. S. Stevens, 1961a. Reprinted from *Sensory Communication*, W. A. Rosenblith, Editor, by permission of the M.I.T. Press, Cambridge, Massachusetts. Copyright © 1961 by the Massachusetts Institute of Technology.)

ratio of the two exponents is equal to the predicted slope of the logarithmic equal sensation function. The power equations for the two modalities can be stated in the general form:

$$\psi_1 = \phi_1{}^a,$$
$$\psi_2 = \phi_2{}^b. \tag{13.4}$$

If the observer equates ψ_1 and ψ_2 by cross-modality matching at various intensity levels, the equation for the equal sensation function should be

$$\phi_1{}^a = \phi_2{}^b. \tag{13.5}$$

This equation is a power function which states that stimuli in one modality, ϕ_1, when raised to the power a will result in the same sensory magnitude, ψ, as will a stimulus in another modality, ϕ_2, when raised to the power b. In logarithmic form this equation becomes

$$a \log \phi_1 = b \log \phi_2 \tag{13.6}$$

or

$$\log \, \phi_1 = \frac{b}{a} \log \, \phi_2, \qquad (13.7)$$

which is the formula for a straight line with a slope equal to the ratio of the exponents of the power function of the two modalities (b/a).

It has been proposed by Stevens that cross-modality matching provides a test of the validity of the power law because results obtained using one procedure can be used to predict results obtained by an entirely different procedure. The results of a large number of experiments using cross-modality validation techniques are consistent with the power law (S. S. Stevens, 1975). In the experiments, observers made cross-modality comparisons of vibration and loudness, vibration and electric shock, electric shock and loudness, loudness and ten perceptual continua, and force of handgrip and nine perceptual continua. The experiments involving force of handgrip provide a dramatic illustration of the use of this scale-validation technique. The sensation of muscle tension has been measured by the methods of magnitude estimation and magnitude production (J. C. Stevens & Mack, 1959). Observers squeezed a device called a hand dynanometer. A force gauge attached to the instrument provided a measure of the physical force exerted by the response. Observers judged the magnitudes of sensations produced by squeezes of varied physical force. When sensation magnitude was plotted against physical force, the psychophysical function was a power function with an exponent of 1.7. S. S. Stevens (1975) has summarized the results of a series of experiments in which observers squeezed a hand dynamometer to produce sensations of tension that were equal in magnitude to sensations of varied magnitudes on nine other perceptual continua (J. C. Stevens, Mack, & S. S. Stevens, 1960; J. C. Stevens & S. S. Stevens, 1960). The equal sensation functions obtained in these experiments are shown in Figure 13.8. The slope of each function is in accordance with the prediction based on the magnitude functions for force of handgrip and the other continuum involved (Table 13.3). In another study (S. S. Stevens, 1966a), the loudness of a sound was matched to the intensities of sensations on ten other perceptual continua. In all cases, the slopes of the equal sensation functions were accurately predicted from the magnitude estimation functions of the two modalities. The results of an experiment by Bond and S. S. Stevens (1969), in which 5-year-olds were used as observers, indicate that cross-modality matching probably does not depend on prior experience with scales of physical stimuli or on the ability to translate sensations into numbers. The observers adjusted the intensity of a light to match the loudness of a 500-Hz tone of variable intensity. The results were essentially identical for five children between the ages of 4 years, 2 months and 5 years, 8 months, and a group of five adults. The authors concluded that hypotheses con-

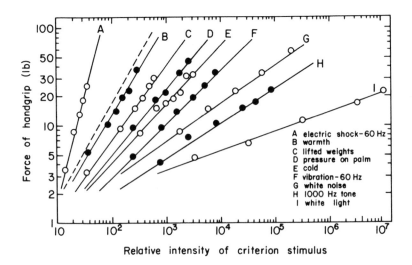

FIG. 13.8. Equal sensation functions obtained by matching force of handgrip to various stimuli in other modalities. Each point is based on the median judgments of 10 or more observers. The dashed line has a slope of 1.0. (From S. S. Stevens, 1961a. Reprinted from *Sensory Communication*, W. A. Rosenblith, Editor, by permission of the M.I.T. Press, Cambridge, Massachusetts. Copyright © 1961 by the Massachusetts Institute of Technology.)

TABLE 13.3
Predicted and Obtained Exponents for Matching
Force of Handgrip to Nine Other Continua[a]

	Exponent obtained by handgrip	Predicted value
Electric shock	2.13	2.06
Warmth on arm	0.96	0.94
Heaviness of lifted weights	0.79	0.85
Pressure on palm	0.67	0.65
Cold on arm	0.60	0.59
Vibration, 60 Hz	0.56	0.56
Loudness of white noise	0.41	0.39
Loudness of 1000-Hz tone	0.35	0.39
Brightness of white light	0.21	0.20

[a]After S. S. Stevens, 1975. (Reprinted from S. S. Stevens, *Psychophysics: Introduction to Its Perceptual, Neural and Social Prospects.* Copyright © 1975 by John Wiley & Sons, Inc. Reprinted by permission of John Wiley & Sons, Inc.)

cerning prior learning fail to account for cross-modality matching data. It seems more reasonable to assume that judgments of sensation magnitude depend primarily on the operation of sense organs and that the sense organs of children function like those of adults.

The use of cross-modality matching as a procedure for validating the power law has been criticized on the grounds that magnitude estimation scales can be transformed by various mathematical functions that leave the predicted cross-modality matching function unchanged (Ekman, 1964; MacKay, 1963; Shepard, 1978; Triesman, 1964; Zinnes, 1969). Thus, the psychophysical law could be some function other than a power function, such as Fechner's logarithmic law, which becomes transformed into the observed power functions of magnitude estimation through a nonlinear sensory response law. If this were true, it is still possible that the cross-modality matching function will be a power function with an exponent equal to the ratio of the exponents of the two magnitude estimation functions. Thus, although cross-modality matching provides a very good test of the internal consistency of the observer's judgments it does not provide proof of the validity of the psychophysical law.

A Scaling Method

Cross-modality matching can be used for a variety of scaling problems for which it is not practical to have observers assign numbers to their sensations. An example of such a problem is the measurement of clinical pain. Instead of only asking patients how they feel, some physicians have adopted the procedure of asking them to adjust the loudness of a noise presented through earphones to match the intensity of their discomfort. The intensity of the patient's pain is calculated by converting his noise adjustment into psychophysical loudness units. This procedure has been used to quantify the effectiveness of medications for relieving a patient's distress (Peck, 1966). The success of the procedure has warranted the commercial production of a device called a thymometer that can be used to quantify pain from loudness matches.

Cross-modality matching has also been used to study clinical patients with hearing defects. Thalmann (1965) examined a group of ten patients who had hearing thresholds about 50 dB higher than normal in one ear, but had normal hearing in the other ear. Five of the patients had been diagnosed as having conductive hearing loss whereby sound is not effectively transmitted through the mechanical elements of the auditory system to the receptors. The hearing loss of the other five patients was attributable to problems in the auditory nervous system. In the experiment, patients adjusted the intensity of a 150-Hz vibration on the fingertip to match the

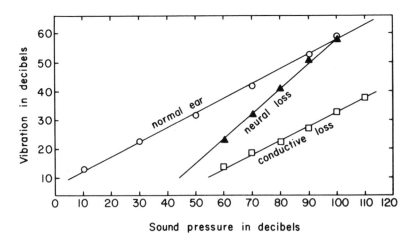

FIG. 13.9. Cross-modality matches of patients with normal hearing in one ear and a hearing loss in the other. Each patient adjusted vibration to match loudness in the normal ear and in the abnormal ear. The circles represent the results for the normal ear. The triangles and squares show matches when the stimuli were presented to ears with neural hearing loss and to ears with conductive hearing loss, respectively. (From S. S. Stevens, 1975; after Thalmann, 1965.) (Reprinted from S. S. Stevens, *Psychophysics: Introduction to Its Perceptual, Neural and Social Prospects.* Copyright © 1975 by John Wiley & Sons, Inc.)

loudness of a 1000-Hz tone delivered to the defective ear on some trials and to the normal ear on other trials. The results are seen in Figure 13.9. When the tone was delivered to the normal ear, a linear function on log–log axes with the predicted slope was obtained. The matching function for ears with conductive loss had the same slope as the function for normal ears, but it was displaced to a position about 50 dB higher up on the intensity scale. It is apparent that a conductive hearing loss has the effect of attenuating sounds at all intensities by a constant number of decibels. A very different picture of the hearing problem emerges from examining the results for the ears with neural loss. The unusually steep function for the ear with neural loss indicates that the exponent for the loudness function is abnormally high. Once the sound intensity exceeds the high threshold, loudness grows at a very rapid rate as intensity is increased. It can be seen from Figure 13.9 that at high intensity levels the loudness of the defective ear eventually catches up with the loudness of the normal ear. This phenomenon, found in neural hearing loss and in masking experiments, has been called recruitment. Since the matching functions are distinctly different for normal ears, ears with conductive loss, and ears with neural loss, cross-modality matching provides a valuable diagnostic method for identifying various kinds of auditory defects.

MODIFICATIONS OF THE POWER LAW

In most psychophysical experiments, $\psi = k\phi^a$ has been found to be a very accurate statement of the relation between sensory magnitude judgments and stimulus magnitude. However, for weak stimuli near absolute threshold, this equation becomes highly inaccurate. When log apparent magnitude is plotted against log stimulus magnitude, the relationship is linear (a power function) only at the higher stimulus values. At stimulus values near absolute threshold, the relationship is concave downward. Fortunately, this deviation from the power law can be eliminated by a slight modification of the equation. The power law has been found to hold for the entire range of perceptible stimuli when a constant ϕ_0 is subtracted from the values of ϕ. According to some investigators, the constant ϕ_0 represents the absolute threshold. Thus, subtraction of ϕ_0 from ϕ may be equivalent to specifying the stimulus in effective units above threshold rather than in units above the zero point on the physical scale. The general form of the power function becomes

$$\psi = k(\phi - \phi_0)^a, \tag{13.8}$$

where ϕ_0 is the value of the absolute threshold. This procedure of correcting the stimulus scale so that its zero point corresponds to the zero point on the psychological scale has been successfully applied to psychophysical scales such as brightness (J. C. Stevens & S. S. Stevens, 1963), loudness (Scharf & J. C. Stevens, 1961), temperature (S. S. Stevens, 1961a), cutaneous vibration (Gescheider & Wright, 1968; S. S. Stevens, 1959b), cutaneous apparent successiveness (Gescheider, 1967), and the taste of salt (McBurney, 1966).

In an experiment by Gescheider and Wright (1968), the effect of adaptation upon the form of the psychophysical magnitude function for cutaneous vibration of the fingertip was investigated. The family of curves presented in Figure 13.10 represents the relationship between sensation magnitude and the amplitude of 60-Hz vibration applied for 5, 60, 120, 180, and 360 sec following termination of an intense adapting stimulus of 10 min duration. It is apparent that each of the sensation magnitude functions deviates from linearity by becoming concave downward for the range of stimulus values near the absolute threshold.

To test the applicability of the revised power law to cutaneous vibration following recovery from adaptation, sensation magnitude was plotted as a function of $\phi - \phi_0$, that is, vibration amplitude in microns above absolute threshold (Figure 13.11). To obtain $\phi - \phi_0$, the appropriate empirically determined value of ϕ_0 for each adaptation-recovery time was subtracted from the corresponding values of ϕ for that particular adaptation-recovery time. Figure 13.11 illustrates that this transformation of the stimulus scale produced a power function over the entire range of stimulus intensities.

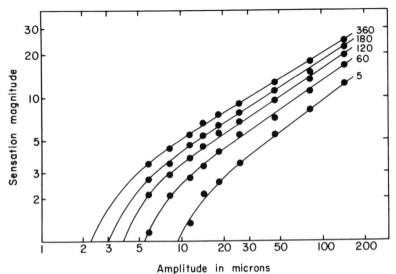

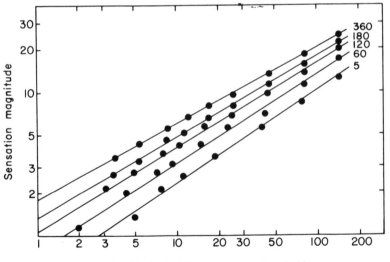

FIG. 13.10. Psychophysical magnitude functions for 60-Hz vibration of the fingertip after varying durations of recovery time from the effects of a 10-min adaptation period during which the fingertip was continuously stimulated by intense 60-Hz vibration. (From Gescheider & Wright, 1968. Copyright 1968 by the American Psychological Association. Reprinted by permission.)

FIG. 13.11. Psychophysical magnitude functions for 60-Hz vibration of the fingertip after varying durations of recovery time from adaptation. Stimulus intensity was expressed in vibration amplitude above absolute thresholds measured at the various recovery times. (From Gescheider & Wright, 1968. Copyright 1968 by the American Psychological Association. Reprinted by permission.)

314

In most experiments, however, ϕ_0 is not generally determined experimentally, since such factors as the particular psychophysical method employed and the location of the observer's decision criterion would greatly affect its value. Instead, it is usually determined indirectly by finding the value of ϕ_0 that will work; that is, by finding one that will produce a power function over the entire range of stimulus values. In describing a mathematical procedure for estimating ϕ_0, Ekman (1959) pointed out that the value of ϕ_0 is sometimes negative. When ϕ_0 is negative, the use of Equation (13.8) implies that ψ is greater than zero when $\phi = 0$. Subtraction of a negative value of ϕ_0 from zero yields a positive value of ψ. Ekman identified the positive value of ψ when ϕ was zero as sensory noise resulting from the spontaneous activity of the nervous system and proposed another form of the power law:

$$\psi = \psi_0 + \phi^a, \qquad (13.9)$$

where ψ_0 is the basic sensory noise to which the sensory magnitude produced by an external stimulus, ϕ^a, is added to determine the total subjective magnitude, ψ, for a particular stimulus value, ϕ.

It should be understood that Equations (13.8) and (13.9) represent two distinct hypotheses about the growth of sensory magnitude with increases in stimulus intensity. In Equation (13.8), the subtraction of a constant from stimulus intensity implies that sensation magnitude is a power function of effective stimulation above threshold. On the other hand, the use of Equation (13.9) implies a correction for sensory noise, rather than threshold. Equation (13.9) states that sensation magnitude is proportional to stimulus intensity raised to a power plus a constant which has been interpreted to represent sensory noise. There have been several other equations proposed as modified power laws, and the problem has been reviewed by Marks and J. C. Stevens (1968). It is not possible to select a single equation which applies accurately to data obtained under all circumstances. It is likely that different equations will be applicable for different experimental situations.

The work of Zwislocki (1965) illustrates the application of one particular modified power function to the problem of auditory masking. Hellman and Zwislocki (1964) carefully measured loudness functions for a 1000-Hz tone presented to observers against noise backgrounds of various levels of intensity. Zwislocki's formulation of the power law for loudness may be written in the form

$$L_S = k(E_S + E_N)^\theta - E_N^\theta. \qquad (13.10)$$

The loudness of the signal, L_S, is equal to a constant, k, times the sum of the energy of the signal, E_S, and the energy of the noise, E_N, raised to a power, θ, minus the energy of the noise raised to a power, θ. This formulation takes into account analytic properties of the auditory system and permits the calculation of the loudness of the total acoustic event, the random noise alone, or the signal. When we listen to a signal in the presence of relatively loud noise, the signal does not sound loud if it is barely audible above the noise background, even though it is very intense; yet the noise sounds loud, and the overall acoustic event sounds loud. Zwislocki's (1965) formula permits us to calculate the loudness of a signal by subtracting the loudness of the noise from the loudness of the signal plus noise.

When the noise is external, its energy can be measured and its value specified in the equation. However, internal noise produced by spontaneous activity in the sensory system must be specified in terms of equivalent stimulus energy. Zwislocki (1965) has provided the means for making the necessary calculations. It is assumed that masking by internal noise determines the threshold of audibility for a signal presented in external conditions of quiet. Research in auditory psychophysics has conclusively revealed that when a tone is masked by noise, only the frequencies in the noise close to the frequency of the tone do the masking. The range of frequencies in the noise that bracket the frequency of a tone signal and act as a masker is called the *critical band*. It has been determined that when a tone is barely audible against a noise background, the energy in one critical band is approximately 2.5 times that of the signal (see Scharf, 1961). Zwislocki employed these concepts, which had been developed from experiments in which external noise was used to mask tones, to arrive at a procedure for calculating the equivalent sound energy of internal noise. It was simply proposed that the equivalent sound energy of internal noise is 2.5 times the threshold energy of a barely audible tone presented in quiet.

More complicated computations are required to calculate the equivalent sound energy of internal noise that has a wider frequency spectrum than the critical band for a particular tone. These procedures are fully developed in Zwislocki's (1965) paper. The virtues of Zwislocki's formulation are that it integrates certain notions of critical band theory and signal detection theory with psychophysical data on loudness scales; that it makes physiological sense; and that it accurately describes how signals sound in noisy situations.

POWER TRANSFORMATIONS

S. S. Stevens (1966b) has described some situations in which modified or unmodified power function equations fail to correspond to the psychophysical data. In some situations, the observer judged a stimulus in the presence of an inhibitory stimulus, such as a bright glaring background light in the case of vision, or a masking noise in the scaling of auditory stimuli. Psychophysical magnitude functions obtained under these conditions appear to consist of two separate power functions, each with its own exponent. For stimuli more intense than the inhibitory stimulus, the exponent is approximately the same as it would be in the absence of the inhibitory stimulus. But for stimuli weaker than the inhibitory stimulus, the exponent is often much larger than it would be in the absence of the inhibitory stimulus.

If a white stimulus is viewed against a black background, the cube-root brightness function (exponent .33) is generally obtained. If, however, the white target is surrounded by an area of illumination, the cube-root function is obtained only for stimuli that are more intense than the surrounding illumination. For stimuli less intense than the "surround," the data also follow a power function; but instead of the .33 exponent, a larger value is found. On log–log coordinates, the function abruptly becomes steeper for stimuli below than above the intensity of the surround. Figure 13.12 depicts a family of such functions for different intensities of the surround. The surrounding stimulus seems to have an inhibitory effect on the perception of weaker stimuli but not on the perception of stimuli more intense than the surround. In most studies, it is found that the change in the power function exponent is always at the intensity of the inhibiting stimulus. The inhibiting stimulus has the effect of transforming to a higher value the power function exponent for weaker stimuli, while having little, if any, effect on the exponent for stronger stimuli. The degree to which the inhibiting stimulus changes the exponent of weaker stimuli depends on its intensity. It can be seen from Figure 13.12 that as the

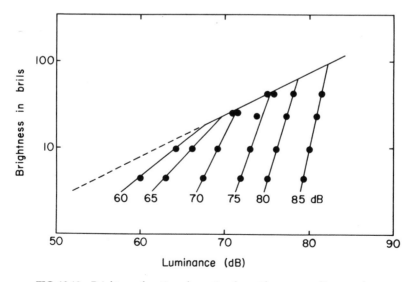

FIG. 13.12. Brightness functions for a stimulus with a surrounding annulus background of various intensities. (From Horeman, 1965.)

intensity of the inhibiting surround is increased, the transformation of the exponent increases. An intense surround 85 dB above threshold resulted in large amounts of inhibition, as indicated by the extremely high exponent for the weaker stimuli. On the other hand, a weaker surround of 60 dB above threshold caused less inhibition, and consequently, the difference between the exponents for weaker and stronger stimuli was not as extreme.

A change in the exponent of a psychophysical magnitude function due to the effects of some particular variable is called a *power transformation*. The investigation of power transformations can be a fruitful approach in the psychophysical study of sensory systems. S. S. Stevens (1966b) has extended this approach to the study of inhibition in general. He applied the analysis to the problem of auditory masking and hearing loss due to neural defects as well as to the problem of visual inhibition. For example, Stevens has argued that the loudness function may exhibit a power transformation due to a masking stimulus. The exponent for the loudness function may be considerably higher for stimuli weaker than a masking noise than for stimuli more intense than the masker. Stevens points out the close analogy between the results of visual and auditory experiments in which inhibitory stimuli are presented. In both modalities, the inhibiting stimulus increased the exponent for weaker stimuli while having little or no effect on the exponent for stronger stimuli.

MEMORY PSYCHOPHYSICS AND THE POWER LAW

An interesting extension of psychophysical ratio scaling procedures to problems beyond the study of sensory systems has been the application of magnitude estimation to the measurement of memory images. In these experiments, observers are presented with stimuli to which they associate names. At some time later, the observer is presented with the name and required to judge the magnitude of the associated memory image of the stimulus. It has generally been found that the remembered stimulus, as has been found to be true of the perceived stimulus, is a power function of stimulus intensity (Algom, 1992). For example, Moyer, Bradley, Sorensen, Whiting, and Mansfield (1978) had observers either assign numbers, by magnitude estimation, to the perceived size of visually presented objects or to the remembered sizes of the objects. In the memory condition, the observer was told to imagine each stimulus as its prelearned name was called out, and to then magnitude estimate its size. In the perceptual condition, the observer magnitude estimated the size of the visual stimulus while looking at it. Whether the observer estimated the stimulus directly or from memory, the numerical values of magnitude estimations plotted as a function of the size of the stimulus were well fitted by power functions. For example, perceived area was related to physical area by a power function with an exponent of .64, and for remembered area, the exponent was .46. For several perceptual dimensions including brightness, loudness, lifted weight, roughness, haptic extent, taste, odor, and pain, power functions have been found to describe the relation between the magnitude of the remembered stimulus and stimulus intensity (Algom, 1992).

As Algom (1992) pointed out, often the exponent for remembered stimuli is smaller than that of perceived stimuli. Two alternative hypotheses have been proposed to account for this interesting finding. In the *reperception hypothesis* (Kerst & Howard, 1978; Moyer, Bradley, Sorensen, Whiting, & Mansfield, 1978) stimulus intensity is first transformed into sensation magnitude according to Stevens' power law, $\varphi = k\phi^a$. Following this transformation, a second transformation occurs in which sensation magnitude (φ) is converted into the intensity of a memory image (M). This second transformation can also be described by a power function,

$$M = k'\varphi^a, \tag{13.11}$$

where M is the intensity of the memory image and k' and a are constants. The values of k and k' in the two power functions are determined by the units of measurements and a is the exponent of the power functions. According to the reperception hypothesis, the value of the exponent a is the same for converting stimulus intensity into sensation magnitude and for converting sensation magnitude into memory image magnitude. By substituting for φ, it is possible to write the following power function equation to describe the transformation of stimulus intensity to memory image magnitude:

$$M = k'(k\phi^a)^a \tag{13.12}$$

which stated simply is

$$M = A\phi^{a^2} \tag{13.13}$$

where A is the new scaling factor. Thus, the reperception hypothesis predicts that the exponent for memory images should be equal to the square of the exponent for sensation magnitude. The .46 exponent obtained by Moyer et al. (1978) for remembered area was close to the .41 value predicted by squaring the .64 exponent for perceived area.

An alternative hypothesis to explain the lower exponents for memory than for perception is the *uncertainty hypothesis*, which states that observers experience greater uncertainty in making judgments of the magnitudes of memory images than when making judgments of the magnitudes of perceptions. According to this hypothesis, this uncertainty either causes observers to become conservative, restricting the range of their judgments (Kerst & Howard, 1978), or to remember the stimulus range as wider than it is (Algom, Wolf, & Bergman, 1985). Because either the narrowing the range of magnitude estimations or increasing the stimulus range can result in a reduction of the exponent of the power function, it is predicted that memory exponents should be lower than perceptual exponents.

The results of most studies are consistent with both the reperception and uncertainty hypotheses. Both hypotheses predict the generally observed phenomenon that when the perceptual exponent is less than 1.0, memory exponents are smaller than perceptual exponents. A different prediction from the two hypotheses is seen only on those relatively rare occasions when the perceptual exponent is greater than 1.0. In these cases, the prediction for the reperception hypothesis is that the memory exponent should be higher than the perception exponent, because when the perception exponent is squared, its value increases. On the other hand, according to the uncertainty hypothesis, the memory exponent should always be lower than the perception exponent, no matter what its value. Uncertainty should always reduce the observer's response range or increase the stimulus range. Thus, the critical experiment would be to measure perceptual and memory magnitude estimation functions under conditions in which the exponent describing the perceptual function is greater than 1.0. Such an experiment was conducted by Algom and Lubel (1994) who had women estimate the painfulness of labor contractions either immediately or 8 to 48 hours after they occurred. During labor, the magnitudes of uterine contractions were biometrically measured. One group of 13 women made magnitude estimations of the perceived pain of contractions and 33 women estimated the remembered pain. In the perceptual condition, the woman judged the intensity of pain felt at each of five contractions selected by the experimenter. In the memory condition, the woman was required to associate colors with each of five similarly selected contractions. After either 8, 24, or 48 hours from the time of labor, the woman was again presented with the colors and asked to magnitude estimate the pain she remembered to be associated with each color. Magnitude estimations of the women in both the perceptual and the memory conditions were plotted as a function of the peak pressure of their uterine contractions. Consistent with the reperception hypothesis and inconsistent with the uncertainty hypothesis, the exponents of the power functions fitted to the data of individual observers were higher when judgments were made of remembered pain than when made to the perceived pain. The average exponent for perceived pain was 1.39, whereas the exponents for pain remembered 8, 24, and 48 hours after labor were 1.63, 2.0, and 1.75 respectively. Also significant is the fact that

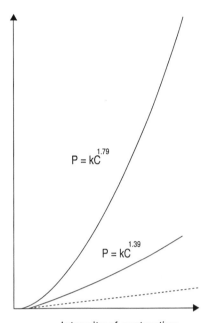

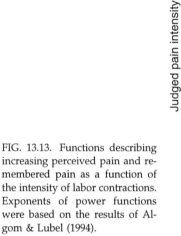

FIG. 13.13. Functions describing increasing perceived pain and re-membered pain as a function of the intensity of labor contractions. Exponents of power functions were based on the results of Al-gom & Lubel (1994).

Intensity of contraction

the exponents for remembered pain do not deviate substantially from the value predicted from the reperception hypothesis ($1.39^2 = 1.92$).

What adaptive function could be served by a higher exponent for remembered than for perceived pain? Examination of Figure 13.13, in which pain in unspecified units is plotted as a function of contraction intensity in unspecified units, may provide the answer. One function has the form of the average perceived pain function, reported by Algom and Lubel with its exponent of 1.39, and the other has the form of their average remembered pain function with its exponent of 1.79. It is clear that although both perceived and remembered pain grow as a positively accelerated function of contraction intensity, the growth rate for remem-bered pain is greater than that of perceived pain. The rapid growth rate of the expansive function for perceived pain relative to linear (dashed line) or negatively accelerated compressive functions serves to bring on the experience of intense pain rapidly as stimulus intensity increases and approaches the point of injury to the person. This arrangement is adaptive because the rapid welling up of intense pain causes the individual to take action to reduce pain and avoid serious injury. According to Algom and Lubel, the even more expansive function for remembered pain may com-prise an advanced warning device in which remembered pain triggers withdrawal and other actions aimed at avoiding further injury to a part of the body that has already sustained damage and pain. In the case of labor pain, there are obviously motives that compete with that of avoiding pain and injury that impel a woman to go through the experience of child bearing more than once.

SCALING OF SOCIAL CONSENSUS
AND THE POWER LAW

What is the esthetic value of a work of art? What is the social status of a particular occupation? What is the political importance of various heads of government? What is the seriousness of various criminal offenses? These are questions of human judgment and represent only a few of the socially significant problems to which ratio scaling methods have been applied. Advances have not occurred without some resistance, however. Social scientists have been skeptical of the psychophysicists' claim that psychological processes can be measured on a ratio scale while the stimuli that elicit them can only be specified on a nominal scale. In resorting to ranking procedures or biased category scales, social scientists must admit that the most they can say about the psychological values of two stimuli is that one is greater than the other.

The endeavors of psychologists to obtain precise quantitative measurements of social consensus are as old as psychophysics itself. The work of Fechner on experimental esthetics was the first important attempt to scale the psychological value of nominally specifiable stimuli on a quantitative scale. The fundamental concepts of Fechner's sensory psychophysics were extended to the measurement of esthetic judgments. Thus, according to Fechner, esthetic stimuli that are equally discriminable are equally different psychologically. In the 1920's, Thurstone retained Fechner's basic logic and worked out the law of comparative judgment as a mathematical model for converting measures of discriminability into psychological scale values. Thurstone was particularly interested in applying the method to socially significant problems such as the measurement of preferences for nationalities and the judged seriousness of offenses.

It has only been very recently that ratio scaling methods have been extensively applied to the scaling of nonsensory variables. The logic of ratio scaling in these cases is no different than it is for scaling loudness, brightness, or any other sensory process that has a quantifiable stimulus. The only requirements are that stimuli be nominally specified and that observers are able to match numbers or other stimuli to the strength of their psychological impressions. Generally, it is found that if an observer assigns numbers to impressions, or if she adjusts the intensity of a stimulus such as a tone or light to impressions, the same psychological scale emerges from the data. This finding constitutes strong support for the validity of the procedure.

Beyond the fact that ratio scaling procedures result in the highest level of measurement, a great advantage of their use is in the relative ease of application. Large amounts of data can be obtained quickly, and data analysis is uncomplicated. The category scales that have been so popular among social scientists are also extremely efficient. A person is simply asked to assign each of a number of items to one of a limited number of categories. The category scale, however, yields, at best, an interval scale of measurement. Often, biasing factors render it no better than an ordinal scale. S. S. Stevens (1975) noted that it would be possible to generate a ratio scale by a slight rewording of the instructions to the observer. He would simply be told to use any number which seems appropriate, rather than to use a restricted set of categories.

The applicability of ratio scaling to problems of social significance has been clearly demonstrated in a study by Sellin and Wolfgang (1964) on the measurement of criminality. In part of this extensive three-year project, 38 juvenile court judges, 286 police officers, and 245 students made judgments of the seriousness of 21 criminal offenses. Since there was an impressive invariance for the results of such diverse observers as judges, policemen, and students, it seems probable that there is a general consensus in the society on the seriousness of a wide variety of criminal offenses. Furthermore, according to Sellin and Wolfgang (1964), "[T]his agreement transcends simple qualitative concordance: it extends to the estimated degree of seriousness of these offenses" (p. 268). For example, it is now possible to make quantitative statements about how much more serious armed robbery is than car theft.

Several tests of the validity of the data supported the claim that a ratio scale of judgments of the seriousness of criminal offenses had been achieved. In one of these tests, the magnitude estimations were found to meet the ratio measurement requirement of additivity. Crimes that combined two offenses were judged to be equal in seriousness to the sum of the judgments made for the two separate offenses. The mean magnitude estimation for the crime of breaking into a building and stealing $5.00, for example, was approximately equal to the mean magnitude estimation for breaking into a building plus the mean magnitude estimation for stealing $5.00.

Among the 21 crimes ranging from minor offenses to murder, there were the crimes of stealing $5.00, $20.00, $50.00, $1,000.00, and $5,000.00. It is interesting that the judged seriousness of the crime was found to grow as a power function with an exponent of .17 of the amount of money stolen. This finding represents an extension of the power law far beyond the original problems of sensory processes. The exponent of .17 indicates that for a crime to be considered twice as serious as another, the amount stolen must be approximately 65 times as great. This result cannot be interpreted as a simple reflection of how the psychological value of money grows with the actual amount of money. The exponent of .17 is much smaller than the .5 value for the utility of money proposed by Cramer in the 18th century and more recently confirmed experimentally by Galanter (1962) and Galanter and Pliner (1974). Obviously, factors in addition to the perceived worth of the stolen money determined judgments of the seriousness of the crime.

Sellin and Wolfgang were also interested in the question of whether or not the punishment fits the crime. Are the punishments given by the state consistent with the seriousness of the crimes as judged by members of society? Magnitude estimation of the judged seriousness of crime was found to be a power function with an exponent of .7 of the maximum penalty stated in terms of time in jail prescribed by the Pennsylvania Penal Code. Since the exponent was not 1.0, the penalty expressed by time in jail is not proportional to the seriousness of the offense. However, before being able to conclude that the Pennsylvania Penal Code is a violation of justice, we would have to determine the psychophysical magnitude function for the relation between the judged severity of a jail term and the actual time in jail. If the psychological severity of the term in jail increases as a power function with an exponent of .7 of the actual time in jail, then the judged severity of the punishment is proportional to the judged seriousness of the crime. Both the judged seriousness of the crime and the judged severity of the punishment would be the same function of the duration of the jail term. An exponent of less than 1.0 would indicate that people judge the severity of the punishment to be a negatively accelerating function of actual time in jail. Thus, a term of two years in jail would be judged to be less than twice as punishing as a term of one year in jail.

Later, Gescheider, Catlin, and Fontana (1982) reported that ratio scale values of the judged seriousness of crimes increased as a power function of the duration of jail terms prescribed by the New York State Penal Code. As in the Sellin and Wolfgang study, the penalty expressed as time in jail was not proportional to the judged seriousness of the crime. The exponent of the power function was .5. Judged severity of punishments was also found to be a power function of the duration of the jail term, and the exponent of this function was .5. Since the judged seriousness of the crime and the judged severity of the punishment were both related to the duration of the jail term by the same function, a power function with an exponent of .5, it was concluded that the severity of punishment was proportional to the seriousness of the crime.

The study by Sellin and Wolfgang illustrates that important social problems can be investigated with the methods originally developed to study sensory processes. The use of the highly efficient ratio scaling methods in such new areas has a promising future. In many of the studies of social consensus, more than one scaling method was employed. The scales derived from ratio scaling have been found to systematically deviate from those obtained by Thurstonian confusion scaling or category scaling. One of the most consistent findings in psychophysics is that the Thurstonian scale is a logarithmic function of the ratio scale. Many experiments have been conducted in which the same stimuli were scaled by both Thurstonian and ratio scaling procedures. When Case V is used, the Thurstonian scale values are almost always a linear function of the logarithm of the corresponding ratio scale values.

Many of the first studies of psychophysical ratio scaling of nonmetric stimuli were done by Gösta Ekman and his associates at the University of Stockholm. The logarithmic relation between ratio and Thurstonian scales was consistently found in these studies. When observers judged the quality of 18 samples of handwriting by the method of paired comparison and by a ratio estimation procedure, two distinct scales were produced. The Thurstonian scale was a logarithmic function of the ratio estimation scale (Ekman & Künnapas, 1962a). The same relation was found between scales derived by the two methods when observers judged 17 drawings of a tree made by sixth-grade students (Ekman & Künnapas, 1962b). The logarithmic relation was again found when students judged the political importance of 11 Swedish monarchs who lived between 1550 and 1850 (Ekman & Künnapas, 1963), and when the prestige of occupations was judged (Künnapas & Wikström, 1963). The systematic difference between the results from the two methods might have caused the investigators to become skeptical about their procedures. Instead, the finding has become a basis for understanding why different methods produce different scales under some conditions and the same scale under other conditions. The significance of the logarithmic relation between ratio and Thurstonian scales will be clarified in Chapter 14 in our evaluation of the different scaling methods.

PROBLEMS

13.1. Plot log Y against log X for Y_1, Y_2, and Y_3. Determine the best-fitting straight lines by the method of least squares. Write the power function equation for each function. Plot Y against X for Y_1, Y_2, and Y_3.

X_1	Y_1	X_2	Y_2	X_3	Y_3
1	2.3	13	1.0	1	2.9
4	5.5	20	3.3	4	10.5
10	8.7	30	7.8	8	17.0
20	15.6	40	18.0	12	30.2
40	22.0	50	32.6	20	43.0
60	27.3	60	45.1	30	61.0
80	36.1	70	73.2	40	85.7
100	39.7	80	100.3	50	100.0

13.2. Plot Y as a function of X for Y_1 and Y_2. Plot log Y as a function of log X for Y_1 and Y_2. Why do both of these functions have a slope of 1.0 on the log-log plot?

X_1	Y_1	X_2	Y_2
10	10	10	5
20	20	20	10
30	30	30	15
40	40	40	20
50	50	50	25

13.3. Starting with a stimulus value of 3.0 with a corresponding sensation value of 1.0, compute a series of six successive ϕ values when c is .4, and then compute a series of six successive ψ values when k is .3. Plot log ψ as a function of log ϕ, and determine the power function equation that describes the results.

14

Some Fundamental Issues
in Psychophysical Scaling

In this final chapter, a few controversial issues in scaling that have led to advances in psychophysical methodology and theory are considered. Some of the questions raised in this chapter have yet to be answered. For example, is the power law an accurate description of the relationship between stimulus and sensation and, if so, is the physiological correlate of the power law to be found in the rules by which sensory receptors transduce environmental stimulation into neural activity? What is the explanation for the finding that different scaling procedures produce different psychological scales? What are the best ways to scale psychological experiences that vary simultaneously along several psychological dimensions at the same time? What are the integrating principles in psychophysics that make fundamental connections between the diverse experimental findings and theories of psychophysics?

INTERPRETATIONS OF THE POWER LAW

There is little doubt that the power function represents the best description of the relationship between an observer's magnitude estimation judgments and stimulus intensity. However, there is more than one possible interpretation of this finding.

Sensory Transducer Theory

One interpretation of the power law is that it reflects the operation of sensory mechanisms as they transduce stimulus energy into neural activity. S. S. Stevens (1970, 1971b) has proposed that, because the neural output of the sensory system is a power function of stimulus intensity, the observer's judgments will also be a power function of stimulus intensity. Thus, for Stevens the exponent of a psychophysical power function may tell something about the basic transducer properties of sensory receptors.

Since the classic work of Adrian and Matthews (1927) on the eye of the eel, many investigators have assumed that the relationship between the neural output of a receptor and stimulus energy is logarithmic. Adrian and Matthews reported that the frequency of neural impulses increased as a logarithmic function of light intensity, and they concluded that the results were consistent with Fechner's general psychophysical law as applied to the perception of brightness in humans. S. S. Stevens (1970) replotted Adrian and Matthews' data and found that a better description of the results is that impulse frequency for the eel's visual system grows as a power function with an exponent of .32 of light intensity. The exponent for the psychophysical function for the perception of brightness by human observers is .33 for stimuli that are not point sources or brief flashes.

It is apparent that the way in which Adrian and Matthews interpreted their data was greatly influenced by the general acceptance of Fechner's law. At the time of their experiment, Fechner's law was the only psychophysical theory of the perception of stimulus intensity which was under general consideration. Stevens' reevaluation of the Adrian-Matthews data is subject to the same limitations imposed by available theory. Perhaps an even closer approximation to the true input-output relation for the eel will come with subsequent advances in psychophysical theory. However, it does appear that, based on Stevens' evaluation of the Adrian-Matthews data, we can now say that a power function is better than the logarithmic function as a description of the transducer action of the eel's visual system.

How general is the finding that the neural output of a sensory system increases as a power function of stimulus input? In a review of experimental work on neuroelectric recording in sensory systems, S. S. Stevens (1970, 1971b) concluded that the results of a number of studies using different species, including man, indicate that neural activity grows as a power function of stimulus intensity. Furthermore, in many cases the exponent of the power function for neural activity had a similar value to those determined in psychophysical experiments under similar stimulus conditions.

When Stevens replotted the results of Hartline and Graham (1932) on the frequency of action potentials recorded from a single fiber of the compound eye of the horseshoe crab *Limulus*, he found that the frequency of impulses increased as a power function with an exponent of .29 of light intensity. Based on an evaluation of data from another study on *Limulus* by Fuortes and Hodgkin (1964), Stevens proposed that the amplitude of the electrical activity of the receptor increased as a power function with an exponent of .32 of stimulus intensity.

Not all of the experiments reviewed by S. S. Stevens (1970, 1971b) revealed that there is such a close correspondence between the exponents of the neural input-output functions and the comparable psychophysical functions. Many of the differences might be accounted for in terms of species differences, differences in experimental conditions, and electrophysiological recording methods that are in various stages of refinement. It was Stevens' view, however, that sensory modalities having large psychophysical function exponents have large neural function exponents, and modalities that have small psychophysical function exponents have small neural function exponents.

One of the problems of attempting to correlate neurophysiological and psychophysical data is that the two sets of data are almost always obtained from different species. No doubt much could be learned if a method were developed for training animals to make ratio discriminations of sensory magnitude. In the absence of such methods, comparisons of animal neurophysiological data and human psychophysical data will be our main source of information on the problem.

There have, however, been some attempts to directly compare psychophysical and neurophysiological data from humans. In one successful experiment, recordings were made from the taste nerve while the observer made magnitude estimations of taste substances such as sucrose, sodium chloride, and citric acid applied in various concentrations to the tongue (Borg, Diamant, Ström, & Zotterman, 1967). The experiment was possible only because the observers were patients having surgery in which a branch of the chorda tympani taste nerve became accessible to a recording electrode. The patients required surgery that involved removal of the eardrum to expose the middle ear. Since a branch of the taste nerve passes through the middle ear on its way from the tongue to the brain, psychophysical and electrophysiological data on the sense of taste could be obtained from the same observer. A very close correspondence was found between the two sets of data (Figure 14.1). Both the response of the taste nerve and the judgments of the observer increased as a power function of the concentration of the substance placed on the tongue. Furthermore, the exponents were the same for the neural and psychophysical responses.

The results of electrophysiological experimentation on neurons indicate that we are at the beginning of a period where direct observations will be made of the nonlinear transformations of stimulus energy that have been implied for many years by psychophysical data and theory. In his 1969 Nobel address, Delbrück recognized the importance of this problem:

Sensory physiology in a broad sense contains hidden as its kernel an as yet totally undeveloped but absolutely central science: transducer physiology, the study of the conversion of the outside signal to its first "interesting"

output. I use the word "interesting" advisedly because I wish to exclude
. . . the primary photochemical reactions of the visual system . . . Transducer
physiology proper comes after this first step, where we are dealing with
devices of the cell unparalleled in anything the physicists have produced
so far with respect to sensitivity, adaptability, and miniaturization. (Delbrück, 1970, p. 1313)

Whether or not research in Delbrück's "central science" will reveal that
the power functions observed in psychophysical experiments can be accounted for mainly in terms of the operation of sensory transducers will
be seen in the future. The small amount of data existing on this problem
seems to indicate that power functions frequently describe the neurophysiological input–output relationship in the receptor, in the peripheral
sensory nervous system, and in the brain.

One tentative conclusion based on very limited information has been
that a power transformation of the stimulus is made at the receptor and
that all subsequent transformations as the information is conducted toward the brain are linear. S. S. Stevens (1970) reported that at the 1966
Ciba Symposium, Sir John Eccles expressed the opinion that after the
sensory transducer has performed its operation on the input, neural
information undergoes a series of linear transformations at each succeed-
ing synaptic junction. In the same discussion, Mountcastle expressed the
opinion that the nonlinear relationship between stimulus and sensation
may be localized at the receptor level. This position is essentially Stevens'

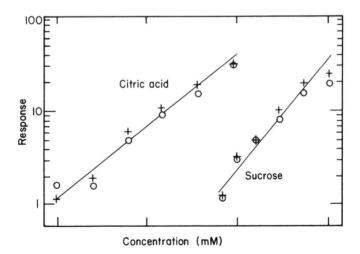

FIG. 14.1. Neural response (open circles) and magnitude estimation
(crosses) as a function of concentration of taste solutions applied to the
tongue. (From Borg et al., 1967.)

sensory transducer theory. Obviously, more work on recording neural activity at various points along the sensory nervous system is needed to give Stevens' transducer theory a firm empirical foundation.

Perhaps as important as measuring more intensity functions in the nervous system is the development of theoretical models for the data already available. In a theoretical analysis of receptor intensity functions, Zwislocki (1973, 1974) pointed out that when intensity characteristics of sensory receptors are recorded over a sufficient range of stimulus intensities, they fit neither Fechner's logarithmic functions nor Stevens' power function. Instead, intensity functions are S shaped. The low end of the function becomes flat when the receptor output cannot become lower because of its spontaneous activity level. As stimulus intensity is increased, receptor output increases; but because the receptor eventually saturates in its ability to respond to further increases in intensity, the function again becomes flat at high intensities. Zwislocki was, however, able to show that if spontaneous activity level, the saturation point, and threshold effects were mathematically taken into account, the remaining receptor activity was a power function of stimulus intensity. According to Zwislocki's calculations on empirical intensity functions from a variety of different receptors, it is possible that receptors of all sensory modalities have power exponents of either .5 or 1.0. Only taste and temperature receptors had exponents of 1.0; all others were .5. Zwislocki made the additional suggestion that, if threshold and neural noise factors were taken into account, psychophysical judgments that seem to parallel the peripheral neural output may also obey the rule by increasing as a function of stimulus energy raised to the power of either .5 or 1.0. The obvious exceptions to this generalization are vision and audition, where the psychophysical exponents are often clearly smaller than the receptor exponents. According to Zwislocki, the difference between receptor and psychophysical data in these cases may be due to the fact that receptors respond over an energy range of only a few log units, while the dynamic range of visual and auditory sensation extends over 12 or more log units of energy. That the psychophysical exponent is lower than the neural exponent may result from the interaction of several receptor processes with sensitivities staggered along the intensity scale.

Zwislocki's formulation is attractive because it represents an attempt to simplify further the relation between stimulus and sensation. The large differences among power exponents for various modalities and stimulus conditions in both the receptor domain and the psychophysical domain may be the result of differences in thresholds, neural noise levels, and saturation points of receptors. With the exception of vision and audition, psychophysical and receptor exponents may parallel each other with power function exponents of either .5 or 1.0. The visual and auditory psychophysical exponents of .33 may result from the interaction of different receptor populations, each having the .5 and 1.0 exponent but operating at different stimulus energy levels.

The fate of sensory transducer theory may depend primarily on the success of theoretical analyses like Zwislocki's. Marks (1974b) has strongly emphasized the importance of evaluating the validity of a particular psychophysical magnitude function in the context of the study of sensory processes in general. Throughout his book, he has clearly demonstrated that power functions generated by ratio scaling methods are often precisely predictable from our current understanding of sensory processes such as temporal summation, spatial summation, adaptation, and inhibition. The analyses of Zwislocki and Marks are important examples of attempts to integrate the ratio scaling data into the very substantial body of psychophysical and physiological facts and theory presently available on sensory processes.

Criticisms of the Sensory Transducer Theory

A strong argument against the sensory transducer theory has been made by Poulton (1968). He argued that exponents for different psychophysical magnitude functions varied in size more because of changes in experimental conditions than because of changing characteristics of different sensory receptors. In viewing the evidence, Poulton found several situational factors that may influence psychological processes involved in judging sensory magnitude: (a) the range of stimulus values, (b) the distance of the stimulus from the threshold, (c) the value of the standard stimulus, (d) the size of the difference between the standard stimulus and the first comparison stimulus presented, (e) whether the range of numbers the observer is permitted to use is infinite or finite, and (f) the sensation magnitude value that the observer is instructed to use for the standard stimulus.

The brightness sensation magnitude function with its exponent of .33 (J. C. Stevens & S. S. Stevens, 1963) and the sensation magnitude function for electric shock with its exponent of 3.5 (S. S. Stevens, Carton, & Shickman, 1958) have been thought to reflect differences between the two sensory systems. Poulton (1968) questioned the validity of this assumption and attempted to account for differences in exponents of different sensory systems in terms of the experimental conditions under which they were determined. In Poulton's model, the observer's judgment is determined by sensation magnitude, which is some function of the transducer properties of the sensory system plus the operation of a number of judgment-biasing factors such as those listed above. The exponents determined in psychophysical scaling experiments, rather than giving us information about the sensory nervous system, may simply reflect situational parameters of the experiment. For example, Poulton proposed that differences in size of exponents for different modalities may be more a function of the range of stimuli employed than of the operation of sensory transducers.

According to Poulton, an inverse relationship between stimulus range and power exponent exists because there is a tendency for the observer's judgments to cover a constant range of log sensation magnitudes for all sensory modalities. Since the log of the range of stimulus intensity values used in experiments is not the same for different modalities, the exponents must be different. The greater the log stimulus intensity range, the lower the exponent must be if the log range of sensation magnitude judgments tends to be constant. For example, the stimulus range for electric current applied to the fingertip was less than one log unit and the exponent was 3.5, while the stimulus range for light presented to the eye was six log units and the exponent was .33. The large difference in exponents could simply be an artifact of the tendency for observers to vary their judgments over a certain range of values for both electric shock and brightness.

Poulton states that there is a highly significant negative correlation (τ = −.60, p < .001) between the exponent values and log stimulus intensity ranges reported in 21 studies conducted by S. S. Stevens and his associates. The correlation is not perfect because, presumably, the observers' judgments were also determined by the transducer properties of the sensory systems. However, the differences in exponents may tell us more about the range of stimulus intensities employed than about the sensory system. In psychophysics, we would like to be able to learn something about the sensory system from the observer's judgments; but according to Poulton, this is not possible using magnitude estimation procedures because of judgmental biases inherent in the method which obscure the very sensory process that we wish to study. Poulton finds these judgmental biases interesting, but for most psychophysicists, who are interested in sensory processes, they cause only frustration.

R. Teghtsoonian (1971) has suggested that Poulton underestimated the closeness with which power exponents are related to the stimulus range employed. Based on his own statistical analysis of the same 21 studies Poulton considered, Teghtsoonian concluded that at least 87% of the variance in exponents can be accounted for by variation in stimulus range. Teghtsoonian, however, interpreted the high negative correlation of −.94 between stimulus range and exponent as support for Stevens' transducer theory rather than as evidence against it. He hypothesized that the ratio of the strongest to the weakest possible sensory magnitude for a sensory system is approximately constant for all modalities. In this hypothesis, the approximate constancy in the range of the observer's judgments is due to the underlying constancy in the range of sensory magnitudes rather than to the judgmental rigidity assumed by Poulton to be inherent in the magnitude estimation procedure. Variances in power exponents are due to variation in the *dynamic range* of stimuli (ratio of the greatest to the smallest stimulus to which the observer is responsive) when the range of sensation magnitude is constant. Thus, according to Teghtsoonian (1971), "In this context, the various receptor systems can be regarded as performing the necessary expansions or compressions required to map the widely varying dynamic ranges into this constant range of subjective magnitudes" (p. 74). Teghtsoonian's hypothesis is illustrated in Figure 14.2, in which sensation magnitude is plotted as a function of stimulus intensity above absolute threshold. The three curves are power functions with different exponents. The range of sensation magnitudes from threshold to the maximum is constant, but the dynamic ranges of stimulus intensity differ greatly for the three hypothetical modalities.

S. S. Stevens (1971a) has pointed out an important exception to Teghtsoonian's interesting rule in the case of odor perception. Odors often have a short stimulus range and a low exponent. Stevens (1957) himself reported an exponent of only .2 for the odor of benzaldehyde. A similar low value has more recently been reported by Berglund, Berglund, Engen, and Ekman (1971). The odor of benzaldehyde has a relatively short range compared with loudness or brightness. Nevertheless, it is an interesting hypothesis that exponents vary in nature, at least to some extent, so that sensory systems can accommodate particular ranges of stimulation. If this hypothesis is correct, the brightness exponent of .33 and the electric shock exponent of 3.5 are not reflections of an artifact in experimental procedure, as suggested by Poulton, but instead reflect real differences in the input–output functions of the two sensory systems.

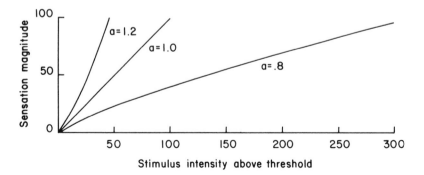

FIG. 14.2. Three power functions with exponents of .8, 1.0, and 1.2. The functions describe how sensory modalities with different dynamic ranges of stimulation could have identical ranges of sensory magnitude.

The Measurement of Sensations

Some behaviorally oriented psychologists have argued that psychophysics is based on the fallacious notion that private events such as sensations can be measured (e.g., Savage, 1966, 1970; Zuriff, 1972). Many critics of psychophysics strongly disagree with the use of subjective terms such as sensation, perception, sensory magnitude, and apparent magnitude because they seem to refer to events that cannot be observed in a scientific experiment. The distinction made frequently by psychophysicists between a physical stimulus continuum and a corresponding psychological continuum is rejected as unnecessary and misleading. To claim that subjective events on a psychological continuum have been measured is considered illogical, since such events are not publicly observable. The distinction between a physical stimulus continuum and a psychological continuum has been very useful to psychophysicists, however, since it separates the stimulus from the effects that the stimulus has on the organism's sensory system. In psychoacoustics, for example, it makes sense to describe the response of the auditory system as varying along continua of loudness and pitch while the stimulus varies in intensity and frequency of vibration. Likewise, in visual research investigators often describe responses of the visual system as varying on continua of brightness, hue, and saturation as the intensity and wavelength characteristics of light are manipulated. It is the fact that the brightness or loudness experienced by an observer cannot be publicly verified that has led the radical behaviorist to reject such subjective concepts as meaningless.

The radical behaviorists appear to fear that the use of subjective-sounding terms to describe the responses of sensory systems, no matter how well they are defined or how much it facilitates the research effort, may cause a regression of psychology to the morass of confusion generated by the mind–body dualism of early experimental psychology. An examination of the writings of such critics of psychophysics will reveal that their arguments, although interesting, have little bearing on the design, analysis, and interpretation of psychophysical experiments. However, a brief discussion of the issue seems in order if for no other reason than to reassure the reader that psychophysicists are not engaged in some kind of futile attempt to solve the mind–body problem.

Is psychophysics based on the fallacious notion that private events can be measured? In a scholarly analysis of the problem, Savage (1966, 1970) proposed that the concept of sensation magnitude be abandoned and suggested that psychophysical scaling procedures be regarded as procedures for measuring perceptual abilities. His argument is based on the assumption that psychophysicists like S. S. Stevens have mistakenly attempted to measure private events. It is true that private events can never be measured, since such attempts could never be verified publicly. However, Savage's arguments for the rejection of subjective-sounding concepts, as pointed out by Stevens in a rebuttal at the end of Savage's 1966 article, are mainly over the use of words and have little substance when it comes to the design and conduct of psychophysical experiments. Stevens pointed out that the operations in an experiment, rather than particular words, are important in scientific investigation.

When S. S. Stevens said he had measured subjective sensation, he was intending to communicate the fact that a certain paradigm of operations had been employed. The specifics of these operations are discussed in detail by Stevens (1966c), and many of them have already been described in this book. The basic operation in the study of sensation magnitude is the matching performed by an observer. For example, in magnitude estimation of loudness, the observer is required to match the loudness of various stimuli with various values on the number scale, while in cross-modality matching he may be required to match the loudness of a tone to the brightness of lights of various intensities. According to Stevens, the focal issue centers on the use of the observer as a comparator. Sensory magnitude is simply measured by a systematic investigation of the observer's behavior as he performs as a matching comparator. Zwislocki (1991) pointed out that the matching operation is one that is natural in the sense that humans and animals do it every day. Squirrels and monkeys match the distances of their jumps to their estimations of the distances between tree branches. Birds maintain correct distances among themselves when flying in a flock. The hunter must match the angle at which a spear is thrown and the subjective impression of perceived effort to the subjective impression of distance from the animal. Thus, *natural measurement*, according to Zwislocki, should be defined as matching common attributes of things and events. This idea has profound implications. For example, psychophysical measurement of sensation magnitude should be relatively easy and highly reliable because it requires only ordinal judgments. The observer must simply judge whether one psychological magnitude located on one continuum is less than, greater than, or equal to a psychological magnitude located on another continuum. A match is made when the psychological magnitudes are judged to be equal. At this point, the two corresponding physical values are recorded by the experimenter. The matching continuum can be impressions of number size, as in magnitude estimation, or impressions of stimulus intensity, as in cross-modality matching. In either case, the principle is the same. The observer matches one psychological continuum to another. This operation is essentially all that is meant by the term sensory magnitude. It should be evident that the term refers rather specifically to a class of publicly observable experimental operations. The experimental results produced by such operations can be easily replicated by several investigators. The reliability of the results can be established, and their usefulness can be evaluated in terms of how they relate to other experimental data and to psychophysical theories.

If the problem is only with the use of words, one might argue that psychophysicists should drop the use of subjective-sounding terms such as subjective magnitude so that they would not be misinterpreted. In the appended comments to Savage's article, S. S. Stevens' explanation for his use of subjective-sounding terms is that they refer to a configuration of defining operation rather than to scientifically unmanageable private entities. We should therefore think of subjective magnitude, sensory magnitude, or whatever it is called, as a scientific construct. It appears to be advantageous to use words such as subjective, sensory, perceptual, or apparent to identify the construct, since these words refer to a specific kind of judgment an observer will make in a psychophysical experiment. Stevens (1966a) explained that:

> From an experienced photographer you can get two estimates of the light level, depending on whether you ask him to judge the physical or apparent level. And for the apparent or subjective value he will give widely different estimates if you vary the states of adaptation of his eyes. Similarly, a sound engineer can estimate the decibel level of a noisy factory, or, under a different *Aufgabe*, he can judge apparent loudness. (pp. 36–37)

Stevens' point is well illustrated by an experiment of M. Teghtsoonian's (1965). She found the exponent for the power function of apparent size to be .76, but when she asked the observers to judge the physical area, they changed their basis of judgment, and the exponent became 1.03. The exponent of nearly 1.0 indicates that when the observers tried to judge physical area they were, on the average, almost perfectly accurate. Obviously, different psychological processes were being investigated in the two parts of the experiment. Telling the observers to give their judgment of the apparent or subjective magnitude of a stimulus rather than to estimate its physical value appears to encourage them to make a direct response to the stimulus which is unaffected by mediating thoughts concerning physical measurement scales. Since the use of subjective terms as part of the instructions to the observer makes a large difference in the experimental data, such subjective concepts should be retained. The important point is that for purposes of scientific communication, these concepts are not references to vague, mentalistic, inaccessible private events, but rather are operationally defined scientific concepts.

The Physical Correlate Theory

Warren is another investigator who has questioned the validity of the assumption that sensation can be quantified (Warren, 1958, 1969; Warren & Warren, 1963). He claimed that instead of making judgments of sensory magnitude, observers make judgments of some physical attribute associated with the stimulus. Similar arguments have recently been made by Lockhead (1992) who claims that observers are capable of making judgments of the characteristics of objects but not the attributes of their own perceptions. According to the physical correlate theory, it is through past experience that observers learn to attend to some particular physical attribute when they are required in a psychophysics experiment to make sensation magnitude judgments of stimuli. The varying power function exponents found for different sense modalities do not reflect the operating characteristics of different biological transducers, but instead are thought to be determined by the observer's responding to particular physical attributes of different stimuli.

A psychophysical power function with an exponent of approximately 1.0 for the judgment of duration may simply indicate that observers, through years of experience, have become capable of making judgments of duration that are linearly related to stimulus duration. A sound that is twice as long as another sound will be judged to be twice as long in apparent duration. According to the physical correlate theory, the observer does not call one stimulus twice as long as another because this response indicates how his apparent durations are perceived. Instead, he makes this judgment because through experience he has learned the physical cues that correspond to a doubling of duration. In instrumental conditioning language, the observer has learned through years of reinforcement and extinction to make the correct response to a stimulus of a particular duration. Consequently, the observer's judgments on the psychophysical task are determined by physical attributes of the stimulus rather than by the duration of the sensation. Contrary to sensory transducer theory, apparent duration, if it exists, is certainly not measured by the observer's judgments of the stimulus. What is measured, according to the physical correlate theory, is the observer's ability to discriminate among stimuli of various durations. The present example does not offer a test of the two theories, but instead illustrates how they can account for the same data. Some basis for evaluation of the two theories is provided by examining the results of experiments on loudness and brightness scaling.

Unless a person is an acoustical engineer, he or she would probably not have the opportunity to learn to make accurate judgments of the energy level of sound. Most people do, however, learn to make fairly accurate judgments of the distance of a sound. Warren (1963) has proposed that the distance between the observer and a sound source is the physical attribute to which the observer responds when he makes judgments of loudness in a laboratory situation. For example, if sound A is twice as far from the observer as sound B, then sound A should be judged to be half as loud as sound B. Because of the inverse square law, however, the sound energy at the observer's ears would not be half as great for A as for B, but only 25% as great. Thus, if the physical correlate theory is correct, loudness judgments should be proportional to the square root of sound energy; that is, the loudness function should be $L = kI^5$ when L is loudness, k is a constant, and I is sound energy. S. S. Stevens (1972b), in a review of the many experiments on loudness scales, concluded that the best estimate of the exponent for loudness is .33. Warren, Sersen, and Pores (1958), in an article on the applicability of the physical correlate theory to loudness judgments, claimed that when pure tones are presented through earphones under conditions that eliminate reflections, the highly unusual quality of the stimulus prevents the observer from accurately using distance information. According to the authors, it is only under these unnatural conditions that the exponent for the loudness function is .33. When auditory stimuli were generated through a loudspeaker in a room which produced reverberations within the range normally encountered, the loudness function $L = kI^5$, which is predicted from physical correlate theory, was obtained. Further evidence in support of the physical correlate theory of loudness was presented by Warren (1963).

It is possible that the biological transducer theory and the physical correlate theory are both correct. It may be that under conditions in which observers hear sounds in the familiar setting of a reverberating field, they find it most natural to judge their loudness by their apparent distance. Certainly such sounds would be clearly localized as sound sources with relative positions in respect to other objects in the environment. Under these conditions, the observer may find it impossible to avoid making what Titchener (1905) called the *stimulus error*.[1] The early psychophysicists thought that the observer made the stimulus error when he failed to judge his sensations and instead made judgments based on what he knew about the stimulus. Perhaps the relatively unfamiliar setting of a reverberation-free environment, such as those employed by the dozens of investigators who found the exponent for loudness to be approximately .33, permitted observers to judge correctly the magnitude of their sensations of loudness. The physical correlate theory may be correct when the observer is encouraged to make judgments about the physical attributes of stimuli, but the sensory transducer theory may apply in situations where the observer has been trained to avoid making the stimulus error of judging objects instead of sensations.

Warren (1969) has reviewed the evidence supporting the physical correlate theory for brightness judgments. Most people having little experience in measuring light are unable to make accurate estimates of light intensity, yet they are constantly making judgments of the brightness of objects. According to Warren, individuals are familiar with the way in

---

[1]For an excellent analysis of the stimulus error in psychological experiments, see E. G. Boring (1921).

which an object's appearance changes as the distance between the object and the source of light that illuminates it changes. It is assumed that when an observer is asked to make brightness judgments in a laboratory situation, he bases his responses upon this familiar effect. A judgment of "half as bright" should occur when the stimulus intensity has been reduced by exactly the same amount as would occur when the distance between an object and a light source is doubled. Because of the inverse square law, if object A is twice as far from an illuminating light source as object B, then object A will receive 25% as much illumination. Therefore, a perceived brightness ratio of one-half should require a stimulus energy ratio of one-quarter, and the brightness function should be $B = kI^{.5}$, where B is judged brightness, k is a constant, and I is light energy.

Warren (1969) has claimed that exponents other than .5 are obtained only under very restricted and unnatural viewing conditions. For example, S. S. Stevens, based on data from experiments by Hanes (1949a, 1949b) and data from his own experiments (Stevens, 1961a; Stevens & Galanter, 1957), has proposed that the exponent for brightness is .33. This value was obtained for a dark-adapted eye when the observer viewed a small luminous disc (about 5°) against a dark background. Warren (1969), in a review of the experimental evidence for a brightness exponent of .5, reports that the .5 exponent is consistently obtained when stimuli are presented in a fashion closely resembling conditions under which the eyes are normally used (i.e., large stimuli with eyes adapted to the stimulus level). S. S. Stevens (1963), on the other hand, argues that the exponent for brightness may vary over a wide range depending on conditions of adaptation and glare. According to Stevens, .5 is a limited case and therefore does not constitute evidence in support of Warren's theory.

The interpretation of loudness judgment data, in which it was suggested that both the biological transducer theory and the physical correlate theory may be correct, is equally applicable to brightness judgment data. When stimuli are viewed as objects, the brightness exponent may be close to .5. Under these conditions, the observer may be attending to the stimulus correlate of changing luminance with changes in light source distance. Under conditions where it is difficult to identify the stimulus as an object, or when the observer has been trained to avoid viewing the stimulus as an object, the stimulus error is not made, and the exponent may vary over a wide range depending on how the viewing conditions affect the operating characteristics of the sensory transducers. Brightness functions obtained in both of these two different ways are important, since one set of functions applies to sensory transducers, while the other applies to object perception. However, since the primary aim of psychophysical research has been to determine the operating characteristics of sensory systems, the work of Warren and his associates has been regarded by many psychophysicists as interesting but irrelevant.

In response to a paper in which Warren (1981) reviewed his work on the physical correlate theory of psychophysical scaling, Gescheider (1981) pointed out that, while Warren's work is an attack on the traditional sensory process hypothesis of psychophysical scaling, it does not constitute an adequate test of the hypothesis. The sensory process hypothesis that psychophysical scales of stimulus intensity reflect the operation of sensory mechanisms as they transduce and code stimulus energy into neural activity can be tested only within the context of our knowledge of sensory processes. Psychophysical scales generated by ratio scaling procedures are often precisely predictable from our understanding of temporal summation, spatial summation, adaptation, inhibition, and other sensory processes. It is this approach in which psychophysical scaling data are predicted from knowledge of sensory processes that will determine the final verdict on the sensory process hypothesis. The experiments by Warren and his associates that appear to support an alternative hypothesis have little if any bearing on the sensory process hypothesis.

EVALUATION OF SCALING METHODS

Comparison of Scaling Methods

Agreement among scientific results obtained under different conditions and by different methods is often thought to constitute a type of validation of the particular finding. Therefore, the forms of the psychophysical magnitude functions obtained by the various confusion, partition, and ratio scaling methods should be essentially the same if the scales are valid. When correspondence between the different scales is lacking, the validity of each scaling method is questionable. A careful examination of each method should be made to determine (a) which if any of the methods yield valid results, and (b) the reason for the lack of agreement among the results of the different methods.

On metathetic continua, all three kinds of psychophysical scales show remarkable agreement. For example, the form of the mel scale of pitch is the same when constructed by summating jnd's, equisectioning pitch intervals, and making ratio judgments (S. S. Stevens, 1954; S. S. Stevens & Galanter, 1957). When the scale values obtained by one method are plotted against the scale values obtained by another method for various stimulus values, the relationship is a straight line. Furthermore, the pitch scale for pure tones corresponds almost exactly to a graph of how the point of maximum vibration on the basilar membrane of the inner ear changes as a function of frequency. Thus, psychological pitch is approximately linearly mapped out on the basilar membrane.

On prothetic continua, ratio scales, partition scales, and discrimination scales are nonlinearly related. S. S. Stevens (1961a), comparing scales constructed by magnitude estimation, jnd summation, and category rating, states that

> ... on all prothetic continua the magnitude scale is a power function, the discriminability (jnd) scale approximates a logarithmic function, and the category scale assumes a form intermediate between the other two. Over the different sense modalities, these relations among the three scales are strikingly invariant; they constitute one of the really stable aspects of psychophysics. (p. 9)

The difference between scales obtained by magnitude estimation, jnd scaling, and category scaling is illustrated in Figure 14.3. The three measures were applied to the apparent duration of a noise stimulus. Magnitude estimation judgments and category scale judgments on a scale of 1 to 7 are shown by a smooth curve drawn through the data points and the dashed curve is the function obtained by summation of the jnd's (Stevens, 1957). The results for each scaling procedure can be read from separate Y axes. It is clear that the forms of the functions are different, with that of magnitude estimation being almost linear, that of summated jnd's being approximately logarithmic, and with the form of the category scaling lying somewhere between the two.

Why do the three scaling methods result in comparable scales on metathetic continua but not on prothetic continua? S. S. Stevens has taken the position that on metathetic continua, the three scaling methods measure the same aspect of the sensory response—discriminability.

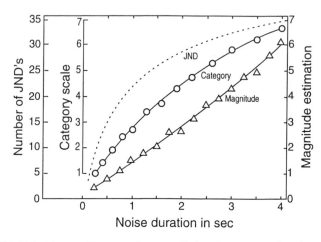

FIG. 14.3. Three scaling procedures applied to the apparent duration of a noise stimulus. (From Stevens, 1957.) Reprinted with permission.

Because metathetic continua are qualitative, relating to the "what" and "where" of sensory experience, the important consideration in scaling would seem to be the measurement of the amount of difference between sensations. Discrimination scales such as summated jnd's give a direct measure of the discriminability of sensations. Partition scales are in agreement with discrimination scales because, when the observer is asked to partition the continuum into psychologically equal segments, he apparently bases his judgments on the discriminability of sensations and creates a series of segments, each of which contains the same number of jnd's. When a ratio scaling method is used, the observer will judge one sensation to be twice as great as another sensation if the second sensation corresponds to twice the number of summated jnd's as the first. Thus, on metathetic continua all three kinds of scaling methods seem to result in valid psychological scales of the discriminability of sensation.

On prothetic continua, the relevant aspect of the sensory response is not discriminability but sensation magnitude. However, as on metathetic continua, the discrimination and partition scales measure discriminability when applied to the prothetic continua. Discriminability of sensations is certainly important, but it should not be confused with sensation magnitude. On prothetic continua, the discriminability of two sensations does not correspond to the difference in magnitude between the two sensations. Sensation magnitude is assumed to be directly and validly measured only by the ratio scaling methods.

Marks (1974c) argued that there is strong evidence for the validity of ratio scales of sensory magnitude. He cited as evidence internal consistency of the data as determined by cross-modality matching and intramodality matching. He also argued that the validity of magnitude-estimation data is supported by *psychosensory laws*, in which measures of sensory magnitude enter into simple lawful relationship, such as loudness summation and the multiplicative relation between measures of density and volume to produce loudness. Thus, the requirement that valid psychophysical measurements must interrelate with one another in laws in the same way that valid physical measurements do (Luce, 1972) seems to be met in these instances.

Although Marks and others make a strong case for the valid measurement of sensory magnitude by magnitude estimation and other ratio scaling procedures, Anderson (e.g., 1970, 1976, 1982) and others have argued for the validity of category judgments. In Anderson's functional-measurement approach (Anderson, 1981), the sensory scale and the psychosensory law are simultaneously determined in experimental designs in which different dimensions of the stimulus are factorially manipulated. It is Anderson's view that psychosensory (psychological) laws obey simple algebraic rules such as addition, averaging, and multiplication as revealed by category scaling. It is significant that category ratings are almost always nonlinearly related to magnitude estimations. Because category ratings and magnitude estimations yield different results, it has been frequently argued that the results of one method are valid, whereas those of the other are invalid. Anderson and his associates have consistently argued that because the results of category scaling reveal psychosensory (psychological) laws that can be described by simple, algebraic equations of information integration, the category scale must be valid. Moreover, the magnitude-estimation scale, because of its nonlinear relation with the category scale, must be invalid. It is noteworthy, however, that studies in which magnitude estimation was used in a functional-measurement design also yielded simple algebraic equations of information integration (e.g., Algom & Cohen-Raz, 1984; Algom, Raphaeli, & Cohen-Raz, 1986; Algom, Wolf, & Bergman, 1985; Marks, 1982). Now which scale is valid?

The problem is that the two scaling methods yield scales that pass a variety of validity tests, yet are nonlinearly related. It would appear that something must be wrong with the validity test or, as Marks (1974c) first proposed, each of the two types of scale produces valid measurements but of fundamentally different psychophysical processes. Marks' proposal is that ratio-scaling methods, when applied correctly, yield valid measures of sensory magnitude, and category-scaling methods, when applied correctly, yield valid measures of sensory dissimilarity. The sensory magnitudes and sensory dissimilarities of stimuli are considered to be equally meaningful dimensions of perceptual experience, each being tapped most effectively by a different scaling procedure.

Functional Measurement

Problems of perceptual integration and the psychological (psychosensory) law have been studied extensively in a number of areas other than sensory psychophysics. Anderson has been one of the most productive investigators in this area. His work started with problems of social judgment, but has extended to areas including decision theory, learning and motivation, psycholinguistics, and developmental psychology (Anderson, 1982). It has been Anderson's view that psychological laws in these areas obey simple arithmetic rules such as addition and multiplication. The laws can be discovered by what Anderson calls *functional measurement*. In functional measurement, two or more stimuli produce separate subjective impressions. When the stimuli are combined, these impressions are integrated by some rule that is the psychological law. The person is required to make an overt rating response of his subjective impression. The psychological law is discovered through an examination of how the person's ratings change when the combination of stimuli are changed. Typically, an experiment consists of presenting stimuli in all possible combinations to an observer who rates the combination on some psychological dimension.

In one of his early studies, Anderson (1962) employed a rating scale method to investigate person perception. The observer's task was to rate, on a 20-point scale, the likableness of each of nine persons described by two different personality traits. The adjectives *level-headed, unsophisticated,* and *ungrateful* were paired in all possible combinations with *good-natured, bold,* and *humorless.* The data shown in Figure 14.4 indicate that the likableness of a person is the sum of the likableness ratings of the separate adjectives. The parallel functions in Figure 14.4 indicate that the effect of a particular adjective on an observer's ratings is the same when combined with any other adjective. For example, when the first adjective is changed from ungrateful to unsophisticated and combined with the second adjectives of good-natured, bold, and humorless, ratings of likableness increase by approximately the same amount. Perception of one adjective does not seem to affect perception of the other, but instead the effect of one adjective on the observer's rating simply adds to the effect of the other adjective. It is also significant that the additive effects of the adjectives on likableness ratings appear with both observers FF and RH even though RH considered *unsophisticated* to be almost as desirable as *level-headed,* while FF regarded *unsophisticated* to be midway between *ungrateful* and *level-headed.* The important feature of this experiment is the demonstration that, through psychophysical measurement, a cognitive process such as the impression

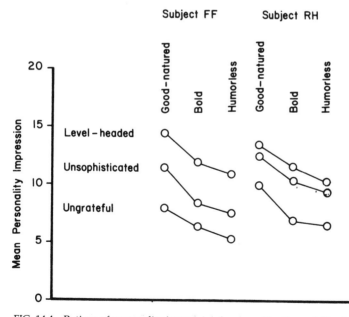

FIG. 14.4. Ratings of personality impression from combinations of descriptive adjectives. (Data from Anderson, 1962.)

of someone obtained from a description can be broken down into component parts that relate to each other through a psychological law of addition. How do these cognitive integration processes develop in individuals? According to Anderson (1982), children as young as 3 years of age are able to integrate cognitive information by adding its effects together. For example, the judged naughtiness of an act depends on the summation of the judged harm or damage of the act and the intention of the offender. The results shown in Figure 14.5 show that no matter what the severity of consequence, the intention of the act has a constant influence on the judged naughtiness of the act (Leon, 1980). It is also evident that children place greater importance on the severity of consequences than do adults. The curves are somewhat steeper for children than for adults. Also, the intention of the offender is less important for children than for adults, as shown by the smaller separation of the children's curves for intentions of accident, displaced aggression, and malice.

According to Anderson (1980), children are very good at cognitive integration and in general show much more cognitive ability than has been recognized by most child psychologists. The use of simple scaling methods with children to discover psychological laws is becoming a powerful method for studying cognitive development.

The work of Anderson and his associates represents an important application of scaling methods to the problem of determining how indi-

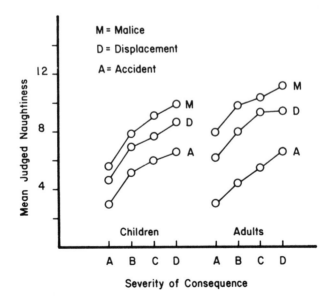

FIG. 14.5.   Ratings of naughtiness of acts are the sum of the intention behind the act and the damage caused by the act. (Data from Leon, 1980.)

viduals integrate information. The work also has important implications for the validity of scaling methods. In their studies, the method of category rating has been used. It is significant that the category rating method almost always gives different results than magnitude estimation. Because they yield different results, one might argue that both methods cannot be valid. Anderson's evidence for the validity of his category scaling procedures is his finding that psychological laws discovered by this method can be stated as simple algebraic equations such as the summation of psychological states. The results of the experiment seem to simultaneously validate the psychological law of additivity of psychological impressions and the category scaling procedure. The problem with this logic is that demonstration of summation of experimentally obtained scale values cannot validate both the proposed psychological law of summation and the proposed linear sensory response law (*psychomotor law* in Anderson's terms) at the same time. To prove the linearity of the sensory response law, and thus the validity of the category rating procedure, the psychological law must be *assumed*; but at the same time, to prove the psychological law, the linear sensory response law must be *assumed*. For example, in the study of offensive acts, a psychological law was *assumed* in which the naughtiness of an act is the sum of the perceived consequence and the perceived intention of the offender. The fact that the observer's ratings were additive was considered evidence for a valid scale in which the category values assigned by observers were linearly related to their subjective impression of naughtiness. This conclusion would be fine if there were some independent ways of testing the assumed psychological law that perceived consequence and intention summate. Unfortunately, no independent way of testing this psychological law has yet been devised. Instead, the validity of this law of summation of consequences and intentions is supported by the data only when a linear sensory response law is *assumed*.

It is true that the results of Leon's (1980) experiment are consistent with a model in which psychological states obey an adding rule and the sensory response law is linear. The problem is that other models, with other psychological and sensory response laws, can also account for Leon's data. As was true in attempting to formulate psychological laws of perceived volume, density, and loudness of sounds, it is impossible to validate the psychological scale by simply demonstrating that the results are consistent with some simple psychological law of subjective impressions. For example, the results obtained in Leon's experiment would also be predicted from a model in which perceived intention and consequence combined multiplicitively rather than additively to produce perceived naughtiness and in which the relationship between perceived naughtiness and the observer's rating response was logarithmic rather than linear.

To illustrate how the two models can predict the same results in a functional measurement experiment, consider the hypothetical psycho-

TABLE 14.1
Psychological Values of Naughtiness Corresponding to
Three Consequences of an Act and Two Intentions

Psychological Naughtiness					
Consequence				Intention	
$\dfrac{X}{2}$	$\dfrac{Y}{4}$	$\dfrac{Z}{6}$		$\dfrac{A}{2}$	$\dfrac{M}{4}$

logical values of naughtiness corresponding to three consequences of increasing severity (X, Y, and Z) and the two intentions of accident (A) or malice (M) presented in Table 14.1. In the first model, it is assumed that naughtiness (N) is equal to consequence (C) plus intentions (I), and that rating scale values (R) are proportional to naughtiness (N):

Model 1
$$N = C + I \qquad R \propto N$$

In the top row of Table 14.2, the amount of naughtiness corresponding to accident has been added to the naughtiness of each of the three consequences. In the bottom row of the table, the amount of naughtiness corresponding to an act of malice is added to the naughtinesses of the three consequences. Assuming that the rating response is proportional to the perceived total naughtiness of the act, the predicted results, as seen in Figure 14.6, are two parallel functions when rating responses are plotted as a function of consequence for the two intentions. This prediction fits the data of Leon (1980) well (Figure 14.5).

In the second model, it is assumed that the naughtiness of an act is equal to its consequence multiplied by its intention, and that the psychological rating is proportional to the logarithm of perceived naughtiness.

TABLE 14.2
Psychological Impressions of the Naughtiness of an Act
Determined by the Summation of Impressions of the
Act's Consequences and the Actor's Intentions

	Total Naughtiness		
Accident + consequence	$\dfrac{A + X}{4}$	$\dfrac{A + Y}{6}$	$\dfrac{A + Z}{8}$
Malice + consequence	$\dfrac{M + X}{6}$	$\dfrac{M + Y}{8}$	$\dfrac{M + Z}{10}$

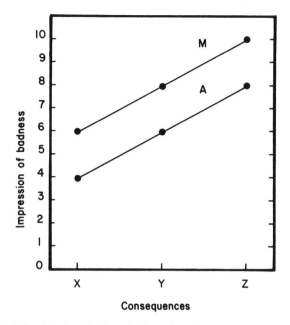

FIG. 14.6.   Predicted results from the hypothesis that perceived naughtiness is equal to the perceived consequences plus the perceived intentions of an act. It is also assumed that the observer's rating responses are proportional to perceived naughtiness.

Model 2

$$N = C \times I \qquad\qquad R \propto \log N$$

In the top row of Table 14.3, the amount of naughtiness of each consequence has been multiplied by the naughtiness of an accident; and in the bottom row, these same amounts of naughtiness have been multiplied by the naughtiness of an act of malice. Assuming that the rating response is proportional to the logarithm of the total naughtiness of the act, we must

TABLE 14.3
Psychological Impressions of the Naughtiness of an Act
Determined by the Multiplication of Impressions of the
Act's Consequences and the Actor's Intentions

	Total Naughtiness		
Accident × consequence	$\dfrac{A \times X}{4}$	$\dfrac{A \times Y}{8}$	$\dfrac{A \times Z}{12}$
Malice × consequence	$\dfrac{M \times X}{8}$	$\dfrac{M \times Y}{16}$	$\dfrac{M \times Z}{24}$

TABLE 14.4
Logarithms of Values in Table 14.3

	Log Total Naughtiness		
Accident × consequence	A × X	A × Y	A × Z
	.6	.9	1.08
Malice × consequence	M × X	M × Y	M × Z
	.9	1.2	1.38

convert the values in Table 14.3 to logarithms in order to predict the rating response of the observer. The logarithms of the psychological values are seen in Table 14.4 and are plotted in Figure 14.7. This prediction also agrees with Leon's data (Figure 14.5).

Anderson claims that through functional measurement it is possible to simultaneously discover a psychological law and validate the scaling method. The exercise above shows that this is not possible when more than one model can account for the data, and only one of them can be correct. Functional measurement does not provide a way to decide among alternative models. Unless information beyond that gained in the func-

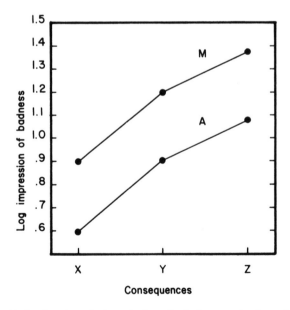

FIG. 14.7. Predicted results from the hypothesis that perceived naughtiness is equal to the perceived consequences multiplied by the perceived intention of an act. It is also assumed that the observer's rating responses are proportional to log naughtiness.

tional measurement experiment is available to support the hypothesized psychological law, we have no reason to accept it and therefore no reason to accept the hypothesis that the observers' category ratings are linearly related to their conception of naughtiness. There is also no reason to accept Anderson's (1982) argument that experiments like his, in validating category rating scales, prove that magnitude estimation scales are invalid.

Instead, perhaps Marks (1974c, 1979b) is correct in his contention that both types of scale are valid with magnitude estimation measuring psychological magnitude and category scales measuring psychological dissimilarity. This could provide the explanation for why, as mentioned earlier, functional measurement has revealed simple psychological (psychosensory) laws determined by both category and magnitude estimation scaling.

The strength of functional measurement is that it provides a method for discovering the psychological laws that govern the interaction of mental processes. Discovering these laws has become one of the most important research problems in modern psychophysics. It should be kept in mind, however, that psychological laws that obey simple algebraic rules suggest, but do not prove, the validity of the psychophysical scale.

Ekman's Law

At the University of Stockholm, an effort was made by Ekman to establish a precise theoretical formulation that would account for the difference between psychophysical scales derived by ratio scaling and discrimination scaling. Ekman's (1956, 1959) principle, known as *Ekman's law*, states that the psychological size of the jnd is a linear function of sensation magnitude. The formulation states that

$$\Delta \psi = k\psi, \tag{14.1}$$

where $\Delta \psi$ is a change in sensation magnitude that is just noticeable, ψ is the starting value of sensation magnitude, and k is a constant. This equation, which applies to the psychological continuum, is exactly analogous to Weber's law, $\Delta \phi = c\phi$, which applies to the physical stimulus continuum. The c in Weber's law refers to the constant fraction by which all values of ϕ must be changed to produce a just noticeable difference in sensation; the k in Ekman's law refers to the constant fraction by which all values of ψ must be changed to produce a just noticeable difference in sensation.

The first empirical evidence for Ekman's law came from an experiment by Harper and S. S. Stevens (1948) in which a psychological scale for heaviness, called the veg scale, was constructed. Harper and Stevens determined the weights which were judged to be half as heavy as standard weights of 20, 40, 70, 100, 300, 500, 1000, and 2000 gm. From the fractionation data, a sensation magnitude scale was constructed which turned out to be a power function with an exponent of 1.45. From the data of Oberlin (1936) on the size of Δφ for heaviness for different values of φ, it was possible for Harper and Stevens to calculate Δψ values for different values of ψ. This could be done graphically by simply converting φ into ψ and Δφ into Δψ for several values of ψ. Figure 14.8 illustrates the procedure for a single value of φ. In the experiment by Harper and Stevens, a linear relation was found between Δψ and ψ. Also in support of Ekman's law, Ekman (1959) reported that Δψ is proportional to ψ for visual velocity and auditory time.

In essence, Ekman's law is a statement that variability in sensory magnitude is proportional to the average sensory magnitude value. The derivation of Harper and Stevens that Δψ is proportional to ψ is complemented by the finding that the standard deviation is proportional to the mean magnitude estimation over a fairly wide range of stimulus values (Eisler, 1962, 1963). But even if relevant experimental data were absent, Ekman's hypothesis would seem very reasonable. Weber's law indicates that the variability of discrimination measured in the physical stimulus domain obeys the proportionality rule. Furthermore, in other sciences the variability of measurements is often proportional to the average value of the measurements. In measuring properties such as distance, duration, and weight, the result is frequently stated as a value in the appropriate units plus or minus some percentage, and the standard deviation is generally proportional to the mean. As early as 1874, Brentano speculated

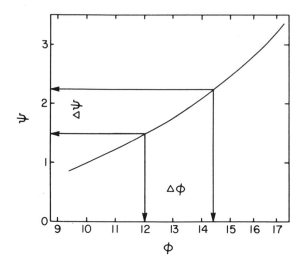

FIG. 14.8. Hypothetical psychophysical magnitude function. If the value of Δφ is known for a particular stimulus intensity, the corresponding value of Δψ can be determined from the psychophysical magnitude function.

that the relativity of variability applies in the psychological as well as in the physical domain. Had Brentano's idea been seriously considered, it would probably have resulted in the derivation of the power function as the psychophysical law. In contrast to Fechner, Brentano proposed that the psychological size of the jnd was not a constant value but was instead a constant ratio on the sensory continuum. Fechner's law, based on the less reasonable assumption that variability and, consequently, the jnd are constant all along the sensory magnitude continuum, carried the day and remained dominant for another 80 years.

Stevens' power law implies that both Ekman's law and Weber's law are valid. Since in the power law log ψ is linearly related to log ϕ, as ϕ is increased by some constant ratio (constant number of log units), ψ will also increase by some other constant ratio (constant ratio of log units). For example, the power function, with its exponent of .33 for loudness, indicates that every time we increase stimulus energy by 8.2 times (.91 log unit) we cause a doubling of loudness (.30 log unit). The loudness exponent is .30/.91 = .33.

In another example, we can increase ϕ by a constant ratio, c (Weber's law), and cause ψ to increase by the constant ratio, k (Ekman's law). Suppose that c is .5 and k is .2. Successive $\Delta\phi$ values along the ϕ scale can be calculated from Weber's law ($\Delta\phi = c\phi$). By adding $\Delta\phi$ to ϕ, successive values of ϕ are obtained in a series of ϕ values separated by difference thresholds. In this example, each ϕ value is .5 times greater than the previous value. Calculation of a series of ϕ values from Weber's law is shown below. In this example, the value of c in the equation $\Delta\phi = c\phi$ is equal to .5.

$\phi_1 = 1.0$
$\phi_2 = \phi_1 \times c + \phi_1 = 1.00 \times .5 + 1.00 = 1.50$
$\phi_3 = \phi_2 \times c + \phi_2 = 1.50 \times .5 + 1.50 = 2.25$
$\phi_4 = \phi_3 \times c + \phi_3 = 2.25 \times .5 + 2.25 = 3.37$
$\phi_5 = \phi_4 \times c + \phi_4 = 3.37 \times .5 + 3.37 = 5.09$

Through Weber's law, we have been able to calculate a series of stimulus values, ϕ, that increase by the constant ratio, c. It is also possible, through Ekman's law ($\Delta\psi = k\psi$), to calculate a series of sensation values, ψ, that increase by the constant ratio, k. The ψ values corresponding to the ϕ values can be calculated by determining successive values of $\Delta\psi$ along the ψ scale. In this example, the value of k is equal to .2. Calculation of a series of ψ values from Ekman's law is shown below.

$\psi_1 = 5$
$\psi_2 = \psi_1 \times k + \psi_1 = 5.0 \times .2 + 5.0 = 6.0$
$\psi_3 = \psi_2 \times k + \psi_2 = 6.0 \times .2 + 6.0 = 7.2$

$\psi_4 = \psi_3 \times k + \psi_3 = 7.2 \times .2 + 7.2 = 8.6$

$\psi_5 = \psi_4 \times k + \psi_4 = 8.6 \times .2 + 8.6 = 10.3$

The calculations above have resulted in a series of ϕ values that increase according to Weber's law and a corresponding series of ψ values that increase according to Ekman's law. The relationship between sensation magnitude and stimulus intensity is illustrated in Figure 14.9, in which ψ is plotted as a function of ϕ. The negatively accelerated function is a result of the fact that while the values of ϕ increase by the constant ratio of .5, the corresponding values of ψ are increasing by the smaller ratio of .2. That this curve is a power function is clearly illustrated in Figure 14.10, in which a linear function is seen when log ψ is plotted against log ϕ. Thus, when Weber's law is true for the ϕ dimension, and Ekman's law is

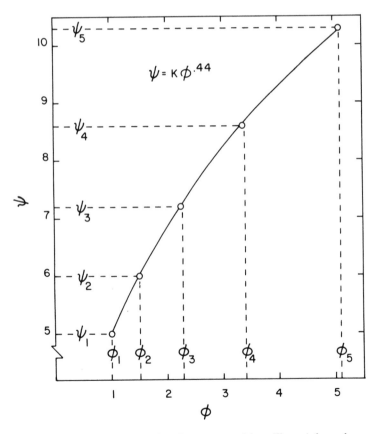

FIG. 14.9. Sensation magnitude values computed from Ekman's law when $k = .2$ plotted as a function of stimulus intensity values computed from Weber's law when $c = .5$.

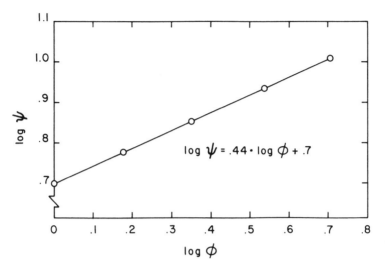

FIG. 14.10. Logarithm of sensation magnitude values computed from Ekman's law when $k = .2$ plotted as a function of the logarithm of stimulus intensity values computed from Weber's law when $c = .5$.

true for the ψ dimension, the relation between ϕ and ψ is a power function. The exponent of a particular psychophysical power function would be determined by the values of c and k. In this particular example, as indicated by the slope of the log-log function of Figure 14.10, the exponent is .44.

As was stated earlier, R. Teghtsoonian (1971) has hypothesized that the ratio of the weakest to the strongest ψ experienced is the same for all sensory modalities, even though the stimulus ranges are different. This hypothesis suggests that there may be only one value of k that applies to all modalities. Teghtsoonian, using power functions and c values for nine different modalities, found k to be nearly constant at about .03. If further research substantiates this finding, Ekman's law may be more precisely stated as

$$\Delta\psi = .03\psi \qquad (14.2)$$

The Fechnerian jnd scale, which generally shows the number of empirically determined jnd's above threshold to be a logarithmic function of ϕ, becomes a power function when each successive jnd above threshold is regarded as a constant ratio increment in sensation. Had Fechner assumed Weber's law to be applicable to both ϕ and ψ dimensions, he would have proposed a psychophysical power law rather than a logarithmic law.

If Ekman's law bridges a gap between jnd scales and psychophysical ratio scales, it should also bridge the gap between other confusion scales and psychophysical ratio scales. For example, there appear to be some interesting relationships between Stevens' power law, Ekman's law, and Thurstone's law of comparative judgment. The finding that $\Delta\psi$ increases linearly with ψ implies that the variance of a distribution of ψ values on the psychological continuum would be proportional to the mean of the distribution. Generally, Thurstone's Case V is applied to paired comparison proportions to derive a psychophysical scale. The resulting Thurstonian scale, in which ψ is not a power function of ϕ, appears to be an artifact of the incorrect assumption that variability in psychological units, $\Delta\psi$ or σ_ψ, is constant along the psychological continuum. Recall that when Ekman and his fellow workers scaled various nonmetric stimuli by both paired comparison and ratio methods, the Thurstonian Case V values were a logarithmic function of the ratio scale values. This is precisely the result we would expect if the ratio scale is valid and each added unit on the Thurstonian Case V or jnd scale is equivalent to a constant ratio increment on the psychological continuum. Suppose that stimuli A, B, and C yielded Thurstonian scale values of 1, 2, and 3, respectively, and ratio scale values of 3, 6, and 12, respectively. Each Thurstonian unit corresponds to a doubling of the ratio scale value (a constant ratio increment). A logarithmic transformation of the ratio scale values yields values of .48, .78, and 1.08, which are linearly related to the Thurstonian scale values of 1, 2, and 3.

S. S. Stevens (1966d) has pointed out that had Thurstone gone further in proposing various cases for the solution of his law and proposed a Case VI in which σ_ψ is assumed to be directly proportional to ψ, paired comparison scales and psychophysical ratio scales would be linearly related. If Thurstone had applied this solution to paired comparison of measurable stimuli of variable intensity, he would most likely have proposed a psychophysical power law.

It should be recalled that ROC curves obtained in signal detection experiments frequently indicate that the variance of the SN distribution increases with signal strength. Ekman's law appears to serve a valuable function of unifying data from experiments on such seemingly diverse topics as signal detection, discrimination, magnitude estimation, and paired comparison judgments.

MULTIDIMENSIONAL PSYCHOPHYSICS

Thus far, we have considered scaling methods that are designed to measure an observer's psychological experiences along a single dimension. For example, magnitude estimation, and category scaling have been used to measure the loudness of sounds, the brightness of lights, and the intensity of pain produced by noxious stimuli. This approach has been very useful in helping us to understand the basic dimensions of sensory experiences and how they relate to physical stimulation of the sense organs. The approach depends on the ability of the observer to make accurate judgments of sensory magnitude along a single dimension as the stimulus is changed. This task is not always easy because, in many situations, changing the stimulus changes the sensory experience in more than one dimension. For example, the loudness of a low, midrange, or high frequency tone becomes louder as its intensity is increased, but at the same time the pitch of the low frequency tone becomes lower, the pitch of the high frequency tone becomes higher, while the pitch of tones in the midrange of frequencies remains the same. As a consequence of the changes in pitch that accompany changes in the loudness of low and high frequency sounds, the observer may have difficulty separating these two sensory dimensions in order to make independent judgments of each. The problem is compounded when the multiple dimensions along which the subjective impression of stimuli vary cannot be clearly defined. For example, pieces of paper may look different to you but it may not be clear what and how many dimensions underlie your ability to discriminate among them. Your visual perceptions of the stimuli may differ in a number of ways including hue, saturation, brightness, size, and shape. How can we separate and identify these dimensions? Fortunately, methods of *multidimensional scaling* have been developed that permit identification of the number of independent underlying subjective dimensions associated with the perception of differences among stimuli. Furthermore, with these methods, each stimulus can be assigned psychological scale values along each of the identified psychological dimensions. From such a result, it is then possible to determine how the different dimensions combine to determine the psychological distances among different stimuli.

It is essential that the same unit of measurement apply to each of the underlying dimensions on which the psychological impression of stimuli varies. For example, the psychological distance between two colored stimuli that are different in hue (which color), saturation (amount of color) and brightness (intensity of sensation) is meaningful only if hue, saturation, and brightness are measured with a common unit. To achieve this common unit, observers are required to make judgments of similarity (or dissimilarity) of stimuli on a common scale. Thus, the first step in multidimensional scaling is to obtain measures of the psychological distance, as determined by similarity judgments, for all possible combinations of pairs of stimuli used in the experiment. The greater the judged similarity of two stimuli, the smaller is their presumed psychological distance. From these similarity measurements, it is then possible to mathematically derive the underlying dimensions determining them and to locate each stimulus on each of the dimensions. In our example of colored stimuli, observers would judge the similarities between members of pairs of colored papers and, from performing a multidimensional scaling analysis on the results, it might be determined that there were three underlying psychological dimensions contributing to the judgments. Each stimulus could then be specified with regard to its scale value on each of the three dimensions. Attempts would then be made to identify and label the underlying dimensions. This is where theory and, perhaps, additional experimentation could become important. For example, previous research and theories of visual perception might make it reasonable to propose that the underlying dimensions in this particular case are hue, saturation, and brightness.

The dimensions revealed by multidimensional scaling can often be represented in a multidimensional space. A common assumption for defining the multidimensional space is Euclidean. *Euclidean space* is the space of every day experience in which the shortest distance between two points is a straight line, and a position in space can be defined in terms of values on a set of coordinates. For example, in Figure 14.11 the two-dimensional space has two coordinates, X and Y, and any point within this space is specified in terms of two coordinate values—one for X and one for Y. Knowing the coordinate values for any two points within the

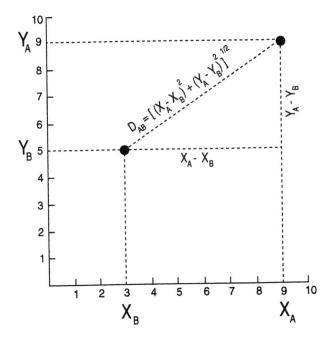

FIG. 14.11. Two-dimensional space in which Euclidean distance and city-block distances are illustrated.

Euclidean space, it is possible to solve for the distance between points through the use of the Pythagorean theorem that stated that square of the hypotenuse of a right triangle is equal to the square of its base plus the square of its height. The principle is illustrated in Figure 14.11 for points A and B. The distance between A and B is determined by the equation:

$$D_{AB} = [(X_A - X_B)^2 + (Y_A - Y_B)^2]^{1/2} \qquad (14.3)$$

in which the distance between points A and B, D_{AB}, is equal to the square root of the sum of the squared difference between the coordinate values of the two points on the X dimension, $(X_A - X_B)^2$, and the squared difference between the points on the Y dimension, $(Y_A - Y_B)^2$. In the present example, D_{AB} is equal to $[(9 - 3)^2 + (9 - 5)^2]^{1/2} = 7.21$.

In multidimensional scaling, the distances between stimuli are estimated from experimental observations and a model is used to compute the coordinate values for each stimulus. An example is seen in Figure 14.12, in which a model called ALSCAL was used to recreate the position of cities within the United States based on distances between the cities (Schiffman, Reynolds, & Young, 1981). The ALSCAL procedure attempted to arrive at coordinate values for each city such that the distances in the derived space were a constant ratio of the actual flying distances. The map derived through multidimensional scaling, in this case, is an accurate representation of the actual location of the cities relative to each other.

Thus far, we have considered a case of multidimensional scaling in which the multidimensional space defining the position of stimuli is Euclidean and, therefore, easy to understand graphically. Another type of

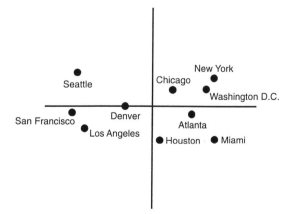

FIG. 14.12.   ALSCAL analysis of intercity flying distances. (From Schiffman, Reynolds, & Young, 1981.)

space, also easy to understand graphically, is a *city-block* metric, in which the distance between stimuli, D_{AB}, is given as the sum of the individual component distances along the individual dimensions. In the example given in Figure 14.11, the value of D_{AB} is 10 because

$$D_{AB} = (X_A - X_B) + (Y_A - Y_B) \qquad (14.4)$$

which is

$$10 = (9 - 3) + (9 - 5).$$

The difference between Euclidean and city-block space is seen in Figure 14.11. Consider Euclidean space as defining the distance between two points as the distance the crow flies to get from one point to another, and consider this same distance in city-block space as the distance you must walk partially around a block to get from one point to another in a city.

A generalized formula that describes the distance, D, between two points in Euclidean or city-block space is

$$D = (\Sigma d^n)^{1/n} \qquad (14.5)$$

where d is the distance along one of the component dimensions, and n is equal to or greater than one. In our example, the values of d were 6 on the X dimension and 4 on the Y dimension. In city-block space $n = 1.0$ and in Euclidean space $n = 2$. Thus, the value of D is $(6^1 + 4^1)^1 = 10$ in city-block space and $(6^2 + 4^2)^{1/2} = 7.21$ in Euclidean space. Both Euclidean and city-block spaces are examples of *Minkowski-n space*, in which the value of n can take on various values equal to or greater than 1. Minkowski distances calculated with value of n greater than 2 are more difficult to conceptualize than city-block or Euclidean space, but they can easily be calculated through equation 14.5? For example, had a Minkowski-n space, in which n = 3 been used in our example, the value of D would be $(6^3 + 4^3)^{1/3} = 6.54$.

The answer to the question of which space, city-block, Euclidean, or Minkowski with n greater than 2, provides that best fit to the data seems to depend on the nature of the stimuli that the observer must judge. Torgerson (1958) noted that the city-block space seemed to fit the data better when psychological dimensions were "obvious, and compelling" to the observer (p. 254). Under these conditions, the psychological distance between two stimuli (D) is the sum of the distances along the individual dimensions (Σd). This was found to be true by Attneave (1950) when he discovered that the city-block space provided the best representation of similarity judgments of visual stimuli that varied along such clearly distinguishable dimensions as form, size, and hue. Thus, the overall psychological distance between two visual stimuli was found to be equal to the sum of the psychological distances between the two stimuli on these three dimensions of form, size, and hue. The psychological distances on the individual dimensions simply added up to produce the overall psychological distance. On the other hand, Euclidean space is often found to represent the data well when the underlying psychological dimensions, such as pitch and loudness or hue and saturation, are not easily separated by the observer. In this case, the distances between the stimuli on the individual psychological dimensions do not combine in a simple additive fashion to produce the overall distance. City-block and Euclidean spaces are used more frequently than Minkowski space, where n is neither 1 (city-block) nor 2 (Euclidean). In those cases in which the n is greater than 2, the dimension on which the two stimuli are most different is emphasized in determining the value of D_{AB} (Schiffman, Reynolds, & Young, 1981).

Whichever space, city-block, Euclidean, or Minkowski with n greater than 2, is used, the problem is one of determining scale values for stimuli from judgments of similarities. When the data for similarity judgments are subjected to analysis through one of several available multidimensional scaling programs (see Schiffman, Reynolds, & Young, 1981), the coordinates for each stimulus are established on the minimal number of dimensions needed to adequately represent the results. According to Melara (1992), the attractiveness of multidimensional scaling derives from the presumed properties of the space formed by the dimensions it extracts. Melara (1992) pointed out that two fundamental characteristics are associated with this space: (a) it serves as a psychological model and (b) it is metric. As a model, the spatial relations among stimuli, as defined by the values of the coordinates of the space, provide a representation of the psychological similarities among stimuli. Psychologically similar stimuli are close to one another in the multidimensional space and psychologically dissimilar stimuli are far apart. Melara defined the metric properties of multidimensional space in terms of three conditions that must be satisfied for the distance between a pair of points for a scale to be a metric (Beals, Krantz, & Tversky, 1968). *Symmetry* is demonstrated when the distance from X to Y is the same as from Y to X, *positivity* dictates that distances can never be negative, and *triangle inequality* requires that the sum of distances among three points (X to Y plus Y to Z) can never be less than that between any two of the points (e.g., X to Z). By satisfying these three conditions, called *metric axioms*, it may be possible to measure an observer's experiences as they vary along multiple psychological dimensions.

How does one arrive at a model with metric properties that specifies, in multidimensional space, the location of stimuli relative to each other? In a

TABLE 14.5
Table of Proximities

	S_A	S_B	S_C	S_D
	Stimuli			
S_A	X	10	24	50
S_B	10	X	14	40
S_C	24	14	X	26
S_D	50	40	26	X

very general sense, the answer to this question is that we attempt to construct a model of the psychological distances between stimuli that corresponds as closely as possible to the psychophysically measured distances. Let us call the psychological distances in the model *MDS* (*multidimensional scaling distances*) and the psychophysically judged distances *proximities*. The MDS model must account for the proximities by postulating as few dimensions as possible.

Consideration of two hypothetical sets of data illustrates how decisions are made about how many dimensions a particular MDS model should have. Imagine that similarity judgments have been made between four stimuli presented in pairs in all possible combinations. The similarity judgments have been converted to dissimilarities that are presented in Table 14.5 as proximities, which represent the psychological distances between stimuli. We must now ask the fundamental question: How many dimensions in a MDS model are needed to describe these proximities? The answer, in this case, is one. A model is seen in Figure 14.13, in which the distances between stimuli in the model (MDS distances) exactly correspond to the psychophysically measured proximities. Had the MDS model not fit the empirically determined proximities perfectly, the MDS computer program might still have produced an acceptable one-dimensional model that fit the data well but not perfectly. MDS programs produce estimations of the goodness of fit of models with 1, 2, 3, 4, ... n number of dimensions. *Stress* is one estimate of goodness of fit that

One dimensional solution

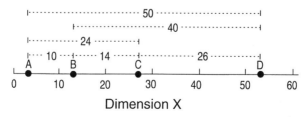

Dimension X

FIG. 14.13.   One-dimensional model of hypothetical proximities of Table 14.5.

shows how far the MDS solution distances deviate from their corresponding proximities. Another measure of goodness of fit is $1-R^2$, which is the proportion of variance in the proximities not accounted for by the correlation between proximities and MDS distances. In our hypothetical example, stress and $1-R^2$ are both zero, indicating a perfect fit of the model to the data. A plot of MDS distances as a function of corresponding proximities show a perfect correspondence between the two (Figure 14.14).

Let us now consider a second hypothetical set of data that cannot be adequately described by a model with one dimension. The proximities in Table 14.6 clearly cannot be accommodated by the one-dimensional model illustrated in Figure 14.15. When we plot the MDS model distances as a function of the proximities we find substantial differences between the two (Figure 14.16). Thus, in this case stress and $1-R^2$ would be high. However, when a two-dimensional MDS model is applied to these same data, a perfect fit is found in which stress and $1-R^2$ are 0.0. The stimuli are plotted in two-dimensional MDS space in Figure 14.17 and, in Figure 14.18, a perfect correspondence between MSD distances and proximities is shown.

When actual experiments are conducted and MDS analysis performed, such perfect fits to the data as illustrated in our hypothetical examples

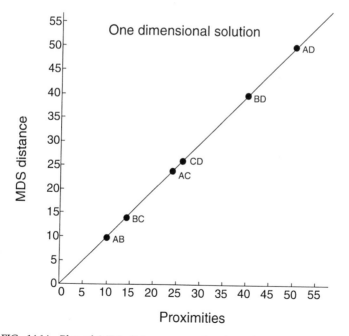

FIG. 14.14. Plot of MDS distances as a function of proximities for a one-dimensional solution to the hypothetical data of Table 14.5.

TABLE 14.6
Table of Proximities

	Stimuli			
	S_A	S_B	S_C	S_D
S_A	X	40	47.5	55
S_B	40	X	14	43.5
S_C	47.5	14	X	32.5
S_D	55	43.5	32.5	X

are rarely found. Stress and $1-R^2$ values are generally above 0.0. The problem then is to decide the number of dimensions (coordinate axes) in the MSD space. Should there be two, three, four, or just one? The decision is often based on an examination of changes in the goodness of fit of the model with increases in the number of dimensions in the model. In general, goodness of fit improves as the number of dimensions in the model increases. If these values are plotted as a function of the number of dimensions, there will frequently be an elbow in the curve. The number of dimensions at the elbow usually specifies the number of dimensions considered for the model. The values of stress and $1-R^2$ found in an MDS study of tactile texture perception are seen in Figure 14.19 (Hollins, Faldowski, Rao, & Young, 1993).

Let us now consider, in some detail, the tactile texture perception study conducted by Hollins and his associates. The object of the study was to examine the psychological dimensionality of tactile surface texture perception. The experience that occurs when one draws a finger across the surface of an object is complex. Besides gaining information about the shape of the object, the observer receives impressions about the nature of its surface. For example the object may feel hard or soft, rough or

One dimensional solution

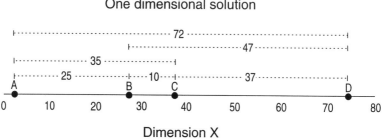

FIG. 14.15. One-dimensional model of hypothetical proximities of Table 14.6.

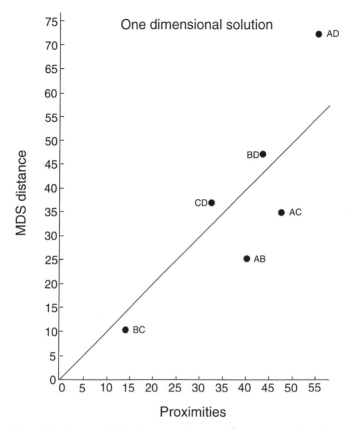

FIG. 14.16. Plot of MDS distances as a function of proximities for a one-dimensional solution to the hypothetical data of Table 14.6.

smooth. Are roughness and hardness independent psychological dimensions? Are there other independent psychological dimensions of the tactile perception of surfaces? MDS analysis of the similarity judgments of 17 tactile surfaces chosen from a wide range of materials including wax paper, sandpaper, felt, velvet, cork, styrofoam, brick, wood, leather, sponge, and unglazed ceramic tile indicated the existence of three independent dimensions. The MDS program used in this experiment, ALSCAL, attempts to approximate the proximities of the observer's judged dissimilarities between stimuli by calculating interstimulus distances (D is equation 14.5) within the MDS space. This is done for 1, 2, 3, 4, 5 ... n dimensional solutions and for each of these solutions, measures of goodness of fit such as stress and $1-R^2$ are given. Hollins and his associates considered the outcomes of these solutions when applied to their data

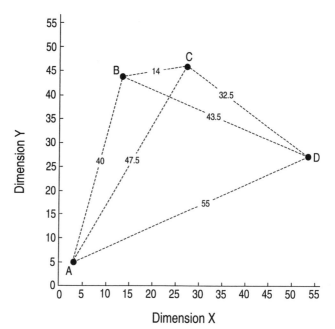

FIG. 14.17. Two-dimensional model of hypothetical proximities of Table 14.6.

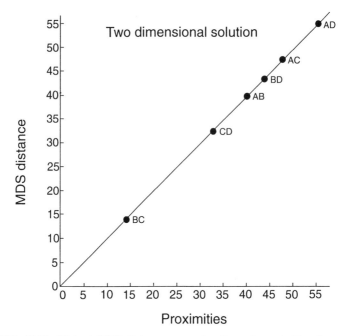

FIG. 14.18. Plot of MDS distances as a function of proximities for a two-dimensional solution to the hypothetical data of Table 14.6.

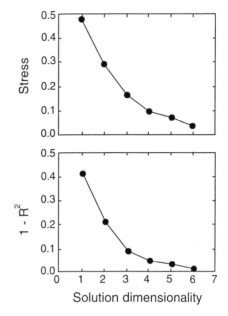

FIG. 14.19. Measures of goodness of fit as a function of the number of dimensions in the MDS solution. (From Hollins, Faldowski, Rao, & Young, 1993.)

and concluded that three dimensions were needed to adequately account for their observers' judgments. The possibility of including a fourth dimension was considered but rejected because it would be difficult to interpret and its inclusion, as seen in Figure 14.19, yields only a slight improvement in $1-R^2$.

Figure 14.20 shows the three-dimensional solution for tactile texture perception. The bold-faced front of the box represents the plane of the box closest to the viewer and from the viewer's perspective is tilted slightly down and rotated slightly to the left. The viewer is also looking

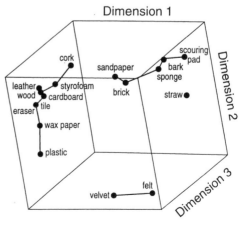

FIG. 14.20. Three-dimensional model of tactile surface texture judgments. (From Hollins, Faldowski, Rao, & Young, 1993.)

at the outside surfaces of the "ceiling" and right "wall" of the box. Values on the MDS solution increase on Dimension 1 as they change from left to right, values increase on Dimension 2 as they change from bottom to top of the box, and values on Dimension 3 increase as they change from the rear to the front of the box. Notice that felt and velvet are similar to one another and different from other stimuli. They are both very low on Dimension 2, which the investigators eventually identified as the perceptual dimension of soft–hard. Straw is also unlike other stimuli and sits alone on the rear wall of the box at a position very low on Dimension 3, about midway on Dimension 2 and relatively high on Dimension 1. Dimension 1 was identified as smooth–rough and Dimension 3 was thought possibly to be springy–nonspringy caused by the compressional elasticity of the material. Straw and other materials high in compressional elasticity, such as the scouring pad, cork, and styrofoam, are high on the dimension of springiness. The three-dimensional MDS solution also contained two bands of stimuli. The stimuli within each band are connected by lines. One band, on the left side of the cube, consisting of plastic, wax paper, an eraser, tile, cardboard, wood, leather, styrofoam, and cork all tend to be on the smooth end of Dimension 1. The other band on the right side of the cube, consisting of sandpaper, brick, sponge, bark, and scouring pad are located at the rough end of Dimension 1.

The process of determining the identity of the dimensions discovered by an MDS analysis of similarity judgments can be greatly facilitated by conducting a second experiment in which, preferably, the same observers who made similarity judgments of stimuli also make rating of these same stimuli on various psychological attributes. Hollins and his associates, for example, were able to identify two of their three dimensions in this way. Because of the high correlation between Dimension 1 MDS values and the ratings of objects on a smooth–rough scale, Dimension 1 was identified as the smooth–rough psychological attribute of tactile objects. Likewise, MDS solutions on Dimension 2 were highly correlated with hard–soft ratings and, therefore, Dimension 2 in MDS space was identified as representing the hard–soft attribute. Because in this study, no ratings of springiness were made, the identification of springiness as the attribute of Dimension 3 was made with less confidence than the identification of the attributes of Dimension 1 and Dimension 2.

Our discussion of multidimensional scaling has consisted of a description of the purpose of the method and the general logic on which it is based. The example given on tactile attributes provides an overview of the methodology used to obtain and interpret an MDS solution. In order to conduct an MDS experiment, specific procedures of data gathering and analysis must be followed. This detailed information is found in sources specifically devoted to multidimensional scaling (e.g., Shiffman, Reynolds, & Young, 1981).

CONCLUSION

For nearly 150 years, the goal of measuring sensation magnitude has been fundamental to psychophysics, yet many problems remain today. For example, different scaling techniques often produce different results. Either all or some of the methods produce invalid results, or the different methods are validly measuring different aspects of perception. It has been argued that the solution to this problem depends on the development of *fundamental psychophysics* defined by Ward (1992) as an attempt to find "a core of concepts and relations from which all the rest of psychophysics can be derived" (p. 190). We have a tremendous amount of experimental data accumulated since the birth of psychophysics, and we have many concepts such as spatial and temporal summation, adaptation, masking, contrast, stimulus variability, sensory-system variability, to name but a few, to explain them. The basic question is whether there are a few fundamental concepts that, when properly interrelated, will explain all of psychophysics. In recent years, several proposals have been made for such a *fundamental psychophysical theory*. For example, for Norwich (1993), the fundamental principles of psychophysics came from information theory in which the critical event is the flow of information rather than stimulus energy as in more traditional psychophysical theories. From a few basic principles of information flow, Norwich was able to explain sensory adaptation, Fechner's law, and Stevens' law. A somewhat different approach can be seen in Link's (1992), *Wave Theory of Difference and Similarity*. According to this theory, on each trial, the observer samples the stimulus continuously over time and the result is the envelope of a time-amplitude waveform. At any point during the sampling process the value sampled from the stimulus wave is subtracted from a value sampled from a referent wave, and the result is a comparative wave. The differences between the sampled wave and the referent wave cumulate over time until the sum exceeds the observer's threshold. The response to the stimulus starts as a quantized action of sensory receptor modeled by a Poisson process, which allows for the prediction of sensation magnitude functions. This theory, in contrast to that of Norwich, focuses on stimulus energy rather than stimulus information. Finally, the nonlinear nature for the process of judging sensory stimuli as they are first converted to sensory magnitude and then to internal and overt responses has found formal mathematical expression in the work of Gregson (1988).

It is my hope that, in the not-too-distant future, psychophysics will make a quantum leap forward with the emergence and wide acceptance of a fundamental theory. Such a theory would provide the explanation of the many fascinating and diverse phenomena discovered in psychophysical laboratories during the past 147 years since Fechner founded the discipline. Perhaps it will be one of the theorists just mentioned to which we will pay tribute for advancing the field to the next level.

Appendix

TABLE A
z Scores and Ordinate Values (O) of the Normal
Distribution Corresponding to Proportions (p)

p	z	O	p	z	O	p	z	O	p	z	O
.01	−2.33	.026	.26	−.64	.325	.51	.03	.399	.76	.71	.310
.02	−2.05	.049	.27	−.61	.331	.52	.05	.398	.77	.74	.303
.03	−1.88	.068	.28	−.58	.337	.53	.08	.398	.78	.77	.297
.04	−1.75	.086	.29	−.55	.343	.54	.10	.397	.79	.81	.287
.05	−1.65	.102	.30	−.52	.348	.55	.13	.396	.80	.84	.280
.06	−1.56	.118	.31	−.50	.352	.56	.15	.394	.81	.88	.271
.07	−1.48	.133	.32	−.47	.357	.57	.18	.393	.82	.92	.261
.08	−1.41	.148	.33	−.44	.362	.58	.20	.391	.83	.95	.254
.09	−1.34	.163	.34	−.41	.367	.59	.23	.389	.84	.99	.244
.10	−1.28	.176	.35	−.39	.370	.60	.25	.387	.85	1.04	.232
.11	−1.23	.187	.36	−.36	.374	.61	.28	.384	.86	1.08	.223
.12	−1.18	.199	.37	−.33	.378	.62	.31	.380	.87	1.13	.211
.13	−1.13	.211	.38	−.31	.380	.63	.33	.378	.88	1.18	.199
.14	−1.08	.223	.39	−.28	.384	.64	.36	.374	.89	1.23	.187
.15	−1.04	.232	.40	−.25	.387	.65	.39	.370	.90	1.28	.176
.16	−.99	.244	.41	−.23	.389	.66	.41	.367	.91	1.34	.163
.17	−.95	.254	.42	−.20	.391	.67	.44	.362	.92	1.41	.148
.18	−.92	.261	.43	−.18	.393	.68	.47	.357	.93	1.48	.133
.19	−.88	.271	.44	−.15	.394	.69	.50	.352	.94	1.56	.118
.20	−.84	.280	.45	−.13	.396	.70	.52	.348	.95	1.65	.102
.21	−.81	.287	.46	−.10	.397	.71	.55	.343	.96	1.75	.086
.22	−.77	.297	.47	−.08	.398	.72	.58	.337	.97	1.88	.068
.23	−.74	.303	.48	−.05	.398	.73	.61	.331	.98	2.05	.049
.24	−.71	.310	.49	−.03	.399	.74	.64	.325	.99	2.33	.026
.25	−.67	.319	.50	.00	.399	.75	.67	.319			

Values of d' for p(c) Values Obtained in a Forced-Choice Task

p(c)	2	3	4	5	6	7	8	9	10
.01	-3.29	-2.42	-2.02	-1.77	-1.59	-1.46	-1.35	-1.26	-1.18
.02	-2.90	-2.08	-1.69	-1.45	-1.28	-1.14	-1.04	-0.95	-0.88
.03	-2.66	-1.86	-1.48	-1.24	-1.07	-0.94	-0.84	-0.75	-0.68
.04	-2.48	-1.69	-1.32	-1.09	-0.92	-0.79	-0.69	-0.61	-0.53
.05	-2.33	-1.56	-1.19	-0.96	-0.80	-0.67	-0.57	-0.49	-0.41
.06	-2.20	-1.44	-1.08	-0.85	-0.69	-0.57	-0.47	-0.38	-0.31
.07	-2.09	-1.34	-0.98	-0.76	-0.60	-0.48	-0.38	-0.29	-0.22
.08	-1.99	-1.25	-0.90	-0.68	-0.52	-0.39	-0.29	-0.21	-0.14
.09	-1.90	-1.17	-0.82	-0.60	-0.44	-0.32	-0.22	-0.14	-0.07
.10	-1.81	-1.09	-0.75	-0.53	-0.37	-0.25	-0.15	-0.07	0.00
.11	-1.73	-1.02	-0.68	-0.46	-0.31	-0.19	-0.09	-0.01	0.06
.12	-1.66	-0.96	-0.62	-0.40	-0.25	-0.13	-0.03	0.05	0.12
.13	-1.59	-0.89	-0.56	-0.34	-0.19	-0.07	0.03	0.11	0.18
.14	-1.53	-0.83	-0.50	-0.29	-0.13	-0.01	0.08	0.16	0.23
.15	-1.47	-0.78	-0.45	-0.23	-0.08	0.04	0.13	0.21	0.28
.16	-1.41	-0.72	-0.39	-0.18	-0.03	0.09	0.18	0.26	0.33
.17	-1.35	-0.67	-0.35	-0.13	0.02	0.13	0.23	0.31	0.37
.18	-1.29	-0.62	-0.30	-0.09	0.06	0.18	0.27	0.35	0.42
.19	-1.24	-0.57	-0.25	-0.04	0.11	0.22	0.32	0.39	0.46
.20	-1.19	-0.53	-0.21	0.00	0.15	0.26	0.36	0.44	0.50
.21	-1.14	-0.48	-0.16	0.04	0.19	0.31	0.40	0.48	0.54
.22	-1.09	-0.44	-0.12	0.08	0.23	0.35	0.44	0.52	0.58
.23	-1.04	-0.40	-0.08	0.12	0.27	0.38	0.48	0.56	0.62
.24	-1.00	-0.35	-0.04	0.16	0.31	0.42	0.52	0.59	0.66
.25	-0.95	-0.31	0.00	0.20	0.35	0.46	0.55	0.63	0.70
.26	-0.91	-0.27	0.04	0.24	0.38	0.50	0.59	0.66	0.73
.27	-0.87	-0.23	0.08	0.28	0.42	0.53	0.62	0.70	0.77
.28	-0.82	-0.20	0.11	0.31	0.46	0.57	0.66	0.74	0.80
.29	-0.78	-0.16	0.15	0.35	0.49	0.60	0.69	0.77	0.83
.30	-0.74	-0.12	0.19	0.38	0.53	0.64	0.73	0.80	0.87
.31	-0.70	-0.08	0.22	0.42	0.56	0.67	0.76	0.84	0.90
.32	-0.66	-0.05	0.26	0.45	0.59	0.70	0.79	0.87	0.93
.33	-0.62	-0.01	0.29	0.48	0.63	0.74	0.83	0.90	0.97

(Continued)

p(c)	2	3	4	5	6	7	8	9	10
.34	−0.58	0.02	0.32	0.52	0.66	0.77	0.86	0.93	1.00
.35	−0.55	0.06	0.36	0.55	0.69	0.80	0.89	0.96	1.03
.36	−0.51	0.09	0.39	0.58	0.72	0.83	0.92	1.00	1.06
.37	−0.47	0.13	0.42	0.62	0.76	0.86	0.95	1.03	1.09
.38	−0.43	0.16	0.46	0.65	0.79	0.89	0.98	1.06	1.12
.39	−0.40	0.20	0.49	0.68	0.82	0.93	1.01	1.09	1.15
.40	−0.36	0.23	0.52	0.71	0.85	0.96	1.04	1.12	1.18
.41	−0.32	0.26	0.55	0.74	0.88	0.99	1.07	1.15	1.21
.42	−0.29	0.30	0.59	0.77	0.91	1.02	1.10	1.18	1.24
.43	−0.25	0.33	0.62	0.80	0.94	1.05	1.13	1.21	1.27
.44	−0.21	0.36	0.65	0.84	0.97	1.08	1.16	1.24	1.30
.45	−0.18	0.39	0.68	0.87	1.00	1.11	1.19	1.27	1.33
.46	−0.14	0.43	0.71	0.90	1.03	1.14	1.22	1.30	1.36
.47	−0.11	0.46	0.74	0.93	1.06	1.17	1.25	1.33	1.39
.48	−0.07	0.49	0.77	0.96	1.09	1.20	1.28	1.35	1.42
.49	−0.04	0.52	0.81	0.99	1.12	1.23	1.31	1.38	1.45
.50	0.00	0.56	0.84	1.02	1.15	1.26	1.34	1.41	1.47
.51	0.04	0.59	0.87	1.05	1.18	1.29	1.37	1.44	1.50
.52	0.07	0.62	0.90	1.08	1.21	1.32	1.40	1.47	1.53
.53	0.11	0.65	0.93	1.11	1.24	1.35	1.43	1.50	1.56
.54	0.14	0.69	0.96	1.14	1.27	1.38	1.46	1.53	1.59
.55	0.18	0.72	0.99	1.17	1.30	1.41	1.49	1.56	1.62
.56	0.21	0.75	1.02	1.20	1.33	1.44	1.52	1.59	1.65
.57	0.25	0.78	1.06	1.23	1.37	1.47	1.55	1.62	1.68
.58	0.29	0.82	1.09	1.27	1.39	1.50	1.58	1.65	1.71
.59	0.32	0.85	1.12	1.30	1.43	1.53	1.61	1.68	1.74
.60	0.36	0.89	1.15	1.33	1.46	1.56	1.64	1.71	1.77
.61	0.40	0.92	1.19	1.36	1.49	1.59	1.67	1.74	1.80
.62	0.43	0.95	1.22	1.39	1.52	1.62	1.70	1.77	1.83
.63	0.47	0.99	1.25	1.42	1.55	1.65	1.73	1.80	1.86
.64	0.51	1.02	1.29	1.46	1.58	1.68	1.77	1.83	1.89
.65	0.54	1.06	1.32	1.49	1.62	1.72	1.80	1.87	1.92
.66	0.58	1.09	1.35	1.52	1.65	1.75	1.83	1.90	1.96

(Continued)

p(c)	2	3	4	5	6	7	8	9	10
.67	0.62	1.13	1.39	1.56	1.68	1.78	1.86	1.93	1.99
.68	0.66	1.16	1.42	1.59	1.72	1.81	1.89	1.96	2.02
.69	0.70	1.20	1.46	1.63	1.75	1.85	1.93	2.00	2.05
.70	0.74	1.24	1.49	1.66	1.79	1.89	1.96	2.03	2.09
.71	0.78	1.28	1.53	1.70	1.82	1.92	2.00	2.06	2.12
.72	0.82	1.31	1.57	1.73	1.86	1.95	2.03	2.10	2.16
.73	0.87	1.35	1.60	1.77	1.89	1.99	2.07	2.13	2.19
.74	0.91	1.39	1.64	1.81	1.93	2.03	2.10	2.17	2.23
.75	0.95	1.43	1.68	1.85	1.97	2.06	2.14	2.21	2.26
.76	1.00	1.47	1.72	1.89	2.01	2.10	2.18	2.24	2.30
.77	1.05	1.52	1.76	1.93	2.05	2.14	2.22	2.28	2.34
.78	1.09	1.56	1.81	1.97	2.09	2.18	2.26	2.32	2.38
.79	1.14	1.61	1.85	2.01	2.13	2.22	2.30	2.36	2.42
.80	1.19	1.65	1.89	2.05	2.17	2.26	2.34	2.40	2.46
.81	1.24	1.70	1.94	2.10	2.22	2.31	2.38	2.45	2.50
.82	1.29	1.75	1.99	2.14	2.26	2.35	2.43	2.49	2.55
.83	1.35	1.80	2.04	2.19	2.31	2.40	2.47	2.54	2.59
.84	1.41	1.85	2.09	2.24	2.36	2.45	2.52	2.59	2.64
.85	1.47	1.91	2.14	2.29	2.41	2.50	2.57	2.64	2.69
.86	1.53	1.97	2.20	2.35	2.46	2.55	2.63	2.69	2.74
.87	1.59	2.03	2.25	2.41	2.52	2.61	2.68	2.74	2.80
.88	1.66	2.09	2.32	2.47	2.58	2.67	2.74	2.80	2.86
.89	1.73	2.16	2.38	2.53	2.64	2.73	2.80	2.86	2.92
.90	1.81	2.23	2.45	2.60	2.71	2.80	2.87	2.93	2.98
.91	1.90	2.31	2.53	2.67	2.78	2.87	2.94	3.00	3.05
.92	1.99	2.39	2.61	2.75	2.86	2.95	3.02	3.08	3.13
.93	2.09	2.49	2.70	2.84	2.95	3.03	3.10	3.16	3.22
.94	2.20	2.59	2.80	2.94	3.05	3.13	3.20	3.26	3.31
.95	2.33	2.71	2.92	3.06	3.16	3.24	3.31	3.37	3.42
.96	2.48	2.85	3.05	3.19	3.29	3.37	3.44	3.50	3.55
.97	2.66	3.02	3.22	3.35	3.45	3.53	3.60	3.65	3.70
.98	2.90	3.25	3.44	3.57	3.67	3.75	3.81	3.87	3.91
.99	3.29	3.62	3.80	3.92	4.01	4.09	4.15	4.20	4.25

Note. From Hacker and Ratcliff (1979). Reprinted with permission.

Problem 1.1

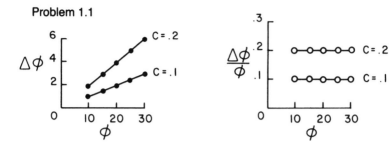

Problem 1.2 and 1.3

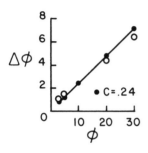

Problem 1.4

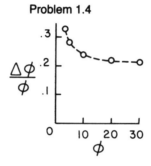

Problem 1.5

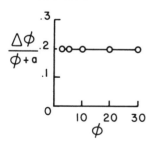

Problem 1.6

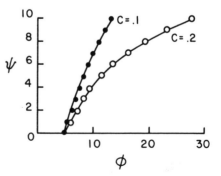

Problem 1.7

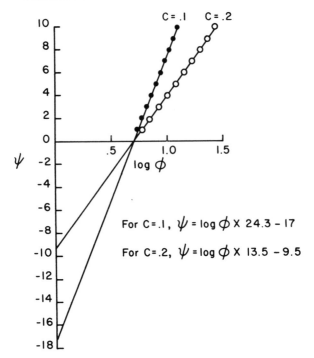

For C=.1, $\psi = \log \phi \times 24.3 - 17$

For C=.2, $\psi = \log \phi \times 13.5 - 9.5$

Problem 1.8 See pages 12–14.

Problem 2.1

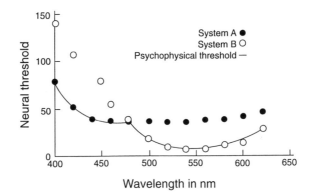

Problem 2.2

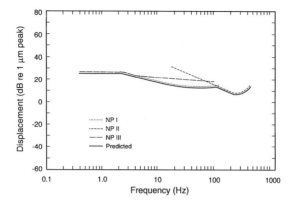

Problem 3.1

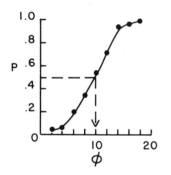

Problem 3.2

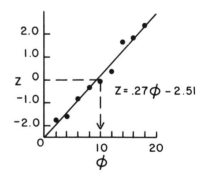

Problem 3.3

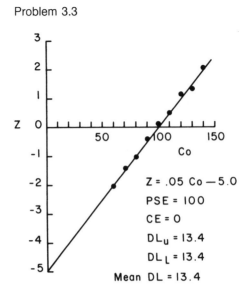

$$Z = .05 \ Co - 5.0$$
$$PSE = 100$$
$$CE = 0$$
$$DL_u = 13.4$$
$$DL_l = 13.4$$
$$Mean \ DL = 13.4$$

Problem 3.4

	A	D	A	D	A	D	Mean
T_U	122.5	117.5	112.5	117.5	127.5	122.5	120.0
T_L	92.5	87.5	92.5	82.5	87.5	77.5	86.7

$$IU = 120 - 86.7 = 33.3$$

$$PSE = \frac{120 + 86.7}{2} = 103.4$$

$$Mean \ DL = 16.65$$

$$CE = 3.4$$

Problem 3.5

$$PSE = 100.66$$
$$CE = .66$$
$$DL = 15.18$$

Problem 4.1

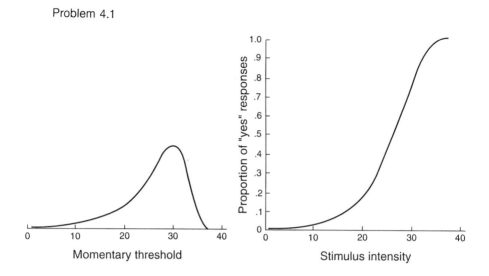

Problem 4.2 $p = .31$

Problem 4.3

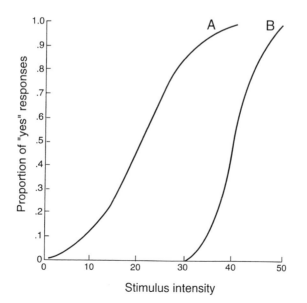

Problem 4.4

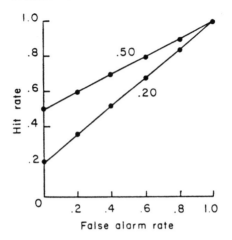

Problem 5.1

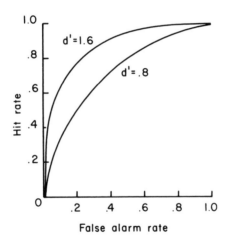

Problem 5.2

Observer	d'	β
1	1.91	.935
2	2.06	.226
3	.70	.900
4	.47	1.144
5	1.53	.141

Problem 5.3

$$\text{For } p(S) = .30 \quad \beta_{\text{opt}} = \frac{.70}{.30} \times \frac{2 - (-1)}{2 - (-1)} = 2.33$$

$$\text{For } p(S) = .70 \quad \beta_{\text{opt}} = \frac{.30}{.70} \times \frac{2 - (-1)}{2 - (-1)} = .43$$

Problem 5.4

$$P_{\text{opt}} = \frac{.5}{.5} \times \frac{(1) - (-.5)}{(2) - (-1.5)} = \frac{1.5}{3.5} = .43$$

Problem 6.1

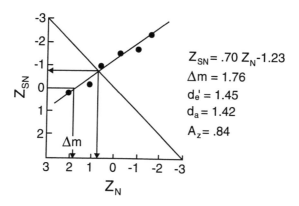

$Z_{SN} = .70\ Z_N - 1.23$

$\Delta m = 1.76$

$d_e' = 1.45$

$d_a = 1.42$

$A_z = .84$

Problem 7.1

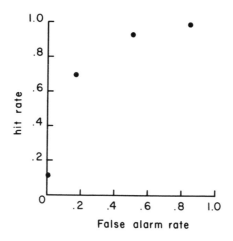

Problem 9.1   See Figure 9.1 for an example.

Problem 9.2

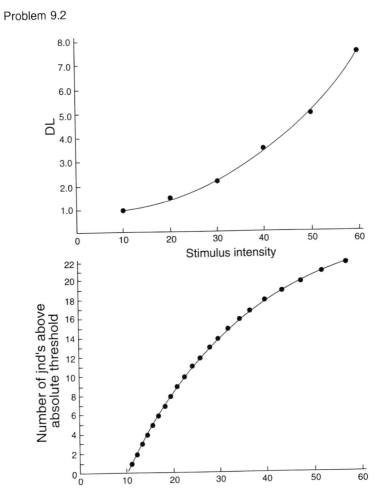

Problem 9.3

p values

[greater than]	A	B	C	D	E
A		.58	.72	.90	.97
B			.64	.84	.95
C				.77	.89
D					.71

p values

[greater than]	A	B	C	D	E
A	X	.58	.72	.90	.97
B	.42	X	.64	.84	.95
C	.28	.36	X	.77	.89
D	.10	.16	.23	X	.71
E	.03	.05	.11	.29	X

z values

	A	B	C	D	E
A	X	.20	.58	1.28	1.88
B	− .20	X	.36	.99	1.65
C	− .58	− .36	X	.74	1.23
D	− 1.28	− .99	− .74	X	.55
E	− 1.88	− 1.65	− 1.23	− .55	X

$z\sqrt{2}$

	A	B	C	D	E	Mean
A	X	.28	.82	1.80	2.65	1.39
B	− .28	X	.51	1.40	2.33	.99
C	− .82	− .51	X	1.04	1.73	.36
D	− 1.80	− 1.40	− 1.04	X	.78	− .865
E	− 2.65	− 2.33	− 1.73	− .78	X	− 1.87

Problem 10.1

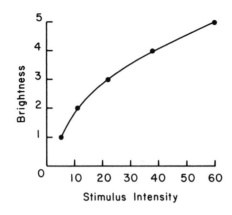

Problem 10.2

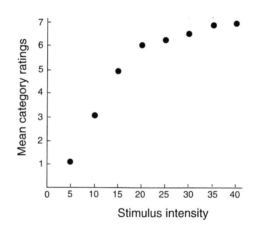

Problem 11.1 Answers depend on individual experimental results.

Problem 11.2

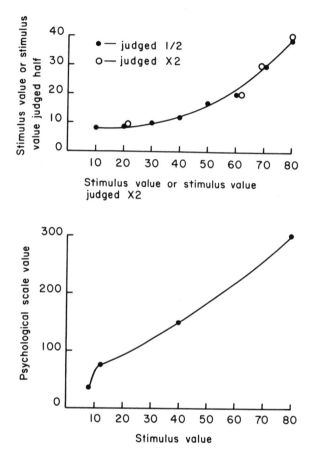

Problem 11.3

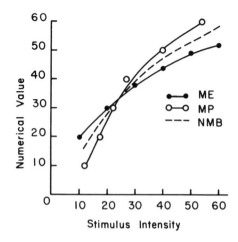

Problem 12.1

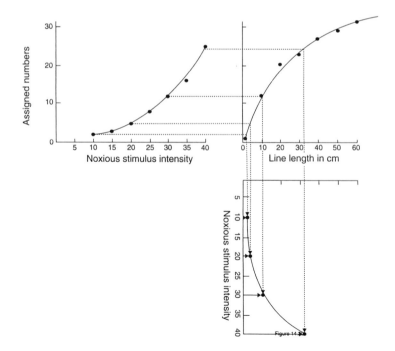

Problem 12.2a

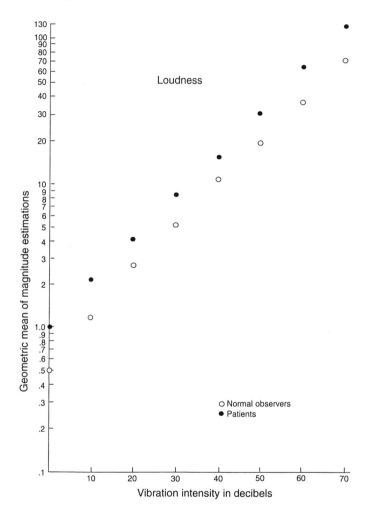

Problem 12.2b

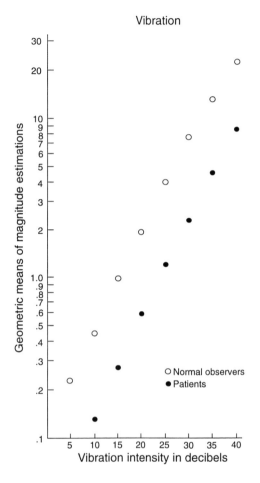

Problem 12.2c

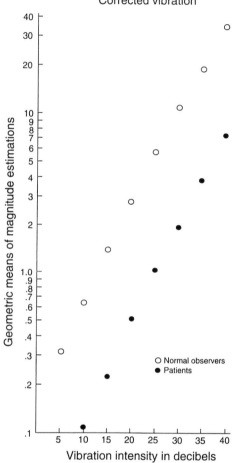

Corrected vibration

Problem 13.1

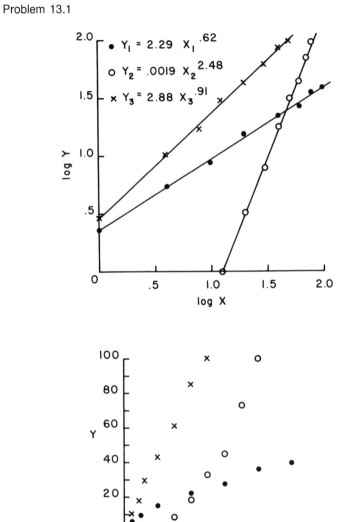

Problem 13.2

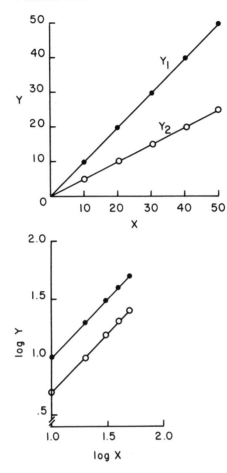

Problem 13.3

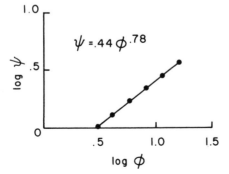

$\psi = .44 \, \phi^{.78}$

Glossary

A'. A nonparametric index of signal detectability.

A_z. A measure of signal detectability consisting of the proportion of the area of the entire ROC graph that lies beneath the ROC curve. This proportion is calculated by first fitting a z-score ROC curve to the data and then computing $z(A)$ from Δm and the slope, S, $(z(A) = S (\Delta m)/\sqrt{1+S^2})$. A_z is determined by converting $z(A)$ from a z-score to a proportion.

Absolute Magnitude Estimation. A scaling procedure in which observers are required to make magnitude estimations of stimuli such that their subjective impression of the size of a number assigned to a stimulus matches their subjective impression of the stimulus.

Absolute Threshold. Traditionally defined as the smallest amount of stimulus energy necessary to produce a sensation. In more modern and less subjective terms, the absolute threshold is defined as the smallest amount of stimulus energy necessary to achieve some criterion level of performance, such as correct responses 75% of the time, in a stimulus detection task.

Action Spectrum. Combinations of wavelength and light intensity that produce the same response. Action spectra have been measured for photochemical, neurophysiological, and psychophysical responses. In each case, the results are plotted as a graph in which the intensity of light needed to produce some specified response is plotted as a function of wavelength.

Adaptation-Level Theory. Helson's theory that a stimulus is perceived and judged within a frame of reference determined by the values of other stimuli in the situation and by the recent stimulus history of the observer. The frame of reference establishes the adaptation level which, in turn, determines the stimulus that is perceived as having a medium value. All other stimuli are judged relative to this value.

Additivity. Measurements are additive when the measurement of A and B combined is equal to the sum of separate measurements of A and B. When possible, this is used as a test of the validity of a set of measurements.

Analytical Psychophysics. Psychophysical measurements that permit the testing of hypotheses about the nature of biological mechanisms that underlie sensory perception.

Assimilation. The observer's judged magnitude of a particular stimulus tends to be greater when the stimulus follows the presentation of a stronger stimulus than when it follows the presentation of a weaker stimulus.

Best PEST. An adaptive procedure for measuring threshold in which maximum-likelihood statistics are used to estimate a psychometric function with a logistic form.

Bezugs System. A frame of reference from everyday life experiences that provide the context for judging specific stimuli in the laboratory situation.

$\beta opt.$ A value of the likelihood ratio corresponding to the optimal criterion for maximizing payoff in a detection task.

C. A measure of response bias expressed as $C = 0.5 [Z_{SN} + Z_N]$. The value of C is zero when the observer's criterion is located at the point where the N and SN distributions cross.

C′. A measure of response bias in which the value of C is expressed as a proportion of the value of d′.

Catch Trial. Trials, randomly presented within a series of stimulus trials, on which no stimulus is presented. Catch trials were used in early psychophysical testing in attempts to train observers to never report a stimulus when it is not perceived and presumably below threshold. The proportion of these trials on which the observer reported the presence of a stimulus consists of the false alarm rate. In classical threshold theory, the false alarm rate was interpreted as a guessing rate for reporting the presence of a stimulus when it failed to exceed the threshold.

Category Ratio Scale. A method for controlling for individual differences in the use of numbers in scaling in which adjectives such as extremely strong, strong, moderate, weak, and extremely weak, and so on, are associated with specific numbers forming a verbally labeled category scale. The numbers, however, are chosen so that the results are linearly related to magnitude estimation scales and, therefore, this type of category scale is considered to be a ratio scale.

Category Scales. A type of partition scale in which the observer is presented with several stimuli and told to assign them to a specified number of categories on a psychological dimension.

City-Block Space. A type of multidimensional space in which the distance between two stimuli is given as the sum of the individual component distances along the individual dimensions. This space often is found to represent the multidimensional scaling data well when the stimuli varies along clearly distinguishable dimensions.

Class A Observations. Observations in which two stimuli are adjusted so that they elicit the same response from the observer. These include threshold experiments and matching experiments, in which the sensations produced by the different stimuli are identical.

Class B Observations. Observations in which the experimenter determines how the sensory response of the observer changes as the stimulus changes.

Classical Threshold Theory. An early theory in psychophysics in which it is assumed that observers report the presence of a stimulus when it exceeds a momentary threshold within the nervous system.

Comparison Stimulus. A stimulus that varies in its value from trial to trial and is compared with a standard stimulus that has the same fixed value on each trial.

Confidence Rating Procedure. The observer makes ratings of the confidence that the signal was presented or that it was not presented. From the proportions of times that each confidence rating was used when the signal was presented and when it was not, an ROC curve can be constructed.

Confusion Scaling. Scales in which psychological magnitudes of stimuli are inferred from measures of stimulus discriminability. The fewer times two stimuli are confused the greater is their discriminability and the greater is the difference in their psychological magnitudes.

Constant Error. A stimulus value equal to the value of the point of subjective equality minus the value of the standard stimulus.

Contrast Effects. Context effect in which the judged magnitude of a stimulus is greater if presented with weaker than with stronger stimuli.

Correction for Guessing. Equation used in classical psychophysics to correct the proportion of "yes" responses on stimulus trials for guessing. In this procedure the guessing rate is taken as the false alarm rate determined over a number of trials on which no stimulus is presented.

Criterion (β). Likelihood ratio corresponding to the observer's criterion. The value of β is calculated by dividing the ordinate of the SN distribution at criterion by the ordinate of the N distribution at criterion. These two values are determined from $1.0 -$ hit rate and $1.0 -$ false alarm rate, respectively, that are converted to ordinate values through Table A.

Criterion Response Technique. Method, also known as the method of response invariance, in which the investigator seeks to determine combinations of stimulus variables that generate identical responses. For example, in visual psychophysics, the investigator, by measuring absolute thresholds for detecting light, can specify combinations of light intensity and wavelength that always result in the same responses of detecting the stimulus 50% of the time.

Cross-Modality Matching. The observer is required to adjust the intensity level of a stimulus in one modality so that its sensation magnitude matches that of a stimulus presented in another modality. For example, the observer may be asked to adjust the brightness of a light so that it matches the loudness of a sound.

Cross-Modality Matching Function. A graph in which the intensities of stimuli in one modality judged to be equal in sensation magnitude to the intensities of stimuli in another modality are plotted against each other.

d'. A measure of signal detectability, equal to the difference between the means of the SN and N distributions divided by the standard deviation of the N distribution.

d_a. A measure of signal detectability in which the difference between the means of the N and SN distributions is expressed as the root-mean-square average of the standard deviations of the two distributions.

d_e'. A measure of signal detectability in which the difference between the means of the SN and N distributions are expressed in units equal to the average of the standard deviations of the N and SN distributions.

Δm. A measure of signal detectability, equal to the difference between the means of the SN and N distributions expressed in standard deviation units of the N distribution. Used in situations where the standard deviations of the SN and N distributions are unequal.

Dark Adaptation. A progressive decrease in the visual detection threshold as a function of how long the observer has been in the dark after prior stimulation by light. The threshold decreases over a period of approximately 5 to 8 minutes for cone stimulation and over 40 to 60 minutes for rod stimulation.

Descriptive Psychophysics. Psychophysical measurements that provide quantitative descriptions of the capacities of sensory systems.

Difference Threshold. Also known as the DL for the German *Differenz Limen*. The smallest amount of stimulus change ($\Delta\phi$) required to produce a discriminable change in sensation. In more modern and less subjective terms, the difference threshold is defined as the smallest amount of stimulus change necessary to achieve some criterion level of performance, such as correct responding 75% of the time, in a discrimination task. The discrimination task always requires the observer to discriminate between two stimuli that are physically different. The question is how different do the two stimuli have to be for a designated level of performance to be achieved.

Differencing Strategy. A possible strategy used by the observer in the same–different task, in which a difference between two stimuli is reported when the absolute difference between two sensory observations is greater than some criterion.

Direct Scaling. Methods in which measurements of psychological magnitudes are derived directly from the observer's judgments (e.g., magnitude estimation and category scaling).

Discriminal Difference. The size of the difference between two discriminal processes for a single presentation of S_A and S_B.

Discriminal Dispersion. The standard deviation of discriminal processes as they vary on the psychological continuum. The term was used by Thurstone in describing his law of comparative judgment.

Discriminal Process. A psychological event (e.g., a sensation) having some value on the psychological continuum. The term was used by Thurstone in describing his law of comparative judgment.

Discrimination Scales. Psychophysical scales based on the principle that the difference between the psychological magnitudes of two stimuli increases as a function of the ability of the observer to discriminate between them.

DL Scales. Scales in which the difference in the psychological magnitudes of two stimuli is specified as the number of jnd's separating them.

Dol Scale. DL scale of pain in which the unit of measurement is the dol consisting of two jnd's of pain.

Ekman's Law. States that the psychological size of the jnd is a linear function of sensation magnitude rather than constant as proposed by Fechner.

Empirical Threshold. The intensity of a stimulus required for a specified level of performance by an observer. Examples are the intensity of the stimulus corresponding to reporting the stimulus 50% of the time in the method constant stimuli, or correctly detecting the stimulus 75% of the time in a two-alternative forced choice task, or achieving a d' value of 1.0 in the yes–no TSD procedure. Empirical thresholds are sometimes called statistical thresholds.

Energy Threshold. The intensity of the stimulus at which the observer's performance is better than that observed in the absence of a stimulus.

Equal Sensation Function. A graph showing the stimulus values of one modality plotted against those stimulus values of another modality that result in judgments of equal sensory magnitude.

Equisection Scales. A type of partition scale in which the observer is required to section the psychological continuum into equal psychological distances.

Errors of Expectation. In the method of limits, the tendency for the observer to falsely anticipate the arrival of the stimulus at threshold and prematurely report that the stimulus is above threshold before it really is.

Errors of Habituation. Tendency for the observer to develop a habit of repeating the same response when the threshold is measured by the method of limits.

Equal Sensation Contours. A graph describing the intensities of stimuli needed to keep sensation magnitude constant as some dimension of the stimulus such as the wavelength of light or the frequency of sound varies.

Euclidean Space. A type of multidimensional space in which the shortest distance between two points is a straight line. This space often is found to represent multidimensional scaling data very well when the underlying psychological dimensions are not easily separated by the observer but are approximately equally important in determining the perception of differences among stimuli.

Fechner's Law. G. T. Fechner, in his *Elements of Psychophysics* (1860), proposed that sensation magnitude (ψ) is a logarithmic function of stimulus intensity (ϕ). Fechner found support for his idea in Weber's Law, which had shown that a series of intensity values, each separated by a difference threshold ($\Delta\phi$) increase, in value as a geometric progression in which each successive value increased by a constant fraction. Fechner's Law follows from the assumption that Weber's Law is true and that jnd's corresponding to each successive difference threshold represent a constant increment in sensation magnitude.

Fixed Threshold. A theoretical threshold within the observer that is assumed to be fixed in its value and, therefore, is unchanging from one time to another. In the theory of the fixed threshold the form of the psychometric function is assumed to be due to fluctuations in the stimulus rather than to fluctuations in a momentary threshold.

Forced-Choice Procedure. The observer is given two or more observation intervals, one of which contains a signal. The observer is required to choose which observation interval contained the signal.

Four Channel Model of Mechanoreceptor. Theory that there are four separate channels, each with its own receptor type, for the detection of mechanical stimuli applied to glabrous skin.

Functional Measurement. An approach to the investigation of psychological (psychosensory) laws in which the observer makes judgments of stimuli that vary along more than one psychological dimension. The goal of this approach is to determine the rules by which the psychological impression of the stimulus is produced by integration of the underlying psychological dimensions.

Geometric Mean. The antilog of the mean of a series of log X values.

Independent-Observation Strategy. A possible strategy used by the observer in the same–different task in which the observer compares the independent sensory observations produced by each stimulus with a criterion and calls two stimuli different only if the resulting two sensory observations fall on different sides of the criterion.

Indirect Scaling. Methods in which measurements of psychological magnitude are derived from data on how well observers can tell one stimulus from another. Fechnerian jnd scales and Thurstonian scales are examples.

Internal Noise. Background activity within a sensory system, generated spontaneously in the absence of an external stimulus, which may limit the detectability and discriminability of signals.

Interval Scale. A set of measurements in which the intervals between the scale values represent differences or distances between amounts of the property measured. Any linear transformation performed on the results leaves the scale invariant.

Interval of Uncertainty. The range of the stimulus dimension over which an observer cannot perceive a difference between the comparison and the standard stimuli, as determined by the classical methods of constant stimuli and limits.

Invariance. A measurement scale exhibits the property of invariance if the scale when transformed by some mathematical function does not lose its significance. For example, any monotonic transformation of an ordinal scale will maintain the rank order of the measurements and, thus, leave the scale invariant.

Just Noticeable Difference (jnd). The term traditionally was used in reference to the just noticeable difference in sensation associated with a measured difference threshold. The difference threshold was the measured physical difference between two stimuli required to achieve a just noticeable difference in sensation. In recent times the term just noticeable difference (jnd) has been used interchangeably with the term difference threshold (DL).

Law of Comparative Judgment. A mathematical model, proposed by L. L. Thurstone, for analysis of paired comparison judgments. Application of the law allows one to convert the proportion of times stimulus B is judged greater, on some dimension, than stimulus A into the average difference in psychological magnitude between the two stimuli.

Likelihood Ratio. The likelihood, expressed as probability density, of sensory observation χ occurring, given that it is a sample from the signal-plus-noise distribution, divided by the likelihood of the same value of χ occurring, given that it is a sample from the noise distribution.

Line Length Matching. The procedure of scaling sensation magnitude by requiring the observer to match the apparent length of lines to the sensation magnitudes of stimuli within the modality under investigation. In the use of this method, it is assumed that the apparent length of lines is linearly related to their physical length. Thus, the physical length of a line that appears to be equal in subjective magnitude to a stimulus in another modality is an acceptable measurement of sensation magnitude.

Magnitude Estimation. A scaling method in which the observer is required to make numerical estimations of the sensory magnitudes produced by various stimuli.

Magnitude Matching. A method for controlling the individual difference in the use of numbers in magnitude estimation in which the observer judges the sensory magnitudes of stimuli from two different modalities on a single, common scale. One of the modalities serves as a control modality, in which sensation magnitudes are assumed to be the same across individuals, and the other modality is the test modality under investigation. The magnitude estimations in the control modality are used to calibrate those in the test modality. The experimental question is whether individuals or groups of individuals differ in their perception of stimuli within the test modality.

Magnitude Production. A scaling method in which the observer is required to adjust stimuli to produce a psychological magnitude of some designated numerical value.

Maximum-Likelihood Methods. Adaptive procedures for measuring threshold in which the intensity of the stimulus presented on each trial is determined by a statistical estimation of the observer's threshold that is made from all of the results obtained from the beginning of the test run.

Master Scaling. A method for controlling for individual differences in the use of numbers in magnitude estimation in which the results of individuals or groups of individuals are converted to a master scale so that the responses of all individuals can be compared on a common scale with a common unit.

Memory Psychophysics. The use of psychophysical scaling procedures to investigate characteristics of remembered stimuli.

Metathetic Continua. Perceptual changes that are of a qualitative nature, such as changes in pitch or hue, rather than quantitative changes (prothetic continua), such as loudness or brightness.

Method of Adjustment. In this method, the observer adjusts the stimulus to correspond to the absolute threshold or, in the case of measuring difference thresholds, the observer adjusts the comparison stimulus so that its subjective intensity matches that of the standard stimulus.

Method of Constant Stimuli. Stimuli of varied intensity are presented several times in a random order to an observer who, in the case of measuring absolute threshold, is required to report the presence or absence of the stimulus or who, in the case of measuring difference thresholds, must report which of two stimuli is more intense.

Method of Equal-Appearing Intervals. A version of category scaling in which it is assumed that observers are capable of keeping the intervals between category boundaries psychologically equal as they assign stimuli to the various categories.

Method of Least Squares. Method for determining the slope and intercept of the straight line that best fitted a set of data points in which for each point, the Y value of the point is plotted as a function of its X value. The method minimizes the sum of the squared deviations of the Y values from the line.

Method of Limits. In a descending series, the value of the stimulus presented to the observer is decreased on successive trials until a stimulus is no longer detected or, in the case of measuring difference thresholds, until a stimulus difference is no longer noticed. In an ascending series, the value of the stimulus is increased on successive trials until a stimulus is detected or, in the case of measuring difference thresholds, until a stimulus difference is no longer noticed.

Method of Paired Comparison. The method most frequently used to collect data for constructing psychological scales based on comparative judgments. The observer is required to make comparative judgments of all possible pairs of stimuli.

Method of Response Invariance. In this method, the investigator seeks to discover different stimulus conditions that leave the psychophysical response constant. An example of the use of this method would be to determine the absolute thresholds, as specified as the intensities of stimuli needed to produce a constant response criterion of 50% correct responding, for the detection of lights of different wavelengths.

Method of Selective Adaptation. In this method, the thresholds of all but one sensory system are elevated through adaptation so that psychophysical thresholds can be determined by only the unadapted system.

Minkowski-n Space. The space of multidimensional scaling in which the distance between two stimuli is found by the equation $D = (\Sigma d^n)^{1/n}$, where D is the psychological distance between two stimuli and d is the distance along one of the component dimensions. When the space is city block, $n = 1$, and when it is Euclidean, $n = 2$.

Modulus. The psychological scale value that the experimenter assigns to the standard stimulus in magnitude estimation. When a standard stimulus is used in magnitude estimation, the observer is instructed to assign numbers to stimuli relative to the value of the modulus of the standard stimulus.

Momentary Threshold. The threshold, which varies over time, that exists at any particular time. This concept is fundamental in classical threshold theory.

Multidimensional Scaling. A method of psychophysical scaling developed to permit identification of the number of independent subjective dimensions associated with the perception of differences among stimuli. With these methods, each stimulus can be assigned psychological scale values along each of the identified psychological dimensions.

"Near Miss" to Weber's Law. The observation in auditory intensity discrimination of sinusoidal stimuli and tactile intensity discrimination of sinusoidal stimuli and noise stimuli that the Weber fraction ($\Delta I/I$) decreases slightly as intensity (I) increases, rather than being constant as predicted from Weber's law.

Neural Quantum Theory. The theory that the dimension of sensory magnitude is not continuous but, instead, consists of a series, starting at absolute threshold and progressing to high levels, of discrete steps.

Noise Distribution. Probability distribution of the variation of internal noise within the observer.

Numerical Magnitude Balance. A scaling method in which the psychophysical scale is the average of scales obtained by magnitude estimation and magnitude production.

Observer Threshold. A theoretical threshold within the observer above which presentation of the stimulus causes the nervous system to be in a detect state which is fundamentally different than the nondetect state within the nervous system which occurs when the stimulus is below threshold.

Oddity Procedure. Method of measuring the discriminability of stimuli in which three or more observation intervals are presented to the observer in which the same stimulus is presented in all but one observation interval and another stimulus is presented in the remaining interval. The observer's task is to select the interval containing the odd stimulus.

Ogive Function. A mathematical function that describes the cumulative normal distribution. If variations in X can be described by a normal distribution then an ogive function is obtained when the proportion of the area under the normal distribution below any value of X is plotted as a function of X.

Ordinal Scale. A set of measurements in which the amount of a property of objects or events can be ranked. The rank number represents the scale value for each measurement. Any monotonic transformation can be performed on the results and leave the scale invariant.

p(A). A measure of signal detectability consisting of the proportion of the area of the entire ROC graph that lies beneath the ROC curve.

p(C). Proportion of correct responses in a forced-choice task.

Paired Comparison Scales. Scales constructed from the proportion of times stimulus A is judged greater than stimulus B on some psychological dimension. The difference between the psychological scale values for two stimulus increases as the proportion of times one is judged to be greater than the other increases.

Parameter Estimation by Sequential Testing (PEST). An adaptive method for measuring thresholds in which the step size for changing signal strength is dependent on the observer's prior performance.

Partition Scales. Scales in which psychological magnitudes of stimuli are inferred from the observer's judgments of the psychological differences among stimuli.

Pay-Off Matrix. In a signal detection task, the costs associated with the incorrect responses of misses and false alarms and the values associated with the correct responses of hits and correct rejections.

PEST. An adaptive procedure for measuring threshold, in which the size of the steps during stimulus change are governed by rules designed to efficiently and accurately determine the threshold.

Phi-Gamma Hypothesis. The hypothesis that the psychometric function should have the ogive form of the cumulative normal distribution. The hypothesis is based on the assumption that momentary thresholds in classical threshold theory are normally distributed.

Phi-Log-Gamma Hypothesis. The hypothesis that psychometric function should have the ogive form of the cumulative normal distribution when response probability is plotted as a function of the logarithm of stimulus intensity. The hypothesis is based on the assumption that Fechner's law is true.

Physical Correlate Theory. Theory that the observer, instead of making judgments of sensory magnitude, makes judgments of some physical attribute associated through learning with the stimulus. For example, observers are thought to judge the distance between themselves and a sound source when asked to judge loudness rather than loudness itself.

Point of Subjective Equality. Value of the comparison stimulus judged to be subjectively equal to the standard stimulus.

Poisson Distribution. A frequency distribution of events that is positively skewed when the mean of the distribution has a low value. In general, as the mean of the distribution increases, its form approaches that of a normal distribution.

Power Law. In 1957, S. S. Stevens proposed that the relationship between sensation magnitude and stimulus intensity is a power function in which sensation magnitude is proportional to stimulus intensity raised to a power. The exponent of the power function depends on the sensory modality and stimulus conditions.

Power Transformation. A change in the exponent of a psychophysical magnitude function due to the effects of some variable such as the presence of a masking stimulus.

Principle of Nomination. Declares that identical neural events give rise to identical psychological events (sensory experiences). The principle essentially says that all psychological states are determined by unique states in the nervous system.

Prothetic Continuum. Perceptual changes that are quantitative such as loudness or brightness rather than qualitative changes (metathetic continuum) such as pitch or loudness.

Proximities. Psychological distances between stimuli estimated from similarity judgments to be used in multidimensional scaling solutions.

Psychological Continuum. A dimension over which a psychological event can vary (e.g., the loudness of sounds, the brightness of lights or the pain of a noxious stimulus). The term was used by Thurstone in describing his law of comparative judgment.

Psychometric Function. A graph in which the proportion of responses in a detection or discrimination task is plotted as a function of the value of the stimulus.

Psychological Laws. Psychological laws in psychophysics describe the relationships among sensations. Psychological laws have also been referred to as *psychosensory laws.* An example is the binaural summation of loudness in which the total loudness of a sound heard with two ears is equal to the sum of the loudness experienced by each ear separately.

Psychophysical Laws. Psychophysical laws describe the relationship between stimulus and sensation. Psychophysical laws are also referred to as the *stimulus transformation.*

Psychophysical Linking Hypothesis. By using class A observations, coupled with the reflexive principle of nomination that identical sensations are based on identical neural events, hypotheses can be formulated about the neural basis of sensory perception.

Psychophysical Magnitude Function. The relationship between judged psychological magnitude and stimulus intensity.

Quantal Fluctuations. Random fluctuations in the number of quanta emitted from a light source, and thought to influence the form of the psychometric function for detecting a visual stimulus.

QUEST. An adaptive procedure for measuring threshold in which maximum-likelihood statistics are used to estimate a psychometric function with the form of a Weibull function.

Range-Frequency Model. Category scaling model of Parducci concerning the effects of the stimulus range and the frequency distribution of stimulus presentations on category responses.

Ratio Estimation. A scaling method in which the observer is required to estimate the ratios of the psychological magnitudes of two stimuli.

Ratio Production. A scaling method in which the observer is required to adjust a variable stimulus while observing a standard stimulus such that the two resulting sensations are in a prescribed ratio.

Ratio Scale. A set of measurements in which the scale, as well as having the properties of order and distance, has a natural origin to represent zero amount of the property. The only transformation that can be performed on the results that leave the scale invariant is multiplication by a constant.

Ratio Scaling. Direct scaling methods in which the observer's task is to make judgments that reflect the ratios of their experienced psychological magnitudes.

Reflexive Principle of Nomination. Declares that when psychological events are identical, neural events are identical. The principle is fundamental to analytical psychophysics because if, through a psychophysical experiment, different stimuli can be discovered that produce identical sensations, then further experiments can be conducted to determine which neural events are also identical. In this way, the underlying neural basis of sensation may be discovered.

Regression Bias. A tendency of observers to be conservative in making judgments, the result of which is for the values of their judgments to regress toward the mean of their judgments.

Reperception Hypothesis. The hypothesis that stimuli are first transformed into perceptions through a power function and then these perceptions are transformed into memories by the same power function transformation.

Response Bias. A tendency for the observer to favor one response over another, which is determined by factors other than the intensity of the stimulus.

ROC Curve. A graph, called the *receiver operating characteristic curve*, in which the performance of the observer is described by plotting the proportion of hits as a function of the proportion of false alarms.

Response Transformation Function. The mathematical function describing the relationship between sensation and sensory responses such as those made in magnitude estimation and category scaling.

Same–Different Procedure. Method for measuring the discriminability of stimuli wherein the observer is presented with pairs of stimuli, in which each member of the pair are either the same or different. The observer's task is to report whether the two stimuli are the same or different.

Sensory Response Laws. Sensory response laws describe the relationship between the observer's sensory responses, such as magnitude estimations or category judgments, and sensation. The sensory response law has also been referred to as the *judgment function* or the *response transformation*.

Sensory Transducer Theory. The theory that the power law observed for psychophysical magnitude functions is a reflection of the operation of sensory mechanisms as they transduce stimulus energy into neural activity.

Sequential Effects. The tendency for the judged sensory magnitude of a stimulus to be systematically related to the value of stimuli presented and responses made on the previous few trials.

Signal-Plus-Noise Distribution. Probability distribution of the variation of the internal state of the observer when a signal is presented against the background of internal noise.

Space Error. Response bias resulting from presenting the standard stimulus and the comparison stimulus in a discrimination task to different receptive areas. Space errors are controlled by presenting the standard stimulus to one receptive area on a random half of the trials and to the other receptive area on the other trials.

Spatial Summation. Occurs when the detection threshold is constant as long as the total energy in the stimulus is the same whether it is concentrated in a very small area of sensory receptors or spread over a larger area of sensory receptors. When threshold is expressed as energy per unit area, it decreases as a function of the size of the stimulus. This phenomenon has been interpreted as an indication that sensory receptors and their associated nerve fibers are capable of summating their activity. In all sensory systems, there are limits to the size of the area over which spatial summation can occur.

Spectral Sensitivity. The term refers to changes in the absolute threshold for vision as the wavelength of light presented to the eye is changed. When the light as presented exclusively to cone receptors by stimulating only the fovea, an area in the center of the retina containing only cones, the resulting spectral sensitivity curve is called the *photopic curve.* When the light is presented to the periphery of the retina, containing both rods and cones, rods, because they are more sensitive than cones, determine threshold and the resulting spectral sensitivity cure is called the *scotopic curve.*

Staircase Method. Version of the method of limits wherein the direction, in which changes in the stimulus value are made, is changed whenever the observer's response changes. Threshold is taken as the average of the stimulus values corresponding to the response reversals.

Standard Stimulus. A stimulus of fixed value presented in discrimination tasks to be compared with a comparison stimulus that varies from trial to trial in its value.

Stimulus Critical Value Function. The *stimulus critical value* is a measured value of the stimulus corresponding to some designated level of detection performance (e.g., absolute threshold determined by some specific method) or discrimination performance (e.g., difference threshold determined by some specific method).

Stimulus-Range Equalizing Bias. The tendency for the observer to use the same response range in judging the sensation magnitudes of stimuli presented within a wide range or a narrow range of stimulus values.

Stimulus Transformation Function. The mathematical function describing the relationship between the stimulus and sensation—also known as the *psychophysical law.*

Stress. An estimate of goodness of fit that shows how far multidimensional scaling distances deviate from their corresponding proximities.

Temporal Summation. Occurs when the detection threshold is constant as long as the total energy in the stimulus is the same, whether it is concentrated in a very brief period of time or spread over a longer period. When threshold is expressed as energy per unit time, it decreases as a function of stimulus duration. The phenomenon has been interpreted as an indication that sensory systems are capable of summating their activity over time. In all sensory systems, there are limits to the duration of stimulation over which summation occurs.

Theory of Signal Detection. In this model, no threshold is assumed. Thus, instead of internal states that are either suprathreshold or subthreshold, a single suprathreshold state is assumed to exist whether a stimulus is presented or not. The value of the suprathreshold state when no signal is presented is described as the noise distribution. The value of the suprathreshold state when a signal is presented is described as the signal plus noise distribution. The observer must decide whether the suprathreshold observation was due to signal or due to noise by setting a decision criterion above which a signal is reported and below which no signal is reported.

Threshold Tracking Method. The observer controls a continuously variable stimulus and the transition points where a stimulus of increasing intensity is first detected and a stimulus of decreasing intensity is first not detected are determined. Threshold is taken as the average of these transition points.

Time Error. Response bias resulting from presenting the standard stimulus and the comparison stimulus in the same sequential order on every trial. Controlled by presenting the standard stimulus first on a random half of trials and presenting the comparison stimulus first on the other trials.

Transitivity. When measurement A is equal to measurement B and measurement C is equal to measurement B, then measurement A must be equal to measurement C if the measurements are transitive. Transitivity tests have been used in psychophysics as a test of the validity of scales.

Two-stage Theory of Magnitude Estimation. Theory that, in magnitude estimation, the observer's response results from a two-stage process in which the stimulus first produces a sensation and then the sensation results in a judgment response.

Uncertainty Hypothesis. The hypothesis that observers experience greater uncertainty in making judgments of the magnitudes of memory images than when making judgments of the magnitude of perceptions.

Up–Down Transformed Response (UDTR) method. An adaptive procedure for measuring threshold, in which the sequence of correct and incorrect responses since the last change in the stimulus determines the value of the next stimulus.

Verbally Labeled Category Scales. Category scales in which numerical values of the category scale are associated with descriptive verbal labels for various psychological states and intensities of these states.

Weber's Law. A principle first discovered by E. H. Weber, a German physiologist, in 1834, that the change in stimulus intensity that can just be discriminated ($\Delta\phi$) is a constant fraction (c) of the level of stimulus intensity (ϕ). The law is expressed as either $\Delta\phi = c\phi$ or alternatively, $\Delta\phi/\phi = c$. The law has wide generality across sensory modalities and stimulus conditions with the exception that the values of $\Delta\phi$ are often a bit too high at low values of ϕ near the absolute threshold. Also, there are some cases, such as hearing pure tones in which a "near miss" to Weber's Law is seen where $\Delta\phi/\phi$ is almost, but not quite, constant as ϕ is changed.

Yes–No Procedure. The observer is given a series of trials, some of which contain a signal and some of which do not, and the task is to report the presence or absence of the signal on each trial.

Z_N. z-score value on the baseline of the N distribution corresponding to the criterion, calculated by subtracting the false alarm rate from 1.0 and converting this proportion to a z score.

Z_{SN}. z-score value on the baseline of the SN distribution corresponding to the criterion, calculated by subtracting the hit rate from 1.0 and converting this proportion to a z score.

References

Abel, E. L. Marijuana and memory: Acquisition or retrieval? *Science*, 1971, *173*, 1038–1040.

Adams, C., Hall, D., Pennypacker, H., Goldstein, G., Hench, L., Madden, M., Stein, G., & Catania, A. Lump detection in simulated human breasts. *Perception and Psychophysics*, 1976, *20*, 163–167.

Adrian, E. D., & Matthews, R. The action of light on the eye: I. The discharge of impulses in the optic nerve and its relation to the electric changes in the retina. *Journal of Physiology*, 1927, *63*, 378–414.

Algom, D. Memory psychophysics: An examination of its perceptual and cognitive prospects. In D. Algom (Ed.), *Psychophysical Approaches to Cognition*. Amsterdam: Elsevier Science Publishers B.V., 1992.

Algom, D., & Cohen-Raz, L. Visual velocity input–output functions: The integration of distance and duration onto subjective velocity. *Journal of Experimental Psychology: Human Perception & Performance*, 1984, *10*, 486–501.

Algom, D., & Lubel, S. Psychophysics in the field: Perception and memory for labor pain. *Perception & Psychophysics*, 1994, *55*, 133–141.

Algom, D., & Marks, L. E. Individual differences in loudness processing and loudness scales. *Journal of Experimental Psychology: General*, 1984, *113*, 571–593.

Algom, D., & Marks, L. E. Range and regression, loudness scales, and loudness processing: Toward a context bound psychophysics. *Journal of Experimental Psychology: Human Perception & Performance*, 1990, *16*, 706–727.

Algom, D., Raphaeli, N., & Cohen-Raz, L. Integration of noxious stimulation across separate somatosensory communication systems: A functional theory of pain. *Journal of Experimental Psychology: Human Perception & Performance*, 1986, *12*, 92–102.

Algom, D., Wolf, Y., & Bergman, B. Integration of stimulus dimensions in perception and memory: Composition rules and psychophysical relations. *Journal of Experimental Psychology: General*, 1985, *114*, 451–471.

Anderson, N. H. Application of an additive model to impression formation. *Science*, 1962, *138*, 817–818.

Anderson, N. H. Functional measurement and psychophysical judgment. *Psychological Review*, 1970, *77*, 153–170.

Anderson, N. H. Algebraic models of perception. In E. C. Carterette & M. P. Friedman (Eds.), *Handbook of Perception* (Vol. 2). New York: Academic Press, 1974.

Anderson, N. H. Integration theory, functional measurement, and the psychological law. In H. G. Geisslerl & Y. M. Zabrodin (Eds.), *Advances in Psychophysics*, pp. 93–130. Berlin: VEB Deutscher Verlag, 1976.

Anderson, N. H. Note on functional measurement and data analysis. *Perception and Psychophysics*, 1977, *21*, 201–215.

Anderson, N. H. Information integration theory in developmental psychology. In F. Wilkening, J. Becker, & T. Trabasso (Eds.), *Information integration by children*. Hillsdale, NJ: Lawrence Erlbaum Associates, 1980.

Anderson, N. H. *Foundation of Information Integration Theory*. New York: Academic, 1981.

Anderson, N. H. Cognitive algebra and social psychophysics. In B. Wegener (Ed.), *Social attitudes and psychophysical measurements*. Hillsdale, NJ: Lawrence Erlbaum Associates, 1982.

Anderson, N. H. Integration psychophysics and cognition. In D. Algom (Ed.), *Psychophysical Approaches to Cognition*, pp. 13–113. Amsterdam: North-Holland, 1992.

Attneave, F. Dimensions of similarity. *American Journal of Psychology*, 1950, *63*, 516–556.

Attneave, F. Perception and related areas. In S. Koch (Ed.), *Psychology: A Study of a Science* (Vol. 4), pp. 619–659. New York: McGraw Hill, 1962.

Banks, W. P. Signal detection theory and human memory. *Psychological Bulletin*, 1970, *74*, 81–99.

Bartoshuk, L. M., Rifkin, B., Marks, L. E., & Bars, P. Taste and aging. *Journal of Gerontology*, 1986, *44*, 51–57.

Beals, R., Krantz, D. H., & Tversky, A. Foundation of multidimensional scaling. *Psychological Review*, 1968, *75*, 127–142.

Békésy, G. Über das Fechner'sche Gesetz und seine Bedeutung für die Theorie der akustischen Beobachtungsfehler und die Theorie des Hörens. *Annalen der Physik*, 1930, *7*, 329–359.

Békésy, G. A new audiometer. *Acta Oto-laryngology*, 1947, *35*, 411–422.

Berglund, B., Berglund, U., Engen, T., & Ekman, G. Individual psychophysical functions for twenty-eight odorants. *Perception and Psychophysics*, 1971, *9*, 379–384.

Berglund, M. B. Quality assurance in environmental psychophysics. In S. J. Bolanowski & G. A. Gescheider (Eds.), *Ratio Scaling of Psychological Magnitude: In Honor of the Memory of S. S. Stevens*, pp. 140–162. Hillsdale, NJ: Lawrence Erlbaum Associates, 1991.

Bernoulli, D. Specimen theoriae novae de mensura sortis. *Commentarii Academiae Scientiarum Imperiales Petropolitanae*, 1738, *5*, 175–192. (Translated by L. Sommer in *Econometrica*, 1954, *22*, 23–36.)

Birnbaum, M. H. Controversies in psychophysical measurement. In B. Wegener (Ed.), *Social Attitudes and Psychophysical Measurement*, pp. 401–485. Hillsdale, NJ: Lawrence Erlbaum Associates, 1982.

Blackwell, H. R. Psychophysical thresholds: Experimental studies of methods of measurement. *Bulletin of the Engineering Research Institute*, University of Michigan, No. 36, 1953.

Blough, D. S. A method for obtaining psychophysical thresholds from the pigeon. *Journal of the Experimental Analysis of Behavior*, 1958, *1*, 31–43.

Bolanowski, S. J., Jr. Contourless stimuli produce binocular brightness summation. *Vision Research*, 1987, *27*, 1943–1951.

Bolanowski, S. J., Gescheider, G. A., & Sutton, S. V. W. Relationship between oral pain and ethanol concentration in mouthrinses. *Journal of Periodontal Research*, 1995, *30*, 192–197.

Bolanowski, S. J., Gescheider, G. A., & Verrillo, R. T. Expansion of the four channel model for touch: Hairy skin. *Somatosensory and Motor Research*, 1994, *11*, 279–290.

Bolanowski, S. J., Jr., Gescheider, G. A., Verrillo, R. T., & Checkosky, C. M. Four channels mediate the mechanical aspects of touch. *Journal of the Acoustical Society of America*, 1988, *84*, 1680–1694.

Bolanowski, S. J., Jr., & Verrillo, R. T. Temperature and criterion effects in a somatosensory subsystem: A neurophysiological and psychophysical study. *Journal of Neurophysiology*, 1982, *48*, 837–856.

Bolanowski, S. J., Jr., Zwislocki, J. J., & Gescheider, G. A. Intersensory generality and psychological units. In S. J. Bolanowski, Jr. & G. A. Gescheider (Eds.), *Ratio Scaling of Psychological Magnitude: A Tribute to the Memory of S. S. Stevens*, pp. 277–293. Hillsdale, NJ: Lawrence Erlbaum Associates, 1991.

Bond, B., & Stevens, S. S. Cross-modality matching of brightness to loudness by 5-year-olds. *Perception and Psychophysics*, 1969, *6*, 337–339.

Borg, G. Perceived exertion as an indicator of somatic stress. *Scandinavian Journal of Rehabilitation Medicine*, 1970, 2, 92–98.

Borg, G. A category scale with ratio properties for intermodal and interindividual comparisons. In H. G. Geissler & P. Petzold (Eds.), *Psychophysical Judgment and the Process of Perception*. Berlin, GDR: VEB Deutscher Verlag der Wissenschaften, 1982.

Borg, G., & Borg, E. Principles and experiments in category-ratio scaling. *Reports from the Department of Psychology*, Stockholm University, 1994, No. 789.

Borg, G., Diamant, H., Ström, L., & Zotterman, Y. The relation between neural and perceptual intensity: A comparative study on the neural and psychophysical response to taste stimuli. *Journal of Physiology*, 1967, *192*, 13–20.

Boring, E. G. A chart of the psychometric function. *American Journal of Psychology*, 1917, *28*, 465–470.

Boring, E. G. The stimulus error. *American Journal of Psychology*, 1921, *32*, 449–471.

Brindley, G. A. *Physiology of the retina and the visual pathways*. London: Edward Arnold Ltd., 1960.

Brooks, D. N. Recognition memory after head injury: A signal detection analysis. *Cortex*, 1974, *40*, 224–230.

Cain, W. S. Differential sensitivity for smell: "Noise" at the nose. *Science*, 1977, *195*, 796–798.

Chapman, C. R., & Feather, B. W. Effects of diazepam on human pain tolerance and pain sensitivity. *Psychosomatic Medicine*, 1973, *35*, 330–340.

Chapman, C. R., Gehrig, J. D., & Wilson, M. E. Acupuncture, pain and signal detection theory. *Science*, 1975, *189*, 65.

Churcher, B. G. A loudness scale for industrial noise measurement. *Journal of the Acoustical Society of America*, 1935, *6*, 216–226.

Clark, W. C. Sensory decision theory analysis of the placebo effect on the criterion for pain and thermal sensitivity (*d'*). *Journal of Abnormal Psychology*, 1969, *74*, 363–371.

Clark, W. C., & Mehl, L. Thermal pain: A sensory decision theory analysis of the effect of age and sex on *d'*, various response criteria, and 50% pain threshold. *Journal of Abnormal Psychology*, 1971, *78*, 202–212.

Cohn, J. Experimentelle Untersuchungen über die Gefuhlsbetonung der Farben, Helligkeiten, und ihrer Combinationen. *Philosophische Studien*, 1894, *10*, 562–603.

Collins, A. A., & Gescheider, G. A. The measurement of loudness in children and adults by absolute magnitude estimation and cross-modality matching. *Journal of the Acoustical Society of America*, 1989, *85*, 2012–2021.

Cornsweet, T. N. The staircase method in psychophysics. *American Journal of Psychology*, 1962, *75*, 485–491.

Cross, D. V. Sequential dependencies and regression in psychophysical judgments. *Perception & Psychophysics*, 1973, *14*, 547–552.

Curtis, D. W., Attneave, F., & Harrington, T. L. A test of a two-stage model of magnitude judgment. *Perception & Psychophysics*, 1968, *3*, 25–31.

Dai, H., Versfeld, N. J., & Green, D. M. The optimum decision rules in the *same–different* paradigm. *Perception & Psychophysics*, 1996, *58*, 1–9.

Davis, H., & Krantz, F. W. International audiometric zero. *Journal of the Acoustical Society of America*, 1964, *36*, 1450–1454.

Dawson, W. E. Magnitude estimation of apparent sums and differences. *Perception & Psychophysics*, 1971, *9*, 368–374.

DeCarlo, L. T. Intertrial interval and sequential effects in magnitude scaling. *Journal of Experimental Psychology: Human Perception and Performance*, 1992, *18*, 1080–1088.

DeCarlo, L. T. A dynamic theory of proportional judgment: Context and judgments of length, heaviness, and roughness. *Journal of Experimental Psychology: Human Perception and Performance*, 1994, *20*, 372–381.

Delbrück, M. A physicist's renewed look at biology: Twenty years later. *Science*, 1970, *168*, 1312–1315.

Durup, G., & Piéron, H. Recherches au sujet de l'interpretation du phénomène de Purkinje par des différences dans les courbes de sensation des recepteurs chromatiques. *L'Année Psychologique*, 1933, *33*, 57–83.

Eisler, H. Empirical test of a model relating magnitude and category scales. *Scandinavian Journal of Psychology*, 1962, *3*, 88–96.

Eisler, H. Magnitude scales, category scales, and Fechnerian integration. *Psychological Review*, 1963, *70*, 243–253.

Ekman, G. Discriminal sensitivity on the subjective continuum. *Acta Psychologica*, 1956, *12*, 233–243.

Ekman, G. Weber's law and related functions. *Journal of Psychology*, 1959, *47*, 343–352.

Ekman, G. Is the power law a special case of Fechner's law? *Perceptual and Motor Skills*, 1964, *19*, 730.

Ekman, G., Frankenhaeuser, M., Goldberg, L., Hagdahl, R., & Myrstern, A. Subjective and objective effects of alcohol as functions of dosage and time. *Psychopharmacologia*, 1964, *6*, 399–409.

Ekman, G., & Künnapas, T. Measurement of aesthetic value by "direct" and "indirect" methods. *Scandinavian Journal of Psychology*, 1962a, *3*, 33–39.

Ekman, G., & Künnapas, T. Scales of aesthetic value. *Perceptual and Motor Skills*, 1962b, *14*, 19–26.

Ekman, G., & Künnapas, T. A further study of direct and indirect scaling methods. *Scandinavian Journal of Psychology*, 1963, *4*, 77–80.

Ellermeier, W., Westphal, W., & Heidenfelder, M. On the "absoluteness" of category and magnitude scales of pain. *Perception & Psychophysics*, 1991, *49*, 159–166.

Elliot, L. Discrimination and response bias for CV syllables differing in voice onset time among children and adults. *Journal of the Acoustical Society of America*, 1986, *80*, 1250–1255.

Engen, T. Psychophysics: Discrimination and detection. In J. W. Kling & L. A. Riggs (Eds.), *Woodworth & Schlosberg's experimental psychology* (3rd ed.). New York: Holt, 1971.

Engen, T., & Tulunay, Ü. Some sources of error in half-heaviness judgments. *Journal of Experimental Psychology*, 1956, *54*, 208–212.

Estes, W. K. The problem of inference from curves based on group data. *Psychological Bulletin*, 1956, *53*, 134–140.

Falmagne, J. C. The generalized Fechner problem and discrimination. *Journal of Mathematical Psychology*, 1971, *8*, 22–43.

Falmagne, J. C. Foundation of Fechnerian psychophysics. In D. H. Krantz, R. C. Atkinson, R. D. Luce, & P. Suppes (Eds.), *Contemporary Developments in Mathematical Psychology:*

Measurement, Psychophysics, and Neural Information Processing (Vol. 2), pp. 129–159. San Francisco: Freeman, 1974.

Falmagne, J. C. *Elements of Psychophysical Theory.* Oxford: Oxford University Press, 1985.

Fechner, G. T. *Element der Psychophysik.* Leipzig: Breitkopf & Härterl, 1860.

Fechner, G. T. *Vorschule der Aesthetik.* Leipzig: Breitkopf & Härterl, 1876.

Fletcher, H., & Munson, W. A. Loudness, its definition, measurement and calculation. *Journal of the Acoustical Society of America,* 1933, 5, 82–108.

Foley, H. J., Cross, D. V., Foley, M. A., & Reeder, R. Stimulus range, number of categories and the "virtual" exponent. *Perception & Psychophysics,* 1983, 34, 505–512.

Foley, H. J., Cross, D. V., & O'Reilly, J. A. Pervasiveness and magnitude of context effects: Evidence for the relativity of absolute magnitude estimation. *Perception & Psychophysics,* 1990, 48, 551–558.

Frankenhaeuser, M., Fröberg, J., Hagdahl, R., Rissler, A., Björkvall, C., & Wolff, B. Physiological, behavioral, and subjective indices of habituation to psychological stress. *Physiology and Behavior,* 1967, 2, 229–237.

Frankenhaeuser, M., Sterky, K., & Järpe, G. Psychophysiological relations in habituation to gravitational stress. *Perceptual and Motor Skills,* 1962, 15, 63–72.

Frederiksen, J. R. Two models for psychological judgment: Scale invariance with changes in stimulus range. *Perception & Psychophysics,* 1975, 17, 147–157.

Fullerton, G. S., & Cattell, J. McK. *On the perception of small differences.* Philadelphia: University of Pennsylvania Press, 1892.

Fuortes, M. G. F., & Hodgkin, A. L. Changes in time scale and sensitivity in the ommatidia of Limulus. *Journal of Physiology,* 1964, 172, 239–263.

Galanter, E. The direct measurement of utility and subjective probability. *American Journal of Psychology,* 1962, 75, 208–220.

Galanter, E., & Pliner, P. Cross-modality matching of money against other continua. In H. R. Moskowitz, B. Scharf, & J. C. Stevens (Eds.), *Sensation and measurement.* Dordrecht, Holland: Reidel, 1974.

Gamble, E. A. McC. The applicability of Weber's law to smell. *American Journal of Psychology,* 1898, 10, 82–142.

Garner, W. R. Context effects and the validity of loudness scales. *Journal of Experimental Psychology,* 1954, 48, 218–224.

Gault, R. H. Touch as a substitute for hearing in the interpretation and control of speech. *Archives of Otolaryngology,* 1926, 3, 121–135.

Gescheider, G. A. Auditory and cutaneous apparent successiveness. *Journal of Experimental Psychology,* 1967, 73, 179–186.

Gescheider, G. A. In defense of a sensory process theory of psychophysical scaling. *The Behavioral and Brain Sciences,* 1981, 4, 194.

Gescheider, G. A., Barton, W. G., Bruce, M. R., Goldberg, J. H., & Greenspan, M. J. The effects of simultaneous auditory stimulation upon the detection of tactile stimuli. *Journal of Experimental Psychology,* 1969, 81, 120–125.

Gescheider, G. A., & Bolanowski, S. J., Jr. Final comments on ratio scaling of psychological magnitude. In S. J. Bolanowski, Jr. & G. A. Gescheider (Eds.), *Ratio Scaling of Psychological Magnitude: In Honor of the Memory of S. S. Stevens,* pp. 295–311. Hillsdale, NJ: Lawrence Erlbaum Associates, 1991.

Gescheider, G. A., Bolanowski, S. J., Jr., & Verrillo, R. T. Sensory, cognitive and response factors in the judgment of sensory magnitude. In D. Algom (Ed.), *Psychophysical Approaches to Cognition,* pp. 575–621. Amsterdam: North-Holland, 1992.

Gescheider, G. A., Bolanowski, S. J., Jr., Verrillo, R. T., Arpajian, D. J., & Ryan, T. F. Vibrotactile intensity discrimination measured by three methods. *Journal of the Acoustical Society of America,* 1990, 87, 330–338.

Gescheider, G. A., Bolanowski, S. J., Zwislocki, J. J., Hall, K. L., & Mascia, C. The effects of masking on the growth of vibrotactile sensation magnitude and on the intensity DL: A test of the equal sensation magnitude—equal DL hypothesis. *Journal of the Acoustical Society of America,* 1994, *96,* 1479–1488.

Gescheider, G. A., Catlin, E. C., & Fontana, A. M. Psychophysical measurement of the judged seriousness of crimes and severity of punishments. *Bulletin of the Psychonomic Society,* 1982, *19,* 275–278.

Gescheider, G. A., Edwards, R. R., Lackner, E. A., Bolanowski, S. J., & Verrillo, R. T. The effects of aging on information processing channels in the sense of touch: III. Differential sensitivity to changes in stimulus intensity. *Somatosensory and Motor Research,* 1996, *13,* 73–80.

Gescheider, G. A., Frisina, R. D., & Verrillo, R. T. Selective adaptation of vibrotactile thresholds. *Sensory Processes,* 1979, *3,* 37–48.

Gescheider, G. A., Herman, D. D., & Phillips, J. N. Criterion shifts in the measurement of tactile masking. *Perception & Psychophysics,* 1970, *8,* 433–436.

Gescheider, G. A., & Hughson, B. A. Stimulus context and absolute magnitude estimation: A study of individual differences. *Perception & Psychophysics,* 1991, *50,* 45–57.

Gescheider, G. A., Verrillo, R. T., Capraro, A. J., & Hamer, R. D. Enhancement of vibrotactile sensation magnitude and predictions from the duplex model of mechanoreception. *Sensory Processes,* 1977, *1,* 187–203.

Gescheider, G. A., & Wright, J. H. Effects of sensory adaptation on the form of the psychophysical magnitude function for cutaneous vibration. *Journal of Experimental Psychology,* 1968, *77,* 308–313.

Gescheider, G. A., Wright, J. H., & Polak, J. W. Detection of vibrotactile signals differing in probability of occurrence. *Journal of Psychology,* 1971, *78,* 253–260.

Gescheider, G. A., Wright, J. H., Weber, B. J., & Barton, W. G. Absolute thresholds in vibrotactile signal detection. *Perception and Psychophysics,* 1971, *10,* 413–417.

Goff, G. D. Differential discrimination of frequency of cutaneous mechanical vibration. *Journal of Experimental Psychology,* 1967, *74,* 294–299.

Graham, C. H., Brown, R. H., & Mote, F. A., Jr. The relation of size of stimulus and intensity in the human eye: I. Intensity thresholds for white light. *Journal of Experimental Psychology,* 1939, *24,* 255–573.

Green, D. M. Stimulus selection in adaptive psychophysical procedures. *Journal of the Acoustical Society of America,* 1990, *87,* 2662–2674.

Green, D. M., & Swets, J. A. *Signal detection theory and psychophysics.* New York: Wiley, 1966.

Greene, L. C., & Hardy, J. D. Spatial summation of pain. *Journal of Applied Physiology,* 1958, *13,* 457–464.

Gregg, L. W. Fractionation of temporal intervals. *Journal of Experimental Psychology,* 1951, *42,* 307–312.

Gregson, R. A. M. *Nonlinear psychophysical dynamics.* Hillsdale, NJ: Lawrence Erlbaum Associates, 1988.

Grossberg, J. M., & Grant, B. F. Clinical psychophysics: Applications of ratio scaling and signal detection methods to research on pain, fear, drugs, and medical decision making. *Psychological Bulletin,* 1978, *85,* 1154–1176.

Guilford, J. P. *Psychometric methods.* New York: McGraw-Hill, 1954.

Gulick, W. L., Gescheider, G. A., & Frisina, R. D. *Hearing: Physiological Acoustics, Neural Coding, and Psychoacoustics.* New York: Oxford, 1989.

Hacker, M. J., & Ratcliff, R. A revised table of d' for M-alternative forced choice. *Perception & Psychophysics,* 1979, *26,* 168–170.

Hamer, R. D. *Vibrotactile masking: Evidence for a peripheral energy threshold.* Syracuse, NY: Syracuse University, 1979. (Institute for Sensory Research, PhD and Special Report No. ISR-S-18)

Hanes, R. M. A scale of subjective brightness. *Journal of Experimental Psychology*, 1949, *39*, 438–452. (a)

Hanes, R. M. The construction of subjective brightness scales from fractionation data: A validation. *Journal of Experimental Psychology*, 1949, *39*, 719–728. (b)

Hardy, J. D., Wolff, H. G., & Goodell, H. Studies on pain: Discrimination of differences in pain as a basis of a scale of pain intensity. *Journal of Clinical Investigation*, 1947, *26*, 1152–1158.

Harper, R. S., & Stevens, S. S. A psychological scale for weight and a formula for its derivation. *American Journal of Psychology*, 1948, *61*, 343–351.

Hartline, H. K., & Graham, C. H. Nerve impulses from single receptors in the eye. *Journal of Cellular and Comparative Physiology*, 1932, *1*, 277–295.

Hautus, M. J., Irwin, J. R., & Sutherland, S. Relativity of judgements about sound amplitude and the asymmetry of the same-different ROC. *Quarterly Journal of Experimental Psychology*, 1994, *47A*, 1035–1045.

Hecht, S. Vision II. The nature of the photoreceptor process. In C. Murchison (Ed.), *Handbook of general experimental psychology*. Worcester, MA: Clark University Press, 1934.

Hecht, S., Haig, C., & Chase, A. M. Influence of light adaptation on subsequent dark adaptation of the eye. *Journal of General Physiology*, 1937, *20*, 831–850.

Hecht, S., Shlaer, S., & Pirenne, M. H. Energy, quanta, and vision. *Journal of General Physiology*, 1942, *25*, 819–840.

Heller, O. Hörfeldaudiometrie mit dem Verfahren der Kategorienunterteilung (KU). *Psychologische Beiträge*, 1985, *27*, 478–493.

Hellman, R. P. Growth of loudness at 1000 and 3000 Hz. *Journal of the Acoustical Society of America*, 1976, *60*, 672–679.

Hellman, R. P., Scharf, B., Teghtsoonian, M., & Teghtsoonian, R. On the relation between the growth of loudness and the discrimination of intensity for pure tones. *Journal of the Acoustical Society of America*, 1987, *82*, 448–452.

Hellman, R. P., & Zwislocki, J. J. Some factors affecting the estimation of loudness. *Journal of the Acoustical Society of America*, 1961, *33*, 687–694.

Hellman, R. P., & Zwislocki, J. J. Monaural loudness function of a 1000-cps tone and internal summation. *Journal of the Acoustical Society of America*, 1963, *35*, 856–865.

Hellman, R. P., & Zwislocki, J. J. Loudness function of a 1000-cps tone in the presence of a masking noise. *Journal of the Acoustical Society of America*, 1964, *36*, 1618–1627.

Hellman, R. P., & Zwislocki, J. J. Loudness determination at low sound frequencies. *Journal of the Acoustical Society of America*, 1968, *43*, 60–64.

Hellström, A. The time-order error and its relatives: Mirrors of cognitive processes in comparing. *Psychological Bulletin*, 1985, *97*, 35–61.

Helson, H. Adaptation level as a basis for quantitative theory of frames of reference. *Psychological Review*, 1948, *55*, 297–313.

Helson, H. Adaptation level theory. In S. Koch (Ed.), *Psychology: A study of a science* (Vol. 1), pp. 565–621. New York: McGraw-Hill, 1959.

Helson, H. *Adaptation level theory—An experimental and systematic approach to behavior*. New York: Harper and Row, 1964.

Herbart, J. F. *Psychologie als Wissenschaft, neu gegrundet Auferfahrung, Metaphysik, und Mathematik*. Königsberg, Germany: Unzer, 1824.

Hilgard, E. R. Pain as a puzzle for psychology and physiology. *American Psychologist*, 1969, *24*, 103–113.

Hollins, M., Faldowski, R., Rao, S., & Young, F. Perceptual dimensions of tactile surface texture: A multidimensional scaling analysis. *Perception & Psychophysics*, 1993, *54*, 697–705.

Hollins, M., Goble, A. K., Whitsel, B. L., & Tommerdahl, M. Time course and action spectrum of vibrotactile adaptation. *Somatosensory and Motor Research*, 1990, *7*, 205–221.

Holmes, T. H., & Rahe, R. H. The social readjustment rating scale. *Journal of Psychosomatic Research*, 1967, *11*, 213–218.

Horeman, H. W. Relation between brightness and luminance under induction. *Vision Research*, 1965, *5*, 331–340.

Hsia, Y., & Graham, C. H. Spectral sensitivity of the cones in the dark adapted human eye. *Proceedings of the National Academy of Science*, 1952, *38*, 80–85.

Ingham, J. G. Individual differences in signal detection. *Acta Psychologica*, 1970, *34*, 39–50.

Irwin, J. R., Stillman, J. A., Hautus, M. J., & Huddleston, L. M. The measurement of taste discrimination with the same-different task: A detection-theory analysis. *Journal of Sensory Studies*, 1993, *8*, 229–239.

Jastrow, J. The psycho-physic law and star magnitudes. *American Journal of Psychology*, 1887, *1*, 112–127.

Jesteadt, W., Luce, R. D., & Green, D. M. Sequential effects in judgments of loudness. *Journal of Experimental Psychology: Human Perception and Performance*, 1977, *3*, 92–104.

Jones, F. N. A forced-choice method of limits. *American Journal of Psychology*, 1956, *69*, 672–673.

Kenshalo, D. R., Decker, T., & Hamilton, A. Spatial summation on the forehead, forearm, and back produced by radiant and conducted heat. *Journal of Comparative and Physiological Psychology*, 1967, *63*, 510–515.

Kerst, S. M., & Howard, J. H., Jr. Memory psychophysics for visual area and length. *Memory & Cognition*, 1978, *6*, 327–335.

König, A., & Brodhun, E. Experimentelle Untersuchungen ueber die psychophysiche Fundamental-formel in Bezug auf den Gesichtssinn. *Sitzungsberichte Preussische Akademie Wissenschaften*, Berlin, 1889, *27*, 641–644.

Krantz, D. H. Threshold theories of signal detection. *Psychological Review*, 1969, *76*, 308–324.

Künnapas, T., & Wikström, I. Measurement of occupational preferences: A comparison of scaling methods. *Perceptual and Motor Skills*, 1963, *17*, 611–694.

Laming, D., & Marsh, D. Some performance tests of QUEST on measurements of vibrotactile thresholds. *Perception & Psychophysics*, 1988, *44*, 99–107.

Leon, M. Integration of intent and consequence information in children's moral judgment. In F. Wilkening, J. Becker, & T. Trabasso (Eds.), *Information integration by children*. Hillsdale, NJ: Lawrence Erlbaum Associates, 1980.

Levitt, H. L. Transformed up-down methods in psychophysics. *Journal of the Acoustical Society of America*, 1971, *49*, 467–477.

Lieberman, H. R., & Pentland, A. P. Computer technology: Microcomputer-based estimation of psychophysical thresholds: The best PEST. *Behavior Research Methods & Instrumentation*, 1982, *14*, 21–25.

Link, S. W. *The wave theory of difference and similarity*. Hillsdale, NJ: Lawrence Erlbaum Associates, 1992.

Lockhart, R. S., & Murdock, B. B., Jr. Memory and the theory of signal detection. *Psychological Bulletin*, 1970, *74*, 100–109.

Lockhead, G. R. Psychophysical scaling: Judgments of attributes or objects? *Behavioral and Brain Sciences*, 1992, *15*, 543–601.

Luce, R. D. A threshold theory for simple detection experiments. *Psychological Review*, 1963, *70*, 61–79.

Luce, R. D. What sort of measurement is psychophysical measurement? *American Psychologist*, 1972, *27*, 96–106.

Luce, R. D., & Galanter, E. Discrimination. In R. D. Luce, R. R. Bush, & E. Galanter (Eds.), *Handbook of Mathematical Psychology* (Vol. 1), pp. 191–243. New York: Wiley, 1963.

Luce, R. D., & Green, D. M. The response ratio hypothesis for magnitude estimation. *Journal of Mathematical Psychology*, 1974, *11*, 1–14.

Ludvigh, E., & McCarthy, E. F. Absorption of visible light by the refractive media of the human eye. *Archives of Ophthalmology*, 1938, *20*, 37–51.

Lusted, L. B. Signal detectability and medical decision-making. *Science*, 1971, *171*, 1217–1219.

MacKay, D. M. Psychophysics of perceived intensity: A theoretical basis for Fechner's and Stevens' laws. *Science*, 1963, *139*, 1213–1216.

Macmillan, N. A., & Creelman, C. D. Response bias: Characteristics of detection-theory, threshold-theory, and "nonparametric" indexes. *Psychological Bulletin*, 1990, *107*, 401–413.

Macmillan, N. A., & Creelman, C. D. *Detection theory: A user's guide*. Cambridge: Cambridge University Press, 1991.

Markowitz, J., & Swets, J. A. Factors affecting the slope of empirical ROC curves: Comparison of binary and rating responses. *Perception and Psychophysics*, 1967, *2*, 91–97.

Marks, L. E. Spatial summation in the warmth sense. In H. R. Moskowitz, B. Scharf, & J. C. Stevens (Eds.), *Sensation and measurement*. Dordrecht, Holland: Reidel, 1974. (a)

Marks, L. E. *Sensory processes*. New York: Academic Press, 1974. (b)

Marks, L. E. On scales of sensation: Prolegomena to any future psychophysics that will come forth as sciences. *Perception & Psychophysics*, 1974, *16*, 358–376. (c)

Marks, L. E. *The unity of the senses: Interrelations among the modalities*. New York: Academic Press, 1978. (a)

Marks, L. E. Binaural summation of the loudness of pure tones. *Journal of the Acoustical Society of America*, 1978, *64*, 107–113. (b)

Marks, L. E. Phonion: Translation and annotation concerning loudness scales and the processing of auditory intensity. In N. J. Castellan, Jr., & F. Restle (Eds.), *Cognitive theory* (Vol. 3). Hillsdale, NJ: Lawrence Erlbaum Associates, 1978. (c)

Marks, L. E. Summation of vibrotactile intensity: An analog to auditory critical bands? *Sensory Processes*, 1979, *3*, 188–203. (a)

Marks, L. E. A theory of loudness and loudness judgment. *Psychological Review*, 1979, *86*, 256–285. (b)

Marks, L. E. Sensory and cognitive factors in judgments of loudness. *Journal of Experimental Psychology*, 1979, *5*, 426–443. (c)

Marks, L. E. Psychophysical measurement: Procedures, tasks, scales. In B. Wegener (Ed.), *Social Attitudes and Psychophysical Measurement*, pp. 43–71. Hillsdale, NJ: Lawrence Erlbaum Associates, 1982.

Marks, L. E. Reliability of magnitude matching. *Perception & Psychophysics*, 1991, *49*, 31–37.

Marks, L. E. The contingency of perceptual processing: Context modifies equal-loudness relations. *Psychological Science*, 1992, *3*, 285–291.

Marks, L. E., & Algom, D. *Psychophysical Scaling* (in press).

Marks, L. E., Borg, G., & Ljunggren, G. Individual differences in perceived exertion assessed by two new methods. *Perception & Psychophysics*, 1983, *34*, 280–288.

Marks, L. E., & Stevens, J. C. Individual brightness functions. *Perception and Psychophysics*, 1966, *1*, 17–24.

Marks, L. E., & Stevens, J. C. The form of the psychophysical function near threshold. *Perception and Psychophysics*, 1968, *4*, 315–318.

Marks, L. E., & Stevens, J. C. Spatial summation of warmth: Influence of duration and configuration of the stimulus. *American Journal of Psychology*, 1973, *86*, 251–267.

Marks, L. E., Stevens, J. C., Bartoshuk, L. M., Gent, J. F., Rifkin, B., & Stone, V. K. Magnitude-matching: The measurement of taste and smell. *Chemical Senses*, 1988, *13*, 63–87.

Marks, L. E., Szczesiul, R., & Ohlott, P. On the cross-modality perception of intensity. *Journal of Experimental Psychology: Human Perception and Performance*, 1986, *12*, 517–534.

McBurney, D. H. Magnitude estimation of the taste of sodium chloride after adaptation to sodium chloride. *Journal of Experimental Psychology*, 1966, *72*, 869–873.

McGill, W. J., & Goldberg, J. P. A study of the near-miss involving Weber's law and pure-tone intensity discrimination. *Perception & Psychophysics*, 1968, *4*, 105–109. (a)

McGill, W. J., & Goldberg, J. P. Pure-tone intensity discrimination and energy detection. *Journal of the Acoustical Society of America*, 1968, *44*, 576–581. (b)

Melara, R. D. The concept of perceptual similarity: From psychophysics to cognitive psychology. In D. Algom (Ed.), *Psychophysical Approaches to Cognition*. Amsterdam: North-Holland, 1992.

Mellers, B. A. Evidence against "absolute" scaling. *Perception & Psychophysics*, 1983, *33*, 523–526.

Miller, E., & Lewis, P. Recognition memory in elderly patients with depression and dementia: A signal detection analysis. *Journal of Abnormal Psychology*, 1977, *86*, 84–86.

Miller, G. A. Sensitivity to changes in the intensity of white noise and its relation to masking and loudness. *Journal of the Acoustical Society of America*, 1947, *19*, 609–619.

Montgomery, H. Direct estimation: Effect of methodological factors on scale type. *Scandinavian Journal of Psychology*, 1975, *16*, 19–29.

Moyer, R. S., Bradley, D. R., Sorensen, M. H., Whiting, J. C., & Mansfield, D. P. Psychophysical functions for perceived and remembered size. *Science*, 1978, *200*, 330–332.

Munsell, A. E. O., Sloan, L. L., & Godlove, I. H. Neutral value scales: I. Munsell neutral value scale. *Journal of the Optical Society of America*, 1933, *23*, 394–411.

Noreen, E. D. Optimal decision rules for some common psychophysical paradigms. In S. Grossberg (Ed.), *Mathematical Psychology and Psychophysiology: Seminars in Applied Mathematics* (Vol. 13), pp. 237–280. Providence, RI: American Mathematical Society, 1981.

Norman, D. A. Neural quantum controversy in sensory psychology. *Science*, 1973, *181*, 468–469.

Norwich, K. H. *Information, sensation, and perception*. Orlando, FL: Academic Press, 1993.

Oberlin, W. K. Variation in intensive sensitivity to lifted weights. *Journal of Experimental Psychology*, 1936, *19*, 438–455.

Parducci, A. Category judgment: A range-frequency model. *Psychological Review*, 1965, *75*, 407–418.

Parducci, A. Contextual effects: A range-frequency analysis. In E. C. Carterette & M. P. Friedman (Eds.), *Handbook of Perception: Psychophysical judgment and measurement* (Vol. 2), pp. 127–141. New York: Academic Press, 1974.

Parker, S., & Schneider, B. Non-metric scaling of loudness and pitch using similarity and difference estimates. *Perception & Psychophysics*, 1974, *15*, 238–242.

Parker, S., & Schneider, B. The stimulus range effect: Evidence of top-down control of sensory intensity in audition. *Perception & Psychophysics*, 1994, *56*, 1–11.

Pascal, B. *Pensées*. New York: Dutton, 1958. (originally published, 1670)

Peck, R. E. The application of thymometry to the measurement of anxiety. *International Journal of Neuropsychiatry*, 1966, *2*, 337–341.

Pentland, A. Maximum likelihood estimation: The best PEST. *Perception & Psychophysics*, 1980, *28*, 377–379.

Petrus, B. W., & Bolanowski, S. J. Mechanics of Pacinian corpuscles, 1996. Unpublished manuscript.

Plateau, J. A. F. Sur la mesure des sensations physiques, et sur la loi que lie l'intensité de ces sensations à l'intensité de la cause excitante. *Bulletins de l' Academie Royale des Sciences, des Lettres, et des Beaux-Arts de Belgique*, 1872, *33*, 376–388.

Pollack, I., & Norman, D. A. A non-parametric analysis of recognition experiments. *Psychonomic Science*, 1964, *1*, 125–126.

Popper, R. D., Parker, S., & Galanter, E. Dual loudness scales in individual subjects. *Journal of Experimental Psychology: Human Perception and Performance*, 1986, *12*, 61–69.

Poulton, E. The new psychophysics: Six models for magnitude estimation. *Psychological Bulletin*, 1968, *69*, 1–19.

Poulton, E. C. Models of bias in judging sensory magnitude. *Psychological Bulletin*, 1979, *86*, 777–803.

Pradhan, P. L., & Hoffman, P. J. Effect of spacing and range of stimuli on magnitude estimation judgments. *Journal of Experimental Psychology*, 1963, *66*, 533–541.

Rahe, R. H., Romo, M., Bennett, L., & Siltanen, P. Recent life changes, myocardial infarction, and abrupt coronary death: Studies in Helsinki. *Archives of Internal Medicine*, 1974, *133*, 221–228.

Riesz, R. R. Differential intensity sensitivity of the ear for pure tones. *Physical Review*, 1928, *31*, 867–875.

Robinson, D. W., & Dadson, R. S. A re-determination of the equal loudness relations for pure tones. *British Journal of Applied Physics*, 1956, *7*, 166–181.

Rodieck, R. W. *The vertebrate retina*. San Francisco: Freeman, 1973.

Rollman, G. B. Cognitive effects in pain and pain judgments. In D. Algom (Ed.), *Psychophysical approaches to cognition*, pp. 515–574. Amsterdam: North-Holland, 1992.

Ross, S., & Katchmer, L. The construction of a magnitude function for short time intervals. *American Journal of Psychology*, 1951, *64*, 397–401.

Rowley, R. R., & Studebaker, G. A. Monaural loudness–intensity relationships for a 1000 Hz tone. *Journal of the Acoustical Society of America*, 1969, *45*, 1193–1205.

Savage, C. W. Introspectionist and behaviorist interpretations of ratio scales of perceptual magnitudes. *Psychological Monographs*, 1966, *80*(19, Whole No. 627).

Savage, C. W. *The measurement of sensation*. Berkeley: University of California Press, 1970.

Scharf, B. Complex sounds and critical bands. *Psychological Bulletin*, 1961, *58*, 205–217.

Scharf, B., & Stevens, J. C. The form of the loudness function near threshold. *Proceedings of the 3rd International Congress on Acoustics, Stuttgart, 1959* (Vol. I). Amsterdam: Elsevier, 1961.

Schiffman, S. S., Reynolds, M. L., & Young, F. W. *Introduction to Multidimensional Scaling: Theory, Methods and Applications*. New York: Academic Press, 1981.

Schneider, B. Individual loudness functions determined from direct comparisons of loudness intervals. *Perception & Psychophysics*, 1980, *27*, 493–503.

Schneider, B., & Parker, S. Does stimulus context affect loudness or only loudness judgments? *Perception & Psychophysics*, 1990, *48*, 409–418.

Schneider, B., Parker, S., & Stein, D. The measurement of loudness using direct comparisons of sensory intervals. *Journal of Mathematical Psychology*, 1974, *11*, 259–273.

Schneider, B., Parker, S., Valenti, M., Farrell, G., & Kanow, G. Response bias in category and magnitude estimation of difference and similarity for loudness and pitch. *Journal of Experimental Psychology: Human Perception and Performance*, 1978, *4*, 483–496.

Sellin, T., & Wolfgang, M. E. *The measurement of delinquency*. New York: Wiley, 1964.

Shepard, R. Metric structures in ordinal data. *Journal of Mathematical Psychology*, 1966, *3*, 287–315.

Shepard, R. N. On the status of "direct" psychological measurement. In C. W. Savage (Ed.), *Minnesota Studies in the Philosophy of Science* (Vol. 9), pp. 441–490. Minneapolis: University of Minnesota Press, 1978.

Shepard, R. N. Psychological relations and psychological scales: On the status of "direct" psychophysical measurement. *Journal of Mathematical Psychology*, 1981, *24*, 21–57.

Sivian, L. J., & White, S. D. On minimum audible sound fields. *Journal of the Acoustical Society of America*, 1933, *4*, 288–321.

Snodgrass, J. G., & Corwin, J. Pragmatics of measuring recognition memory: Application to dementia and amnesia. *Journal of Experimental Psychology: General*, 1988, *117*, 34–50.

Sorkin, R. D. Extension of the theory of signal detectability to matching procedures in psychoacoustics. *Journal of the Acoustical Society of America*, 1962, *34*, 1745–1751.

Stenson, H., Kleinmuntz, B., & Scott, B. Personality assessment as a signal detection task. *Journal of Consulting and Clinical Psychology*, 1975, *43*, 794–799.

Stevens, J. C., & Guirao, M. Individual loudness functions. *Journal of the Acoustical Society of America*, 1964, *36*, 2210–2213.

Stevens, J. C., & Mack, J. D. Scales of apparent force. *Journal of Experimental Psychology*, 1959, *58*, 405–413.

Stevens, J. C., Mack, J. D., & Stevens, S. S. Growth of sensation on seven continua as measured by force of handgrip. *Journal of Experimental Psychology*, 1960, *59*, 60–67.

Stevens, J. C., & Marks, L. E. Spatial summation and the dynamics of warmth sensation. *Perception and Psychophysics*, 1971, *9*, 291–298.

Stevens, J. C., & Marks, L. E. Cross-modality matching functions generated by magnitude estimation. *Perception & Psychophysics*, 1980, *27*, 379–389.

Stevens, J. C., Plantinga, A., & Cain, W. S. Reduction of order and nasal pungency associated with aging. *Neurobiology of Aging*, 1982, *3*, 125–132.

Stevens, J. C., & Stevens, S. S. Warmth and cold: Dynamics of sensory intensity. *Journal of Experimental Psychology*, 1960, *60*, 183–192.

Stevens, J. C., & Stevens, S. S. Brightness function: Effects of adaptation. *Journal of the Optical Society of America*, 1963, *53*, 375–385.

Stevens, S. S. A scale for the measurement for a psychological magnitude: Loudness. *Psychological Review*, 1936, *43*, 405–416.

Stevens, S. S. *Handbook of experimental psychology*. New York: Wiley, 1951.

Stevens, S. S. On the brightness of lights and loudness of sounds. *Science*, 1953, *118*, 576. (Abstract)

Stevens, S. S. Pitch discrimination, mels, and Koch's contention. *Journal of the Acoustical Society of America*, 1954, *26*, 1075–1077.

Stevens, S. S. The measurement of loudness. *Journal of the Acoustical Society of America*, 1955, *27*, 815–820.

Stevens, S. S. The direct estimation of sensory magnitude—loudness. *American Journal of Psychology*, 1956, *69*, 1–25.

Stevens, S. S. On the psychophysical law. *Psychological Review*, 1957, *64*, 153–181.

Stevens, S. S. Problems and methods of psychophysics. *Psychological Bulletin*, 1958, *55*, 177–196.

Stevens, S. S. Cross-modality validations of subjective scales for loudness, vibrations, and electric shock. *Journal of Experimental Psychology*, 1959, *57*, 201–209. (a)

Stevens, S. S. Tactile vibration: Dynamics of sensory intensity. *Journal of Experimental Psychology*, 1959, *57*, 210–218. (b)

Stevens, S. S. Ratio scales, partition scales and confusion scales. In H. Gulliksen & S. Messick (Eds.), *Psychological scaling: Theory and applications*. New York: Wiley, 1960.

Stevens, S. S. The psychophysics of sensory function. In W. A. Rosenblith (Ed.), *Sensory communication*. Boston: MIT Press, 1961. (a)

Stevens, S. S. Is there a quantal threshold? In W. A. Rosenblith (Ed.), *Sensory communication*. Boston: MIT Press, 1961. (b)

Stevens, S. S. The basis of psychophysical judgments. *Journal of the Acoustical Society of America*, 1963, *35*, 611–612.

Stevens, S. S. Matching functions between loudness and ten other continua. *Perception and Psychophysics*, 1966, *1*, 5–8. (a)

Stevens, S. S. Power-group transformations under glare, masking, and recruitment. *Journal of the Acoustical Society of America*, 1966, *39*, 725–735. (b)

Stevens, S. S. On the operation known as judgment. *American Scientist*, 1966, *54*, 385–401. (c)

Stevens, S. S. A metric for social consensus. *Science*, 1966, *151*, 530–541. (d)

Stevens, S. S. Neural events and the psychophysical law. *Science*, 1970, *170*, 1043–1050.

Stevens, S. S. Issues in psychophysical measurement. *Psychological Review*, 1971, *78*, 426–450. (a)

Stevens, S. S. Sensory power functions and neural events. In W. R. Loewenstein (Ed.), *Handbook of sensory physiology* (Vol. 1). Berlin and New York: Springer-Verlag, 1971. (b)

Stevens, S. S. A neural quantum in sensory discrimination. *Science*, 1972, *177*, 749–762. (a)

Stevens, S. S. Perceived level of noise by Mark VII and db(E). *Journal of the Acoustical Society of America*, 1972, *51*, 575–601. (b)

Stevens, S. S. *Psychophysics: Introduction to its perceptual, neural and social prospects.* New York: Wiley, 1975.

Stevens, S. S., Carton, A. S., & Shickman, G. M. A scale of apparent intensity of electric shock. *Journal of Experimental Psychology*, 1958, *56*, 328–334.

Stevens, S. S., & Galanter, E. H. Ratio scales and category scales for a dozen perceptual continua. *Journal of Experimental Psychology*, 1957, *54*, 377–411.

Stevens, S. S., & Guirao, M. Loudness, reciprocality, and partition scales. *Journal of the Acoustical Society of America*, 1962, *34*, 1466–1471.

Stevens, S. S., Guirao, M., & Slawson, A. W. Loudness, a product of volume times density. *Journal of Experimental Psychology*, 1965, *69*, 503–510.

Stevens, S. S., Morgan, C. E., & Volkmann, J. Theory of neural quantum in the discrimination of loudness and pitch. *American Journal of Psychology*, 1941, *54*, 315–355.

Stevens, S. S., & Volkmann, J. The relation of pitch to frequency: A revised scale. *American Journal of Psychology*, 1940, *53*, 329–353.

Stiles, W. S. A. Color vision: The approach through increment-threshold sensitivity. *Proceedings of the National Academy of Sciences*, 1959, *45*, 100–114.

Stone, L. A. Bases for psychiatric impairment severity judgments: Psychophysical power functions? *Studia Psychologica*, 1968, *10*, 194–199.

Stuiver, M. *Biophysics of the sense of smell.* Unpublished doctoral dissertation. University of Gronigen, Netherlands, 1958.

Swets, J. A. Indices of signal detectability obtained with various psychophysical procedures. *Journal of the Acoustical Society of America*, 1959, *31*, 511–513.

Swets, J. A. Is there a sensory threshold? *Science*, 1961, *134*, 168–177.

Swets, J. A. The relative operating characteristics in psychology. *Science*, 1973, *182*, 990–1000.

Swets, J. A. Form of empirical ROCs in discrimination and diagnostic tasks. *Psychological Bulletin*, 1986, *99*, 100–117.

Swets, J. A. Measuring the accuracy of diagnostic systems. *Science*, 1988, *240*, 1285–1293.

Swets, J. A. The science of choosing the right decision threshold in high-stake diagnostics. *American Psychologist*, 1992, *47*, 522–532.

Swets, J. H., & Pickett, R. M. *Evaluation of Diagnostic Systems: Methods From Signal Detection Theory.* New York: Academic Press, 1982.

Swets, J. A., Pickett, R. M., Whitehead, S. F., Getty, D. J., Schnur, J. A., Swets, J. B., & Freeman, B. A. Assessment of diagnostic technologies. *Science*, 1979, *205*, 753–759.

Swets, J. A., Tanner, W. P., Jr., & Birdsall, T. G. *The evidence for a decision-making theory of visual detection.* University of Michigan: Electronic Defense Group Technical Report No. 40, 1955.

Swets, J. A., Tanner, W. P., Jr., & Birdsall, T. G. Decision processes in perception. *Psychological Review*, 1961, *68*, 301–340.

Tanner, T. A., Haller, R. D., & Atkinson, R. C. Signal recognition as influenced by presentation schedules. *Perception & Psychophysics*, 1967, *2*, 349–358.

Tanner, W. P., Jr., & Swets, J. A. A decision-making theory of visual detection. *Psychological Review*, 1954, *61*, 401–409.

Tanner, W. P., Jr., Swets, J. A., & Green, D. M. *Some general properties of the hearing mechanism.* University of Michigan: Electronic Defense Group Technical Report No. 30, 1956.

#31 Sat Nov 17 2001 11:12AM
Item(s) checked out to Sabella, Mark.

TITLE: EPS Interlibrary Loan
BARCODE: 31208002242818
DUE DATE: Dec 15 2001

TITLE: EPS Interlibrary Loan
BARCODE: 31208002242883
DUE DATE: Dec 15 2001

TITLE: EPS Interlibrary Loan
BARCODE: 31208002242222
DUE DATE: Dec 15 2001

Taylor, M. M., & Creelman, C. D. PEST: Efficient estimates on probability functions. *Journal of the Acoustical Society of America*, 1967, *41*, 782–787.

Teghtsoonian, M. The judgment of size. *American Journal of Psychology*, 1965, *78*, 392–402.

Teghtsoonian, R. On the exponents in Stevens' law and the constant in Ekman's law. *Psychological Review*, 1971, *78*, 71–80.

Teghtsoonian, R. Range effects in psychophysical scaling and a revision of Stevens' Law. *American Journal of Psychology*, 1973, *86*, 3–27.

Teghtsoonian, R., & Teghtsoonian, M. Range and regression effects in magnitude scaling. *Perception & Psychophysics*, 1978, *24*, 305–314.

Thalmann, R. Cross-modality matching in a study of abnormal loudness functions. *Laryngoscope*, 1965, *75*, 1708–1726.

Thorndike, E. L. Handwriting. *Teachers College Record*, 1910, *11*, No. 2.

Thurstone, L. L. A law of comparative judgment. *Psychological Review*, 1927, *34*, 273–286.

Thurstone, L. L. The phi-gamma hypothesis. *Journal of Experimental Psychology*, 1928, *9*, 293–305.

Thurstone, L. L. *The measurement of values.* Chicago: University of Chicago Press, 1959.

Titchener, E. B. *Experimental psychology: Quantitative.* New York: Macmillan, 1905.

Tonndorf, J., & Khanna, S. M. Submicroscopic displacement amplitudes of the tympanic membrane (cat) measured by a laser interferometer. *Journal of the Acoustical Society of America*, 1968, *44*, 1546–1554.

Torgerson, W. S. *Theory and methods of scaling.* New York: Wiley, 1958.

Triesman, M. Sensory scaling and the psychophysical law. *Quarterly Journal of Experimental Psychology*, 1964, *16*, 11–22.

Tryon, W. W. Psychophysical scaling and hierarchy construction. *Journal of Behavior Therapy and Experimental Psychiatry*, 1977, *8*, 53–56.

Ulehla, Z. J., & Adams, D. K. Detection theory and expectations for social reinforcers: An application to aggression. *Psychological Review*, 1973, *80*, 439–445.

Urban, F. M. The future of psychophysics. *Psychological Review*, 1930, *37*, 93–106.

Vallbo, A. B., & Johansson, R. S. Skin mechanoreceptors in the human hand: Neural and psychophysical thresholds. In Y. Zotterman (Ed.), *Sensory functions of the skin in primates*. Oxford: Pergamon Press, 1976.

Vendrik, A. J. H., & Eijkman, E. G. Psychophysical properties determined with internal noise. In D. R. Kenshalo (Ed.), *The skin senses*. Springfield, IL: Charles C. Thomas, 1968.

Verrillo, R. T. Effect of contactor area on the vibrotactile threshold. *Journal of the Acoustical Society of America*, 1963, *35*, 1962–1966.

Verrillo, R. T. Vibrotactile sensitivity and the frequency response of the Pacinian corpuscle. *Psychonomic Science*, 1966, *4*, 135–136.

Verrillo, R. T. Cutaneous sensation. In B. Scharf (Ed.), *Experimental sensory psychology*. Scott, Foresman & Co., 1975.

Verrillo, R. T. Stability of line-length estimates using the method of absolute magnitude estimation. *Perception and Psychophysics*, 1983, *33*, 261–265.

Verrillo, R. T., Fraioli, A. J., & Smith, R. L. Sensory magnitude of vibrotactile stimuli. *Perception & Psychophysics*, 1969, *6*, 366–372.

Verrillo, R. T., & Gescheider, G. A. Enhancement and summation in the perception of two successive vibrotactile stimuli. *Perception and Psychophysics*, 1975, *18*, 128–136.

Verrillo, R. T., & Gescheider, G. A. Effect of double ipsilateral stimulation on vibrotactile sensation magnitude. *Sensory Processes*, 1976, *1*, 127–137.

Verrillo, R. T., & Gescheider, G. A. Effect of prior stimulation on vibrotactile thresholds. *Sensory Processes*, 1977, *1*, 292–300.

Versfeld, N. J., Dai, H., & Green, D. M. The optimum decision rules for the oddity task. *Perception & Psychophysics*, 1996, *58*, 10–21.

Wald, G. Human vision and the spectrum. *Science*, 1945, *101*, 653–658.

Wald, G. The receptors of human color vision. *Science*, 1964, *145*, 1007–1017.

Ward, L. M. Repeated magnitude estimations with a variable standard: Sequential effects and other properties. *Perception and Psychophysics*, 1973, *13*, 193–200.

Ward, L. M. Critical bands and mixed-frequency scaling: Sequential dependencies, equal-loudness contours, and power function exponents. *Perception & Psychophysics*, 1990, *47*, 551–562.

Ward, L. M. Mind in psychophysics. In D. Algom (Ed.), *Psychophysical approaches to cognition* (pp. 187–249). Amsterdam: North-Holland Elsevier, 1992.

Warren, R. M. A basis for judgments of sensory intensity. *American Journal of Psychology*, 1958, *71*, 675–687.

Warren, R. M. Reply to S. S. Stevens. *Journal of the Acoustical Society of America*, 1963, *35*, 1663–1665.

Warren, R. M. Visual intensity judgments: An empirical rule and a theory. *Psychological Review*, 1969, *76*, 16–30.

Warren, R. M. Measurement of sensory intensity. *The Behavioral and Brain Sciences*, 1981, *4*, 175–223.

Warren, R. M., Sersen, E. A., & Pores, E. A basis for loudness judgments. *American Journal of Psychology*, 1958, *71*, 700–709.

Warren, R. M., & Warren, R. P. A critique of S. S. Stevens' "new psychophysics." *Perceptual and Motor Skills*, 1963, *16*, 797–810.

Watson, A. B., & Pelli, D. G. QUEST: A Bayesian adaptive psychometric method. *Perception & Psychophysics*, 1983, *33*, 113–120.

Weber, E. H. *De pulsu, resorptione, auditu et tactu: Annotationes anatomicae et physiologicae.* Leipzig: Koehlor, 1834.

Wetherill, G. B., & Levitt, H. Sequential estimation of points on a psychometric function. *British Journal of Mathematical and Statistical Psychology*, 1965, *18*, 1–10.

Wickelgren, W. A., & Norman, D. A. Strength models of serial position in short-term recognition memory. *Journal of Mathematical Psychology*, 1966, *3*, 316–347.

Wilska, A. Eine Methode zur Bestimmung der Horschwell enamplituden des Trommelfels bei verschiedenen Freguenzen. *Skandinavisches Archiv für Physiologie*, 1935, *72*, 161–165.

Wolpe, J. Quantitative relationships in the systematic desensitization of phobias. *American Journal of Psychiatry*, 1963, *119*, 1062–1068.

Wright, A. A. Psychometric and psychophysical theory within a framework of response bias. *Psychological Review*, 1974, *81*, 322–347.

Zinnes, J. L. Scaling. *Annual Review of Psychology*, 1969, *20*, 447–478.

Zuriff, G. E. A behavioral interpretation of psychophysical scaling. *Behaviorism*, 1972, *1*, 118–133.

Zwislocki, J. J. An analysis of some auditory characteristics. In R. D. Luce, R. R. Bush, & E. Galanter (Eds.), *Handbook of mathematical psychology* (Vol. III). New York: Wiley, 1965.

Zwislocki, J. J. On intensity characteristics of sensory receptors: A generalized function. *Kybernetik*, 1973, *12*, 169–183.

Zwislocki, J. J. A power function for sensory receptors. In H. R. Moskowitz, B. Scharf, & J. C. Stevens (Eds.), *Sensation and measurements*. Dordrecht, Holland: Reidel, 1974.

Zwislocki, J. J. Group and individual relations between sensation magnitudes and their numerical estimates. *Perception and Psychophysics*, 1983, *33*, 460–468.

Zwislocki, J. J. Natural measurement. In S. J. Bolanowski, Jr. & G. A. Gescheider (Eds.), *Ratio scaling of psychological magnitude*. Hillsdale, NJ: Lawrence Erlbaum Associates, 1991.

Zwislocki, J. J., & Goodman, D. A. Absolute scaling and sensory magnitudes: A validation. *Perception and Psychophysics*, 1980, *28*, 28–38.

Zwislocki, J. J., & Jordan, H. N. On the relations of intensity jnd's to loudness and neural noise. *Journal of the Acoustical Society of America*, 1986, *79*, 772–780.

Zwislocki, J. J., Ketkar, I., Cannon, M. W., & Nodar, R. H. Loudness in enhancement and summation in pairs of short sound bursts. *Perception and Psychophysics*, 1974, *16*, 91–95.

Zwislocki, J., Maire, F., Feldman, A. S., & Rubin, H. On the effect of practice and motivation on the threshold of audibility. *Journal of the Acoustical Society of America*, 1957, *30*, 254–262.

Zwislocki, J. J., & Sokolich, W. G. On loudness enhancement of a tone burst by preceding tone burst. *Perception and Psychophysics*, 1974, *16*, 87–90.

Author Index

425

Subject Index